Anglo-Saxon Texts

12

THE OLD ENGLISH METRICAL CALENDAR

(*MENOLOGIUM*)

Anglo-Saxon Texts

ISSN 1463–6948

Editorial Board
MICHAEL LAPIDGE
MARY CLAYTON
LESLIE LOCKETT
RICHARD MARSDEN
ANDY ORCHARD

Anglo-Saxon Texts is a series of scholarly editions (with parallel translations) of important texts from Anglo-Saxon England, whether written in Latin or in Old English. The series aims to offer critical texts with suitable apparatus and accurate modern English translations, together with informative general introductions and full historical and literary commentaries.

Previously published volumes in the series are listed at the back of this book

THE OLD ENGLISH METRICAL CALENDAR (*MENOLOGIUM*)

Edited with a translation by
KAZUTOMO KARASAWA

D. S. BREWER

© Kazutomo Karasawa 2015

All rights reserved. Except as permitted under current legislation
no part of this work may be photocopied, stored in a retrieval system,
published, performed in public, adapted, broadcast,
transmitted, recorded or reproduced in any form or by any means,
without the prior permission of the copyright owner

First published 2015
D. S. Brewer, Cambridge
Paperback edition 2021

ISBN 978 1 84384 409 9 hardback
ISBN 978 1 84384 599 7 paperback

D. S. Brewer is an imprint of Boydell & Brewer Ltd
PO Box 9, Woodbridge, Suffolk IP12 3DF, UK
and of Boydell & Brewer Inc.
668 Mt Hope Avenue, Rochester, NY 14620–2731, USA
website: www.boydellandbrewer.com

A CIP catalogue record for this book is available
from the British Library

The publisher has no responsibility for the continued existence or accuracy
of URLs for external or third-party internet websites referred to in this book,
and does not guarantee that any content on such websites is,
or will remain, accurate or appropriate

In memoriam
Fr Richard H. Randolph SJ, Fr Clarence Gallagher SJ
and Fr Ian Brayley SJ

Contents

List of Figures	ix
Preface	xi
Acknowledgements	xiii
Abbreviations	xiv

Introduction

1.	The Title	1
2.	Editorial History	3
3.	The Manuscript and Its Context	5
4.	Sources	15
5.	Analogues	18
6.	Structure	33
7.	Entries	40
8.	The Relationship between the Prose and the Verse *Menologium*	44
9.	Purpose	52
10.	Language	55
11.	Prosody	64
12.	Date and Place of Composition	70

The Old English Metrical Calendar (*Menologium*): Text and Translation — 73

    Commentary — 86

Appendices

1.	The Prose *Menologium*	131
2.	Metrical Calendar of York	138
3.	*Félire Adamnáin*	154
4.	*Enlaith betha*	156
5.	List of Anglo-Saxon Calendars	161

6.	Immovable Feasts Marked in Anglo-Saxon Calendars	164
7.	Vigils in Anglo-Saxon Calendars	180
8.	Dates of the Solar Turning Points in Anglo-Saxon Calendars	181
9.	Latin and Old English Month-names in Old English Written Tradition and in the Verse *Menologium*	182

Glossary	201
Bibliography	213
Index	225

Figures

1. Byrhtferth's diagram summarising the quaternary structure of the natural/solar year — 35
2. Byrhtferth's diagram summarising the basic structure of the year — 39

Both figures are reproduced by permission of the Council of the Early English Text Society.

Preface

The Old English verse *Menologium* is a lively poem which takes the reader through the cycle of the year: the changing months and seasons of the natural year and the feasts and commemorations of the liturgical year, from Christmas and back to Christmas. Written in the characteristic heroic diction and traditional metre of Old English poetry, it opens with a eulogy to the birth of Christ as Heavenly Ruler, 'glory of kings' and 'guardian of the kingdom of heaven', in a passage reminiscent of the well known *Cædmon's Hymn*. The months and seasons are personified as they leave the 'dwelling places' or 'come to town' and there follow short cameo narratives akin to the poem *Fates of the Apostles* commemorating the apostles, martyrs and confessors of the Church. At one point the poem even quotes directly from the Old English *Metrical Psalms*. As a summary of the basics of the Christian, as well as the natural, year current in late Anglo-Saxon England, the *Menologium* is a unique and important piece of Old English poetry. Like Chronicle poems such as *The Coronation of Edgar*, and like the computistical treatises of Ælfric and Byrhtferth, the poem is didactic and informative on the regular feasts of the year, and it could well have been used as a practical timepiece for reading the dates of the Anglo-Saxon Chronicle, for which it serves as a kind of Prologue in the manuscript.

In the last 300 years, the fact that at least seventeen different edited texts of the *Menologium*, published or unpublished, have been available demonstrates the high level of interest among Anglo-Saxonists. It is, however, also true that the interest has not necessarily led to serious critical analysis; the *Menologium* scholarship which began with George Hickes in the early eighteenth century has become inactive,[1] and there remains ample room for debate, even of such fundamental issues as its overall nature and purpose, structure and content, and sources and analogues. With this situation in mind, the present critical edition is offered, along with a full introduction covering these fundamentals of the poem.

The *Menologium* in fact exhibits several notable features. Together with *Maxims II*, it occurs in its unique manuscript (London, British Library, Cotton Tiberius B.i) just before the C-text of the Anglo-Saxon Chronicle. No other extant Chronicle manuscripts contain any introductory poem, and this raises

---

[1] Only six studies on the poem itself (including three editions and one translation) are listed in Greenfield and Robinson, *A Bibliography*, which covers the studies published by the end of 1972. In the Old English Newsletter Bibliography Database (http://oenewsletter.org/OENDB/index.php), covering more than 23,000 books and articles published between 1973 and 2009 and later, only five studies are found apart from three of my own, when searched by the keyword 'menologium'. The keywords 'metrical calendar' and 'calendar poem' yield no results for the *Menologium* (last consulted on 4 October 2014).

Preface

such questions as what is the relationship between the poem and the Chronicle, why the C-text alone is accompanied by two poems, and why the *Menologium* was chosen as one of them. Perhaps in conjunction with this, the poem, while dealing mostly with the 'universal feasts', is based on a strikingly local-English or even British perspective, expressed in its actual words: Britain and its inhabitants, the Angles and the Saxons, are repeatedly mentioned throughout the poem, as well as their ruler, 'king of the Saxons', whose command extends over the 'spacious kingdoms' of Britain.

Also Anglo-Saxon is the specific set of feasts and festivals listed in the poem. The poem is a rare work that concisely summarises the late Anglo-Saxon method of comprehending the annual cycle of feasts, festivals, solar turning points, seasons and months, and their interrelationships. In this respect, the prose *Menologium*, one of the analogous works often compared with the poem, is the only text that is really comparable. As reflected both in the structure and in the choice of entries, the prose and the verse *Menologium*, both following basically the same systematic scheme, belong to the same literary/educational tradition, whereas the analogues in Latin and Old Irish, following different principles and composed/used for different purposes, represent different traditions. Its vernacular style reflects its independence of other traditions. Various grammatical, prosodic and vocabulary-related peculiarities are found, such as a tendency to adhere to standard metrical patterns even at the cost of grammatical and/or conventional word forms; there is a notable dependence on learned prosaic words including Latin month-names and other computistical terms and a rare and heavy use of Old English month-names.

In short, the *Menologium* raises many intriguing questions, which I shall explore further in the Introduction, while the Commentary and the Glossary will deal with smaller issues regarding the reading of the text. For ease of comparison with the *Menologium*, I have supplied various Appendices; these provide edited texts and English translations of analogous works in Latin, Old English and Old Irish; they also include a discussion of the use of Latin and vernacular month-names in the Anglo-Saxon written tradition.

Acknowledgements

I have been working on the *Menologium* for nearly ten years and during this period have been helped by many people. First of all, I would like to thank the members of Campion Hall, Oxford, where I did much of my research, and where I wrote and revised many parts of this volume, especially the late Richard H. Randolph, the late Clarence Gallagher, the late Ian Brayley, Gerard J. Hughes (former Master of Campion Hall), Kevin J. Cathcart (Professor Emeritus at University College, Dublin), Joseph Munitiz (former Master of Campion Hall), Norman Tanner (Professor Emeritus at the Pontifical Gregorian University, Rome), M. Antoni J. Üçerler (University of San Francisco) and Jack Mahoney (Professor Emeritus at the University of London), who advised on Latin and Italian, read through various parts of this book to check my English, and gave advice and comments about the issues regarding the liturgical year, the saints and other related topics. I would also like to thank Mark Atherton (Regent's Park College, Oxford), who read the volume through and gave me helpful comments and suggestions, and Rebecca Rushforth, who kindly provided me with photocopies of microfilm printouts of an Anglo-Saxon calendar, which were otherwise far from my reach. I would also like to thank Hideki Watanabe (Osaka University), who once presided at my presentation on the *Menologium* and gave me useful comments, and Matsuji Tajima (Professor Emeritus at Kyushu University), who as an external examiner read my doctoral thesis on the poem. Thanks also to Mary P. Richards (Professor Emeritus at the University of Delaware), Andrea Di Maio (Pontifical Gregorian University, Rome), Joseph S. O'Leary (Sophia University, Tokyo), Peter Evan (Seikei University, Tokyo) and my colleagues at Komazawa University, Tokyo, especially David M. Pierce and Sarah Moate, for their help and encouragement. I also express my thanks to the various staff of the British Library, the Bodleian Library and the Parker Library for granting me access to the manuscripts I needed to consult, and for useful advice and assistance.

Financial support for the preparation of this edition was given by Japan's Ministry of Education, Culture, Sports, Science and Technology, KAKENHI Grant Number 22720113 and by the Rintaro Fukuhara Memorial Research Foundation.

Abbreviations

Editions of the Old English Metrical Calendar (Menologium)

Bouterwek	K. W. Bouterwek, ed., *Calendcwide i.e. Menologium Ecclesiæ Anglo-Saxonicæ Poeticum* (Gütersloh, 1857)
Dobbie	E. V. K. Dobbie, ed., *The Anglo-Saxon Minor Poems*, ASPR 6 (New York, 1942)
Earle	J. Earle, ed., *Two of the Saxon Chronicles Paralleled with Supplementary Extracts from the Others* (Oxford, 1865)
Ebeling	'*Menologium*' edited in F. W. Ebeling, *Angelsæchsisches Lesebuch* (Leipzig, 1847)
Fox	S. Fox, ed., *Menologium seu Calendarium Poeticum* (London, 1830)
Fritsche	P. Fritsche, *Darstellung der Syntax in dem altenglischen Menologium* (Berlin, 1907)
Greeson	Hoyt St Clair Greeson, Jr, 'Two Old English Observance Poems: *Seasons for Fasting* and *The Menologium* – An Edition', diss., University of Oregon, 1970
Grein	'*Menologium*' in C. W. M. Grein, ed., *Bibliothek der angelsächsischen Poesie in kritisch bearbeiteten Texten und mit vollständigem Glossar*, II.2 (Göttingen, 1858)
Grimaldi	M. Grimaldi, *Il 'Menologio' poetico anglosassone: introduzione, edizione, traduzione, commento* (Naples, 1988)
Hart	C. Hart, 'Appendix 23.1: The Old English Verse Menologium', in *Learning and Culture*, vol. 2.1 (Lewiston, 2003), pp. 197–215
Hickes	G. Hickes, *Linguarum Vett. Septentrionalium Thesauri Grammatico-critici et Archæologici*, Pars prima (Oxford, 1703)
Imelmann	R. Imelmann, *Das altenglische Menologium* (Berlin, 1902)
Jones	C. A. Jones, ed., *Old English Shorter Poems, vol. 1: Religious and Didactic* (Cambridge, MA, 2012)
O'Brien O'Keeffe	K. O'Brien O'Keeffe, ed., *The Anglo-Saxon Chronicle: A Collaborative Edition*, vol. 5: MS. C (Cambridge, 2001)
Plummer	C. Plummer, ed., *Two of the Saxon Chronicles*, 2 vols, reissued with a bibliographical note by Dorothy Whitelock (Oxford, 1952)
Rositzke	H. A. Rositzke, ed., *The C-Text of the Old English Chronicles*, Beiträge zur englischen Philologie 34 (Bochum-Langendreer, 1940)
Wülker	'Heiligenkalender' in R. P. Wülker, ed., *Bibliothek der*

Abbreviations

angelsächsischen Poesie begründet von Christian W. M. Grein,
II.2 (Leipzig, 1894)

Other Abbreviations

ÆCHom I	The first series of Ælfric's *Catholic Homilies*, ed. P. Clemoes, EETS ss 17 (Oxford, 1997)
ÆCHom II	The second series of Ælfric's *Catholic Homilies*, ed. M. Godden, EETS ss 5 (Oxford, 1979)
ASPR	Anglo-Saxon Poetic Records
AST	Anglo-Saxon Texts
BL	London, British Library
BT	J. Bosworth and T. N. Toller, eds., *An Anglo-Saxon Dictionary Based on the Manuscript Collections*, 2 vols. (Oxford, 1898, 1921)
BTC	A. Campbell, ed., *An Anglo-Saxon Dictionary Based on the Manuscript Collections of Joseph Bosworth: Enlarged Addenda and Corrigenda to the Supplement by T. Northcote Toller* (Oxford, 1972)
ByrEnch	Byrhtferth's *Enchiridion*, ed. P. S. Baker and M. Lapidge, EETS ss 15 (Oxford, 1995)
Campbell	A. Campbell, *Old English Grammar* (Oxford, 1959)
CCCC	Corpus Christi College, Cambridge
CH	John R. Clark Hall, ed., *A Concise Anglo-Saxon Dictionary*, 4th ed. with a supplement by H. D. Meritt (Cambridge, 1960)
CSASE	Cambridge Studies in Anglo-Saxon England
CSML	Cambridge Studies in Medieval Literature
DNR	Isidore of Sevilla's *De natura rerum*, ed. in ePL
DOE	*Dictionary of Old English, A–G Online*, ed. A. diPaolo Healey et al. (Toronto, 2007)
DOEC	*Dictionary of Old English Corpus*, ed. A. diPaolo Healey et al. (Toronto, 2009)
DTA	Ælfric's *De Temporibus Anni*, ed. M. Blake, AST 6 (Cambridge, 2009)
DTR	Bede's *De Temporum Ratione*, ed. C. W. Jones in *Bedae Opera de Temporibus* (Cambridge, MA, 1943)
EETS	Early English Text Society
os	original series
ss	supplementary series
EHR	*English Historical Review*
eMGH	Monumenta Germaniae Historica, http://ezproxy.ouls.ox.ac.uk:3386/eMGH/Default.aspx
ePL	Patrologia Latina Database, http://pld.chadwyck.co.uk
Gneuss	H. Gneuss, *Handlist of Anglo-Saxon Manuscripts: A List of*

Abbreviaitons

	Manuscripts and Manuscript Fragments Written or Owned in England up to 1100, MRTS 241 (Tempe, 2001)
Gneuss and Lapidge	H. Gneuss and M. Lapidge, *Anglo-Saxon Manuscripts: A Bibliographical Handlist of Manuscripts and Manuscript Fragments Written or Owned in England up to 1100* (Toronto, 2014)
HBS	Henry Bradshaw Society
Hogg	R. M. Hogg, *A Grammar of Old English*, vol. 1: Phonology (Oxford, 1992)
Hogg and Fulk	R. M. Hogg and R. D. Fulk, *A Grammar of Old English*, vol. 2: Morphology (Chichester, 2011)
JEGP	*Journal of English and Germanic Philology*
Ker	N. R. Ker, *Catalogue of Manuscripts Containing Anglo-Saxon* (Oxford, 1957)
MÆ	*Medium Ævum*
MCH	Metrical Calendar of Hampson, ed. P. McGurk, 'The Metrical Calendar of Hampson: A New Edition', *Analecta Bollandiana* 104 (1986), 79–125
MCR	Metrical Calendar of Ramsey, ed. M. Lapidge, 'A Tenth-Century Metrical Calendar from Ramsey', *Revue Bénédictine* 94 (1984), 326–69; repr. in M. Lapidge, *Anglo-Latin Literature 900–1066* (London, 1993), pp. 343–86
MCW	Metrical Calendar of Winchcombe, ed. M. Lapidge, 'A Tenth-Century Metrical Calendar from Ramsey', *Revue Bénédictine* 94 (1984), 326–69
MCY	Metrical Calendar of York, ed. A. Wilmart, 'Un témoin anglo-saxon du calendrier métrique d'York', *Revue Bénédictine* 46 (1934), 41–69
Mitchell	B. Mitchell, *Old English Syntax*, 2 vols (Oxford, 1985)
MRTS	Medieval and Renaissance Texts and Studies
NQ	*Notes and Queries*
OED2	J. Simpson and E. Weiner, eds., *The Oxford English Dictionary*, 2nd ed. 20 vols (Oxford, 1989)
OEM	*The Old English Martyrology*, ed. C. Rauer, AST 10 (Cambridge, 2013)
PASE	Prosopography of Anglo-Saxon England, http://www.pase.ac.uk/index.html
PM	The prose *Menologium* (i.e. PMC and PMH)
PMC	The prose *Menologium* recorded in CCCC, MS 422
PMH	The prose *Menologium* recorded in BL, MS Harley 3271
VM	The verse *Menologium*
WS	West Saxon
eWS	early West Saxon
lWS	late West Saxon
x	times (e.g., 8x means eight times)

Introduction

1
The Title

Ever since Hickes, the poem has generally been called the *Menologium*, although many modern scholars have regarded this as inappropriate. Dobbie, for instance, regards it as 'not quite appropriate',[1] Hart 'not wholly appropriate'[2] and Henel 'nicht recht passend'.[3] Baker also says that the poem is 'mistakenly known as the "Menologium"',[4] Lapidge writes that it 'normally passes under the utterly inappropriate title "Menologium"'[5] and Fulk and Cain refer to it as the 'misnamed *Menologium*'.[6] Some have even avoided using it, adopting some other title such as 'Old English Metrical Calendar'.[7] The main problem with the title is that it is originally a term for a certain service-book used in the Eastern Church,[8] with which the Old English poem has nothing to do.

When Hickes entitled the poem 'Calendarium seu Menologium Poeticum' in his *editio princeps*[9] published at the beginning of the eighteenth century, he seems to have had in mind a sort of martyrology arranged by the month, for which the term had been used in Western religious orders since the seventeenth century; in fact, he repeatedly refers to the *Old English Martyrology* as *Menol(ogium) Sax(onicum)*.[10] The word 'menologium' used to be applied, more often in Latin

---

[1] Dobbie, ed., *The Anglo-Saxon Minor Poems*, p. lxii.
[2] Hart, *Learning and Culture* II.1, p. 177.
[3] Henel, *Studien*, p. 71.
[4] Baker, 'OE Metrical Calendar', p. 312.
[5] Lapidge, 'The Saintly Life', p. 262.
[6] Fulk and Cain, *A History of Old English Literature*, p. 133.
[7] Lapidge, 'The Saintly Life', Baker, 'OE Metrical Calendar', Neville, *Representations*, and Gneuss and Lapidge, *Anglo-Saxon Manuscripts*, prefer this title, avoiding using the traditional one. Malone adopts the title 'Old English Calendar Poem' for his translation of the poem published in 1969, although he seems usually to use the traditional title as in his earlier book. See Malone, 'The Old English Period (to 1100)', pp. 35 and 70. Other than these instances, Bouterwek names the poem *Calendcwide* in his edition of the poem published in 1857, while Wülker calls it *Heiligenkalender* in his *Grundriss*, p. 367 and in *Bibliothek* II.2, p. 282. None of these alternative titles has ever been accepted widely.
[8] For instance, see Malone, 'Old English Calendar Poem', p. 193. The word came from medieval Latin *menologium* < later Greek μηνολόγιον.
[9] Hickes, *Linguarum* I.1, pp. 203–21.
[10] Hickes, *Linguarum* I.1, pp. 218–19. Elstob, *An English-Saxon Homily*, Appendix 26, and Kemble, *The Saxons in England* I, pp. 423–4, also use the term in this meaning.

Introduction

writing but also in English (often in the form 'menology'), to various works with characteristics similar to a martyrology arranged by the month, especially in the seventeenth and eighteenth centuries.[11] This led to its use for the *Old English Martyrology* as well as for the verse *Menologium*. Its use both in Latin and in English for this sort of work does not seem to have been unusual in the nineteenth century;[12] the Old English poem, in other words, was not named irrelevantly after some Greek service-book; rather, the use of the term for this sort of work has become obsolete in English, and as a result, it has come to seem irrelevant.

Thus its use for the poem does not seem totally inappropriate given its semantic history, but I also admit that it does not always represent the nature of the poem effectively. Following the advice of the editor of this series, therefore, I decided to entitle the book *The Old English Metrical Calendar (Menologium)*. I have retained the traditional title in parentheses partly because it is the only widely-known title by which people would search for the poem, and partly because 'The Old English Metrical Calendar' itself sounds more like the name of a literary genre (as with 'Latin metrical calendar') than the title of a particular work. Despite the convention of printing titles of Old English poems in italics, in fact, the alternative title in question has scarcely ever been printed in italics even by those preferring it, which may reflect its heterogeneity as the title of a poem. Throughout this volume, at any rate, I shall use the traditional title, partly for the sake of convenience; 'The Old English Metrical Calendar' is rather lengthy to be used repeatedly, while the abbreviation OEMC, which does not mean anything, is worse than *Menologium*. The use of the traditional title is preferable also from the viewpoint of consistency, since it is firmly established and is hardly avoidable; it is used in nearly all the books and articles referring to the poem, from which I quote. The title has also been used for the prose *Menologium* for more than eighty years and this is another good reason to follow the tradition. As I shall argue below, the prose and the verse *Menologium* are closely related, perhaps based on the same *Menologium* template; their close affinity is rightly reflected in the title they have in common. Moreover, alternative titles such as 'Old English Metrical Calendar' and 'Old English Calendar Poem' obscure the close relationship between the prose and the verse *Menologium*, whereas they

---

[11] For this use of the term in Western monastic orders, see Thurston, 'Menologium', pp. 191–2. In his dictionary, Dr Johnson defines the word menology as 'a register of months' and the only passage he quotes as an example of it is that referring to 'the Roman martyrology'. See Johnson, *A Dictionary of the English Language*, s.v. menology. In Jesuit houses in Britain, moreover, the tradition of reading an English menology of previous Jesuits continued at supper into the last century (Jack Mahoney, SJ, private communication).

[12] For examples of its use for this sort of work, see *OED*2, s.v. menology 1b, which lists examples of the word 'applied esp. to the OE. metrical church calendar first printed by Hickes in 1705', i.e. the verse *Menologium*, but quotations include some instances of its use for other works.

may also suggest a closer relationship with Latin metrical calendars and/or Old Irish calendar poems, which is, in my opinion, not the case (for details, see pp. 18–32 below).

2
Editorial History

The *Menologium* has been edited by at least seventeen editors (though not always based on the original manuscript), which is a good number for a short minor poem. Hickes's edition is included in his *Linguarum Veterum Septentrionalium Thesaurus* (*pars prima* dated 1703) and is furnished with a translation and notes both in Latin. Fox's edition published in 1830, the first independent edition with a brief commentary and the first English translation, is basically a re-presentation of Hickes's text with some corrections, modifications and errors. Hickes entitles the poem 'Calendarium seu Menologium Poeticum', while Fox modifies it as 'Menologium seu Calendarium Poeticum', which may have contributed to the establishment of the title *Menologium*.

The first edition in Germany is included in an Old English reader by Ebeling published in 1847. His text is based chiefly on Hickes's and takes over almost all the misspelt words (often neglecting Fox's corrections), while he adds many more. He also follows Hickes as regards the title. Other than the text itself, it includes only very brief textual notes.

The first independent edition in Germany, entitled *Calendcwide i.e. Menologium ecclesiæ Anglo-Saxonicæ Poeticum*, published by Bouterwek in 1857, includes the Old English text and interlinear glosses and substantial notes, both in Latin. Bouterwek often follows the traditional reading handed down from Hickes and Fox rather than the manuscript reading, but at several points he suggests a new reading introducing radical emendations, none of which have been accepted by any later editors. It was first pointed out in this edition that lines 60–2 are a quotation from the *Metrical Psalms*.

Another independent edition in Germany is a doctoral dissertation by Imelmann published in 1902. It provides the first substantial introduction on the manuscript, language, metre and style, purpose, sources and analogues, place and date of origin, etc., but fails to include commentary and glossary. As regards the text, Imelmann tends to introduce unnecessary emendations, while he often omits words in the manuscript, adds words not in the original, and also changes spellings and word orders. Fritsche includes a revised version of Imelmann's text in his thesis on the syntax of the *Menologium* published in 1907. His modifications are minute and his text inherits the problems of Imelmann's. He enumerates syntactic features of the poem but provides no discussion on the poem itself.

The poem is sometimes included in collections of Old English poems such as those by Grein, Wülker, Dobbie and Jones. Grein's text is printed at the

Introduction

beginning of the second volume of his *Bibliothek der angelsächsischen Poesie* series published in 1858. It provides the text and only very brief footnotes without any introduction. Grein adopts his own peculiar spelling conventions, whereas he often follows earlier editors rather than the original text when they differ from the original. Unlike earlier editions, his text is nearly free from misspellings, but it includes one incomprehensible mistake; he prints *vinter* 'winter' (124a) instead of *sumor* 'summer' in the original. Wülker includes the poem under the title *Heiligenkalender* in the revised edition of the same series published in 1894. As far as the *Menologium* is concerned, his text seems to be a new edition rather than a revised version of Grein's. In comparison with earlier editions, his is edited relatively faithfully to the original, and is accompanied by extensive textual notes and also a few explanatory notes but it does not include any introduction to the poem.[13]

The edition of the poem most widely used hitherto is included in the sixth volume of the Anglo-Saxon Poetic Records published by Dobbie in 1942. It includes an introduction neatly summarising major views on the poem as well as detailed explanatory notes. Generally, Dobbie follows the original faithfully and in that sense his text is much more reliable than those of earlier editors, which are often full of changes and emendations. He is the first editor who correctly divides the poem into the four sections designed by the poet himself and duly followed by the scribe in the manuscript. As pointed out by Stanley, however, it is also true that Dobbie, when editing the poem, introduces emendations more readily than he usually does in his texts of other poems in the same series.[14] In fact, Greeson and Grimaldi, two of the most serious editors of the poem, reject many of Dobbie's own emendations as well as those of earlier editors adopted by Dobbie.

Two editions are derived from Dobbie's, those by Hart and Jones. Hart's is attached to his study on the poem and is provided with an English translation. He discusses its contents and sources, and its concordance with the Ramsey Calendar and Byrhtferth's *Enchiridion*, and concludes that the poet is Byrhtferth (for details, see below). Hart's text is intended to be 'based closely on' Dobbie's,[15] but numerous misspelt words and a significant change in the order of the original text (in lines 43–7) make it much less reliable. He also introduces his own sectioning. Jones's text, on the other hand, is fairly closely based on Dobbie's with only a few modifications, while he introduces his own hyphenation and sectioning. This is the most recent edition to date, included in a volume gathering Old English religious and didactic poems in the Dumbarton

---

[13] Wülker gives an overview of the studies on the poem in his earlier work. See Wülker, *Grundriss*, pp. 367–8.

[14] Stanley writes that 'Dobbie, who is usually careful in considering the emendations proposed by earlier editors and commentators, seems less so in his edition of the verse *Menologium*'. See Stanley, 'The Prose *Menologium* and the Verse *Menologium*', p. 260.

[15] Hart, *Learning and Culture* II.1, p. 197.

Oaks Medieval Library series published in 2012. It is provided with an English translation, brief introduction and textual and explanatory notes.

Four more editions, those by Earle, Plummer, Rositzke and O'Brien O'Keeffe, are included in the editions of the Anglo-Saxon Chronicle. Whether or not this is clearly stated, they are all semi-diplomatic editions, and are equally problematic, falling between critical and diplomatic, which causes various inconsistencies in their texts.[16] Earle, Plummer and Rositzke provide only very brief introductions and a few notes, whereas O'Brien O'Keeffe furnishes a detailed introduction to the manuscript, the scribal practices and the language as well as detailed notes on scribal practices.

None of the three full-fledged editions are widely circulated: Greeson's 'Two Observance Poems' (1970) and Karasawa's 'The Verse *Menologium*' (2007) are unpublished doctoral dissertations, while Grimaldi's *Il 'Menologio'* (1988), written in Italian, is difficult to obtain. Besides the text, all these editions include an English or Italian translation, introduction, commentary and glossary. Their texts are faithful to the original with minimal emendations and changes; they, therefore, reject many of the emendations adopted in Dobbie's edition. Greeson, in his introduction, focuses especially on the development of the genre of metrical calendar and its art, whereas Grimaldi summarises major views on the poem presented by various scholars and discusses the genre of martyrology and menologium. Karasawa provides extensive introductions to both the prose and verse *Menologium* as well as a discussion on the relationship between the two.

3

The Manuscript and Its Context

The Manuscript

The verse *Menologium* is uniquely preserved in London, British Library, MS Cotton Tiberius B.i, which contains the following items:[17]

1. The Old English *Orosius* (fols. 3r–111v);[18]
2. The *Menologium* (fols. 112r–114v);[19]

---

[16] See Karasawa, 'The Verse *Menologium*', pp. 29–34, and also Karasawa, 'Some Problems'.
[17] For general information about this manuscript as a whole, see Ker, *Catalogue*, pp. 251–4; and Doane, ed., *Anglo-Saxon Manuscripts*, pp. 1–6. The latter includes a microfiche facsimile of the whole manuscript.
[18] For the edition of this item, see Bately, ed., *Old English Orosius*.
[19] For the editions of this item, see the previous section. Its printed facsimile is included in Robinson and Stanley, *Old English Verse Texts*.

Introduction

3. *Maxims II* (fol. 115r–v);[20]
4. The C-text of the Anglo-Saxon Chronicle (fols. 115v–164r).[21]

Since the C-text of the Chronicle seems to have been 'written at one time to 1044 and probably to "þæt bisceoprice" in the 1045 annal',[22] while it seems to keep 'a near-contemporary record from then until 1066',[23] its compilation is thought to have begun in the 1040s.[24] This must also be when the *Menologium* and *Maxims II* were written down, since these poems and the beginning part of the Chronicle (up to AD 490) are written in the same hand.[25] As Ker dates the first and the second part respectively as s. xi[1] and s. xi[2],[26] the first part (item 1 above), written in four hands of s. xi[1],[27] seems slightly earlier than the rest (items 2–4) written by seven mid-eleventh-century hands (and one twelfth-century hand transcribing a supply-text on fol. 164r).[28] Of these texts, Plummer says 'it is impossible to say whether it [i.e. the Chronicle including the two poems] and the Orosius originally belonged together or not',[29] whereas Conner claims that 'the Orosius seems to have been added later'.[30] O'Brien O'Keeffe's recent study, on the other hand, observes that the grid and ruling at the beginning of the second part seemingly follow those of the first part, which suggests that the second part was added to the already existing first part rather than the other way around.[31]

---

[20] For the edition of this item, see Dobbie, ed., *The Anglo-Saxon Minor Poems*, pp. 55–7. See also Williams, ed., *Gnomic Poetry*. Its printed facsimile is included in Robinson and Stanley, *Old English Verse Texts*.

[21] For the edition of this item, see O'Brien O'Keeffe, ed., *The Anglo-Saxon Chronicle*. See also Rositzke, *The C-Text of the Old English Chronicles*.

[22] Ker, *Catalogue*, p. 252.

[23] Baxter, 'MS C of the Anglo-Saxon Chronicle', p. 1194.

[24] Keynes also writes that the manuscript 'was produced ... in the mid-1040s'. See Keynes, 'Manuscripts of the *Anglo-Saxon Chronicle*', p. 546.

[25] Ker, *Catalogue*, p. 253; Bately, ed., *Old English Orosius*, p. xxv; and O'Brien O'Keeffe, ed., *The Anglo-Saxon Chronicle*, pp. xxvi–xxvii.

[26] Ker, *Catalogue*, pp. 251–3. Gneuss also dates the first part as s. xi[1], while the rest as s. xi med. See Gneuss, *Handlist*, p. 68. See also Gneuss and Lapidge, *Anglo-Saxon Manuscripts*, pp. 294–6.

[27] For the date of the first four hands, see Bately, ed., *Old English Orosius*, p. xxv.

[28] For details of these eight hands responsible for the second part, see O'Brien O'Keeffe, ed., *The Anglo-Saxon Chronicle*, pp. xxvi–xxxviii.

[29] Plummer, ed., *Two of the Saxon Chronicles* II, p. xxx. The words in square brackets are mine.

[30] Conner, ed., *The Anglo-Saxon Chronicle*, p. xix.

[31] According to O'Brien O'Keeffe, from fol. 35 on, 'the page is ruled for 27 lines, and the measurements of the written space of the *Orosius* ... [are] 130mm ..., while the height of the writing grid is 215–18mm'. The quire (quire 15) containing the *Menologium*, *Maxims II* and the beginning of the Chronicle is also ruled for 27 lines and 'the writing grid ... is ruled consistently to be 130mm wide', while 'the outer sheet of the quire is ruled for a length of 212mm, although its inner two sheets are ruled for 215 and 218mm ... matching the normal dimensions for the second writing grid of the *Orosius* ...'.

Jorgensen accepts this and writes that 'the whole collection seems to have been assembled around a copy of the Old English *Orosius*'.[32]

The place of origin of the manuscript is not totally clear but it has generally been assigned to Abingdon.[33] John Joscelyn identified it as an Abingdon manuscript in the list of the manuscripts of the Anglo-Saxon Chronicle between 1565 and 1567,[34] and Robert Cotton, following Joscelyn, is said to have written 'Cronica Saxonica Abbingdoniæ ad annum 1066' at the head of fol. 112r, where the *Menologium* begins.[35] Whitelock writes that 'It has several references to Abingdon affairs and was doubtless the product of that house, where it seems to have remained.'[36] In a recent study, Conner tries to prove the Abingdon origin of the manuscript, saying 'ever since John Joscelyn ... we have found no unassailable arguments to attribute the manuscript elsewhere', enumerating numerous pieces of evidence.[37] In the introduction to her recent edition of the C-text of the Anglo-Saxon Chronicle, on the other hand, O'Brien O'Keeffe raises doubts about the traditional attribution of the manuscript to Abingdon, and ascribes its origin to Christ Church, Canterbury.[38] Although she admits that 'further work must be done on the evidence connecting the C-text to Canterbury'[39] and the traditional Abingdon provenance is still much more widely current,[40] her view is interesting in relation to the *Menologium*, since it contains a few words possibly indicating Kentish phonological/orthographical features and some suggest its close connection with Canterbury.[41] Moreover, the calendar in Oxford, Bodleian Library, MS Bodley 579, which shows close affinities with the prose *Menologium*, a very close analogue of the verse *Menologium*, in terms

---

See O'Brien O'Keeffe, ed., *The Anglo-Saxon Chronicle*, pp. xx–xxv. See also O'Brien O'Keeffe, 'Reading the C-Text', pp. 138–41.

[32] Jorgensen, ed., *Reading the Anglo-Saxon Chronicle*, p. 9.

[33] Gneuss notes 'prob. Abingdon' for the first part and 'Abingdon' for the second. See Gneuss, *Handlist*, p. 68. See also Swanton, *The Anglo-Saxon Chronicle*, p. xxiv and Jorgensen, ed., *Reading the Anglo-Saxon Chronicle*, p. 6.

[34] O'Brien O'Keeffe, ed., *The Anglo-Saxon Chronicle*, p. lxxiv. The list is preserved in London, British Library, MS Cotton Nero C.iii, fol. 208r. For the edition and photographic reproduction of the list, see Graham and Watson, *The Recovery of the Past*.

[35] Plummer, ed., *Two of the Saxon Chronicles*, p. 273 and Ker, *Catalogue*, p. 252 ascribe the note to John Joscelyn, but according to O'Brien O'Keeffe, it post-dates Joscelyn and is to be ascribed to Robert Cotton. See O'Brien O'Keeffe, ed., *The Anglo-Saxon Chronicle*, p. lxxvii. See also Doane, ed., *Anglo-Saxon Manuscripts*, p. 1.

[36] Whitelock et al., *The Anglo-Saxon Chronicle*, p. xiii.

[37] Conner, ed., *The Anglo-Saxon Chronicle*, pp. lxxi–lxxxi. The quotation is from p. lxxi.

[38] O'Brien O'Keeffe, ed., *The Anglo-Saxon Chronicle*, pp. lxxiv–xcii.

[39] O'Brien O'Keeffe, ed., *The Anglo-Saxon Chronicle*, p. xcii.

[40] See, for instance, Baxter, 'MS C of the Anglo-Saxon Chronicle', pp. 1189–1227 and Jorgensen, ed., *Reading the Anglo-Saxon Chronicle*, p. 6.

[41] Imelmann, *Das altenglische Menologium*, pp. 53–4. For the possible Kentish spellings, see p. 56 below.

of its choice of high feasts, is possibly of Canterbury provenance (for details, see pp. 31–2 below).[42]

The scribe of the *Menologium*, *Maxims II* and the first part of the Chronicle seems to have copied his exemplars carefully. For instance, O'Brien O'Keeffe observes that the different styles of capitals he uses at the beginnings of these works suggest that he 'basically imitated the capital displays from his exemplars'.[43] As far as the *Menologium* is concerned, he seems to have followed the exemplar faithfully, preserving not only the style of the capitals at the beginning but also the sectioning of the poem and grammatical and spelling irregularities as in lines 55b, 56b, 88b, 104b, 106b, 111b, 120b, 130b, 140b, 164a, 173b, 181b, 184b, 193b, 206a and 218b (for details, see below). As I shall argue below, his sectioning of the poem reflects the poet's design, while grammatical and spelling irregularities often seem to have been intentionally caused by the poet himself in many cases for metrical purposes. Especially the latter points, together with the use of capitals noted by O'Brien O'Keeffe, suggest that the scribe copied the text mechanically without making any major changes. This may also indicate that the exemplar he used, as well as the extant text, is not very far away from the lost original since it seems to preserve features of the original text to a considerable degree. The present text itself, however, is not the original, which is obvious from the time lag of more than forty years between the date of composition and that of copying. Textual defects, including the two defective lines (71 and 76) and two misrepresentations of numerals (in lines 107 and 188), may well have also come into existence during the process of textual transmission.

Throughout the poem, the scribe uses a medial point to indicate the end of a half line, though he sometimes fails to do so by omitting or misplacing it.[44] Other than a medial point, *punctus versus* appears ten times (following lines 10b, 20b, 22b, 26b, 47b, 55b, 82b, 153a, 175b and 231b), in many cases with a rubric capital following it. Among these instances, those following lines 22b, 26b, 47b, 82b, 175b and 231b may be genuine,[45] while the others seem to be formed later by adding a downward stroke below the scribal medial point. The perhaps genuine *punctus versus* tends to mark a longer pause; those following lines 22b and 82b coincide with the end of a sentence, while those following lines 47b, 175b and 231b mark the ends of the sections or the poem.[46] However, the use of *punctus versus* is sparing and it is not used for most of the longer

---

[42] See Gneuss, *Handlist*, p. 95; and Gneuss and Lapidge, *Anglo-Saxon Manuscripts*, p. 456.
[43] O'Brien O'Keeffe, ed., *The Anglo-Saxon Chronicle*, p. l.
[44] He omits the points following lines 14b, 37b, 38a, 100b, 122a, 126b, 134a, 139a, 146a, 148a, 178a, 185a, 188a, 197a, 200b, 202a, 206a, 224a and 230a, while he seems to misplace the points in lines 59a, 67, 77b, 79b and 102a.
[45] See O'Brien O'Keeffe, ed., *The Anglo-Saxon Chronicle*, p. xlvii, where she also mentions line 35b, but *punctus versus* does not appear there.
[46] Regarding the sectioning of the poem, see pp. 33–9 below.

pauses including the end of the second section (in line 119b), whereas it is used in the middle of a sentence at least once at the end of line 26b.

The *punctus elevatus* also appears in several places, but most or all of them seem to be added by a later hand who added a virgule above the scribal medial point changing it into a *punctus elevatus*. By doing so, the later punctuator intends to mark the caesura, but occasionally he adds a virgule above the wrong point as if he intended to mark the end of a long-line. Once a virgule is misplaced, it often takes several half-lines for the punctuator to recover the right order.[47] In one case, it takes nearly twenty lines (88–107) for him to recognise the mistake. After repeating the same mistake several times, he quits adding a virgule at line 130 with only one exception at line 153b.

Rubrics are used only for capitals (but not all capitals are rubrics). Huge rubrics are used at the beginning of the poem (fol. 112r1), while a huge rubric *h* is also used on the margin at the beginnings of the second and the fourth sections (fol. 112v13 and fol. 114r18). The third section also begins with a large rubric wynn (fol. 113v6).[48] Thus larger rubrics are used only to mark the beginning of the poem and of the sections. In combination with a larger rubric (and in one case also with *punctus versus*), the scribe twice uses a wide blank space to mark the end of the section (fol. 112v12 and fol. 113v6).

Smaller rubrics are occasionally used to mark the beginning of a sentence and also for the initials of proper names. There are also two instances of capital *A*'s filled with red/orange; both are on the first page (fol. 112r9 and 15), and both mark the beginning of a sentence. Ordinary brown capitals are also occasionally used, basically to mark the beginnings of sentences or for the initials of proper names. There are, however, some cases where they are used for the initials of ordinary words in the middle of a sentence. On the whole, the use of smaller rubrics, *A*'s filled with red/orange and brown capitals are sporadic and irregular.

Accents are also used sporadically. According to O'Brien O'Keeffe, thirty-four of them may be genuine, while the others (some seventeen) are later additions.[49] They are often placed above a monophthongal long vowel in a monosyllabic word or element as in *áá, ǽgleawe, ǽr, fús, hér, líf, rímcrǽftige, sǽgrund, tó, tún, þá, ús, tíd/tíid/tííd, tíreadige, unrím*. Yet accents are also used for the same type of vowel in a disyllabic word, as in *éce* and *tíída*. Though less frequently, they are also placed above a monophthongal short vowel as in *óf, lóf, sé, úp, wícum*. Thus there seem to be no strict rules behind the use of the accent marks.

---

[47] Disorders are found in the following lines: 19–22, 37–41, 54–5, 58, 66–8, 71–2, 76–9, 88–107, 112–16, 121–7.

[48] The wynn at 9 mm is not exceptionally tall; there are several capital thorns of similar height, i.e. 8–9 mm. See O'Brien O'Keeffe, ed., *The Anglo-Saxon Chronicle*, pp. 3–10. However, the wynn in question looks larger than the capital thorns of similar height because it is much wider and bolder; it is obviously different from the thorns of similar height.

[49] O'Brien O'Keeffe, ed., *The Anglo-Saxon Chronicle*, p. liii. Dobbie, ed., *The Anglo-Saxon Minor Poems*, p. cxlii, on the other hand, lists fifty-one accents, of which O'Brien O'Keeffe says seventeen 'are clearly the work of later readers'.

Introduction

The scribe uses the following abbreviations when copying the *Menologium*:

1. Line above *a*, *i* and *u* for *m* (*-ā* for *-am*; *-ī* for *-im*; *-ū* for *-um*);
2. Line above *n* for *ne* (*þæn̄* for *þænne*);
3. Line above *nn* for *e* (*þæn̄n̄* for *þænne*);
4. Line above *t* for *er* (*æf[t̄]* for *æfter*);
5. ⁊ for *and/ond* ;
6. þ̄ for *þæt* ;
7. ⁹ for *us* (*martin⁹* for *Martinus*);
8. : for *us* (*Iacob:* for *Iacobus*).

As regards the last case, it seems probable, despite O'Brien O'Keeffe's suggestion,[50] that the abbreviation *:* was added by a scribe at some stage of textual transmission rather than that it preserves the original text; the form *Iacob* without the Latin ending is more plausible from the viewpoints of metre and the poet's prosodic habits (for details, see pp. 66–8 below). Otherwise, all the abbreviations are acceptable as reflecting the original reading. Other than these, the scribe also uses Roman numerals twice, i.e., *.III.* (fol. 112r27) and *xi.* (fol. 112v6).

The Manuscript Context

Unlike most of the other Chronicle manuscripts, London, British Library, MS Cotton Tiberius B.i contains another major work on history, the Old English *Orosius*, alongside the Chronicle. Since most of it consists of these two historical works, the manuscript as a whole seems intended to be a record of world and domestic historical events. Among other Chronicle manuscripts, London, British Library, MS Cotton Otho B.xi (G), combining the Chronicle and the Old English translation of Bede's *Ecclesiastical History*,[51] comprises a larger volume of domestic history, whereas our manuscript is unique in that it combines world and domestic histories. It is also unique among the Chronicle manuscripts in that the Chronicle is preceded by two Old English poems.

Ever since Robert Cotton rightly suggested it in the aforementioned note at the head of fol. 112r, the *Menologium* and *Maxims II* have been considered to be prologues to the C-text of the Anglo-Saxon Chronicle.[52] Although early editors

---

[50] O'Brien O'Keeffe, ed., *The Anglo-Saxon Chronicle*, p. 5. All the editors, earlier or later, of the poem adopt the form without the ending *-us*.

[51] The greater part of this manuscript was lost in the fire at the Cotton Library in 1731, but thanks to the sixteenth-century transcription by Laurence Nowell its contents are known to us. It also contained a West-Saxon royal genealogy and laws. For the manuscript and its contents, see, for instance, Ker, *Catalogue*, pp. 230–4; Swanton, *The Anglo-Saxon Chronicle*, pp. xxii–xxiii; Gneuss, *Handlist*, p. 67; and Gneuss and Lapidge, *Anglo-Saxon Manuscripts*, pp. 280–1.

[52] See, for instance, Earle, ed., *Two of the Saxon Chronicles*, p. xxix; Dobbie, ed., *The Anglo-Saxon Minor Poems*, pp. lx–lxi; Whitbread, 'Two Notes'; Whitelock et al., *The*

sometimes print these poems together with consecutive line numbers as if they were one work,[53] these two poems seem originally to have been regarded as two different works, which seems appropriate if we compare their topics and styles. The scribe, in fact, begins both the *Menologium* and *Maxims II* with a line in capitals: at the beginning of the former, the scribe writes 'CRIST WÆS ACEN/ NYD CYNINGA WULdor', beginning with a huge ornamental capital *C* in black and red put around a picture of an eagle probably symbolising Christ;[54] and the latter begins at the top of a new leaf (fol. 115r) with a line in red capitals reading 'CYNING SCEAL RICE HEALDAN …', with an especially large capital *C* at the beginning of the sentence. The scribe's use of different styles of capitals at the beginnings of these poems suggests that the poems were two different works copied from two different exemplars by different scribes.[55] Paralleled by *Maxims I* in the Exeter Book and other similar works in other Germanic languages,[56] *Maxims II* is based on a Germanic and especially Anglo-Saxon tradition of gnomic verses, and it seems most reasonable to consider that it was originally a separate piece which happened to be placed side by side with the *Menologium* in this manuscript. Dobbie, thus, says that 'there can be little doubt that the two poems were originally separate pieces',[57] whereas Bredehoft assigns them to two different poets based on metrical and phraseological evidence.[58]

The relationship between these two poems is quite obscure – as Williams writes, 'there is no internal connection'.[59] Amodio also writes that it is 'something of a mystery'[60] why the scribe decided to include the two short poems, while Dobbie says *Maxims II* 'has no relationship in subject matter to either the *Menologium* or the Chronicle'.[61] Based on some seasonal/nature descriptions near the beginning of *Maxims II* (lines 5b–9), Whitbread conjectures that the

---

Anglo-Saxon Chronicle, p. xiii; Wrenn, *A Study of Old English Literature*, p. 166; Bollard, 'The Cotton Maxims'; Greenfield and Calder, *A New Critical History of Old English Literature*, p. 235; O'Brien O'Keeffe, ed., *The Anglo-Saxon Chronicle*, p. xx; and Fulk and Cain, *A History of Old English Literature*, p. 133.

[53] See Hickes, *Linguarum*; Fox, *Menologium*; and Ebeling, *Angelsächsischen Lesebuch*. Rask also refers to the ending part of *Maxims II* as 'the conclusion of the *Menologium Saxonicum*' (Rask, *A Grammar of the Anglo-Saxon Tongue*, p. 138). In the editions by Fox and Ebeling, though the line numbers are consecutive, a dividing line is drawn between the *Menologium* and *Maxims II*. CH also adopts consecutive line numbers for the two poems as in MEN 245, referring to *Maxims II* 13 under the heading of *clibbor*.

[54] See Greeson, 'Two Old English Observance Poems', p. 4.

[55] See O'Brien O'Keeffe, ed., *The Anglo-Saxon Chronicle*, p. 1.

[56] As regards the Germanic tradition of gnomic verses, see, for instance, Williams, ed., *Gnomic Poetry*, pp. 1–81; Larrington, *A Store of Common Sense*; and Cavill, *Maxims in Old English Poetry*, pp. 25–40.

[57] Dobbie, ed., *The Anglo-Saxon Minor Poems*, p. lx.

[58] Bredehoft, *Authors*, p. 125. For further details as to metrical features of these poems, see pp. 66–9 below.

[59] Williams, ed., *Gnomic Poetry*, p. 103.

[60] Amodio, *The Anglo-Saxon Literature Handbook*, p. 312.

[61] Dobbie, ed., *The Anglo-Saxon Minor Poems*, p. lxi.

Introduction

scribe, having a copy of these two poems as two consecutive items already, decided to use the *Menologium* as a suitable preface to the Chronicle and then continued to copy *Maxims II* because he just read the first ten or so opening lines of *Maxims II* and noticed that 'it dealt with the year's seasons in much the same style' as that of the *Menologium*.[62] Through this rather cursory conjecture, Whitbread suggests that *Maxims II* is included in the manuscript chiefly due to the scribe's insufficient understanding of it, and therefore it has almost nothing to do with the manuscript context.

As in the case of Whitbread, the *Menologium*, as a calendar poem, has often been viewed as suitable for a preface to the Chronicle,[63] while the position of *Maxims II* is much more obscure. Earle regards it, together with the *Menologium*, as a work illustrating 'the condition of some branches of knowledge and culture which are cognate to the study of history',[64] which is a vague observation. Greenfield and Evert conjecture that perhaps the *Menologium*, presenting the year as a cycle of important holidays, is included in the manuscript to balance 'the extremely linear historical view of the Chronicle', while *Maxims II*, according to them a poem on the limitations of knowledge, may be appropriate as a preface to 'an ambitious intellectual endeavor such as the Chronicle'.[65] Their conjectures do not seem to have been convincing enough to exert any significant influence upon later scholarship. In fact, all the other Chronicle manuscripts may well suggest otherwise; they pay no recognisable attention to either the balance between the linear historical and the cyclic perspectives or the reminder of the limitation of knowledge. Robinson, on the other hand, discusses features shared by the *Menologium*, *Maxims II* and the Chronicle; they are all some sorts of lists, 'thematically united by a shared concern with time' and revealing 'a similar perspective on historical time', in which attention is called to the relation between antiquity and the (Anglo-Saxon) present. As Robinson himself admits, however, it is also true that 'thematic similarities by their nature are less demonstrable'.[66]

The adoption of the two poems as a preface to the C-text of the Chronicle, which is unparalleled elsewhere in the Chronicle manuscripts, may be explained in relation to another of its unique features: the primacy of the Old English *Orosius*, to which the rest seems to have been added. The *Orosius* first relates the geography of the 'world' and human history from the Deluge to the

---

[62] Whitbread, 'Two Notes', pp. 192–3.
[63] See the studies mentioned in footnote 52. See also Robinson, 'Old English Literature in Its Most Immediate Context', and Head, 'Perpetual History'.
[64] Earle, ed., *Two of the Saxon Chronicles*, p. xxix.
[65] Greenfield and Evert, 'Maxims II', p. 354. When referring to the cyclicity of the year and the 'linear historical view of the Chronicle', Greenfield and Evert may be under the influence of Hennig, 'The Irish Counterparts', where the cyclic and the linear historical conceptions of time are discussed in terms of the *Menologium* and some Old Irish calendar poems. For Hennig's influence upon *Menologium* studies, see pp. 21–6 below.
[66] All the quotations are from Robinson, 'Old English Literature in Its Most Immediate Context', p. 28.

foundation of Rome, and then deals with Roman history up to the author's time, together with Greek, Persian and Macedonian histories. It deals (largely) with pre-Christian/non-Christian foreign events, whose dates are indicated in terms of the foundation of the city of Rome by phrases such as: *ær/æfter þæm þe Romeburg getimbred wæs X wintra* ... 'X years before/after the city of Rome was founded ...'. The Chronicle, on the other hand, deals chiefly with domestic events mostly in Christian times and all the events are dated in terms of the birth of Christ. The only event before the birth of Christ in the C-text of the Chronicle, that is, Julius Caesar's failed expedition to Britain, is dated in the following manner: *ÆR CRISTES GEFLÆscnesse .lx.*[67] 'sixty (years) before Christ's incarnation'. The date is counted from the birth of Christ and the event recorded is in a sense a 'domestic' one; its perspective is quite different from that of the *Orosius* which deals chiefly with pre-Christian/non-Christian foreign events whose dates are always counted from the foundation of the city of Rome.

Placed between the *Orosius* and the Chronicle, the two poems may be intended to bridge the gap between these two works based on different perspectives. As a brief summary of the Christian year beginning with the reference to the birth of Christ, the *Menologium* serves clearly to mark the change in the systems of dating followed in these two historical works. Near the beginning of the poem, at the same time, the ancient Romans are mentioned as those who formerly called the first month of the year *Ianuarius* (9b–10) and once reckoned the beginning of *Februarius* (17b–19a), and they are contrasted with 'us' Anglo-Saxons who call the Epiphany *twelfta dæg* 'Twelfth Day' (in the vernacular) here in Britain (11–15a) and to whom *forma monað*[68] and *Solmonað* (rather than *Ianuarius* and *Februarius*) come (7–9a, 15–17a) (in the present tense in contrast with the past tense in the cases of the ancients). This contrast between ancient/foreign and present/domestic people at the beginning serves to mark the aforementioned shift of perspective. A similar contrast occurs once more in lines 165b–7a. The domestic perspective is emphasised throughout the poem by repeated references to *us* Anglo-Saxons (lines 8b, 12b, 34b, 72b, 108b, 131b etc.), or *Engle and Seaxe* (185b),[69] and also to *Bryten* 'Britain' (lines 14b, 40a, 98b, 104b, 155b).[70] In fact, such a frequent use of the word *Bryten* is unparalleled in Old English poetry,[71] and this reflects the poem's especially strong emphasis on its national

---

[67] These words are quoted from O'Brien O'Keeffe, ed., *The Anglo-Saxon Chronicle*, p. 14. My translation.

[68] The Old English term for January, *Æfterra Iula*, is not used in the *Menologium* perhaps because *æfterra* 'latter' is not appropriate for the beginning of the year; it is called *forma monað* (9a) 'the first month' instead.

[69] As far as poetic works are concerned, the phrase *Engle and Seaxe* is attested only twice more in the *Battle of Brunanburh* (70a) and the *Death of Edward* (11a). The word *Seaxe* is used once more in the *Menologium* at 231a.

[70] One more instance, *Brytenricu* (230b), may be added to the list. See the note for line 203b in the Commentary.

[71] In *Guthlac*, *Bryten* is used twice, but once each in *Guthlac A* (175a) and *Guthlac B* (883b), which were composed by two different poets. The other instances of the word in

Introduction

perspective. The Christian, present and domestic perspective is compressed in the concluding lines, where it is said that the poem shows when to hold the holy feasts observed particularly under the rule of the current king of the Saxons (lines 228b–31).[72]

Maxims II, though its relationship with other works in the manuscript is more obscure, is similar in its perspective to the *Menologium*. In the opening lines, the poem directs its audience to post-Roman Britain or Anglo-Saxon England, referring to Roman ruins left in England as *Ceastra ... enta geweorc, þa þe on þysse eorðan syndon* (1b–2) '(Roman) cities, ... works of the giants, which are on this ground'.[73] They are mentioned as things that are to be seen from afar, but the spatial distance mentioned here may also imply the temporal distance, which is more directly expressed by *enta geweorc* 'works of the giants', a set phrase referring to stonework of ancient manufacture.[74] Just as in the case of the concluding remark of the *Menologium*, these opening lines of *Maxims II* reveal that it was written from the post-Roman Anglo-Saxon point of view. Many stock images of Old English poetry used throughout the work also reflect its chief dependence upon the Anglo-Saxon world view.[75] It also occasionally refers to Christian ideas (e.g., 4b, 9b, 35b–6a, 48b–9) and ends with an explicitly Christian passage (lines 57b–66).

From the viewpoint of actual contents, moreover, *Maxims II*, often referring to the social order and values in the traditional Anglo-Saxon aristocratic/warrior society (e.g., 1a, 10b–12, 14–23a, 28b–9a, 31b–3a, 50–7a), has closer ties to the Chronicle, and can function as a bridge between the *Menologium* and the Chronicle. Together with the *Menologium*, therefore, *Maxims II* fits in the larger manuscript context, where these two poems seem to mark the shift from the records of largely pre-Christian/non-Christian foreign events to those of predominantly domestic events in the Christian period.

Some Chronicle manuscripts (i.e., A, B and G), contain laws, royal genealogies, and/or lists of popes, archbishops or bishops.[76] These genealogies and lists themselves are historical records, but listed in chronological order they may also serve as a guide to chronology. In relation to this sort of list as a

---

Old English poems are: *Metres of Boethius* (Metre 20, 99a), *Battle of Brunanburh* (71b), *Death of Edgar* (14a), *Seasons for Fasting* (56b) and *Aldhelm* (5a).

[72] Thornbury argues that these closing lines, where the 'sacred calendar is connected not to the archbishop or pope, but to the Saxon king whose hegemony extends across Britain, ... make clear the *Menologium*'s relation to the Anglo-Saxon Chronicle'. Thornbury, *Becoming a Poet*, p. 231.

[73] See also Robinson, 'Old English Literature in Its Most Immediate Context', p. 28.

[74] The *DOE* (s.v. *ent*) explains the phrase as 'referring to stonework, roads, buildings, artifacts, etc. of ancient manufacture'.

[75] For stock images of Old English poetry found in *Maxims II*, see Shippey, *Poems of Wisdom and Learning*, p. 15.

[76] The A-text is also accompanied by *Acta Lanfranci*, which seems to be treated as a continuation of, or appendix to, the Chronicle; it is placed just after the Chronicle whose last entry is for 1070, while it deals with Lanfranc's archiepiscopate beginning in 1070.

chronological guide, the following observation by Harrison is interesting, since the methodology of listing and counting is quite similar to that followed in the *Menologium*:

> During the summer of 616 a child could have remembered some such words as these: 'King Ethelbert reigned fifty-six years, and before him Eormenric *x* years, and Octa *y* years and Oisc twenty-four years, and that was (about?) thirty-five years before he came across the sea with his father Hengest.'[77]

The *Menologium*, which functions better in the manuscript context discussed above, may be included in place of these sorts of lists. *Maxims II*, on the other hand, may be seen as listing 'the laws of the natural world and of humanity'[78] from the Anglo-Saxon point of view (lines 55b–7a sound especially legal). The poetic 'laws' may have been preferred in place of the real laws perhaps because it is in better harmony with the poetic summary of the Christian year in its length, style and perspective. Thus the *Menologium* and *Maxims II* may have replaced those lists and laws in some other Chronicle manuscripts. Whether or not this is the case, the compiler's choice of these two poems as a preface seems to have much to do with the unique manuscript context in which the Chronicle follows the *Orosius*.

4

Sources

There is no evidence to show that the *Menologium* is a translation, versification, paraphrase, summary or redaction of any other work, and no source for the poem as a whole has ever been identified. It is probable that the poet consulted liturgical calendars when choosing the entries and counting the precise number of days between entries, and in this sense, they may be regarded as the poet's informational source.[79] As we shall see below, perhaps the poet also followed the already existing *Menologium* template, which is preserved better as the prose *Menologium*.[80] Although no one has ever regarded the prose *Menologium*

---

[77] Harrison, *The Framework of Anglo-Saxon History*, p. 124.
[78] Swanton, *The Anglo-Saxon Chronicle*, p. xxiv.
[79] Henel claims that the verse *Menologium* is perhaps an extract from a calendar (*Studien*, p. 90), and Dobbie basically follows this (*The Anglo-Saxon Minor Poems*, p. lxii). Hart, *Learning and Culture* II.1, pp. 180–3, tries to show the close relationship between the *Menologium* and the Ramsey Calendar (Oxford, St John's College, MS 17 (s. xii in.), fols. 16v–21v), although the calendar is more than a century younger than the poem. For details on the close relationship between the *Menologium* and ecclesiastical calendars, see pp. 40–4 below.
[80] For further details, see pp. 44–52 below.

Introduction

as the source of the verse *Menologium*,[81] in fact, it demonstrates by far the closest affinity and these two texts may well be based on fundamentally the same literary/educational tradition (for further details, see below).

There is only one passage in the *Menologium* whose textual source is identified. As Bouterwek first pointed out,[82] lines 60–2 are based on the following passage of the *Metrical Psalms*:

> Þis ys se dæg   þe hine drihten us
> wisfæst geworhte   wera cneorissum,
> eallum eorðtudrum   eadgum to blisse.[83] (Psalm 117.22)

The corresponding passage in the *Menologium* is as follows:

> Þis is se dæg   þæne drihten us
> wisfæst worhte   wera cneorisum,
> eallum eorðwarum   eadigum to blisse. (60–2)

With only minor changes, the passage in the *Menologium* is nearly the same as that in the *Metrical Psalms*. Just before the passage, in line 59, the poet himself says that the words are those sung by *se witega* 'the prophet' rather than his own, making it clear that it is a quotation. Ælfric, in his *Catholic Homilies* (II.16), confirms that this is a part of a song that is based on the words of *witega* and should be sung at Easter.[84] Thus the passage in the *Menologium* is a quotation from the *Metrical Psalms* and the fact furnishes the *terminus a quo* of the poem.[85] This is the only passage in the *Menologium* whose direct textual source can be identified. There are also many half-lines and phrases that may have been taken from other works,[86] but they shall be examined later in the section on the poetic technique of the poet.

Apart from the probable dependence on liturgical calendars and on the *Menologium* template (for details see below), the information on the saints,

---

[81] Stanley writes, for instance, that 'the prose [*Menologium*] cannot be and has never been regarded as the source of the verse [*Menologium*]' ('The Prose *Menologium* and the Verse *Menologium*', p. 259. Square brackets are mine.). Hart, though without justification, speculates that the prose *Menologium* is a condensed translation of the verse *Menologium* (*Learning and Culture* II.1, p. 194).

[82] Bouterwek, *Calendcwide*, p. 23.

[83] The passage is quoted from Krapp, ed., *The Paris Psalter*, pp. 102–3.

[84] For the original text, see Godden, ed., *Ælfric's Catholic Homilies: The Second Series, Text*, p. 167. It is probable that Ælfric, writing his *Catholic Homilies* c. 990–5, is contemporary with the *Menologium* poet. As Hart points out (*Learning and Culture* II.1, pp. 183–5), Byrhtferth's *Enchiridion* IV.1 (c. 1011) quotes the corresponding Latin passage in relation to the Resurrection. For the original text, see Baker and Lapidge, eds., *Byrhtferth's Enchiridion*, p. 212.

[85] See, for instance, Imelmann, *Das altenglische Menologium*, p. 52; Dobbie, ed., *The Anglo-Saxon Minor Poems*, p. lxv; Toswell, 'The Metrical Psalter'; and Bredehoft, *Authors*, pp. 113–14.

[86] See Bredehoft, *Authors*, pp. 113–30.

their feasts and the seasons given in the poem is mostly too brief and/or vague to identify any particular source text.[87] In fact, there may well be no source at all for such simple and commonplace statements as 'Christ was born ... in midwinter' (1–2a) and 'the holy Gregory, noble and famous in Britain, hurried into God's protection' (37b–40a). For the more informative statements, however, their (direct or indirect) informational sources may be located to a certain extent, as listed in the following table:

lines	topics	sources
3b–4a	Naming of Jesus on his eighth day	Luke 2.21 (cf. Matthew 1.21)
21b–2	Presentation of Jesus at the temple	Luke 2.22 (cf. MCY 9 and MCH 22)
44b–7	Vernal equinox and the creation of the sun and the moon[88]	DTR 6
48–54a	The Annunciation	Luke 1.26–33
83–7a	Finding of the Cross	Cf. Ambrose, *De obitu Theodosii*
95b–101a	Gregory's sending Augustine to Britain and Augustine's death	HE I.23–5
104b–6a	Augustine's burial place	HE II.3
158b–60a	Christ's receiving baptism from John the Baptist	Mark 1.4–9
160b–2	John the Baptist as the greatest man	Matthew 11.11
189b–93a	Martyrdom of SS Simon and Jude	*Passio Simonis et Iudae*
211b–14	Martyrdom of St Clement	Bede's *Martyrologium* or *Passio S. Clementis*[89]

The poet's statements are minimal and basic in these passages, and he could have written them even without consulting anything, but the sources listed here may be the ultimate sources of his knowledge, on which he based the poem.

---

[87] Thus no source texts are listed for the *Menologium* in the online Fontes Anglo-Saxonici database at http://fontes.english.ox.ac.uk/ (consulted on 4 October 2014).

[88] Hart points out that the 'Ramsey Calendar' recorded in Oxford, St John's College, MS 17 (fols. 16r–21v) lists the first seven days of the world (*Learning and Culture* II.1, p. 182). The creation of the sun and the moon on the fourth day of creation is listed under *xii Kl. Apr.* (i.e. 21 March) as *iiii. Solem et lunam*. The calendar is edited in Baker and Lapidge, eds., *Byrhtferth's Enchiridion*, pp. 390–416.

[89] See Lapidge, 'The Saintly Life', pp. 248–52.

Introduction

5

Analogues

As a poem closely related to a liturgical calendar, the *Menologium* has often been compared or discussed with Latin metrical calendars and Old Irish calendar poems. Some prefer the title 'Old English Metrical Calendar,' as if emphasising its close affinity to Latin metrical calendars,[90] and some even claim that 'the menologist translates and epitomises the erudite metrical Latin calendar of his house',[91] while others regard it as an Old English counterpart of some Old Irish calendar poems.[92] It is true that these Latin, Old English and Old Irish works are similar in that they are poems dealing with calendric matters but, as I shall presently discuss, these Latin and Old Irish analogues are different from the *Menologium* in their contents, structure, function and nature, and their affinities to the poem do not seem so close as to make us suspect any major connections between them. On the other hand, the prose *Menologium* is by far the closest analogue as rightly reflected in its title. The prose and the verse *Menologium*, seemingly composed for basically the same purpose, present very similar entries, function in the same way and share a peculiar but methodical structure, while differing from Latin metrical calendars and Old Irish calendar poems in all of these respects.

Latin Metrical Calendars

A Latin metrical calendar is a versified liturgical calendar in hexameters showing the dates of the feasts in the Roman reckoning. The 'Metrical Calendar of York' (hereafter MCY),[93] composed in the second half of the eighth century and recorded in two manuscripts,[94] preserves its earliest form. It consists of eighty-two hexameters listing sixty-five feasts, while the 231-line verse *Menologium* lists only twenty-nine feasts, of which twenty-five are shared by MCY.[95] In the early ninth century, MCY was taken to the Continent, where it was widely circulated and continued being redacted. As a result, its continental redactions are extant

---

[90] E.g., Lapidge, 'The Saintly Life', pp. 249–52; Baker, 'OE Metrical Calendar', p. 312; and Neville, *Representations*.
[91] Hart, *Learning and Culture* II.1, p. 194.
[92] Hennig, 'The Irish Counterparts'.
[93] It is edited in Wilmart, 'Un témoin anglo-saxon', pp. 41–69. Occasionally, the title *Martyrologium Poeticum* is also used for the same work as in ePL. For the text, see Appendix 2.
[94] The two manuscripts are: London, British Library, MS Cotton Vespasian B.vi (fol. 104r–v); and Cambridge, Trinity College, MS O.2.24 (fols. 88r–9v).
[95] For details, see Appendix 6.

Analogues

in six French, five German/Swiss and six Italian manuscripts.[96] In the early tenth century, a continental version was re-imported into England and was further refurbished and elaborated so as to contain 365 hexameters covering all the days of the year. This is the so-called 'Metrical Calendar of Hampson' (MCH)[97] and is extant in three manuscripts in its complete form.[98] In the late tenth century, a new metrical calendar of 182 hexameters was composed by an Anglo-Latin poet who drew on both MCY and MCH. This is the 'Metrical Calendar of Ramsey' (MCR), and is extant in only one manuscript, Oxford, St John's College, MS 17.[99] Its early twelfth-century revision, the 'Metrical Calendar of Winchcombe' (MCW),[100] is recorded in a liturgical calendar in London, British Library, MS Cotton Tiberius E.iv (fols. 35r–40v), while some twelve lines of MCR are entered also in a liturgical calendar in the thirteenth-century manuscript London, British Library, MS Cotton Julius D.vii (fols. 35v–41r).[101] The tradition survived even to the fourteenth century, when 'the latest datable Latin example of a metrical calendar', i.e. the Metrical Calendar in the Pembroke Psalter-Hours (MCPH), was composed.[102] Thus Latin metrical calendars, originating in Northumbria in the latter half of the eighth century, were disseminated to the Continent and to other parts of England during the subsequent centuries, and continued to be redacted and used until the fourteenth century and later.

Entries of Latin metrical calendars are often found interpolated in the framework of a liturgical calendar as in the cases of MCH, MCR, MCW, the

---

[96] See Lapidge, 'A Tenth-Century Metrical Calendar from Ramsey', pp. 332–42; and Lapidge, 'The Metrical Calendar in the "Pembroke Psalter-Hours"', pp. 344–5. An Irish redaction is also extant. Apart from these continental and Irish redactions, the following two metrical calendars not directly related to MCY and its derivatives are also known: the Metrical Calendar by Wandelbert of Prüm (813–70); and the Metrical Calendar by Eugenius Vulgarius (fl. tenth century). The former is edited in ePL with the title 'Martyrologium Wandalberti', and in eMGH with the title 'Martyrologium Poetae'. The latter is edited in Meyvaert, 'A Metrical Calendar'.

[97] MCH was first printed in Hampson, *Medii Aevi*, pp. 397–420, but this edition is notorious for its poor quality. See Hennig, 'A Critical Study', pp. 61–74. A new edition is now available in McGurk, 'The Metrical Calendar of Hampson'.

[98] The three manuscripts are: London, British Library, MS Cotton Galba A.xviii (fols. 3r–14v); London, British Library, MS Cotton Tiberius B.v, vol. 1 (fols. 2r–7v); and London, British Library, MS Cotton Julius A.vi (fols. 3r–8v). Apart from these, twenty-seven lines from MCH are recorded in the calendar in Oxford, Bodleian Library, MS Junius 27 (fols. 2r–7v), which is edited in Dumville, *Liturgy and the Ecclesiastical History*, pp. 1–38. For further information, see Lapidge, 'A Tenth-Century Metrical Calendar from Ramsey', pp. 343–5.

[99] MCR is edited in Lapidge, 'A Tenth-Century Metrical Calendar from Ramsey'.

[100] MCW is printed in Lapidge, 'A Tenth-Century Metrical Calendar from Ramsey', pp. 383–6.

[101] For the later history of MCR, see Lapidge, 'A Tenth-Century Metrical Calendar from Ramsey', pp. 375–9.

[102] MCPH is edited in Lapidge, 'The Metrical Calendar in the "Pembroke Psalter-Hours"', pp. 348–59. The quoted phrase is taken from p. 344. The manuscript itself is dated to the third quarter of the fifteenth century (probably 1465 x 1470) (p. 325).

fragment of MCH in Junius 27 and the fragment of MCR in Julius D. vii. As reflected here, they are versified entries of a liturgical calendar not only in their appellation but also in their function. Just like liturgical calendars, Latin metrical calendars reflect local liturgical practices, which underlie the repeated revision yielding different sets of entries. Among the sixty-five feasts mentioned in MCY, for instance, eight are those of Northumbrian saints, i.e. Cuthbert, Ecgberht of Ripon, Wilfrid I of York, Wilfrid II of York, Tatberht of Ripon, Bosa of York, the two Hewalds and Paulinus of York; of these MCH mentions only Cuthbert and Paulinus while MCR mentions Cuthbert alone. Thus MCY mentions six Northumbrian saints who are excluded from both the much longer MCH and MCR. In this way, each Latin metrical calendar is characterised by its regionalism attained by references to local and/or minor feasts not widely shared with others composed/redacted in other places. Just as in the cases of liturgical calendars, in fact, there exist no Latin metrical calendars in which all the traces of regionalism are eliminated by listing only the feasts observed universally.

In comparison, the verse *Menologium* is no more a versified liturgical calendar than the prose *Menologium* is a liturgical calendar. Unlike the cases of Latin metrical calendars, it is impossible to incorporate its entries into the framework of a liturgical calendar; it locates the feasts neither by the Roman reckoning nor in the framework of the Roman month system[103] but follows another major dating system current in Anglo-Saxon England (for details, see below). Judging from the poet's concluding remark (ll. 228b–31), moreover, the verse *Menologium* seems intended for English people in general and is indeed free from such regionalism as differentiated a metrical calendar composed, for instance, in York from that used in Ramsey. The prose *Menologium* is also devoid of this sort of regionalism, which hints, on the one hand, at the verse and the prose's close affinity, and on the other hand, at their remoteness from the traditions of liturgical calendars and Latin metrical calendars.

Hart, claiming that 'we find that all but one of the saints' festivals recorded [in the *Menologium*] appear among the Latin metrical entries of the Ramsey Calendar',[104] conjectures that the *Menologium* poet might well have consulted the (metrical) calendar (i.e. MCR) preserved in Oxford, St John's College, MS 17, fols. 16r–21v.[105] In actual fact, however, MCR includes about five times

---

[103] The use of Roman reckoning, while attested in numerous prose works, is not recorded in Old English poetry except for the reference to *kalendas*. On the other hand, the poet of the *Death of Edgar*, whom Bredehoft identifies as the *Menologium* poet (*Authors*, pp. 113–30), for instance, locates the date of the death of King Edgar in the framework of the Roman month system as the eighth day in the month of July (*Death of Edgar* 4b–10a). The same system is adopted throughout the *Old English Martyrology*.

[104] Hart, *Learning and Culture* II.1, pp. 178–83.

[105] According to Lapidge, the manuscript itself dates back to 1110–11, while the metrical calendar may well have been composed between 992 and 1005 ('A Tenth-Century Metrical Calendar from Ramsey', pp. 349 and 352). The calendar is printed in Baker and Lapidge, eds., *Byrhtferth's Enchiridion*, pp. 391–415.

Analogues

as many entries as are mentioned in the *Menologium*, and the set of feasts it presents is quite different from that in the poem (and more or less the same thing can be claimed about MCH, which includes all the feasts of the saints mentioned in the *Menologium* while presenting far more entries than the poem). Despite Hart's view, MCR does not show particularly close affinity to the verse *Menologium*, while as far as a list of important feasts is concerned, the calendar in Oxford, Bodleian Library, MS Bodley 579 is exceptionally close to the prose *Menologium* and also, though to a slightly lesser degree, to the verse *Menologium*, but I shall return to this issue later when discussing the prose *Menologium* (see also Appendix 6).

On the whole, the Latin and Old English calendar poems are quite different in the general principles they follow and in the scopes they cover, reflecting the difference in the traditions they follow, as well as in their functions, usages and purposes. The *Menologium* is not a simple versification of a liturgical calendar and is not an Old English counterpart of a Latin metrical calendar.

Old Irish Calendar Poems

In his influential article,[106] Hennig compares the verse *Menologium* with Old Irish calendar poems such as *Félire Óengusso*,[107] *Félire Adamnáin*[108] and *Enlaith betha*,[109] pointing out that these Old English and Old Irish works are the only calendar poems written in vernacular languages in early medieval Europe.[110] He argues that the cyclic structure and the integration of saints' feasts into the natural cycle of the year are two characteristics the *Menologium* shares with Old Irish calendar poems. He regards especially *Félire Adamnáin* and *Enlaith betha* as 'obvious Irish counterparts' of the *Menologium*, and claims that these Old Irish and Old English works represent the naturalistic trend of what he calls the Old Irish tradition of the *félire*.[111]

---

[106] It is quoted or mentioned, for instance, in Greeson, 'Two Old English Observance Poems'; Hansen, 'Wisdom Literature', p. 199; Calder and Allen, *Sources and Analogues*, p. 229; Howe, 'The Latin Encyclopedia Tradition', pp. 115–16; Weston, 'Cosmic Pattern', p. 75; Howe, *The Old English Catalogue Poems*, pp. 74–6; Greenfield and Calder, *A New Critical History of Old English Literature*, p. 250; Hansen, *The Solomon Complex*, p. 116; Grimaldi, *Il 'Menologio'*, p. 14; Wright, *The Irish Tradition*, p. 8; Richards, 'Old Wine in a New Bottle', p. 363; and Jones, ed., *Old English Shorter Poems*, p. xl.

[107] Stokes, ed., *Félire Óengusso*.

[108] Byrne, 'Félire Adamnáin'.

[109] The poem is edited in Best and Lawlor, eds., *The Martyrology of Tallaght*, pp. 94–7.

[110] Hennig, 'The Irish Counterparts', p. 100.

[111] Hennig, 'The Irish Counterparts', p. 106. Even before Hennig, Jackson compared the nature descriptions of the *Menologium* with those of some early Irish seasonal poetry. He, however, reached the conclusion that they should be attributed to 'the native elegiac and gnomic tradition' rather than to the influence from Irish seasonal poetry. See Jackson, *Studies in Early Celtic Nature Poetry*, pp. 167–9.

Introduction

Under the influence of Hennig, Greeson, in the introduction to his unpublished edition of the *Menologium*, argues that the Latin metrical calendars and the aforementioned Old Irish calendar poems are 'the Latin and Irish predecessors of the Old English *Menol[ogium]*', and discusses 'the development and descent of the genre'.[112] In discussing possible sources of the poem, Greeson criticises Henel by saying that '[p]ossibly Henel ... did not look far enough afield to the intercultural exchanges of the Anglo-Saxons and the Irish'.[113] Grimaldi, another editor of the poem, follows Hennig and Greeson and writes that the poet must have received the influence of Irish literature, especially with regard to the very close symbolic connection between zodiac signs and the feasts of the saints, between Christ and the sun, and the annual conception of time, which is in fact a common characteristic of Irish calendar poems such as *Félire Óengusso* and *Félire Adamnáin*.[114] Calder and Allen, accepting Hennig's theory, write that 'Dobbie's summary of scholarship on the source of the *Menologium* is ... in need of revision' since it does not mention 'the tradition of the Irish *félire*'.[115] Howe, also under the influence of Hennig, regards '*féliri*' as one of two important analogues, and compares them with the *Menologium*.[116] In a recent article, Richards, following Hennig and Greeson, also says that the *Menologium*'s 'cyclic structure, together with short but lyrical evocations of the seasons, suggests an Irish influence on the poet'.[117] Still more recently Jones, referring to Hennig, also writes that the poem 'resembles a kind of Old Irish metrical calendar, *félire*'.[118] Since Greeson and Grimaldi, the editors of the most recent and most serious editions of the *Menologium*, both adopt Hennig's view in their introductions, the theory of Irish influence, if not very widely accepted (while never seriously challenged either), must have been exerting a certain influence upon the subsequent *Menologium* scholarship as actually attested in the statements by several scholars mentioned above. I shall therefore examine the issue here, reaching the conclusion that the affinities between the Old Irish and Old English poems are too superficial and too general for us reasonably to perceive any substantial connections between them. Even at a glance, those two 'obvious Irish counterparts' look quite different from the *Menologium* in their

---

[112] Greeson, 'Two Old English Observance Poems', pp. 87–178.
[113] Greeson, 'Two Old English Observance Poems', p. 119.
[114] The original Italian passage reads: 'Ma il poeta ha risentito certamente anche degli influssi della letteratura irlandese specialmente per quanto riguarda la stretta connessione simbolica fra i segni zodiacali e festività dei santi, fra Cristo e il sole, la concezione annuale del tempo, che è infatti carattere comune ai calendari irlandesi quali il *Félire Oengusso* o il *Félire Adamnain*.' In a footnote, Grimaldi refers to Hennig and Greeson as her informational sources. The passage is quoted from Grimaldi, *Il 'Menologio'*, p. 14.
[115] Calder and Allen, *Sources and Analogues*, p. 229.
[116] Howe, *The Old English Catalogue Poems*, pp. 74–7.
[117] Richards, 'Old Wine in a New Bottle', p. 363. As revealed in her footnote, Richards's statement is based on Hennig, 'The Irish Counterparts', and Greeson, 'Two Old English Observance Poems'.
[118] Jones, ed., *Old English Shorter Poems*, p. xxvii.

contents, structure and nature, and it is difficult to find any major affinities other than that they are poems treating the liturgical and/or natural cycle of the year.

As Richards summarises in her comment quoted above, the two major topics that have intrigued students of the *Menologium* in relation to Old Irish calendar poems are its cyclic structure and its incorporation of the feasts of the saints into the natural cycle of the year. Hennig argues that the cyclic structure of the *Menologium* hints at the influence of Old Irish calendar poems with a cyclic structure which is of special significance in reflecting an Irish liturgical convention based on the conception of 'cyclical natural time'.[119] According to Hennig, *Félire Óengusso*, Cuimmin's poem on the saints of Ireland,[120] and *Enlaith betha* have this structure; *Félire Óengusso* ends with words nearly identical with those at the beginning thereby referring the reader back to the beginning,[121] while Cuimin's poem and *Enlaith betha* have at the end a kind of cue pointing to the word or letter used at the very beginning.

Despite Hennig's view, the connection between the cyclic structure of these works and the cyclic perception of the liturgical year intertwined into the natural year seems quite obscure in all these works. Although cyclic according to Hennig, Cuimin's poem, for instance, has nothing to do with the cyclicity of the liturgical and natural year, since the feasts mentioned are not arranged in calendrical order while the natural cycle is beyond the scope of the poem. The first five saints mentioned in the poem, for instance, are Patrick, Columba, Brigit, Mochta and Comgall in this order, whose feasts are 17 March, 9 June, 1 February, 9 August and 10 May, respectively. *Enlaith betha*, a poem on the activities of birds and animals annually repeated as if praising the Creator, on the other hand, has little to do with the liturgical year; the feasts of the saints are mentioned only for the purpose of indicating dates (and dates are more often indicated by the Roman reckoning). Its cyclic structure, although it contains a disorder at one point,[122] may represent the cyclicity of birds' and animals' annual activities but not that of the liturgical year. The same cyclic structure, moreover, is introduced into several other poems in the same work, the *Martyrology of Tallaght*,[123] but it never has to do with the cycle of the natural and/or liturgical year, which shows that the structure in question is based primarily on an Old Irish poetic tradition and is not necessarily linked with the cyclic concept of the natural and liturgical year. Thus the liturgical year is not interwoven with the

---

[119] Hennig, 'The Irish Counterparts', p. 102.

[120] I shall hereafter call this poem 'Cuimmin's poem', by which I refer to the poem edited in Stokes, 'Cuimmin's Poem on the Saints of Ireland'.

[121] The words nearly identical with those at the very end of the poem are found in the sixth quatrain in the prologue, which is, according to Hennig, probably because the first five quatrains were added later. See Hennig, 'The Irish Counterparts', p. 102.

[122] In the second stanza, 25 March and then 24 September are mentioned, whereas the third stanza is allotted to 15 April. Greeson notices the disorder, saying that '[w]ith mention of St. Rúadán, April 15 ... the poem resumes the proper order of feasts' ('Two Old English Observance Poems', p. 104).

[123] See Best and Lawlor, eds., *The Martyrology of Tallaght*, pp. 92–127.

Introduction

natural year either in Cuimin's poem or in *Enlaith betha*, nor does their cyclic structure represent the cyclicity of the liturgical year.

Félire Óengusso, on the other hand, is arranged in calendrical order and has a cyclic structure, but as Hennig himself admits, it hardly thinks of the feasts of the saints in connection with the natural cycle.[124] Stokes, the editor of the poem, also says 'in all this long composition there is no trace of imaginative power or of observation of nature'.[125] It consists of the prologue, the main martyrological part, and the epilogue, all of which consist of a number of quatrains. Its cyclic structure is attained by the repetition of nearly identical words at the beginning of prologue and at the end of epilogue. If we carry out a cyclic reading suggested by the cyclic structure, there are, between 31 December and 1 January, some 225 quatrains of epilogue and prologue, which roughly equal the number of quatrains for seven and a half months in the martyrological part. The interval seems too long for the cyclic structure effectively to embody the cyclicity of the liturgical year. The poem also seems too long for a cyclic reading. Thus the cyclic structure of *Félire Óengusso*, having nothing to do with the natural cycle, should be attributed chiefly to the Old Irish poetic tradition rather than to the naturalistic cyclic conception of the liturgical year.

Unlike Cuimin's poem, *Enlaith betha* and *Félire Óengusso*, whose cyclic structures have nothing to do with the intertwinement of liturgical and natural year, *Félire Adamnáin*, one of the two 'obvious Irish counterparts' of the *Menologium* according to Hennig, conceives of the saints in the course of the seasons; but this time it has no cyclic structure. This also suggests that there is no major connection between the cyclic structure and the cycle of the natural and/or the liturgical year. The stanza for spring reads as follows:

> Naoimh ind erraigh errdairc   lim do deoin Dé daltait
> Im Brighit noigh niodhaim   im Grighair im Pattraicc.[126]

> The saints of the glorious spring-time, may they be with me by the will of God's fosterling, together with Brigid, a maiden pure, with Gregory and Patrick.

Similarly, one stanza each is allotted for summer, autumn and winter in this order following that for spring. For spring, three saints are named, as we can see in this quotation, while two saints, i.e. Mary and Michael, are named in the stanza for autumn. Yet no saints are mentioned at all for summer and winter, and it is merely implied that there are many saints to be commemorated in these seasons. Although its structure dividing the whole year into four by the season is fairly clear-cut, what little information given in the poem is vague; it never specifies the dates of the feasts of the few saints it mentions but very roughly indicates in which of the four seasons they are located. Nor does it

---

[124] Hennig, 'The Irish Counterparts', p. 102.
[125] Stokes, ed., *Félire Óengusso*, p. lxvii. Hennig quotes these words.
[126] The passage and translation are both quoted from Byrne, 'Félire Adamnáin'.

clearly define when each season begins and ends, as is done in the *Menologium*. Thus *Félire Adamnáin* is a naturalistic devotional poem rather than a calendar poem and is scarcely comparable with the *Menologium*, which as we shall see, presents precise information about the locations of the feasts within a methodical structure based on a basic division of the year.

Among the Old Irish and Old English poems Hennig discusses, the *Menologium* is the only work that has a cyclic structure and integrates the liturgical year into the natural year at the same time. Yet the cyclic conception of the liturgical year as reflected in the cyclic structure and the intertwinement of the liturgical with the natural year do not seem so peculiar as necessarily to be connected with a particular Old Irish poetic/liturgical tradition. These two characteristics are, for instance, shared with the prose *Menologium*, a brief computistical note accumulating dry information, upon which it is unlikely that the Old Irish calendar poems exerted any major influence. Feasts in ordinary liturgical calendars are also conceived to be of cyclic nature, and are often intermingled with the events of the natural year represented by such entries as the solstices, the equinoxes, the beginnings of the four seasons etc. Since a liturgical calendar is arranged in the framework of the Roman calendar, which is based on a cyclic system, the feasts in the liturgical calendar are conceived of as cyclic rather than linear-historical in nature, like the natural/computistical entries. Embodying the cyclic perception of the liturgical calendar, in fact, the Metrical Calendar by Eugenius Vulgarius has a cyclic structure quite similar to that of the *Menologium*.[127] The cyclic perception of the liturgical year and the integration of the liturgical with the natural year also underlie the ecclesiastical way of stating dates, in which dates are expressed by reference to a feast or a natural/computistical key day.[128] If there is no such cyclic understanding of the liturgical year, and if it is understood only in terms of linear historical time, obviously the feasts of the saints cannot be utilised efficiently to express dates; for instance, St Gregory I's feast can be mentioned to refer to the date 12 March of any year, but, considered linear-historically, it necessarily points to 12 March 604. In the ecclesiastical way of stating dates, moreover, the liturgical and the natural year are intertwined in that it utilises both feasts and natural/computistical events.

Thus neither cyclic perception of the liturgical year nor its intertwinement with the natural year seems so peculiar as necessarily to be attributed to a particular Old Irish poetic tradition, but is more or less universal.[129] Since no

---

[127] See Meyvaert, 'A Metrical Calendar', pp. 349–77. Eugenius Vulgarius (*fl. c.* 887–928) was an Italian priest and scholar learned especially in Greek and Latin literature.

[128] Head, in his 'Perpetual History', does not mention the Irish tradition, while discussing the cyclical nature of the natural and liturgical year in the *Menologium* and its relationship with the ecclesiastical way of stating dates.

[129] Similarly, we can often find a still more clear-cut combination of the liturgical calendar with the natural/computistical cycle in later calendar tables often found in the Book of Hours, where miniatures depict the labours of the months and/or the signs of zodiac of

Introduction

Old Irish calendar poems Hennig discusses seem really comparable with the *Menologium*, which is devoid of clearly Irish elements such as Irish saints and festivals, it is difficult reasonably to detect any major connection between the *Menologium* and the Old Irish calendar poems.[130]

The Prose Menologium

As rightly reflected in its title, the prose *Menologium* is by far the closest analogue of the verse *Menologium*. Henel, the editor of its *editio princeps*,[131] for instance, writes 'Das Verhältnis des Prosa-Menologiums zum Vers-Menologium ist außerordentlich eng'.[132] Dobbie also says 'the prose menologium ... is remarkably similar in content to the verse MENOLOGIUM'.[133] Although they are very similar, it has generally been supposed that they are not related directly to each other. Henel, though not completely denying the possibility that the verse depends on the prose, considers it most plausible that the prose and the verse are of independent origin, suggesting that 'VM [Vers-Menologium] ist also vielleicht Auszug aus einem Kalender, PM [Prosa-Menologium] dagegen aus einem Meßbuch'.[134] Dobbie also writes '[i]t is most probable that the two texts represent independent compilations from missals or from ecclesiastical calendars',[135] while Stanley says 'there is no dependence of the verse on the prose *Menologium*'.[136] Although Hart claims that '[t]he prose text is condensed from the Verse *Menologium*',[137] this is viewed by Henel as least plausible[138] and has otherwise never been suggested (for further details regarding the relationship between the prose and the verse, see pp. 44–52 below).

Two versions of the prose *Menologium* are extant in two different manuscripts: London, British Library, MS Harley 3271, fol. 91r–v (s. xi¹);

> the month. The natural/computistical cycle is often reflected in this type of calendar; for December, a scene of slaughtering a fat pig or baking bread may be depicted, and this leads to the scene of feasting in January, making the whole series of miniatures cyclic. The miniatures of the labours of the months also depict the seasonal scenes and in this respect, the liturgical calendar and the natural cycle are also combined together. See, for instance, Shepherd, 'Anglo-Saxon Labours of the Months', in which the author summarises and compares 'the most common iconographic forms used in calendar decoration from the Classical world, the Anglo-Saxon manuscripts, and medieval representations dating from the twelfth century onward' (pp. 55–9). See also Hill, 'Eleventh Century Labours of the Months'.

[130] For a further discussion, see Karasawa, 'Irish Influence'.
[131] Henel, *Studien*, pp. 71–91.
[132] Henel, *Studien*, p. 78.
[133] Dobbie, ed., *The Anglo-Saxon Minor Poems*, p. lxii.
[134] Henel, *Studien*, p. 90. Square brackets are mine.
[135] Dobbie, ed., *The Anglo-Saxon Minor Poems*, p. lxii.
[136] Stanley, 'The Prose *Menologium* and the Verse *Menologium*', p. 263.
[137] Hart, *Learning and Culture* II.1, p. 194.
[138] Henel, *Studien*, pp. 89–90.

and Cambridge, Corpus Christi College, MS 422, p. 48 (s. xi med.).[139] Apart from minor differences, they are roughly identical, and unless necessary, I do not distinguish them from each other in the following discussion, collectively referring to them as the prose *Menologium*. If need be, however, I call the version in the former manuscript PMH and that in the latter PMC. Both PMH and PMC are included in a series of computistical notes, intended seemingly for elementary students. Harley 3271 contains Ælfric's *Grammar*, which Ælfric himself says is written for *puerulis tenellis* 'immature boys' or *iungum cildum* 'young children',[140] and other elementary notes probably intended for those still learning Latin and computus. Hollis observes that it 'has more of the appearance of a manuscript used in a monastic school',[141] while Chardonnens regards it primarily as a grammatical manuscript with additional notes 'indicative of the range and type of topics that seem to define elementary concerns in learning and education in an early eleventh century monastic setting'.[142] In Corpus Christi College 422, a series of computistical notes including PMC is preceded by the following words:

> Gif ðu ne cunne understandan on ðis ledene þe her beforan awriten is, þonne loca ðu her hu þu scealt þin gear rihtlice gefadian.[143]
> (Corpus Christi College 422, p. 46)
>
> If you cannot understand it in Latin that is written here before, then look here for how you ought to arrange your year properly.

As stated here, the intended users of the computistical notes following these words are not competent in Latin and therefore not far advanced in study. These words also show that the prose *Menologium* is a computistical note for the benefit of elementary students.

The prose *Menologium* summarises the course of the liturgical year, locating the major feasts in the framework of the solar/natural year established by eight temporal indicators: the solstices, the equinoxes, and the beginnings of the four seasons. According to Bede's *De temporum ratione* (ch. 30),[144] it was popularly taught that the solstices and the equinoxes make the fundamental divisions of the liturgical year, while the beginnings of the four seasons are mid-points between any two consecutive solar turning points. The prose *Menologium* adopts this framework of the year and locates each major feast by reference to the number

---

[139] See Ker, *Catalogue*, pp. 309–12 and 119–21; Gneuss, *Handlist*, pp. 38 and 77; and Gneuss and Lapidge, *Anglo-Saxon Manuscripts*, pp. 357–9 and 118–19.

[140] The words in Old English and Latin are quoted from Wilcox, ed., *Ælfric's Prefaces*, pp. 114–15.

[141] Hollis, 'Scientific and Medical Writings', p. 191. Scragg is of the same opinion ('Manuscript Sources of Old English Prose', p. 63).

[142] Chardonnens, 'London, British Library, Harley 3271', p. 24.

[143] This passage is based on Henel, *Studien*, p. 42.

[144] For the original text, see Jones, ed., *Bedae Opera de Temporibus*, pp. 235–7. For an English translation, see Wallis, *Bede: The Reckoning of Time*, pp. 86–9.

of days from one entry to the next. It has nothing to do with the Roman month system, another major way of dividing the year, and is highly ineffectual as a means of consulting the exact dates of the feasts (try, for instance, figuring out the date five weeks and four days after Christmas as the prose *Menologium* directs at the beginning). It is, therefore, most reasonable to suppose that it is fundamentally different from a mere abridgement of a liturgical calendar like the Metrical Calendar of York, in which the exact dates of the feasts are specified.

Another structural feature of the prose *Menologium* worth discussing is its cyclic structure, shared with the verse *Menologium*. Since the influential article by Hennig,[145] as we have seen, the cyclic structure of the verse *Menologium* has often been regarded as a sign of influence from Old Irish calendar poems. It is, however, unlikely that Old Irish poems exerted any influence upon a dry prose computistical note in Old English like the prose *Menologium*. In fact, the formation of its cyclic structure can be explained even without any Irish influence; it is a logical result of the peculiar system of locating entries shared by the prose and the verse *Menologium*. The prose *Menologium*, densely accumulating the formula *and þæs ymbe x niht/wucan* 'and then after *x* nights/weeks', locates each entry both prospectively and retrospectively in terms of the previous and the following entry. At the beginning of the whole chain of interdependent entries, for instance, the Purification is defined as five weeks and four days after Christmas and five days before the beginning of spring. All the other entries can be located in the same way with the exception of Christmas at the very beginning, for which the twofold definition is impossible since no entry precedes it. Only by mentioning it again at the end of the work can it be defined twofold in the same way as all the other entries. This must be why the second reference to Christmas is made at the end, making the whole work cyclic. If the reference to Christmas at the end is omitted, the entry preceding it, the feast of St Thomas, also escapes the twofold definition, located only as three weeks after the feast of St Andrew. Yet its location is made much clearer with the retrospective definition 'four days before Christmas'. Thus, in order to complete the consistent chain of interdependent entries locating each other by twofold, progressive and retrogressive, definitions, it is necessary to refer to Christmas at the beginning and the end. The verse *Menologium*, sharing the same system of locating entries, follows the same logic and has the same cyclic structure.

Apart from the eight temporal indicators, both PMH and PMC refer to exactly the same twenty-nine feasts and festivals, nearly all of which are also mentioned in the verse *Menologium*.[146] Yet there are some differences between the two versions, which may well point to a certain length of textual transmission. The most notable is the discrepancy in the date of the vernal equinox; it coincides with the feast of St Benedict (21 March) in PMH, whereas it falls on the same day as the Annunciation (25 March) in PMC. The former is the date

---

[145] Hennig, 'The Irish Counterparts'.
[146] For details, see pp. 40–3 and Appendix 6.

Analogues

based on the revised Julian calendar officially adopted by the Western Church at the first ecumenical council in Nicaea in 325, whereas the latter is the date based on the original Julian calendar generally followed before 325.[147] Extant Anglo-Saxon calendars reveal that the vernal equinox was often listed against 25 March until the end of the tenth century,[148] whereas 21 March predominates in eleventh-century calendars.[149] The cases of two closely related calendars,[150] in Oxford, Bodleian Library, MS Bodley 579 (fols. 39r–44v; prob. 979 x 987, Canterbury or Glastonbury?) and in London, British Library, Additional MS 37517 (fols. 2r–3r; s. x/xi, Canterbury, Christ Church), show that the date was sometimes 'updated' in calendars compiled toward the end of the tenth century and later. In the former manuscript, which is slightly older than the latter, the vernal equinox is listed against 25 March, whereas the latter has the 'updated' date, 21 March. Since it is unlikely that the date 25 instead of 21 March was newly adopted in the eleventh century, when the vernal equinox was generally listed against 21 March in calendars,[151] the date 25 March adopted in PMC may point to the tenth-century origin of the prose *Menologium*,[152] while the date 21 March in PMH may reflect a revision made toward the end of the century or later.

Another conspicuous difference between PMH and PMC is the references to fast days found only in PMC. Several feasts in PMC are followed by the formula *and þær is fæsten to* 'and there is a fast-day before it', noting that the previous day is a day of fasting. Among those fast days mentioned are included those preceding the feasts of St James the Apostle (25 July), St Bartholomew (25 August) and St Thomas the Apostle (21 December),[153] which are, as far as the extant Anglo-Saxon calendars are concerned, mentioned as vigils only in the eleventh-century calendars, never attested in those compiled in the tenth

---

[147] For the date of the vernal equinox, see Henel, *Studien*, pp. 75–6; and Wallis, *Bede: The Reckoning of Time*, pp. xviii–xix.

[148] E.g., calendars 4, 6 and 7. For details, see Appendix 8. Hereafter I shall refer to Anglo-Saxon calendars by the classification number given in Appendix 5, which is based on the list of calendars in Rushforth, *Saints in English Kalendars*, p. 17. I shall also follow Rushforth as regards the dates and the places of origin of the calendars unless otherwise stated.

[149] E.g., calendars 13–15, 17, 18, 20, 22–5 and 27. For details, see Appendix 8.

[150] For the close relation between these two calendars, see Rushforth, *Saints in English Kalendars*, pp. 25–8.

[151] The two dates sometimes coexist even in the eleventh-century calendars, as in those in calendars 11 and 19, but no eleventh-century calendar lists the vernal equinox against 25 March alone. See Appendix 8.

[152] See Henel, *Studien*, pp. 68–70; and Chardonnens, 'London, British Library, Harley 3271', p. 25.

[153] The other fast days mentioned are those preceding the following feasts: St Paul (30 June), St Laurence (10 August), the Assumption (15 August), St Matthew (21 September), SS Simon and Jude (28 October), All Saints' Day (1 November), and St Andrew (30 November).

century and earlier.[154] Thus it is possible that the references to the fast days in PMC originated in the eleventh century; they may be later additions, if the prose *Menologium* itself dates back to the tenth century. According to PMC, moreover, the day before the feast of St Paul, i.e. 29 June, is a fast day, but the day is never marked as a vigil in Anglo-Saxon calendars and is unlikely to have been a fast day, since that day is the feast of SS Peter and Paul, a much more important feast than the feast of St Paul on the next day.[155] Since in both PMH and PMC the feast of St Peter (29 June) and that of St Paul (30 June) are treated together in the same sentence using the connecting phrase *and on morgen* 'and on the next day', it is difficult to insert the formula for the fast day where it is appropriate, that is, just after the reference to the feast of St Peter. In other words, the shortcoming may have been caused because the reference to the fast day here was added later while the original wording, in which the formula does not really fit, was preserved. Thus the discrepancy between PMH and PMC in this respect is to be attributed to later modifications, and as far as the presence or absence of references to the fast-days, PMH seems to preserve the earlier text.

PMH and PMC sometimes differ also in the formula repeatedly used throughout the work. PMH quite regularly uses the formula *and þæs ymbe x niht bið* … 'and then after *x* nights is …', whereas PMC often mixes *and þæs on x nihton byð* … 'and then in *x* nights is …'.[156] In PMC, *ymbe* and *on* are twice used in apposition with each other as in *ymbe twa ucan and on twam nihton* 'after two weeks and in two nights', which never occurs in PMH. This may imply that the more consistent PMH is more conservative in the use of the preposition. Both PMH and PMC, moreover, use the words *mæsse* 'feast' and *mæssedæg* 'feast-day', but PMH more often uses the former (18 times out of 25), whereas PMC uses them nearly equally (13 versus 12 times). The word *emniht* is always used for equinox in PMH, while PMC always uses *emnihtesdæg*.

Both PMH and PMC contain several misrepresentations of the number of days from one entry to the next. PMH has four misrepresentations, while PMC has five; both texts can be seen as corrupt to a certain degree. Textual corruption is also reflected in other minor shortcomings such as omissions of necessary words and additions of unnecessary words, which often occur especially in PMC.[157] Although they share one misrepresentation of the number of days,[158] all the others as well as most of the minor shortcomings are different, and therefore it is unlikely that the slightly younger PMC is a copy of PMH, nor is it likely that PMH and PMC are based on the same exemplar. All the discrepan-

---

[154] For details, see Appendix 7.
[155] For details, see Appendices 6 and 7.
[156] PMH uses the formula with *ymbe* thirty-six times and that with *on* only twice, whereas PMC uses the *ymbe* formula thirty times and the *on* formula nine times.
[157] For details regarding the misrepresentations and other minor shortcomings, see the text and commentary in Appendix 1. See also Henel, *Studien*, p. 74.
[158] Both say that the feast of St James (25 July) is three weeks and five days after the feast of St Paul (30 June), instead of three weeks and four days.

cies between the two as well as the signs of textual corruption in both suggest that the tradition of the prose *Menologium* had already been established by the time the earlier of the two (i.e. PMH) was copied in the first half of the eleventh century. With fewer misrepresentations and shortcomings and without the references to fast days which seem to have been added later, PMH preserves the original text better but, as inferred from PMC, the date of the vernal equinox seems updated in this version. The verse *Menologium* is closer to PMH in that it follows the revised Julian calendar as regards the date of the vernal equinox, while mentioning no fast days.

The absence of references to St Edward the Martyr and St Dunstan in both PMH and PMC may provide another clue for the date of the original prose *Menologium*. The feasts of St Edward the Martyr and St Dunstan are nearly always marked as high feasts in the calendars compiled after the promulgation of the laws regulating their strict observance in 1008 and 1020 respectively.[159] Thus the absence of these feasts in the prose *Menologium* may well suggest a date of composition before 1008. The verse *Menologium* also lacks references to these feasts.

In addition to this, the treatment of SS Peter and Paul in the prose *Menologium* is also noteworthy. In many calendars, they are listed together against 29 June, while some also list St Paul against 30 June. In the prose *Menologium*, on the other hand, they are treated separately against 29 and 30 June respectively. The same treatments of the feasts are recorded only in calendars 7, 9, 12 and 18 (see Appendix 6). Among these, only calendar 7, recorded in Bodleian Library, MS Bodley 579 (979 x 987, Glastonbury? Canterbury?), includes neither the feast of St Edward the Martyr nor that of St Dunstan. On the other hand, the closely related calendar 9 recorded in British Library, Additional MS 37517 (c. 1000, Christ Church, Canterbury), marks both as high feasts; a revision seems to have been made toward the turn of the century (perhaps even before the strict observance of these feasts were regulated by the laws?). As we have seen above, calendar 7 is also conservative regarding the date of the vernal equinox, as in PMC, while calendar 9 is revised at this point as in PMH.

All things considered, the lost original of the prose *Menologium* seems to have contained all the feasts, festivals and temporal indicators mentioned in the extant versions, while the references to the fast days in PMC seem to have been added later, in the eleventh century. The date of the vernal equinox was originally 25 March as in PMC and was revised to 21 March later as in PMH. The date before the revision, 25 March, as well as the absence of references to the feasts of St Edward the Martyr and St Dunstan, suggests that it had been composed by the end of the tenth century. It is unlikely, however, that the date of composition is considerably earlier than the late tenth century, since the

---

[159] See V Æthelred 16 and I Cnut 17§1. See also p. 43 below.

Introduction

tradition of writing computistical notes in Old English was relatively new, and the manuscripts containing them can be dated only from that period onwards.[160]

The hypothetical original prose *Menologium* shows especially close affinities to the calendar in Bodley 579 (calendar 7) in terms of the selection of high feasts and the dates of the temporal indicators. The prose *Menologium* covers most of the high feasts in calendar 7, while they both treat the feast of SS Peter and Paul in the same way, regard the Major Rogation as high feasts and follow the original rather than the revised Julian calendar as regards the dates of the solstices and the equinoxes. Although there are six high feasts in calendar 7 that are not mentioned in the prose *Menologium*, five of them may have been omitted by the menologist to meet his purpose; summarising the basic framework of the liturgical year rather than giving a full list of high feasts, the menologist seems to have omitted the five high feasts in Christmastide, which is represented by the core feast, the Nativity (the *Menologium* poet does a similar thing for basically the same purpose[161]). If this is the case, the difference between the original prose *Menologium* and calendar 7 is the absence of the feast of St Guthlac in the former and the absence of Lammas Day, which is never mentioned in any calendar, in the latter. Such close affinities are attested nowhere else and there may well be a close relationship between them. The date of the vernal equinox in the original prose *Menologium* was sometimes revised to 21 March when it was copied, as was done around 1000 in calendar 9, which is closely related to calendar 7.[162] PMH reflects this revision. As attested in PMC, however, the original date was sometimes retained while some other revisions such as adding references to fast-days and changing wordings were occasionally made, perhaps in the eleventh century.

While Latin metrical calendars and Old Irish calendar poems are quite different from the verse *Menologium* in every respect, the prose *Menologium* is the only work that is really comparable with the verse *Menologium*. The prose and the verse are remarkably similar in their contents, structure and function, and as I shall discuss below, they may be based on the same *Menologium* template.

---

[160] See Henel, *Studien*, pp. 68–70; and Chardonnens, 'London, British Library, Harley 3271', p. 25.

[161] In the verse *Menologium*, the three high feasts after Christmas – St Stephen (26 December), St John the Apostle (27 December) and the Holy Innocents' Day (28 December) – are omitted. On the other hand, the two feasts at the end of Christmastide, the Circumcision (1 January) and the Epiphany (6 January), are included probably for the reasons I shall discuss below. See pp. 48–50.

[162] Apart from the revision of the date of the vernal equinox, the following feasts are additionally marked as high feasts in calendar 9: SS Hadrian and Fortunatus (9 January), St Edward the Martyr (17 March), St Dunstan (19 May) and St Alban (22 June). Otherwise calendars 7 and 9 are the same as far as marking of high feasts is concerned. Fortunatus is a deacon who was martyred with a bishop, Vitalis, and another deacon, Revocatus, in Smyrna in the third century.

6
Structure

As implied in the title *Menologium* (< later Gk μηνολόγιον, consisting of *μηνός*, 'of the month' plus *λόγος* 'account'), it has often been considered that the work consists of a month-by-month account of the liturgical year, just like a liturgical calendar itself as well as Latin metrical calendars and martyrologies. This may be partly because the dual use of Latin and Old English month-names in the poem is of interest to modern readers and partly because such a division of the year accords with our way of conceiving of the year. In fact, Greeson explains the structure of the poem month by month.[163] However, the poem has a larger structure in which the division by the month is only a subcategory. As I discuss below, the structure, while showing a close affinity with the prose *Menologium*, reflects the nature of the poem and is worth examining here.[164]

The failure to understand the basic structure of the poem by modern scholars is manifested in how it has been sectioned by the editors. Some variously divide the poem into three,[165] four,[166] six,[167] eight,[168] ten,[169] thirty-five[170] or more[171] sections, while many others do not section it at all.[172] The scribe, on the other hand, clearly divides it into four by introducing otherwise reserved combinations of two or more of the following structural features: *punctus versus*, large coloured initials, unusually wide blank spaces and changing lines. As I presently discuss, the scribe's sectioning is based on the structure of the poem established by the poet himself. Dobbie was the first to follow the scribal division,[173] but did not

---

[163] Greeson, 'Two Old English Observance Poems', pp. 111–19.
[164] See Karasawa, 'The Structure of the *Menologium*'. For the discussion on the structure of the poem, see also Weston, 'Cosmic Pattern', pp. 68–102.
[165] Malone, 'The Old English Calendar Poem'.
[166] Dobbie, ed., *The Anglo-Saxon Minor Poems*; Greeson, 'Two Old English Observance Poems'; and Karasawa, 'The Verse *Menologium*'.
[167] Bouterwek, *Calendcwide*.
[168] Earle, ed., *Two of the Saxon Chronicles*; and Plummer, ed., *Two of the Saxon Chronicles*. The latter is a revised edition of the former and the number of the sections into which the poem is divided is the same, but their way of sectioning is slightly different.
[169] Jones, ed., *Old English Shorter Poems*.
[170] Hickes, *Linguarum*; Fox, *Menologium*, and Ebeling, *Angelsächsisches Lesebuch*, basically follow Hickes's sectioning with various changes.
[171] Hart divides the poem into some forty-seven sections, basically allotting a section to an entry (*Learning and Culture* II.1, pp. 198–215).
[172] Grein, *Bibliothek*; Wülker, *Bibliothek*; Imelmann, *Das altenglische Menologium*; Fritsche, *Darstellung*; Rositzke, *The C-Text of the Old English Chronicles*; Grimaldi, *Il 'Menologio'*; and O'Brien O'Keeffe, ed., *The Anglo-Saxon Chronicle*.
[173] Greeson, the only other editor to divide the poem into four, seems simply to follow Dobbie and/or the scribe, unaware of the significance of the sectioning. For his understanding of the structure of the poem, see Greeson, 'Two Old English Observance Poems', pp. 111–19.

Introduction

seem to be aware of its meaning; in fact, he did not totally believe in it, pointing out the somewhat tentative nature of his punctuation and sectioning in lines 119b–20a, and saying that 'The MS. has a large colored capital *W* in *Wide*, but the evidence of capital letters is not necessarily conclusive'.[174] Although Dobbie does not mention it, there is also an unusually wide blank space just before *Wide*, which is another guidepost left by the scribe.

The *Menologium* is divided into four sections as indicated below:

Section 1 (ll. 1–47): from the winter solstice to the vernal equinox;
Section 2 (ll. 48–119): after the vernal equinox to the summer solstice;
Section 3 (ll. 120–175): after the summer solstice to the autumnal equinox;
Section 4 (ll. 176–231): after the autumnal equinox to Christmas (which coincides with the winter solstice).[175]

The poet himself divides the poem into these four sections and the scribe duly follows it, expressing his understanding in the manuscript (or faithfully following his exemplar[176]). The dividing points are the solstices and the equinoxes, reflecting an elementary/popular way of dividing the liturgical year as also adopted in the prose *Menologium*. The poet uses the word *hwæt* at the beginnings of these sections (except at the very beginning of the poem),[177] while he repeats the key terms representing the solstice or equinox just before and after the section boundaries,[178] which seems to function as a sort of anadiplosis, dividing and connecting each section at the same time.

Perceiving all these, the scribe, at the end of line 47 in the edited text (fol. 112v12), where the first section ends, places a *punctus versus*, which he often uses to indicate a longer pause,[179] and begins the next sentence with a huge capital in the margin of the next line leaving the remaining space in line 12 blank, which makes a fairly obvious break in the text. At the end of the second section in line 120 in the edited text, the scribe gives an unusually wide blank space before the beginning of the next section, and begins the new section with a large, red capital (fol. 113v6). At the end of the third section, he places a *punctus versus* (fol. 114r17) and begins a new section with a huge capital in the margin

---

[174] Dobbie, ed., *The Anglo-Saxon Minor Poems*, p. 172.
[175] The last section includes a brief conclusion to the whole poem (lines 228a–31).
[176] It is not certain whether the scribe of the extant manuscript himself is responsible for the visualisation of the poet's sectioning; it seems likely that he faithfully followed the exemplar in which the poem had already been sectioned in this way (cf. the scribe's seemingly mechanical copying of the capitals at the beginnings of the two poems and the Chronicle pointed out by O'Brien O'Keeffe in *The Anglo-Saxon Chronicle*, p. 1). In my discussion here, however, I simply refer to any scribe responsible as 'the scribe'.
[177] The poet does not use the word *hwæt* at the very beginning of Section 3, but still, the pronoun, placed at the beginning of the second sentence of the section, works as a new section marker. For details, see the commentary on line 122b.
[178] See also Weston, 'Cosmic Pattern', pp. 68, 93 and 97.
[179] As regards the punctuation marks used by the scribe, see pp. 8–9 above and also O'Brien O'Keeffe, ed., *The Anglo-Saxon Chronicle*, pp. xlvii–xlviii.

in the next line (fol. 114r18), although this time he does not leave a wide blank space between the two sections, since the last word of the third section happens to be just at the end of line 17 on folio 114r. Thus doubly supported by the poet's and the scribe's practices in the actual text and in the manuscript, it seems reasonable to conclude that the poem is divided into four sections representing the basic framework of the poem.

Based ultimately on the Greek theory of quaternity, Anglo-Saxon textbooks of computus, such as those by Bede, Ælfric and Byrhtferth, often divide the year into four parts at the solstices and the equinoxes just as in the *Menologium*, while they also divide it into four seasons.[180] Byrhtferth, perhaps a younger contemporary of the *Menologium* poet,[181] visualises the idea in the following diagram:[182]

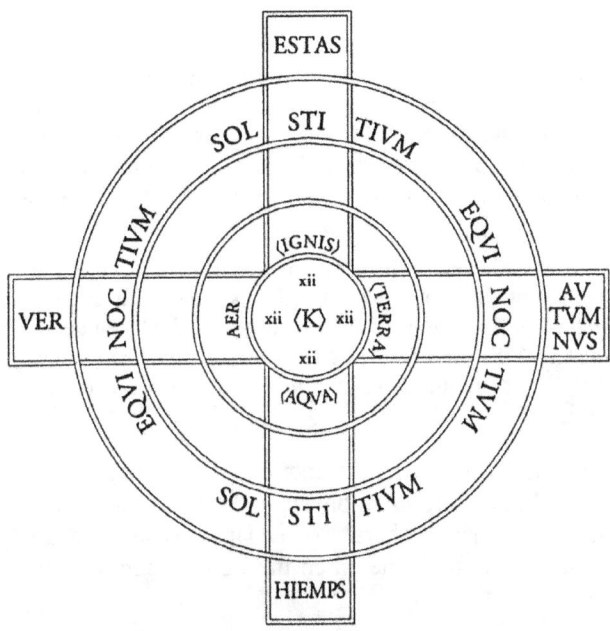

Fig. 1. Byrhtferth's diagram summarising the quaternary structure of the natural/solar year

---

[180] See *DTR* 30 and 35; *DTA* 141–220; and ByrEnch I.1. For the seasons in Anglo-Saxon England or Old English poetry, see also Moorman, *The Interpretation of Nature*, pp. 1–44; Pons, *Le Thème et le Sentiment*; Enkvist, *The Seasons of the Year*, pp. 6–24; Anderson, 'The Seasons of the Year'; and Neville, 'The Seasons in Old English Poetry'.

[181] Hart speculates that the *Menologium* poet is Byrhtferth himself (*Learning and Culture* II.1, pp. 192–3). For the problems of Hart's view, see pp. 47, 89, 91, 96–7, and 106–7. For the date and the authorship of the *Menologium*, see pp. 70–2.

[182] The diagram is taken from Baker and Lapidge, eds., *Byrhtferth's Enchiridion*, p. 10 with the permission of the Council of the Early English Text Society. Its facsimile is printed in Crawford, ed., *Byrhtferth's Manual*, between pages 10 and 11.

Introduction

In this diagram, Byrhtferth superimposes the solar and seasonal divisions of the year with the emphasis on the latter. In terms of the liturgical year, on the other hand, the former division is emphasised as in the case of the *Menologium*, since the beginnings of the solar and the liturgical years coincide with each other on 25 December.

Although the winter solstice officially fell on 21 rather than 25 December, ever since the first ecumenical council in Nicaea in 325,[183] the unofficial date, together with the also unofficial dates of the summer solstice (24 June) and the autumnal equinox (24 September), persisted in Anglo-Saxon England.[184] This may be partly because these days, having nothing to do with the calculation of Easter, were of no significance from the computistical point of view.[185] Yet the persistence seems also to have much to do with the existence of a 'popular' tradition about the coincidence of the key days of the liturgical and the solar year, about which Bede writes as follows:

> Haec quidem gentiles, quibus non dissimilia de tempore etiam perplures ecclesiae tradidere magistri, dicentes: viii kl. apriles in aequinoctio verno dominum conceptum et passum, eundem in solstitio brumali viii kl. ianuarias natum; item beatum praecursorem et baptistam domini viii kl. octobres in aequinoctio autumnali conceptum, et in aestivo solstitio viii kl. iulias natum ... [186] (*DTR* 30)

> These, indeed, are opinions of the heathen not unlike what very many ecclesiastical teachers maintain, namely: the Lord was conceived and suffered on 25 March at the vernal equinox, and was born on 25 December at the winter solstice; similarly, the Lord's blessed precursor and Baptist was conceived on 24 September at the autumnal equinox, and was born on 24 June at the summer solstice.

Bede continues that these teachers further claim that it is appropriate 'that the Creator of eternal light should be conceived and born along with the increase of temporal light and that the herald of penance, who must decrease, should be engendered and born at a time when the light is diminishing'[187] (*DTR* 30).

---

[183] In *DTR* 30, Bede does not mention the exact dates of the autumnal equinox and the solstices but says that they 'ought to be observed a little before [the date] given in the popular treatises' which follow the original rather than the revised Julian calendar. The words in quotations are taken from Wallis, *Bede: The Reckoning of Time*, p. 88. In *DTA* 236–92, Ælfric repeats what Bede says, while Byrhtferth also follows the official dates in 'De mundi natura' in ByrEnch I.1 (see Baker and Lapidge, eds., *Byrhtferth's Enchiridion*, pp. 6–8).

[184] Thus the unofficial dates, while sometimes coexisting with the official ones, are often adopted in Anglo-Saxon calendars. For details, see Appendix 8.

[185] Wallis, for instance, writes that Bede is not interested in fixing the dates of the autumnal equinox and the solstices in *DTR* 30 because 'they are of no computistical consequence' (*Bede: The Reckoning of Time*, p. 88). See also footnote 183 above.

[186] The passage is quoted from Jones, ed., *Bedae Opera de Temporibus*, p. 236.

[187] This translation is taken from Wallis, *Bede: The Reckoning of Time*, p. 87.

Thus many teachers of computus used to associate the four key days of the solar year with the four important feasts of Christ and John the Baptist, thereby accentuating the inevitable importance and meaningfulness of those four days as turning points of the year.[188] The tradition seems to have been especially strong as regards the solstices, since Christmas and the Nativity of St John the Baptist continued to be called, until the end of the Anglo-Saxon period, *middes wintres mæssedæg* or *midwinter*, and *middes sumeres mæssedæg* or *middesumores mæsse*, respectively, while at the same time, *midwinter* and *midsumor* mean the winter and the summer solstices. As I discussed above, the original prose *Menologium* seems closely to follow this tradition,[189] adopting all the unofficial dates of the solar turning points as preserved in PMC.

As reflected in the terms *midwinter* and *midsumor*, the solstices were conceived to be the midpoints of winter and summer, whereas the equinoxes were also conceived to be located in the middle of spring and autumn.[190] According to this way of understanding the year, a year consists of eight parts of roughly equal length, and the liturgical year, beginning with Christmas, which coincides with the (unofficial) winter solstice, can be neatly divided into four at the solstices and the equinoxes, while it can be divided further into eight at the beginnings of the seasons. This is the basic temporal framework adopted in both the prose and verse *Menologium*.

The verse *Menologium* also includes references to the beginnings of the twelve months, superimposing the basic framework of the Roman year. However, not only the aforementioned sectioning but also the peculiar system of locating entries and the cyclic structure caused thereby suggest that the months do not establish the primary temporal framework. In fact, entries are not located in terms of the beginnings of the months, as in 'the fifteenth of March', nor are they located by the Roman reckoning using *kalendae*, *idus* and *nonae* as in 'the ides of March'. Instead, entries are roughly located in terms of the primary temporal framework reflected in the sectioning of the poem, which reveals in which of the quarters of the year they are located. At the same time, they are more precisely located by the two adjacent entries. St Bartholomew's feast (25 August), for instance, is in the third quarter beginning with the summer solstice and is more precisely located as ten days after the Assumption (15 August) and four days before the Decollation of St John the Baptist (29 August). As

---

[188] See also chapters 47 and 48 in *De ratione computandi*, composed in Ireland in the seventh century. In these chapters, the solstices, the equinoxes, the four seasons and the structure of the year are explained based, according to Walsh and Ó Cróinín, on 'the curious doctrine of Pseudo-Anatolius' (*Cummian's Letter*, p. 104). An edition is included in Walsh and Ó Cróinín, eds., *Cummian's Letter*.

[189] In *DTA* 236–92, Ælfric, probably contemporary with the author of the original prose *Menologium*, writes that '[i]t is said by many that the spring equinox occurs rightly on *octaua kalendas aprilis*, that is on Mary's feast day' (25 March). His use of the present tense suggests that this may still have been the case even at the end of the tenth century. The translation is quoted from Blake, ed., *Ælfric's De Temporibus Anni*, p. 87.

[190] See, for instance, *DTR* 35.

Introduction

discussed above, the twofold, progressive and retrogressive, definition of entries leads to the cyclic structure as its logical result, and this is duly fulfilled not only in the prose but also in the verse *Menologium*.

Thanks to the references to the beginnings of the months, the actual dates of the feasts can be calculated by using the information given in the poem. Yet this does not seem to be what it is meant primarily for, since the system of locating entries adopted in this poem is inconvenient for this purpose. For this purpose, it is much more convenient to indicate the number of days from the beginning of the month to each entry rather than the number of days between two consecutive feasts.[191] In most cases, in fact, multiple calculations are required to attain the exact date; there are just six cases where the date can be attained through a simple calculation such as $A + B$.[192] In ten other cases, numbers need to be added twice as in $A + B + C$, whereas in the remaining twenty-six cases, numbers need to be added or subtracted three, four, five or even six times in order to attain the right date. In order to calculate the dates of the feasts, moreover, the number of days from the last feast of the month to the beginning of the next month is unnecessary but the lengths of these intervals are consistently revealed in the poem, which also implies that the main purpose of the poem is not to present the actual dates of the feasts. The cyclic structure shared with the prose *Menologium* also suggests that its primary purpose is to show the interrelationship of adjacent feasts and their locations in the course of the solar/natural year. In this respect, the poem is different from calendars and Latin metrical calendars, in which the dates of the feasts are directly revealed by the Roman reckoning.

The temporal framework adopted in the verse *Menologium* is somewhat similar to that visualised by Byrhtferth in his *Enchiridion* on the opposite page.[193]

Perhaps in order visually to emphasise the division of the year into four at the solstices and the equinoxes,[194] the seasons are represented rather inaccurately; but otherwise the diagram presents the division of the year similar to that of the

---

[191] The way of stating dates in terms of the beginning of the month, as in 'the fifteenth of March', does not seem to have been used very widely in Anglo-Saxon England, but the *Old English Martyrology* adopts this system throughout the work.

[192] These six cases are: Twelfth Night (6 January), the Purification (2 February), the feast of St Gregory the Great (12 March), the Invention of the Cross (3 May), the Nativity of St Mary the Virgin (8 September), the beginning of winter (7 November). All these are the first entry after the reference to the first day of the month, and therefore their dates are attainable simply by adding one to the number of days of the interval the poet reveals. For April, June, July, August, October and December, however, the number of days of the interval itself needs to be calculated (e.g. the Major Rogation (25 April) comes after nineteen and five days after the first of April).

[193] The diagram is taken from Baker and Lapidge, eds., *Byrhtferth's Enchiridion*, p. 76 with the permission of the Council of the Early English Text Society. Its facsimile is printed in Crawford, ed., *Byrhtferth's Manual*, between pages 86 and 87.

[194] The Greek theory of quaternity underlies the diagram as manifested by the references to the four elements themselves: *ignis*, *terra*, *aqua*, and *aer*. Each of these elements is named at the bottom of each bar for the solstices and the equinoxes, and this reflects the special status of the four solar turning points.

Structure

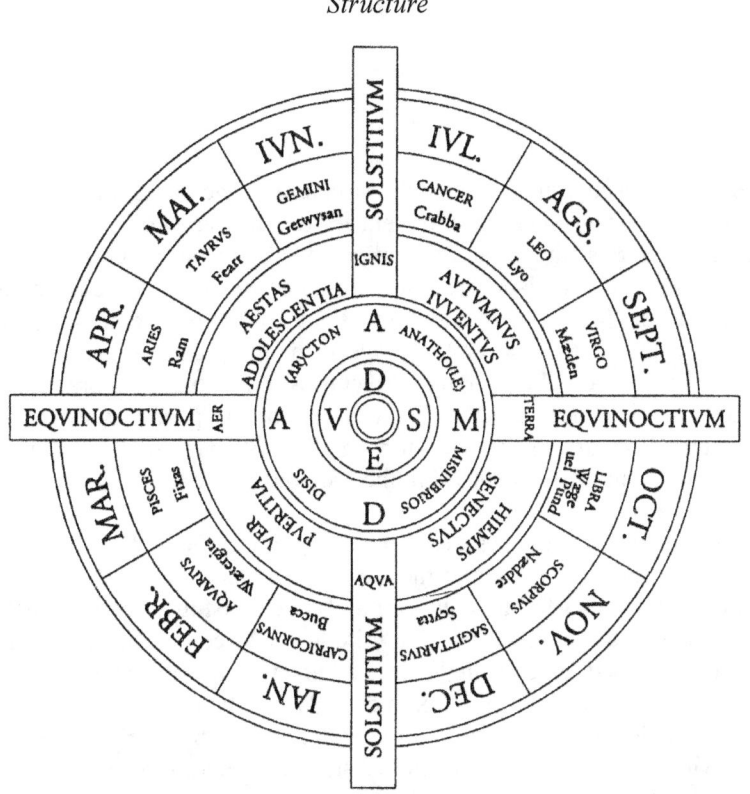

Fig. 2. Byrhtferth's diagram summarising the basic structure of the year.

verse *Menologium*, with the primary division at the solstices and the equinoxes and the subordinate divisions into the seasons and the months. It is noteworthy that this does not seem to have been a common way of structuring the year, superimposing the basic frameworks of the solar, the natural and the Roman year with the primary emphasis on the first; when they were combined together, it was much more usual to think of the solar and the seasonal turning points within the framework of the Roman year as in liturgical calendars and metrical calendars. In other words, the temporal framework of the verse *Menologium* suggests that it is unlikely to be modelled on these sorts of works with which it has often been connected and compared. The formation of the uncommon framework, together with the peculiar system of locating entries, may well point to the poet's indebtedness to, and the renovation of, the *Menologium* template; he basically follows the template, adopting the primary temporal framework established by the solar/natural turning points, but at the same time he renovates it by adding the references to the beginnings of the twelve months, thereby making it possible to show the interrelationship between these two major methods of dividing the year (for the relationship between the prose and the verse, see pp. 44–52 below).

Introduction

7
Entries

As seen in the discussion on the cyclic structure of the poem, the *Menologium* consists of a chain of interdependent entries defining each other. In this chain, two kinds of entries, liturgical and computistical, are intermingled. The poem contains twenty computistical entries, i.e. the solstices, the equinoxes, the beginnings of the four seasons and the first days of the twelve months, whereas it refers to twenty-nine feasts and festivals as the liturgical entries. As discussed in the previous section, the computistical entries function as temporal indicators, while the liturgical ones are the direct targets of the poem, as is verified by the concluding remark of the poet himself (ll. 228b–31). Since I have already discussed the computistical entries in the previous section, here I shall focus on the liturgical entries.

As has generally been observed, the liturgical entries of the *Menologium* are 'major feasts'[195] and 'mostly those of the universal church'.[196] Not all of them are the universal feasts, however; and they constitute only a selection of them rather than a complete list. The criteria for selecting the entries, though sometimes regarded as obscure,[197] is explained to a considerable extent by consulting contemporary Anglo-Saxon calendars, which often mark high feasts by a cross, the letter F,[198] capitals, coloured letters and/or metrical entries.[199] As the following list reveals, most of the feasts mentioned in the *Menologium* are marked as high feasts in more than ten Anglo-Saxon calendars:[200]

---

[195] Stanley, 'The Prose *Menologium* and the Verse *Menologium*', p. 259.
[196] Lapidge, 'The Saintly Life', p. 249. Baker also writes most of the feasts 'were culted by the universal church' ('OE Metrical Calendar', p. 312).
[197] See Amodio, *The Anglo-Saxon Literature Handbook*, p. 311.
[198] It is not known exactly what the letter F stands for, but it seems to indicate higher feasts than the feasts marked with the letter S and those without any mark. Warren says it probably stands for 'Festum' or 'dies feriatus' (*The Leofric Missal*, p. xlv). See also Rushforth, *Saints in English Kalendars*, p. 25.
[199] For metrical entries marking high feasts, see Rushforth, *Saints in English Kalendars*, pp. 22–3. For details regarding high feasts in Anglo-Saxon calendars, see Appendix 6.
[200] The following discussion is based on twenty-three Anglo-Saxon calendars, i.e. calendars 1, 4–7, 8, 9, 11–25 and 27 listed in Appendix 5 and in Rushforth, *Saints in English Kalendars*, p. 17. For calendar 1, I base my discussion on Wilson, ed., *The Calendar of St. Willibrord*; for calendar 5, on Dumville, *Liturgy and the Ecclesiastical History*; for calendar 8, on the microfilm printouts kindly given to me by Dr Rebecca Rushforth and on the table attached to Rushforth, *Saints in English Kalendars*; for calendar 12, on Wilson, ed., *The Missal of Robert of Jumièges*; and for calendars 4, 6, 7, 9, 11, 13–25 and 27, on Wormald, *English Kalendars before A.D. 1100*. I exclude calendars 2, 3, 10 and 26, since they are fragmentary. Among these twenty-three calendars, three (i.e., calendars 1, 14 and 15) mark virtually no important feasts, three (calendars 13, 16, 27) mark very few of them, one (calendar 23) marks relatively few of them and two (calendars 8 and 25) mark them irregularly. Thus there are fourteen calendars that more or less regularly

Entries

	Feast	Attestations
1	Christmas (25 Dec)	20
2	Circumcision (1 Jan)	16
3	Epiphany (6 Jan)	16
4	Purification (2 Feb)	15
5	St Mathias (24 Feb)	15
6	St Gregory (12 March)	17
7	St Benedict (21 March)	14
8	Annunciation (25 March)	15
9	Major Rogation (25 April)	2[201]
10	SS Philip and James (1 May)	11
11	Invention of the Holy Cross (3 May)	10
12	St Augustine of Canterbury (26 May)	12
13	Nativity of St John the Baptist (24 June)	15
14	SS Peter and Paul (29 June)	13
15	St James (25 July)	16
16	Lammas Day (1 Aug)	0
17	St Laurence (10 Aug)	17
18	Assumption (15 Aug)	18
19	St Bartholomew (25 Aug)	12[202]
20	Decollation of St John the Baptist (29 Aug)	13
21	Nativity of St Mary (8 Sept)	17
22	St Matthew (21 Sept)	14
23	Michaelmas (29 Sept)	16
24	SS Simon and Jude (28 Oct)	15
25	All Saints' Day (1 Nov)	16
26	St Martin (11 Nov)	15
27	St Clement (23 Nov)	12
28	St Andrew (30 Nov)	16
29	St Thomas (21 Dec)	15

Most of these feasts are marked as important feasts much more frequently than others in Anglo-Saxon calendars, and this confirms their prominent status.[203]

---

mark high feasts. The numbers in the table are slightly different from those in a similar table in Karasawa, 'The Prose and the Verse *Menologium*', p. 135, partly because of the difference in the number of calendars I consulted and partly because of recounting.

[201] The Major Rogation is marked only twice as a high feast. It is often treated as if it were a computistical entry placed on the right hand side of the leaf, and is marked as such another seven times.

[202] The number includes a case where the saint's name is not revealed but the letter *F* is placed against the date of his feast.

[203] Many of the feasts in calendars are not marked at all. For details regarding the marked feasts, see Appendix 6.

Introduction

However, the Major Rogation and Lammas Day are conspicuous exceptions.[204] They may well be referred to as popular seasonal festivals rather than liturgical feasts comparable with other liturgical entries.[205] Lammas Day, in fact, is a popular festival of the first wheat harvest of the year and was widely known even to unlearned people; in his *Catholic Homilies*, for instance, Ælfric refers to Lammas Day to enable a lay audience (referred to as *eow læwedum mannum* 'you laymen') to locate the feast of St Peter, saying to the effect that the feast is held on the day *þe ge hatað hlafmæsse* (ÆCHom II, p. 222) 'which you call Lammas'.[206] According to the *Menologium* poet himself (73–4a) and some other records from the Anglo-Saxon period,[207] on the other hand, the Major Rogation seems also to have been a day of festival in which people marched in a procession raising and/or visiting relics of saints. The *Menologium* poet says that on the Major Rogation, people lift up relics (*reliquias ræran* in line 73). The day is called *gangdæg* 'walking day'[208] in the prose *Menologium*, while *relicgonge* 'relics-going, visiting of relics' is mentioned in the *Old English Martyrology* (under 25 April, 'Rogation Day') as one of the activities people performed on that day.[209] At the same time, however, the Major Rogation is mentioned rather sparingly in both Old English and Latin works written in Anglo-Saxon England. The verse and the prose *Menologium* and the *Old English Martyrology* are the only works recording its names in Old English (*bentid*, *ænlipiga gangdæg*, and *micelra bena dæg*, respectively), whereas its Latin name, *litania maior*, tends to be used for the Rogationtide, the three days before Ascension Day, which later came to be called *litania minor*.[210] All these may reflect that the status of Major Rogation as a liturgical feast was not as significant as that of the important feasts listed above.[211] This may well be also reflected in the fact that Ælfric's *Catholic Homilies* do not include a homily for the Major Rogation, while containing homilies for many of those feasts listed above and for the Rogationtide.

---

[204] Based on six Anglo-Saxon calendars (i.e., calendars 7, 9, 12, 19, 20 and 24), and one Latin metrical calendar, Henel also points this out, by saying that 'Die Litania maior wird nur im Leof. Miss. und in CCCC 422 als hohes Fest ausgezeichnet, der Lammas Day nirgends' (*Studien*, p. 86). Apart from the metrical entries in calendar 5, which seem to mark high feasts, I do not take any Latin metrical calendars into consideration, because high feasts are not marked at all or at best they are marked only sporadically. For details, see Wilmart, 'Un témoin anglo-saxon'; Lapidge, 'A Tenth-Century Metrical Calendar from Ramsey'; and McGurk, 'The Metrical Calendar of Hampson'.

[205] Piper categorises them as 'die Naturfeste' (*Kalendarien und Martyrologien*, pp. 89–91).

[206] Similarly, Lammas, while it is not treated as a regular entry, is also utilised to locate the 'kalendas' of August in *The Old English Martyrology*, pp. 150–1.

[207] See, for instance, the Council of Clovesho canon 16, 'De diebus Lætaniorum', laid down in 747. Haddan and Stubbs, eds., *Councils and Ecclesiastical Documents* III, p. 368.

[208] For the original meaning of the term, see Hill, 'The *Litaniae maiores*', p. 212.

[209] See *The Old English Martyrology*, pp. 86–7. See also BTC, p. 282, s.v. *gang-dagas*, and Jones, ed., *Old English Shorter Poems*, p. 409.

[210] For the use of *litania maior* for the Rogationtide, see Bazire and Cross, eds., *Eleven Old English Rogationtide Homilies*, pp. xv–xvii, and Hill, 'The *Litaniae maiores*'.

[211] See Hill, 'The *Litaniae maiores*'.

Entries

The following feasts, on the other hand, are not mentioned in the *Menologium*, though they are marked as important feasts nearly as frequently as, or in some cases even more frequently than, those in the list above:

Feast	Attestations
St Edward the Martyr (17 or 18 March)	9
St Cuthbert (20 March)	12
St Dunstan (19 May)	8
St Stephen (26 December)	16
St John (27 December)	16
Holy Innocents (28 December)	15

Strict observance of the feast of St Edward the Martyr was first regulated in V Æthelred 16 in 1008,[212] whereas that of St Dunstan's feast was first regulated in I Cnut 17.1 in the 1020s.[213] Since Anglo-Saxon calendars compiled after these dates and marking important feasts nearly always distinguish them,[214] the absence of references to these feasts in the *Menologium* may well suggest that the poem was composed before these dates.[215]

If we exclude these two feasts from consideration for their late dates of establishment, the *Menologium* includes twenty-seven out of thirty-one liturgical feasts which are frequently marked as high feasts in extant Anglo-Saxon calendars, together with two festivals of less importance from the liturgical point of view. The exclusion of several high feasts and the inclusion of some less important festivals show that the *Menologium* is not a simple list of high feasts compiled from an ecclesiastical calendar or a liturgical book. It is also noteworthy that with the exception of the Circumcision, the Epiphany, the feast of St Cuthbert, and the feast of SS Peter and Paul, the prose *Menologium* treats these feasts and festivals in exactly the same way, which may reflect the very close relationship between the verse and the prose. In fact, there are no two unrelated works from Anglo-Saxon England presenting such close sets of important feasts (for further details, see the next section).

Other than the immovable feasts and festivals, the poet also mentions Easter Day and Ascension Day (ll. 54b–68a), but they are referred to as the feasts unable to be located by the poem; they are outside the scope of the poem and, therefore, not regular entries. In fact, they are mentioned in a digression in relation to the beginning of April probably because the month is called *Eastermonað* 'Easter-month' in Old English. The poet, otherwise always

---

[212] Liebermann, ed., *Die Gesetze* I, pp. 240–1; and Robertson, ed., *The Laws of the Kings of England*, pp. 84–5.

[213] Liebermann, ed., *Die Gesetze* I, pp. 298–9; and Robertson, ed., *The Laws of the Kings of England*, pp. 168–9.

[214] See calendars 11, 12, 17–21 and 24.

[215] Cf. Imelmann, *Das altenglische Menologium*, p. 53. For details about the date of composition, see pp. 70–2 below. As we have seen above, the prose *Menologium* does not contain references to these feasts either.

Introduction

maintaining the precise order of the feasts, exceptionally disregards it here, mentioning Ascension Day before the Major Rogation,[216] which also implies that the poet does not regard it as a regular entry.

8

The Relationship between the Prose and the Verse *Menologium*

After Henel's close study of the prose *Menologium* and its relationship with the verse *Menologium*,[217] nothing much beyond what he argues has been elucidated. As a result, Henel's opinion, or rather a simplified version of it, has been repeated. The following words by Dobbie in his introduction to the poem summarise this received wisdom: 'It is most probable that the two texts represent independent compilations from missals or from ecclesiastical calendars'.[218] Henel himself refers to the following three possibilities: (1) the prose and the verse are independent compilations perhaps from a missal and from a calendar respectively; (2) the prose is an extract from a missal and the verse is a later versification of it; or (3) the prose is derived from the verse. Henel considers that the first possibility is most apt, the second is still not unconditionally declined, while the third is unlikely.[219] As in Dobbie's statement quoted above, the first possibility posed by Henel has been accepted with some modifications by later scholars while the other two are dismissed (though without sufficient justification).[220] As I have argued elsewhere,[221] however, affinities between the prose and the verse seem too close to allow us to dissociate them from each other; even if neither text derived directly from the other, they must be based on a common template, belonging to the same literary/educational tradition. In the following pages, I shall examine their common features and other clues that may support my hypothesis.

Structural affinities

Since Christmas was often regarded as the beginning of the ecclesiastical year in Anglo-Saxon England as well as in many other parts of Western

---

[216] Ascension Day, forty days after Easter, always falls after the Major Rogation (25 April, the latest possible date of Easter).

[217] Henel, *Studien*, pp. 71–91.

[218] Dobbie, ed., *The Anglo-Saxon Minor Poems*, p. lxii.

[219] Henel, *Studien*, pp. 89–90. Stanley also writes 'the prose cannot be and has never been regarded as the source of the verse' ('The Prose *Menologium* and the Verse *Menologium*', p. 259).

[220] Hart is a conspicuous exception (*Learning and Culture* II.1, pp. 193–6). He regards the prose as a condensation of the verse. For details, see below.

[221] Karasawa, 'The Prose and the Verse *Menologium*'.

Europe,[222] the prose and the verse *Menologium* begin with Christmas.[223] What is peculiar to them is that they also end with Christmas, thereby having the same cyclic structure, which is a feature attested nowhere else in works written in Anglo-Saxon England. The only work older than or contemporary with the *Menologium* that I have found to have the same cyclic structure is the Metrical Calendar by Eugenius Vulgarius, an Italian priest who flourished *c*. 887–928, whose works have no known connections with Old English literature.[224] The cyclic structure, as I argued above, is the logical result of the peculiar way of locating entries adopted in both prose and verse, which is itself found nowhere else so densely used as to form the backbone of a work. The prose and the verse are also unique in their use of the basic temporal framework in which the year is divided primarily into four at the four solar turning points – the solstices and the equinoxes – while each compartment is also subdivided into two at its mid-point, i.e. the beginnings of the four seasons. Although this division of the year itself is ordinary, as it was often taught in the course of elementary computistical education,[225] there is no other work systematically listing the locations of the feasts in this temporal framework.

A list of dates or locations of feasts, computistical key days and other events much more commonly follows the framework of the Roman year divided primarily into twelve months each of which has three key days, *kalendae, idus* and *nonae,* to specify dates. Calendar tables embody this way of conceiving of the year, while Latin metrical calendars (including the Metrical Calendar by Eugenius Vulgarius) and the Old Irish calendar poem *Félire Óengusso*, following this system, reveal their close connection with the calendar tradition.[226] It is true

---

[222] For the topic in general, see Cheney and Jones, ed., *A Handbook of Dates*, pp. 9–12. Regarding the beginning of the year in Anglo-Saxon England, see, for instance, Poole, 'The Beginning of the Year'; Whitelock, 'On the Commencement of the Year'; Harrison, 'The Beginning of the Year in England'; Godden, 'New Year's Day in Late Anglo-Saxon England'; and Swanton, *The Anglo-Saxon Chronicle*, pp. xv–xvi.

[223] Imelmann, failing to notice this fact, argues that the *Menologium* poet was influenced by some continental work, which he conjectures as the Gregorian Sacramentary, since they both begin with Christmas while Anglo-Saxon calendars do not (*Das altenglische Menologium*, pp. 43–4). In actual fact, there are many works, continental and Anglo-Saxon, which begin with Christmas, such as *Martyrologium Hieronymianum* (which is dated earlier than the Gregorian Sacramentary), the *Old English Martyrology*, and Ælfric's *Catholic Homilies* (second series). The first series of Ælfric's *Catholic Homilies* begins with the origin of creatures and the Nativity of Christ follows this.

[224] There is no record of his name in writings from the Anglo-Saxon period. According to the PASE database, there is only one record of the name Eugenius, and this is a reference to Pope Eugenius II (reigned 824–7).

[225] See, for instance, *DTR* 30, and also *De ratione computandi* 47–50, edited in Walsh and Ó Cróinín, *Cummian's Letter*.

[226] Many martyrologies such as *Martyrologium Hieronymianum* and the *Old English Martyrology* also follow this system, whether they begin with 25 December or 1 January. The Old Irish *Enlaith betha* also follows the same system, though it is not a systematic list of feasts comparable with Latin metrical calendars, *Félire Óengusso*, or the *Menologium*.

Introduction

that the verse *Menologium* mentions the beginnings of the months or *kalendae*, thereby reflecting the influence from this system, but it is noteworthy that they are structurally subordinated to the other system; the verse *Menologium* primarily follows the same system as the prose *Menologium*, based on the solar/ natural division of the year. As I shall presently argue, moreover, there are some signs that may imply that the references to the beginnings of the months in the verse were added later to the existing *Menologium* template which is better preserved in the prose.

Thus the prose and the verse have in common many peculiar structural features, a combination of which is attested nowhere else. This may suggest a very close relationship between the two, while dissociating them from more or less analogous works such as those in Latin and Old Irish mentioned above.

Topical affinities

Not only the basic temporal framework established by the eight temporal indicators they share but also the main topics, i.e., the feasts, treated in the prose and the verse demonstrate remarkable affinities which are scarcely found elsewhere. It is true, as has often been pointed out, that many of the feasts mentioned in the prose and the verse are universal feasts widely observed, but the issue is not so simple for it to be concluded that 'much of the information is shared, and it could not be otherwise since both the prose and the verse menologia deal only with the major feasts and calendrical events, not with local saints'.[227] In fact, the prose and the verse present by far the closest sets of feasts and there are no other works listing an equally similar set.

Important feasts are, for instance, collectively mentioned in laws such as Alfred 43, V Æthelred 13–16, VI Æthelred 22, VIII Æthelred 16 and I Cnut 14–17,[228] but they, omitting many, list far fewer immovable feasts than the *Menologium*,[229] while often including movable feasts and Sundays which

---

[227] Stanley, 'The Prose *Menologium* and the Verse *Menologium*', p. 259.

[228] As regards the chapter numbers of these laws, I follow Attenborough, ed., *The Laws of the Earliest English Kings* and Robertson, ed., *The Laws of the Kings of England*.

[229] Following Imelmann, *Das altenglische Menologium*, p. 53, Hart claims that the poet composed the poem under the influence of the laws of Æthelred regulating strict observance of important feasts, i.e. V Æthelred 13–19 and VI Æthelred 22–5 (*Learning and Culture* II.1, p. 195). If this is the case, however, the poet should have included the feast of St Edward the Martyr; Æthelred was the first king legally to recognise this as an especially important feast, regulating its strict observance in an independent clause (V Æthelred 16) as if emphasising the importance of the newly established high feast. Hart, while neglecting the conspicuous absence of the feast of St Edward the Martyr, regards the poet's references to St Gregory and many of the Apostles as well as his relatively lengthy treatments of the feasts of St Mary the Virgin as strong clues showing the influence of Æthelred's law, but all his clues seem too general reasonably to show the influence of the law upon the poem.

are mentioned in neither prose nor verse. Ælfric's *Catholic Homilies* present a closer list but the difference is still substantial; while it includes, together with many movable feasts and Sundays, several immovable feasts that are not mentioned in the prose or the verse such as those of Stephen (26 December), John (27 December) and Holy Innocents (28 December), the following immovable feasts and festivals listed in both prose and verse are included neither in the first nor in the second series of *Catholic Homilies*: St Mathias (24 February), Major Rogation (25 April), St Augustine (26 May), St James (25 July), Lammas Day (1 August), and St Thomas (21 December).[230]

The shortest Latin metrical calendar, MCY, mentioning more than twice as many feasts as the prose and the verse *Menologium*, includes the three important feasts after Christmas, which are mentioned in neither prose nor verse, while it omits the following four mentioned in both: the Major Rogation (25 April), Invention of the Cross (1 May), St Augustine (26 May), and Lammas Day (1 August).[231] Calendar tables list far more feasts than are mentioned in the prose and the verse, and even if we extract only those marked as a high feast,[232] the result not only deviates significantly from the list of entries of the prose and the verse *Menologium* but also always varies from one calendar to another.[233] Thus it is true that many of the feasts mentioned in the prose and the verse are major feasts widely observed, but the fact itself does not explain sufficiently why the prose and the verse *Menologium* present so similar a set of feasts; their affinities are, in fact, exceptionally close and no other works are extant that demonstrate equally close affinities.

Apart from the absence of the feasts of St Edward the Martyr and St Dunstan discussed above, one of the most notable features which the prose and the verse have in common is that they both include the Major Rogation and Lammas Day. These festivals, as we have seen above, are conspicuously different from the

---

[230] The feast of St Cuthbert (20 March) mentioned only in the prose *Menologium* is not included in the *Catholic Homilies* either.

[231] Hart conjectures that the poet might well have consulted a calendar whose later copy is preserved in Oxford, St John's College, MS 17, fols. 16v–21v (*Learning and Culture* II.1, pp. 178–83). The calendar includes metrical and non-metrical entries, and the former constitute the unique record of the Metrical Calendar of Ramsey edited in Lapidge, 'A Tenth-Century Metrical Calendar from Ramsey'. Hart writes that 'we find that all but one of the saints' festivals recorded [in the *Menologium*] appear among the Latin metrical entries of the Ramsey Calendar'. This is true but the metrical calendar includes far more entries that are not mentioned in the *Menologium*, while excluding one. Most of the 'concordance' he points out seems commonplace to contemporary calendars and I find no remarkable affinity necessarily connecting the two.

[232] For the marking of high feasts in Anglo-Saxon calendars, see p. 40 above.

[233] For details, see Appendix 6. As Gasquet and Bishop (*The Bosworth Psalter*, pp. 15–16) and Rushforth (*Saints in English Kalendars*, p. 28) say, for instance, the two calendars closely related, i.e. calendars 7 and 9, both marking high feasts by the capital *F*, mark them differently at least at five points. According to Rushforth, calendar 27, in which high feasts are marked by the sign of cross, is very similar to calendar 7 (*Saints in English Kalendars*, p. 53), but they mark high feasts differently at least at nine points.

Introduction

others in their prominence as feasts. The former is marked as a high feast only in two calendars (and the two are calendars no. 7 and no. 9, which are closely related to each other and also possibly related to the prose *Menologium*), while the latter is never treated as an entry in calendars, martyrologies and liturgical books. This may well show that they are not mere compilations from some calendar or liturgical book but are based also on some other, possibly common, principle.

An equally notable feature they share is the exclusion of the three important feasts after Christmas, i.e., the feasts of St Stephen (26 December), St John (27 December) and Holy Innocents (28 December), which are nearly always marked as high feasts in Anglo-Saxon calendars which regularly mark them. Latin metrical calendars usually include all of them. The first series of Ælfric's *Catholic Homilies* includes homilies for all these feasts, while the second series also contains another homily for the feast of St Stephen. Thus a complete list of important Anglo-Saxon feasts would include them; their absence from both the prose and verse *Menologium* may well show that they do not present a simple list of all the important feasts but a select list of them based on some common criterion. The prose *Menologium* also excludes the Circumcision and the Epiphany, both marked in calendars as important feasts as frequently as the other marked feasts. Thus the compiler excludes all the important feasts in Christmastide but its core, Christmas; he seems to present the largest framework of the Anglo-Saxon Christian year leaving details aside.

The sets of feasts and festivals that the prose and the verse *Menologium* present are so close that they share not only some entries of less liturgical importance such as Major Rogation and Lammas Day but also the absence of references to the three important feasts after Christmas. There are no other works presenting two such close sets of feasts,[234] and if we take into account the very close structural affinities discussed above, it seems reasonable to cast suspicion on their intimate interrelationship. It is true that there are several conspicuous differences between the two, but as I shall presently examine, the origins of many of the differences may well be explicable, while the rest of the differences are so minute as to deny their close interrelationship.

Differences between the prose and the verse Menologium

The most conspicuous difference between the prose and the verse *Menologium* is the presence of references to the beginnings of the twelve months in the verse and the absence thereof in the prose. By reference to the beginnings of the

---

[234] As far as I could find, calendar 7 (in Bodley 579), which may have some relation with the prose *Menologium* (see pp. 31–2), presents the closest set of important feasts, but it excludes Lammas Day while it marks as important feasts the three feasts after Christmas and the feast of St Guthlac, which are not included in either the prose or the verse *Menologium*.

months, the verse superimposes the temporal framework based on the Roman year upon that of the solar/natural year shared with the prose. This process results in a peculiar temporal framework rarely found elsewhere;[235] the verse places a prime emphasis on the solar/natural year to which the Roman year is subordinated, while, if they coexist with each other, the former is usually subordinated to the latter as in calendars. Martyrologies are also based primarily on the Roman system, adopting the Roman reckoning and month-by-month accounts,[236] while the solar/natural year, even if having any place in them, is marginal. Missals, often preceded by a calendar, also follow the Roman system, adopting the Roman reckoning while having nothing to do with the solar/natural year. Thus the temporal framework peculiar to the verse *Menologium* shows that it is not a simple versification from a calendar, martyrology, missal etc. It seems more likely that the peculiar temporal framework came into existence by superimposing the framework of the Roman year upon the existing framework of the solar/natural year such as attested in the prose *Menologium*. In fact, this explains some of the features and inconsistencies found only in the verse.

The prose *Menologium* excludes all five important feasts in Christmastide, while the verse excludes the three after Christmas but includes the Circumcision and the Epiphany, which makes a conspicuous difference between the two. In the verse, the first day of January is mentioned due to the integration of the framework of the Roman year, and there seems no reason for the poet summarising the Christian year to avoid mentioning the Circumcision falling on the same day; it is, according to the calendar evidence, as important a feast as many others in the poem. This may well trigger the reference to the Epiphany, an equally important feast, which may establish not only a symmetrical structure mentioning the beginning, midpoint and end of the period but also a conclusion to the narrative regarding the Nativity of Christ, the very first topic of the poem. A sign of the poet's introduction of these two new entries into the existing *Menologium* template may be left in the inconsistency in the way of counting days, which is observed nowhere else in the poem. When locating the Circumcision, the poet says it is on the eighth day counting from Christmas, while it is on the seventh day according to the system of counting days he otherwise consistently follows.[237] Here the poet seems to follow the strong tradition based on the Old and New Testaments, where the Jewish custom of circumcising

---

[235] The diagram in Byrhtferth's *Enchiridion* (Fig. 2 above) is the only analogue I could find.
[236] Martyrologies often begin with Christmas, thereby splitting December into two, but they never follow the solar/seasonal division of the year as the prose and the verse *Menologium* do.
[237] Some, making much of the consistency in the counting system, unconvincingly suggest that here the poet may count from 24 rather than 25 December. Thus this line has often been considered to involve an interpretational difficulty. See Dobbie, ed., *The Anglo-Saxon Minor Poems*, pp. lxiii and 170; and Grimaldi, *Il 'Menologio'*, p. 42. See also Sokoll, 'R. Imelmann', pp. 307–15. For further details, see Karasawa, 'A Note'.

newborn babies on the eighth day of their birth is narrated.[238] This is, at any rate, the only exception to the rule of counting the number of days and therefore may betray the fact that the Circumcision, together with the Epiphany, is a later addition, not belonging to the original *Menologium* tradition as is better preserved in the prose.

Similarly, Easter and Ascension Day, both mentioned only in the verse, may have been added later to the *Menologium* template by the poet. Both are mentioned in a digressive passage (ll. 56–68) as feasts that cannot be located by the poem, and therefore they are not regarded as regular entries. Using both Latin and Old English month-names, the poet must have had good reason to insert a digression on Easter at the beginning of April, since the Old English term for the month is *Eastermonað* 'Easter-month', which he uses just after the digression in line 72.[239] Thus the reference to the beginning of the month (and the use of Old English month-name) may well have triggered a deviation from the *Menologium* tradition. The insertion of the digression, moreover, may also be viewed as causing another inconsistency. At the end of the digression, the poet mentions Ascension Day, which falls forty days after Easter. The earliest possible date of Ascension Day is 5 May,[240] and therefore, the feast is always after the Major Rogation (25 April), the first of May, the feast of SS Philip and James (1 May) and the Invention of the Cross (3 May), but the poet mentions Ascension Day before these entries. Thus the poet, otherwise strictly observing the annual order of the events, neglects it only here in this digression when he refers to Ascension Day. The order may be unimportant since it concerns a movable feast outside the scope of the poem, but at any rate, the digressive nature of the passage itself and the disorder involved therein may represent the extraneous nature of the passage. Thus, inspired by the Old English month-name for April, the poet may have added the digression to the *Menologium* template which he basically follows.

The reference to the bissextile day found only in the verse *Menologium* may well be attributed to another addition made by the poet in connection with the reference to the beginning of the month; the reference is included in a passage on the beginning of March (ll. 29b–37a), where 1 March is said to come one day later than usual in the leap year. According to Byrhtferth and some calendars, however, it is the feast of St Mathias, rather than the beginning of March, that comes one day later than usual in the leap year, when the intercalary

---

[238] See Genesis 17.12, 21.4 and Luke 2.21.

[239] The poet usually uses Latin and Old English month-names almost at the same time, but here he reserves the Old English name for more than fifteen lines until the end of the Easter digression. For the use of Latin and Old English month-names in the poem, see Appendix 9.

[240] The earliest possible date of Ascension Day is often indicated against 5 May in Anglo-Saxon calendars as in calendars 1, 3, 4, 6, 7, 9, 13–16, 20, 24, 27, or rarely against 4 May as in calendar 19. Calendar 20 lists it against both 4 and 5 May.

day is inserted one day before the feast of St Mathias.[241] The poet's inaccurate statement in lines 32–4 may be attributed ultimately to the newly introduced temporal framework mentioning the beginnings of the months; when adding to the *Menologium* template the passage on the beginning of March, the poet also inserted the digressional words on the intercalary day, despite their lack of precision.[242]

The only other major differences in the entries of the prose and the verse *Menologium* are the different treatments of the feast of SS Peter and Paul and the absence of the feast of St Cuthbert from the verse. In the prose, it is said that the feast of St Peter (29 June) comes a day earlier than that of St Paul (30 June). There are only four calendars (i.e., 7, 9, 12, 18) which treat them in the same way, one of which is the calendar in Bodley 579 (no. 7), demonstrating closest affinities to the prose. In many other calendars, on the other hand (i.e., 1, 4–6, 8, 10, 11, 13–27), they are mentioned together against 29 June,[243] and the verse follows this tradition. Judging from the evidence in the extant calendars, the latter tradition seems to have been much more widespread, which may have given the poet a good reason slightly to revise the *Menologium* tradition at this point.

As regards the feast of St Cuthbert, it is difficult to explain why it is included in the prose but excluded from the verse. Possibly it might suggest the existence of variant texts in the *Menologium* tradition, in which the feast of St Cuthbert may or may not be mentioned.

The relationship between the two

As I examined above, the prose and the verse *Menologium* are very similar not only in their general structures but also in their details. Their structural and topical affinities seem close enough for us to regard them as works belonging to fundamentally the same literary tradition, which I call the *Menologium* tradition. The sets of the feasts and festivals they present, though not exactly identical, are closely analogous and there are no other unrelated works listing such similar sets of important feasts. In fact, lists of important feasts in calendars and other works are highly variable, whereas the prose and the verse share not only the presence of most feasts but also the absence of some. They also share references to two seemingly much less important festivals. As the evidence of the calendars shows, it is unlikely for any two unrelated works to list such close sets of feasts

---

[241] For details, see the note for lines 32–4 in the Commentary.
[242] A somewhat similar discrepancy perhaps caused by a later addition of reference to the fast day before the feast of St Paul (30 June) is found in the prose *Menologium*. For details, see p. 30.
[243] Among these calendars 4, 6, 8, 11, 13–25, and 27 also mention St Paul alone against 30 June.

and festivals only by chance, and therefore it seems reasonable to attribute their close affinity in the choice of entries to a common tradition they follow.

While the prose seems to preserve the tradition better in every respect, the verse exhibits significant signs of revision, especially in its style and structure. Unlike the prose, the verse provides not only the dry information on the locations of the feasts but also readable accounts of the feasts, saints, seasons, historical events etc. The poet also introduces a new temporal framework, superimposing the Roman year upon the existing *Menologium* template based on the solar/natural year. It must be through this process that the peculiar temporal framework combining the two with prime emphasis on the latter came into existence; in fact, this type of temporal framework is rarely attested elsewhere in more or less analogous works. The addition of the references to the months also explains the inclusion of some entries and the creation of some discrepancies observed only in the verse. Thus the poet must have utilised the *Menologium* template as the backbone of the poem, to which he added various elements so as to make it more readable and informative.

9

Purpose

Dobbie writes that the purpose of the *Menologium* is 'to furnish readable accounts of the chronology of the Christian year in the vernacular language, for the benefit of those who could not read Latin',[244] while Howe considers that 'it taught the meaning, unity and order of the year as well as of its important elements such as the days and seasons'.[245] On the other hand, Hennig argues that 'the primary object of this work is not to give detailed and exact information on the place and sequence of liturgical feasts, but to give a bird's eye view of the Christian year (in itself a matter supposed to be well known) interwoven with the natural order of time in months and seasons.'[246] Dobbie and Howe seem to consider that the feasts, the months, the seasons and the solar turning points treated in the poem all consist of the chronology of the Christian year and the poet's purpose is to teach it as a whole. Hennig, supposing that the structure of the Christian year itself must have been well known to the audience, places greater emphasis on the interrelationship between the liturgical and the natural year. According to the poet's own words at the end of the poem (ll. 228b–31), the main purpose of the poem is to provide a method of locating the major feasts and festivals observed in contemporary Anglo-Saxon England. Although Malone, based on these words by the poet, considers that the poet 'gives much

---

[244] Dobbie, ed., *The Anglo-Saxon Minor Poems*, p. lxii.
[245] Howe, *The Old English Catalogue Poems*, p. 77.
[246] Hennig, 'The Irish Counterparts', p. 100.

Purpose

that he need not have included' such as the four seasons,[247] it is more reasonable to suppose that the poet introduced the entries from the solar/natural and the Roman year as temporal indicators showing the major temporal frameworks of the year in which each feast is located. The Christian year itself, far from being taken for granted despite Hennig's view, is the main theme of the poem; the poet defines it by locating the major feasts constituting it. It is not so much the Christian year itself as the temporal frameworks that are presupposed; in teaching the major course of the Christian year, the poet utilises the temporal frameworks that are supposed to have been learned elsewhere. If the poem is intended to locate feasts particularly for 'those who kept the sequence of days by reference to past holy days because they did not have or could not use written calendars',[248] the temporal indicators, in themselves having nothing to do with the immovable feasts the poet deals with, would be superfluous. Taking into account the methodical and somewhat peculiar temporal framework established by the temporal indicators, it is unlikely to be a simple list of the number of days between any two consecutive feasts in order for illiterate people to follow on a certain feast day to know when to observe the next feast.

As I have argued above, on the other hand, both the sectioning and the system of locating feasts are inconvenient for specifying the actual dates of feasts in the framework of the Roman month system; it is reasonable to suppose that this is not the primary purpose of the poem. The main target of the poem is the locations rather than the actual dates of the feasts, in terms both of the larger framework of the year established by the temporal indicators and of the adjacent entries. Side by side with the Roman reckoning, there was another major way of dating by reference to a major feast or solar/seasonal key day, such as *on Sancte Georgius mæssedæig* (Anglo-Saxon Chronicle, C 1016) 'on St George's feast', *to middes wintres timan* (*Ælfric's Lives of Saints*, ed. Skeat, II, p. 272) 'at the time of midwinter, i.e. the winter solstice', *VI nihtum ær sumeres cyme* (*Elene* 1227) 'six nights before the coming of summer' etc. In this way of stating dates, not only the solar and seasonal key days but also major feasts work as temporal indicators.

The *Menologium*, as a concise summary of the liturgical as well as the solar/natural year, is useful as a guide to this way of stating dates. Its efficiency for this purpose may be shown by the fact that most of the events whose dates are indicated by reference to an immovable feast or computistical key day in the C-text of the Anglo-Saxon Chronicle are dated within the coverage of the *Menologium*. As far as I could find, there are only four instances out of some

---

[247] Malone, 'The Old English Period', p. 35. Malone, while regarding the Old English month-names as unnecessary elements, does not mention the solar turning points, but an exhaustive list would include them.

[248] Howe, *The Old English Catalogue Poems*, p. 75. Basically the same thing is also argued in Howe, 'The Latin Encyclopedia Tradition', p. 116.

Introduction

sixty-three that are beyond the scope of the poem:[249] the feasts of St Cyricus (under 916), St Britius (1002), St George (1016) and Holy Innocents (1065). This is, moreover, the dating system most frequently adopted in the Chronicle (some 110 instances), although roughly a third (some 31 instances) are those using movable feasts which are outside the scope of the poem.[250] The Roman reckoning is used some thirty-two times[251] and is doubly outnumbered by the ecclesiastical way of stating dates utilising immovable feasts and computistical key days. It is also noteworthy that the two festivals mentioned in both prose and verse *Menologium* but liturgically much less important than the others, i.e. the Major Rogation (1066) and Lammas Day (913, 917, 1009, 1065), are both utilised for the ecclesiastical way of stating dates in the C-text of the Anglo-Saxon Chronicle.

The following instance from the same work is also noteworthy: *& he forðferde on Ealra Halgena mæsseniht .x. nihton ær Martines mæssan æt Tame* (971) 'and he died at Thame on the eve of All Saints' Day, ten nights before St Martin's feast'. The date is doubly specified as 'the eve of All Saints' Day' (31 October), which is 'ten days before St Martin's feast' (judging from the number of days mentioned here, the latter refers to All Saints' Day rather than to its eve). The unnecessary twofold definition attested nowhere else in the manuscript may betray how they conceived the essentials of the Christian year; they remembered the interrelationship of any two consecutive major immovable feasts by reference to their intervals. This is what the prose and the verse *Menologium* instruct, while they also show the interrelationship of the feasts and computistical/seasonal key days, which is essential to locate the feasts in the course of the year. Thus the prose and the verse function as a guide to the ecclesiastical way of stating dates. This may well be one of the reasons why the verse *Menologium* is adopted as a preface to the Anglo-Saxon Chronicle, where that dating system is used more frequently than any other.[252]

---

[249] These sixty-three instances are found under the following years in the C-text of the Anglo-Saxon Chronicle: 763, 827, 879, 886, 898, 901, 913 (2x), 915, MR912, MR913, MR915 (2x), MR916 (2x), MR917, MR918, MR919, 946, 971 (2x), 994, 1002, 1006 (5x), 1009 (3x), 1010 (2x), 1011, 1013, 1014 (2x), 1015 (2x), 1016 (4x), 1021, 1040, 1044, 1046 (2x), 1052 (3x), 1056, 1065 (7x), 1066 (4x). I excluded sixteen instances where only the season is specified as in *by ilcan sumera* 'in the same summer' (897).

[250] These thirty-one instances of the use of movable feasts are found under the following years: 626, 627, 661, 854, 872, 879 (2x), 892, 914, 974, 977, 979, 1002, 1009, 1010 (2x), 1012 (3x), 1014 (2x), 1016 (2x), 1020, 1043 (2x), 1047, 1053 (2x), 1066 (2x).

[251] These thirty-two instances are found under the following years: 538, 540, MR916, 940, 975, 977, 980, 984, 1012 (2x), 1013, 1014, 1017, 1035, 1038, 1042, 1043, 1045 (2x), 1047 (3x), 1048, 1050 (2x), 1051, 1054, 1055, 1056 (2x), 1066 (2x).

[252] Cf. Fulk and Cain, *A History of Old English Literature*, p. 133.

Language

10

Language

Phonology

The phonology of the *Menologium* generally displays characteristics of late West-Saxon or Standard Old English,[253] whereas non-West Saxon features are scarce. The situation is basically the same in *Maxims II* and the C-text of the Anglo-Saxon Chronicle, which follow the poem in the manuscript.[254] In what follows, the principal features of the language of the poem are illustrated based on Campbell, Hogg and/or Hogg and Fulk.[255]

Late West Saxon features of vowels in stressed and partly stressed syllables

(1) *a* for WS *a/o* before nasal (Campbell §130; Hogg §5.5): *gangan* 113, *gangeð* 202, *lange* 107, *man* 73, 161, 229, *manna* 86, *mannum* 57, 219, *manigra* 92, *neorxnawanges* 151, *sang* 59, *strang* 42, *wanan* 141, *wang* 114, *wangas* 90, 206.
 (2) Breaking of *æ* before *l* + consonant (Campbell §143; Hogg §5.15): *bealdum* 225, *behealdan* 113, *ealde* 19, 166, *ealdre* 153, *ealdorþegnas* 130, *ealling* 153, 173, *eallum* 62, *ealra* 199, *healdan* 63, 228, 229, *healdað* 20, 45, 49, 118, 187, 199, *mænifealdlice* 94, *gesealde* 133, *sealtne* 103, *Wealdend* 46, 160, 209, *Wealdendes* 22, 43 (cf. *galgan* 86).
 (3) Diphthongisation of *æ* (both short and long) after palatal *g* and *sc* (Campbell §185; Hogg §5.50): *ageaf* 217, *forgeaf* 223, *metodsceafte* 172, *gesceaft* 227, *sceal* 66, 229, *woruldgesceafta* 115; *gear* 6, *geare* 33, 110, *geardagan* 117.
 (4) *y* (both short and long) for eWS *ie* (Campbell §301; Hogg §5.167): *hyrde* 101, *syx* (76),[256] 203, *ylda* 175, *yldum* 88; *dyre* 192, *gyt* 68, *hy* 190, *hyhst* 110, *nihgontyne* 71, *seofentynum* 25, *gesynra* 129, *tyn* 118, 154, *þreotyne* 116, 170, *geywed* 142, 180.
 (5) *i* (both short and long) for eWS *ie* before palatal consonants (Campbell §301, §316; Hogg §5.167): *ælmihtig* 3, *ælmihtigne* 95, *gebrihted* 137, *emniht*

---

[253] O'Brien O'Keeffe, ed., *The Anglo-Saxon Chronicle*, p. xcvi. For details regarding Standard Old English, see Gneuss, 'The Origin of Standard Old English'; Gretsch, 'Winchester Vocabulary and Standard Old English'; and Hofstetter, 'Winchester and the Standardization of Old English Vocabulary'.
[254] See O'Brien O'Keeffe, ed., *The Anglo-Saxon Chronicle*, p. xcvi.
[255] For the language of the *Menologium*, see also Imelmann, *Das altenglische Menologium*, pp. 9–22; and O'Brien O'Keeffe, ed., *The Anglo-Saxon Chronicle*, pp. xcvi–cx.
[256] This instance is part of fill-in words to compensate for a lost half-line added by editors. Dobbie suggests *siex* here, but *syx* is better since eWS *ie* never occurs in this poem.

Introduction

45, 49, *emnihtes* 175, 180, *niht* 11, 19, 23, 34 etc., *nihtum* 17, 118, 125 etc., *nihtgerimes* 26, 55, 222; *cigð* 184, *igbuende* 185.

(6) *i* for WS *y* (both short and long) before *h*, palatal *c*, palatal *g* and group containing them (Campbell §316): *drihta* 220, *drihten* 60, 96, *drihtne* 192, *drihtnes* 12, 58, 64, 169, 198, 201, *hige* 42, *genihte* 183, *genihtsum* 194, *sigedrihtne* 215.

(7) *y* for WS *i* (both short and long) in proximity to labials (Campbell §318): *byð* 142, 153, 156, 179, *clypiað* 214, *mycel* 9, *mycle* 51, *mycles* 119, *swylc* 141, *swylce* 15, 29, 40, 44 etc., *symbel* 200, *symble* 191, *symle* 136, *gewyderu* 90, *wyle* 112.

(8) lWS smoothing of *ea* to *e* after palatal *g* and before *h* (Campbell §§312–14; Hogg §§5.119–5.121): *agefan* 81, *gerum* 10, *Sexna* 231 (cf. *Seaxe* 185).

(9) lWS *syl-* for WS *sel-* (Campbell §325; Hogg §5.171n2): *sylf* 222, *sylfan* 5, 47, 231.

(10) lWS *þæne* and *þænne* are consistently used for *þone* and *þonne*[257] (Campbell §380; Hogg and Fulk §5.8n2): *þæne* 42, 60, *þænne/ðænne* 23, 32, 33, 37, 58 etc.

(11) lWS *mænig* for WS *manig/monig* (Campbell §193(d)n4): *mænige* 126 (cf. *manigra* 92).

Non-West Saxon features of vowels in stressed and half-stressed syllables

Though scarce, the *Menologium* contains some words with non-West Saxon phonological/orthographical features of vowels in stressed and partly stressed syllables:

(1) Non-lWS *a* for lWS *ea* originated through breaking (Campbell §143; Hogg §5.15): *galgan* 86.

(2) Possibly Kentish *e* for *æ* (Campbell §288; Hogg §§5.189–5.191): *heleþum* 164.

(3) *æ* for *e* possibly due to Kentish hypercorrection (Campbell §§288–9; Hogg §5.189)[258]: *wærþeoda* 127.

(4) Non-WS *eo* for WS *e* through *u*-umlaut (Campbell §210; Hogg §§5.103–5.107)[259]: *meotod* 51, *meotud* 82, *meotudes* 86, 129 (cf. *metodsceafte* 172).

(5) Non-WS *ea* for WS *a* through *u*-umlaut (Campbell §§206–7; Hogg §5.106)[260]: *heaðo-* 14. This is a non-West Saxon form but is 'quite a feature of the W-S transcripts of OE poems' (Campbell §207).

---

[257] The forms *þæne* and *þænne* are also possible in Anglian, but Anglian features are very scarce in the poem and therefore they should be viewed as presenting a late West Saxon feature.

[258] See also Fulk, *A History of Old English Meter*, pp. 284–7.

[259] See also Fulk, *A History of Old English Meter*, p. 302.

[260] See also Fulk, *A History of Old English Meter*, p. 302.

Language

Vowels in unstressed syllables

Vowels in unstressed syllables sometimes suggest the falling together of vowels:

(1) *a* for standard *o* in inflexional endings and others (Campbell §377; Hogg §§6.60–6.61): *torhtast* 111; *þrowade* 25 (cf. *þrowode* 85); *gefrunan* 190, *fundan* 166, *agefan* 81, *hlutan* 192, *sculan* 68, *worhtan* 201; *forþan* 21, 46, 65 (cf. *forþon* 192).

(2) *u* for standard *o* in inflexional endings and others (Campbell §377): *æþelust* 84, *fægerust* 114, 148, *oftust* 56; *besenctun* 122; *meotud* 82, *meotudes* 86, 129 (cf. *meotod* 51, *metodsceafte* 172).

(3) *o* for standard *u* in nominal endings (Campbell §373; Hogg §6.55): *folcbealo* 125, *hælo* 50, *menigeo* 79 and *menigo* 178.

(4) *e* for standard *o* (Campbell §385; Hogg §6.64): *afera* 136, *dogera* 96, *earfeðum* 224, *heofenas* 65, 110, *roderum* 216, *sumere* 137 (cf. *sumor* 89, 119, 124), *swutelra* 129.

(5) *-an* for the standard dative plural ending of nouns *-um* (Campbell §378; Hogg §6.60): *geardagan* 117. This is the only instance and the standard ending is otherwise consistently used.

(6) *y* for standard *e* in the past participle ending of verbs *-ed* : *acennyd* 1 (cf. *acenned* 117, 162, 168). This is the only instance and the standard ending is otherwise consistently used.

Consonants

As regards consonants, the following features and/or irregularities are observed:

(1) *h* for *g* in final position through unvoicing of the final spirant *g*, which often occurs in lWS (Campbell §446; Hogg §7.60–7.61): *burh* 75.

(2) Loss of initial *h* before *r* (Hogg §7.48): *raðe* 75 (cf. *hraþe* 90). Initial *h*, which may drop when directly followed by *l, r, n* or *w*, is otherwise always written down as in *hlafmæssan* 140, *hlutan* 192, *hrime* 35, *hrimes* 204, etc.

(3) Irregular loss of *w* before *u* (Campbell §470): *betux* 162.

(4) Metathesis (Campbell §459; Hogg §§7.93–7.95): *gebrihted* 137, *forste* 205.

Syntax

As regards the syntax of the *Menologium*, there is a detailed study by Fritsche, who enumerates syntactical features of the poem.[261] On the whole, the poem follows the standard syntax of Old English poetry, but it also has several peculiarities as is summarised in the following pages.

---

[261] Fritsche, *Darstellung*.

Introduction

(1) An unusual method of forming numerals

In poetry, larger numerals are expressed usually by 'units + tens/hundreds' as in *fif and sixtig* (*Genesis A* 1169) 'five and sixty', *fif and hundteontig* (*Genesis A* 1131) 'five and a hundred', etc.[262] For the sake of metre and alliteration, on the other hand, the *Menologium* poet often introduces an unusual method of forming numerals by addition:[263] e.g., *III and twa* (30a) 'three and two'; *feower and þreo* (54b) 'four and three'; *twa and feower* (107a) 'two and four'. The other instances are found in lines 71b,[264] 95b, 116a–18a, 210b–11a, 221b.

(2) Juxtaposition of dative and accusative objects after the preposition *ymb/embe*

The preposition *ymb/embe* can take both dative and accusative objects, although '[t]he predominant case with this preposition is the accusative'.[265] Generally, the poet uses accusative objects with *ymb/embe*, but when metrically required, he also uses dative objects. This occurs only when the method of forming numerals by addition is adopted as in *ymb feower niht ... ond twentigum* (133a–4a) 'after four and twenty nights' and *Þænne embe eahta niht* || *and feowerum* (210b–11a) 'then after eight and four nights'.[266] There are two instances, in which the preposition seems to take dative objects alone: *ymb þreotyne ... tyn nihtum eac* (116a–18a) 'after thirteen and also ten nights'; and *ymb twentig þæs ... and seofon nihtum* (187a–8a) 'then after twenty and seven nights'. Here again, the method of forming numerals by addition is adopted. The dative ending *-um* is metrically essential in all these instances and this explains why the poet chooses to use them.[267] The poet does not use dative objects when the preposition immediately precedes the object, in which case, even if the dative object is equally possible from the metrical point of view, the poet consistently uses an accusative object plus *þæs* instead of a dative object as in *embe nigon niht þæs* (41a). The same use of *þæs* is also found in lines 76a,[268] 131a, 137a, 144a, 154a, 174a, 187a.

(3) Sporadic lack of subject-verb agreement

There are two instances where a plural subject is used with a singular verb: *swa hine wide cigð* || *igbuende Engle and Seaxe* (184b–5) 'as the island-dwelling

---

[262] Mitchell, *Old English Syntax* I, p. 220, §558.
[263] Mitchell, *Old English Syntax* I, p. 224, §570.
[264] This instance is based on the reconstruction by modern editors and is not in the manuscript.
[265] See Mitchell, *Old English Syntax* I, pp. 515–16, §1218.
[266] The same technique is used in the reconstructed half-line in line 71b: *þæt embe nihgontyne niht and fifum.*
[267] See also Mitchell, *Old English Syntax* I, p. 224, §571.
[268] Line 76a is not in the manuscript and is a reconstruction by modern editors.

Angles and Saxons widely call it'; and *þæt us wunian ne mot wangas grene* (206) 'so that green fields cannot dwell with us'. Some editors, making much of subject-verb agreement, emend the verb forms to *cigað* and *moton* respectively, although they cause a metrical problem. As I shall argue below, the poet tends to prioritise simple and standard metre even at the cost of standard/consistent word forms,[269] while the use of the singular form here may be justified by sporadic lack of concord when the verb precedes its subject, as pointed out by Stanley[270] following Mohrbutter,[271] Schrader,[272] Bethurum[273] and/or Brook.[274] Since there are several instances outside the poem, while there are two within the poem itself as if establishing each other's authenticity, this may have been a possible, if grammatically less favourable, alternative which the poet chose to adopt. Although Mitchell says that the emendation of *mot* in line 206a to *moton* seems obligatory (while justifying *cigð* in line 184b as a result of 'scribal weakening'),[275] I retain the manuscript readings at these two points, considering that they are authentic and reflect the poet's prosodic characteristics.

(4) *þæt/þætte* clauses occurring with no principal clauses

When preceded by expressions denoting lapse of time, *þæt/þætte* clauses may occur with no principal clauses as in the following instance:[276] *And þæs embe fif niht | þætte fulwihttiid || eces drihtnes | to us cymeð* (lines 11–12), which is to be understood as meaning 'And then [it is] after five nights that the eternal Lord's time of baptism comes to us'. This construction is frequently used in the poem, appearing in lines 15b–17a, 19b–20, 23–4a, 54b–6a, 83–4, 87b–90a, 95b–7, 163–5a, 181–2a, 207b–8, 210b–12, 221b–5 and 226–8a. The words that are to be understood may be 'it is' or 'it was' according to the context. Head suggests that this construction with no principal clause obscures the sense of tense and 'allows for a reading situated in either the present or the past, and within the context of the *Menologium*'s time frame this ambiguity is significant'.[277]

---

[269] See pp. 66–8 below. See also Karasawa, 'Some Problems'.
[270] Stanley, 'The Prose *Menologium* and the Verse *Menologium*', p. 261.
[271] Mohrbutter, 'Darstellung', p. 54.
[272] Schrader, *Studien*, p. 16.
[273] Bethurum, ed., *The Homilies of Wulfstan*, p. 360.
[274] Brook, *An Introduction to Old English*, p. 84.
[275] Mitchell, *Old English Syntax* I, pp. 636–7, §§1522–4.
[276] There are similar examples in other poems and prose works. See Mitchell, *Old English Syntax* II, p. 23, §1973.
[277] Head, 'Perpetual History', p. 156.

Introduction

(5) The adverb *iu* used with the present tense to indicate the future perfect relationship

The adverb *ær* is occasionally used with the present tense to indicate the future perfect relationship, but in the *Menologium*, *iu* is used instead, in the following clause: *þe iu beorna fela* ‖ *Clementes oft | clypiað to þearfe* (213b–14).[278] This clause seems to mean that many people will often have invoked Clement to their benefit (by the time his feast actually comes), which implies people's enthusiastic worship of the saint. As regards this passage, Mitchell writes, 'Here the present tense *clypiað* certifies that the writer is viewing the appeal to Clement as something which is to precede the coming of his feast day'.[279]

(6) Declension of foreign proper names

The poet seems to follow one or other of the contemporary conventions regarding the word forms and declensions of foreign proper names, since similar practices are widely observable in various Old English works.[280] Foreign proper names quite often have declensional endings of Latin origin, but the principles and ideas lying behind the way they function are, in most cases, based on those in Old English rather than those in Latin. The following are examples:

Nominative singular
In most cases, Latin nominative singular forms are retained as in: *Agustus, Andreas, Benedictus, Gregorius, Iohannes, Iudas, Iunius, Laurentius, Maius, Martinus, Martius, Matheus, Mathias, October, Philippus, Simon*. In the case of *Iacobus*, the Latin ending is retained for metrical purposes. Cf. *Iacob* (81a) (see the note for lines 132b–6a in the Commentary).

Genitive singular
The Latin nominative singular masculine ending *-us*, the Latin genitive singular ending *-is*, and the Old English genitive singular ending *-es* are used for the genitive case. This may be because the Latin endings, thanks to the *-s* at the end, sound similar to, and therefore are suggestive of, the Old English genitive ending. The following forms are found in the poem: (with *-us*) *Bartholomeus, Februarius, Iulius, Paulus, Petrus*; (with *-is*) *Aprelis, Nouembris*; and (with *-es*) *Michaheles, Septembres, Zebedes*.

Dative singular
For the dative singular, either Old English *-an* based on the weak declension or Old English *-e* based on the strong declension is used as in the following instances: *Elenan, Rome, Thomase*.

---

[278] Mitchell, *Old English Syntax* I, p. 241, §622.
[279] Mitchell, *Old English Syntax* I, p. 241, §622.
[280] For a similar practice in other works, see Baker, 'The Inflections of Latin Nouns'.

Language

Accusative

Following the Old English declensional system, where nominative and accusative forms of nouns are often the same, the poet uses Latin nominative forms for accusative as in *Agustinus* and *Ianuarius*. *Clementes* is another instance where the poet uses the nominative form as an accusative form.[281] Though its nominative form in Latin is *Clemens*, which is also attested in Old English writings such as the Anglo-Saxon Chronicle (under 101), Ælfric's *Catholic Homilies* (I.37) and his *Lives of Saints* (appearing twice in 'Passion of St. Denis and his Companions'), *Clementes* is another nominative form in Old English as found in the *Old English Martyrology* (under 23 November).[282]

Vocabulary

From the viewpoint of vocabulary and terminology, the *Menologium* poet follows the tradition of Old English poetry to a considerable degree, adopting various poetic clichés and formulaic phrases attested elsewhere.[283] Bredehoft's recent study suggests that the poet follows the literate-formulaic compositional method drawing on various phrases and expressions found in Old English poetic manuscripts available to him.[284] Bredehoft further claims that the poet may have been familiar with the *Metres of Boethius*, the *Metrical Preface to the Pastoral Care*, *Genesis A*, *Andreas*, *Christ B*, *Riddle 40* etc., while he certainly knew the *Metrical Psalms*, from which he quotes in lines 60–2.[285] When quoting from the *Metrical Psalms*, the poet slightly changes the original, replacing *eorðtudrum* (*Metrical Psalms* 117.22, 3a) attested nowhere else with the more familiar *eorðwarum* attested some thirteen times in Old English poetry, which may reflect his preference for standard poetic vocabulary.

Yet it is also true that the poem contains not a few *hapax legomena* and rare words as well as non-poetic/prosaic words and phrases.[286] Nine nonce words are

---

[281] Its accusative form in Latin, *Clementem*, is also used as an accusative form in Old English as in ÆCHom I 37.92, the *Old English Version of Bede's Ecclesiastical History* II 4.22, and the *Old English Martyrology* (under 23 November). It can also be used as a dative form as in ÆCHom I 37.36.

[282] The word form may be based on its Anglicised genitive form developed from the Latin genitive *Clementis*. As seen above, the nominative forms ending with *-us*, *-is* or *-es* are often used also as genitive, which could have promoted the use of genitive forms having these endings also as their nominative forms.

[283] Imelmann enumerates such expressions used in the poem (*Das altenglische Menologium*, pp. 34–6). See also Ten Brink, *History of English Literature* I, p. 92; and Raw, *The Art and Background*, pp. 62–3.

[284] Bredehoft, *Authors*, pp. 113–30.

[285] Bredehoft, *Authors*, pp. 118–20.

[286] For details, see the notes for lines 31b, 32a, 44a, 64b–5a, 74b–5a, 84b, 91b, 111a, 111b, 114a, 125b, 139b, 149a, 150b–1a, 168b, 169b–73a, 190a and 192b–3a in the Commentary.

Introduction

found and they are of varied character: *fulwihttiid* (11b) 'baptismal time'; *bises* (32a) 'intercalary day'; *higestrang* (42a) 'strong in mind'; *rægolfæste* (44a) 'adhering to (monastic) rules'; *stige* (64b) 'ascent'; *bentiid* (75a) 'a Rogation Day'; *agrynt* (111b) 'descends'; *yrmenþeodum* (139b) 'mighty people'; *beornwigan* (225a) 'warrior'. Some are technical words, others are practical ones with commonplace senses, and only a few are poetic. Among these, the use of *stige* is interesting; it exemplifies the poet's use of both prosaic words and phrases and nonce/rare words. When introducing the nonce phrase *drihtnes stige*, the poet seems to have been under the influence of the prosaic expression *drihtnes upstige* (cf. *Cristes upstige*, which is also attested only in prose), but he modified its second element for metrical reasons, dividing it into *stige* plus *up* in the next half-line. In this way, especially when metrically required, the poet occasionally tolerates the use of nonce/rare words. The use of the very rare prosaic word *wisse* (70b) 'certainly' may be explained in the same way (see the note for line 70b in the Commentary).

As in the case of *drihtnes stige*, the poet occasionally introduces prosaic phrases often with some modifications in accordance with metrical and alliterative requirements. The phrases *drihtnes ærist* (58a) 'the resurrection of the Lord', together with similar phrases such as *þæs Hælendes ærist* 'the resurrection of the Saviour' and *Cristes ærist* 'the resurrection of Christ', is otherwise attested only in prose, while such phrases as *ece rice* (224b) 'the eternal kingdom' and *drihtnes modor* (169a) 'the mother of the Lord', both never attested in poetry, must be modified versions of the prosaic phrases *þæt/his ece rice* 'the/His eternal kingdom' and *ure/mine drihtnes modor* 'mother of our/my Lord' with the demonstrative/possessive pronoun omitted for metrical reasons. The phrase *cyninges modor* (21a) 'King's mother' seems to be modelled on such prosaic phrases as *ure/mine drihtnes modor, Cristes modor, Godes modor, þæs Hælendes modor*, etc., while *þeodnes dyrling* (116b) 'the favourite of the Lord', attested nowhere else, seems to be modelled on *Cristes dyrling, dryhtnes dyrling, Godes dyrling*, etc. attested only in prose. Other than these, the following are also prosaic words attested nowhere else in poetry: *ealling* (153b, 173b), *fostorlean* (152a), *gewisse* (124b).[287]

Many other non-poetic words that occur nowhere or very rarely elsewhere in Old English poetry are such computistical or ecclesiastical terms as required by the context of a calendar poem: *bises* (32a), *circul* (67a), *emniht* (45b, 49a, 175a, 180b), *kalend* (7a, 31a), *apostol* (122b), *diacon* (145b), *martira* (69a), *martyrdom* (126a, 145a), and *reliquias* (73a). The word *bises* 'intercalary day', a corrupt form of *bisextus* (via **bisest*),[288] which appears as *bissextus* some fifty-seven times only in prose, is already mentioned above as a *hapax legomenon*, while *circul* 'a cycle (or table) to compute the date of a certain immovable feast' and *diacon* 'deacon' are also attested otherwise only in prose. *Emniht* 'equinox' is

---

[287] See also Karasawa, 'Lexical Choice'.
[288] For the corrupt form, see Campbell, p. 212, §537.

used only once more in poetry, in a technical context in the *Seasons for Fasting* (68), while *reliquias* 'relics of saints' is attested nowhere else other than in *Durham* (19), which was composed much later, probably in the early twelfth century.[289] *Kalend* (without the Latin ending) 'the first day of the month' is attested only in prose works, possibly with two exceptions in the *Solomon and Saturn* (523a) and *Elene* (1228a).[290] *Apostol, martyr,* and *martyrdom* are attested several other times in poetry and are not as rare as the others, but considering their very frequent use in prose, they seem to be used only sparingly in poetry, which may well suggest that they were not regular poetic terms.

Latin and Old English month-names are also non-poetic terms that the poet frequently uses where the context requires them. In poetry, Old English month-names are attested nowhere else,[291] while their Latin correspondents are used only very sparingly, in the *Seasons for Fasting* (49b, 62a, 70a), *Elene* (1228a), and the *Death of Edgar* (8a). For the use of Latin and Old English month-names in this poem, see also Appendix 9.[292]

Although it is probable that the *Menologium* was composed in southern England (see pp. 70–2 below), it sporadically contains words or word forms used predominantly in works of northern origin. The poet's heavy use of the unstressed preposition *in* is a typical example. In purely West-Saxon texts, *on* is clearly preferred to *in* when unstressed, but the latter is used as many as eleven times in the *Menologium* (15a, 39b, 40a, 43a, 75b, 97a, 117a, 134b, 155b, 173a, 201a), whereas it is attested, in other poems of southern origin, only once each in the *Metres of Boethius* (Metre 20, 238a), the *Death of Edgar* (6a) and *Judgment Day II* (190a).[293]

---

[289] For the date of *Durham*, see O'Donnell, 'The Old English *Durham*' and Evan, 'Wordplay'.

[290] It is traditionally conceived that the word *calendcwide* is used in *Solomon and Saturn* (523a), but Anlezark suggests a new reading where *calend* meaning 'month' is the genitive plural form of the word rather than the first element of the compound (*The Old English Dialogues of Solomon and Saturn*, pp. 94 and 137). In *Elene* 1228a, the abbreviation *kł* is used in the phrase *on Maias kł*, but it involves textual problems and Sisam suggests it should be read as *on Maius monað* (*Studies*, p. 14). In her edition of the poem, Gradon follows Sisam's reading (*Cynewulf's 'Elene'*, p. 70).

[291] Old English month-names are used sparingly even in prose, where Latin ones are used predominantly. The *Old English Martyrology* is the only work in which Old English month-names predominate over their Latin counterparts. See Appendix 9.

[292] For these and other instances of the use of words, phrases and word meanings attested chiefly or otherwise exclusively in prose works, see also the notes for lines 21a, 44b–5, 58b, 64b–5a, 67a, 83b, 86a, 87a, 105b–6a, 126a, 148b, 153b, 169a, 198b, 217, 224b and 229a in the Commentary.

[293] See Fulk, *A History of Old English Meter*, pp. 331–2.

Introduction

11

Prosody

Alliteration and rhyme

The poet basically follows the traditional principle of alliteration in Old English poetry with the exception of his treatment of velar and palatal *g*. There are a few instances of crossed alliteration, linked alliteration and rhyming half-lines but it is not certain whether they are intentionally introduced for ornamental purposes. There is a line without alliteration, but it seems certain that it was caused by accident during the textual transmission, rather than intentionally caused by the poet himself. The following is a summary of notable features of alliteration and rhyme in the poem:

(1) Separation of velar and palatal *g*

Traditionally, velar and palatal *g* alliterate with each other, whereas they do not in several later poems such as the *Coronation of Edgar* (10), the *Death of Edgar* (8, 19, 26), the *Death of Edward* (3), and the *Battle of Maldon* (13, 32, 35, 46, 61, 67, 84, 94, 100, etc.).[294] In this respect, the *Menologium* belongs to the younger tradition, separating the two kinds of *g*'s; alliteration on velar *g* is found in lines 39, 100, 101, 113, 171, while that on palatal *g* appears in lines 10 and 109, but they never alliterate with each other.[295] The following half-line is regarded as containing single alliteration on velar *g* : *his gast ageaf* (217a).[296] Velar and palatal *c*, on the other hand, alliterate in one case: *his cyme kalend | ceorlum and eorlum* (31).[297] Yet, unlike the case of *g*, velar and palatal *c* alliterate with each other until the end of the Old English period and therefore do not reveal any instructive information about the date of the poem.[298]

(2) Alliteration between *z* and *s*

There is one instance where *z* and *s* alliterate: *Zebedes afera | and þæs symle scriþ* (136). There are only two other instances of this type of alliteration in

---

[294] Fulk, *A History of Old English Meter*, pp. 258–61. See also Amos, *Linguistic Means*, pp. 100–2.
[295] Fulk, *A History of Old English Meter*, pp. 258–61. See also Bredehoft, *Authors*, p. 114; and Minkova, *Alliteration and Sound Change*, pp. 75–6.
[296] See Fulk, *A History of Old English Meter*, p. 261. This is a half-line of Type B, which is more than twice as likely to contain single alliteration as double alliteration in the a-verse. See Hutcheson, *Old English Poetic Metre*, pp. 132–3.
[297] Alliteration on velar *c* appears in lines 1, 7, 21, 52, 67, 93, 105, 168, 214, while there is no instance where palatal *c* alliterates with itself.
[298] Minkova, *Alliteration and Sound Change*, pp. 72–5.

Prosody

extant Old English poetry: *nis zefferus, | se swifta wind* (*Riddle 40* 68); and *Zeb and Zebee | and Salmanaa* (*Metrical Psalms* 82.9, 2).

(3) Alliteration between *þ* and *th* representing /t/

There is one instance where *þ* alliterates with *th*, a Latin spelling usually representing /t/: *þristhydigum | Thomase forgeaf* (223). This may be an instance of a visual alliteration reflecting a literate rather than an oral compositional method. The same alliteration is attested once elsewhere in Old English poetry: *Swylce Thomas eac | þriste geneðde* (*Fates of the Apostles* 50). Cf. alliteration between *t* and *th* attested only once: *Cumað of Tharsis | tires eadige* (*Metrical Psalms* 71.10, 1).

(4) Requirement of double alliteration in Type 1A*1 verse

As pointed out by Bredehoft,[299] the poet always introduces double alliteration in the on-verse of Type 1A*1 based on Bliss's classification[300] as in lines 1a, 4a, 24a, 35a, 40a, 54a, 66a, 74a, 90a, 98a, 120a, 122a, 127a, 129a, 143a, 153a, 157a, 165a, 180a, 201a, 204a, 205a, 219a, 228a. The following line is the only exception: *Simon and Iudas* (191a), where the use of the foreign proper names seems to underlie the anomaly.

(5) Crossed (*abab*) alliteration

Although it is uncertain whether it is intentionally designed, there are five instances of crossed alliteration of *abab* type: *forma monað. | Hine folc mycel* (9); *Philippus and Iacob, | feorh agefan* (81); *þurh martyrdom, | mære diacon* (145); *embe feower niht | folce genihtsum* (194); and *on syx nihtum | sigelbeortne genimð* (203).

(6) Linked alliteration

Although it may be unintentional, there are four instances of linked alliteration, in which the last lift of the off-verse anticipates the stave of the next line: in lines 42–3, 49–50, 80–1 and 141–2.

(7) Absence of alliteration

There is a line which does not contain any alliteration: *Iohannes in geardagan | wearð acenned* (117). Since this is the only exception, and while the syntax in

---

[299] Bredehoft, *Authors*, p. 123.
[300] The on-verse of the same metrical pattern is occasionally used with single alliteration in *Beowulf* (25 out of 333 instances) and other poems. See Bliss, *The Metre of* Beowulf, p. 122. See also Hutcheson, *Old English Poetic Metre*, pp. 178–9 and 287.

Introduction

the off-verse is also unusual,[301] there must be some defect in the text. Holthausen, moving *wearð* to 115b, suggests the following reading, which Imelmann and Fritsche follow in their texts: *Johannes acenned | in geardagan*.[302] Koch, on the other hand, suggests the addition of *iu* at the beginning of the off-verse,[303] which does not solve the problem regarding the unusual syntax.

(8) Use of rhyming half-lines

There are three half-lines consisting of two rhyming words linked by the conjunction *and* : *ceorlum and eorlum* (31b); *sunnan and monan* (47b); *swutelra and gesynra* (129a). The last two are set phrases attested elsewhere and the poet adopted rather than created these rhyming half-lines.[304] On the other hand, *ceorlum and eorlum* is attested nowhere else, although somewhat similar phrases *ge ceorle and ge eorle* and *ge eorl ge ceorl* are attested in legal texts.[305]

Metre

The poet follows the tradition of Old English poetic metre to a considerable degree, using basic metrical patterns of Types A–E, along with occasional light and heavy verses, but never hypermetric verses. *Maxims II*, placed just after the *Menologium* in the manuscript, abounds with hypermetric verses and, in this respect, the styles of these two works are observably different. Although the poet occasionally fails to follow the metrical tradition, especially when he uses non-poetic foreign words and names, he basically tries to follow the basic traditional metre to the extent that he sometimes seems to make much of metre even at the cost of traditional/standard word forms and/or syntax as summarised in the following paragraphs.[306]

---

[301] As noted by Donoghue, monosyllabic stressed auxiliaries usually come at the end of the verse (*Style in Old English Poetry*, p. 10). The poet otherwise always conforms to this principle, as in lines 52 and 168.

[302] Holthousen, 'C. Plummer', p. 240; Imelmann, *Das altenglische Menologium*, p. 60; and Fritsche, *Darstellung*, p. 10. Later Holthausen suggests another reading: *Iohannes wearð | in geardagum || acenned ...* ('C. W. M. Grein', p. 226).

[303] Kock, *Jubilee*, p. 55.

[304] The phrase *sunnan and monan* in exactly the same form is attested in *Beowulf* (94b), *Christ and Satan* (4b), and *Paris Psalter* (Psalm 73.15, 2a), while the same phrase in different cases, i.e. *sunna and mona*, *sunne and mona*, etc., is also attested in *Daniel* (369a), *Christ B* (606b, 694a), *Paris Psalter* (Psalm 148.3, 1b), etc. The phrase *swutelra and gesynra* in the genitive plural form is attested once more in *Andreas* (565a), while the same phrase in different cases/numbers is also attested in *Riddle 13* (4a), *Riddle 39* (3a) and *Gloria I* (50a).

[305] The phrase is attested in Alfred 4.2 and *Geþyncðo* 1, while its variant *ge eorlisce ge ceorlisce* is used in the prologue of VI Æthelstan.

[306] For the following issues, see also Karasawa, 'Some Problems' and Karasawa, 'Lexical Choice'.

Prosody

(1) Metrical use of conventional and unconventional verb forms

In traditional Old English poetry, the ending -*eþ* is used unsyncopated in the third person singular present forms of long-stemmed verbs, whereas syncopated forms, used in West-Saxon and Kentish prose works, are also used for metrical purposes in later southern poems.[307] The *Menologium* poet uses both forms in order to meet metrical requirements. Conventional unsyncopated forms are metrically required in the following two cases: *þearfe bringeð* (78b); and *welhwær bringeð* (138b). Unconventional forms are more often used as in *þætte nergend sent* (55b), where the replacement of the unconventional *sent* with the conventional *sendeþ* would be metrically problematic with the ending adding a superfluous syllable. Other instances of the same use of unconventional verb forms in order to avoid a superfluous syllable are found in lines 56b, 58b, 88b, 104b, 106b, 111b, 120b, 130b, 140b, 173b, 193b and 218b.

(2) Metrical use of rare, unusual or unconventional words and word forms

The poet occasionally tolerates rare, unusual or unconventional words and word forms in order to accommodate metrical requirements. For instance, the poet twice uses the non-standard monosyllabic *monð* instead of standard *monað* for metrical purposes: *þætte Haligmonð* (164a); and *þæt se teoða monð* (181b),[308] where the second syllable of the disyllabic form would be metrically superfluous. The disyllabic *monað* is used otherwise consistently even when the monosyllabic form is also acceptable as in 56a,[309] 138a, 195a and 219b. When referring to the Ascension of the Lord, the poet, modifying the more usual phrase *drihtnes upstige*, uses *drihtnes stige* (64b), whose second element is a *hapax legomenon*. The phrase *drihtnes upstige* itself is attested only in prose probably because it is devoid of double alliteration required by its metrical pattern, whereas the poet modifies it since the half-line **ne drihtnes upstige* would be metrically problematic. In line 70b, the poet uses the word *wisse* otherwise attested only very rarely, instead of usual *gewisse*, in order to avoid a metrical problem caused by the prefix *ge-*. Similarly, the name of Jacob is otherwise always *Iacob* in poetry as in line 81a, but the poet uses the form with the Latin ending -*us* in line 132b, because the form without the Latin ending causes a metrical problem. For details, see the notes for lines 64b–5a, 70b and 132–6a in the Commentary.

---

[307] See Sievers, 'Zum Codex Junius XI', p. 196; and Fulk, *A History of Old English Meter*, pp. 269–82.

[308] As far as I can find, the monosyllabic form of the word is, while occasionally found in prose works, attested only once more in poetic texts, in the *Death of Edgar* (in the B and C manuscripts): *Iulius monð* (8a), where it seems to be of orthographic rather than metrical nature.

[309] Imelmann and Fritsche emend *monað* in line 56a to *monð*, but this is unnecessary. Even without the emendation, the half-line is metrical; basically the same metrical pattern is used for lines 27a, 36b, 51a and 125b, which they seem to accept as metrical half-lines.

Introduction

(3) Metrical use of singular verbs with plural subjects

There are two cases where a singular verb is used with a plural subject: *swa hine wide cigð* (184b); and *þæt us wunian ne mot* (206a). Some editors retain *cigð*, regarding it as 'scribal weakening' of *cigað*,[310] but the original word form should be attributed to the poet himself rather than to the scribe, since it is metrically required while the emended form causes the same metrical problem as those the poet usually avoids, as discussed under (1) and (2) above. As pointed out by Stanley, following Mohrbutter, Schrader, Bethurum and/or Brook,[311] the use of the singular verb for the plural subject may be justified by sporadic lack of concord when the verb precedes its subject. In the other instance, *mot* is also a metrically required form while in this respect *moton*, though often adopted by recent editors,[312] is problematic in the same way as *cigað* is. Together with the features summarised under (1) and (2) above, these two instances, while establishing each other's authenticity, may show that the *Menologium* poet prefers simple and standard metrical patterns, while he is flexible or somewhat loose in his choice of word forms in that he displays a tendency toward modifying grammatical and/or conventional word forms for metrical purposes even to rather irregular forms if necessary. From this perspective, both *cigð* and *mot* are retained in this present edition.

(4) Metrical use of parasite vowels

There are three instances where parasite vowels are metrically necessary: *tireadige* (13b), *halige dagas* (68a) and *þristhydigum* (223a). The *i* in the adjective suffix *-ig* before inflections beginning with a vowel is historically syncopated, and is metrically disregarded in traditional Old English poetry. However, the metrical use of parasite vowels is occasionally observed chiefly in later poems.[313] See also the note for line 13b in the Commentary.

Though basically conforming to standard metrical patterns, the poet occasionally fails to do so, creating the following non-standard metrical features:

---

[310] As regards the word form *cigð* in this line as the scribal weakening of *cigað*, see Mitchell, *Old English Syntax* I, pp. 636–7. Holthausen defends the manuscript reading from the metrical point of view ('C. W. M. Grein', p. 226), whereas Bouterwek, Grein, Wülker, Dobbie, and Hart emend to *cigað* in their texts of the poem.

[311] Stanley, 'The Prose *Menologium* and the Verse *Menologium*', p. 261. Mohrbutter, 'Darstellung', p. 54; Schrader, *Studien*, p. 16; Bethurum, ed., *The Homilies of Wulfstan*, p. 360; and Brook, *An Introduction to Old English*, p. 84.

[312] Grein, Dobbie, Greeson, O'Brien O'Keeffe, Hart and Jones adopt the emendation in their editions.

[313] For details, see Sievers, 'Zur Rhythmik', pp. 459–61; and Fulk, *A History of Old English Meter*, pp. 194–5.

Prosody

(5) Placement of stressed element in the dip of Type B verse

Although stressed elements are not placed in the dips of traditional Type B verses,[314] there are several such instances in the *Menologium* (6b, 41a, 131a, 137a, 144a, 154a, 174a).[315] Apart from the first instance in line 6b (*habbað foreweard gear*), the other six are those in the following kind of phrase with the stressed element *niht* placed in the second dip between the two lifts, i.e. a numeral and *þæs*: *embe nigon niht þæs* (41a).[316] The same metrical pattern is occasionally found in later poems including the four Chronicle poems, the *Battle of Brunanburh*, the *Capture of the Five Boroughs*, the *Coronation of Edgar* and the *Death of Edgar,* and *Riddle 40*.[317]

(6) Use of half-lines consisting of only three syllables

There are three instances of half-lines that consist of only three syllables: *Agustus* (139a), *Nouembris* (196a) and *Decembris* (220a). The anomaly may be attributed to the use of non-poetic, foreign month-names, although the addition of the word *monð* (in the non-standard monosyllabic form) would easily make these half-lines metrical with no major semantic additions/mutations.

(7) Other anomalies

Other than the half-lines with these non-standard metrical features, the following may be regarded as anomalous: *Februarius fær* 18a[318] and *mid wætere ofewearp* 159a. The following half-line may also be anomalous: *þæs þe Eastermonað* 72a.[319] However, if we scan it as xxS:Sx, assuming the *e* in the vernacular month-name to be a parasite vowel,[320] it is metrical. Cf. *ana in þære easterniht* in the *Descent into Hell* 15a, where the *e* in the compound *easterniht* needs to be underdotted in order to attain a metrical pattern attested elsewhere as in

---

[314] For instance, see Bliss, *The Metre of* Beowulf, pp. 51–3; and Hutcheson, *Old English Poetic Metre*, pp. 204–18.

[315] In addition to these authentic instances, the reconstructed line 76a, though not in the manuscript, also presents another instance: *embe syx niht þæs*.

[316] Bredehoft, *Authors*, p. 123.

[317] Bredehoft, *Authors*, p. 124.

[318] This half-line should be scanned as Sxxx|S, which may be categorised as Type E, but as Hutcheson writes, 'verses of this type that contain no proclitic before the second primary stress are problematic' (*Old English Poetic Metre*, p. 254). For the scansion of *Februarius*, see Campbell, p. 218, §556.

[319] Bredehoft, *Authors*, p. 124.

[320] The element *easter*- 'Easter' is based on the word *eastre* developed from Gmc *austraz/*austran, where the stem is monosyllabic. Cf. Burgundian *austr* and ON *austr*. For its Germanic form and its cognates in other Germanic languages, see Orel, *A Handbook*, p. 30.

reste hine þa rumheort in *Beowulf* 1799a and *ypde swa þisne eardgeard* in the *Wanderer* 85a.[321]

12

Date and Place of Composition

The *Menologium* has been considered of late southern origin[322] and in fact there is nothing in the poem that strongly suggests otherwise; the poet's language generally reveals features of late West Saxon with only a few exceptions, many of which may be attributed to his use of poetic koine.[323] Although the frequent use of unstressed *in* may be exceptional for a poem of southern origin,[324] without any further features that point to its northern origin, it seems reasonable to conclude that it is a southern poem with the unstressed *in* used in an unusual manner.[325]

As regards its date, there are various internal clues pointing to a late date, which in turn may suggest its southern origin. The separation of velar and palatal *g*'s in terms of alliteration, the metrical use of unconventional verb forms and that of parasite vowels, as well as the occasional placement of an accented element in the dip of Type B verses, are features of poems of late southern origin.[326] The *Menologium* is certainly later than the *Metrical Psalms*, from which the poet quotes in lines 60–2.[327] The *Metrical Psalms*, showing metrical features of late poetry, is considered to have been composed in the 'middle-to-late tenth century'[328]

---

[321] However, see also Bredehoft, '*The Battle of Brunanburh*', p. 290, where it is argued that the tradition regarding the parasite vowels had already changed by the time the *Battle of Brunanburh* was composed in the mid-tenth century.

[322] For instance, Imelmann, though assuming its Anglian origin, dates the poem to 950–1008 (*Das altenglische Menologium*, pp. 52–3), Dobbie to 965–1000 (*The Anglo-Saxon Minor Poems*, p. lxv), and Greeson to 950–1000 ('Two Old English Observance Poems', pp. 4–6). Sisam refers to it as 'the late Southern *Menology*' (*Studies*, p. 129), and Fulk includes it into 'the Southern group', accepting Sisam's view (*A History of Old English Meter*, p. 283).

[323] For non-West Saxon phonological features in the Southern group of poems and their relationship with the use of Old English poetic koine, see Fulk, *A History of Old English Meter*, pp. 283–93.

[324] This is one of the reasons Imelmann regards the poet as an Anglian (*Das altenglische Menologium*, pp. 26 and 29), and Jordan considers it possible (*Eigentümlichkeiten*, p. 67).

[325] As regards the views of Imelmann and Jordan mentioned in the previous note, Sisam writes that 'the particular case is unconvincing' (*Studies*, p. 125), while Fulk says that the exceptional use of unstressed *in* is due to 'a more complex isogloss than the distinction between Anglian and Southern dialects' (*A History of Old English Meter*, pp. 331–2).

[326] Fulk, *A History of Old English Meter*, pp. 194, 261 and 269–79.

[327] For this issue, see Toswell, 'The Metrical Psalter'.

[328] Bredehoft, 'Ælfric and Late Old English Verse', p. 106. See also Fulk, *A History of Old English Meter*, pp. 410–14.

Date and Place of Composition

probably in association with the Benedictine monastic revival,[329] to which the *Menologium* also includes a potential allusion (40b–4).[330]

On the other hand, it was composed certainly before 1016, when the Danish dynasty was established, since the poet himself says in his concluding remark (228b–31) that the poem was composed under the reign of an Anglo-Saxon king (and the date after 1042, after the temporary revival of the Anglo-Saxon dynasty due to the coronation of Edward the Confessor, is too late). The absence of reference to the feast of St Edward the Martyr points to the date before 1008, when the strict observance of the feast was regulated by law.[331] The set of important feasts in the poem, as well as its close relationship with the prose *Menologium* probably composed by the end of the tenth century, also suggests the date of its composition by the turn of the century.

Based on especially close lexical links between the *Menologium* and the *Death of Edgar*, which records the king's death in 975, Bredehoft claims that the former was composed in the 970s and attributes these poems as well as three other Chronicle poems, i.e., the *Battle of Brunanburh*, the *Capture of the Five Boroughs* and the *Coronation of Edgar*, to Æthelwold of Winchester (d. 984) or his school.[332] On the other hand, Hart, noticing close lexical affinities between the *Menologium* and the *Death of Edgar*, attributes them, together with the *Coronation of Edgar*, to Byrhtferth of Ramsey (*c*. 970–*c*. 1020), who he speculates was commissioned to compose the *Menologium* by Wulfstan of York perhaps in response to V Æthelred 13–19 issued in 1008.[333] Despite Hart's opinion, however, the poet is unlikely to be Byrhtferth but perhaps an older contemporary of his.[334]

While it is true that the *Death of Edgar* and the *Menologium* indicate especially close metrical and lexical affinities, it is also true that the *Menologium* poet, in comparison with the Chronicle poet, seems a little more tolerant or even loose about anomalies; he tolerates unconventional or ungrammatical word forms, such as *monð* (164a, 181b), *cigð* (184b), *mot* (206a), for the sake of standard metre, while he also tolerates obviously unmetrical half-lines of only three syllables, i.e. *Agustus* (139a), *Nouembris* (196a), *Decembris* (220a). Metrically necessary parasite vowels, while attested three times in the *Menologium* (13a,

---

[329] For the relation between the *Metrical Psalter* and the Benedictine revival, see Dobbie, ed., *The Anglo-Saxon Minor Poems*, p. xvii; Greenfield and Calder, *A New Critical History of Old English Literature*, p. 232; and Bredehoft, 'Ælfric and Late Old English Verse'.

[330] Imelmann, *Das altenglische Menologium*, pp. 52–3; Dobbie, ed., *The Anglo-Saxon Minor Poems*, p. lxv; and Fulk, *A History of Old English Meter*, pp. 261 and 277. See also O'Donnell, 'The Old English *Durham*', p. 155.

[331] Imelmann, *Das altenglische Menologium*, p. 53.

[332] Bredehoft, *Authors*, pp. 125–8.

[333] See Hart, *Learning and Culture* I, p. 122 and II.1, pp. 180–96.

[334] For the problems of Hart's view, see the Commentary below, especially the notes for lines 16b, 32–4, 60–2, 115b–19 and 175a, as well as the section regarding Latin metrical calendars, pp. 18–21 above.

Introduction

68b, 223b), never occur in the Chronicle poems. The Chronicle poet scarcely uses unstressed *in* (found only once in the *Death of Edgar* 6a), while the *Menologium* poet uses it frequently. Thus the *Menologium* and the Chronicle poems do not seem to be the works of the same poet, but still their metrical and lexical affinities are remarkable, and they may have been composed by contemporary poets belonging to the same school, such as that in Winchester, as suggested by Bredehoft.

The Old English Metrical Calendar (*Menologium*)

Text and Translation

Notes on the Text

Italics mark any word which is emended. Editorial additions are marked by [ ]. Abbreviations are expanded without notice. The Tironian sign is expanded as *and*, since it is used more often (five times) than *ond* (used twice). Roman numerals in the manuscript are retained. The sectioning is scribal, while the overall layout, word division and punctuation follow modern convention. Capitalisation also follows modern convention except for those at the beginning of the poem, where I have retained scribal capitalisation. On the left hand side of the page, line numbers are inserted, while folio numbers are given on the right hand side. The end of the manuscript page is indicated in the text by |.

Menologium

CRIST WÆS ACENNYD, CYNINGA WULdor,   112r
on midne winter,   mære þeoden,
ece ælmihtig;   on þy eahteoðan dæg
Hælend gehaten,   heofonrices weard.
5   Swa þa sylfan tiid,   side herigeas,
folc unmæte,   habbað foreweard gear,
for þy se kalend us   cymeð geþincged
on þam ylcan dæge   us to tune,
forma monað.   Hine folc mycel
10   Ianuarius   gerum heton.
And þæs embe fif niht   þætte fulwihttiid
eces drihtnes   to us cymeð,
þæne twelfta dæg   tireadige,
hæleð heaðurofe,   hatað on Brytene,
15   in foldan her.   Swylce emb feower wucan
þætte Solmonað   sigeð to tune
butan twam nihtum,   swa hit getealdon geo,
Februarius fær,   frode gesiþas,
ealde ægleawe.   And þæs embe ane niht
20   þæt we Marian   mæssan healdað,
cyninges modor,   forþan heo Crist on þam dæge,
bearn wealdendes,   brohte to temple.
Ðænne þæs emb fif niht   þæt afered byð
winter of wicum,   and se wigend þa
25   æfter seofentynum   swylt þrowade
nihtgerimes,   nergendes þegen,
Mathias mære,   mine gefræge,
þæs þe lencten on tun   geliden hæfde,
werum to wicum.   Swylce eac is wide cuð
30   ymb III | and twa   þeodum gewelhwær   112v
his cyme, kalend,   ceorlum and eorlum,
butan þænne bises   geboden weorðe
feorðan geare;   þænne he furðor cymeð
ufor anre niht   us to tune,
35   hrime gehyrsted   hagolscurum færð
geond middangeard   Martius reðe,
Hlyda healic.   Ðænne se halga þæs
emb XI niht   æþele scynde
Gregorius   in Godes wære,
40   breme in Brytene.   Swylce Benedictus

15b emb] Dobbie writes 'The letter *e* erased after this word?' (p. 49); embe Bouterwek
25b swylt] swylc with *c* in a later hand on an erasure of *t*; see Commentary

Menologium

Christ, the glory of kings, was born in midwinter, the great Lord, the eternal Almighty, and on the eighth day, the guardian of the heavenly kingdom was called Jesus. At the same time, vast multitudes, innumerable people, hold the beginning of the year, since the first day of the month, the first month, comes to town among us on the same day, as arranged for us. The great people (i.e. the Romans) formerly called it January. (1–10)

And then it is after five nights that the baptismal-tide of the eternal Lord comes to us, which glorious, brave people call Twelfth Day in Britain, here in this land. (11–15a)

Likewise it is after four weeks but two nights that *Solmonath* advances to town, as the wise men, the ancient people learned in the laws (of reckoning) reckoned it, the coming of February. (15b–19a)

And then it is after one night that we celebrate the feast of Mary, the King's mother, since she took Christ, the Ruler's child, to the temple on that day. (19b–22)

Then it is after five nights that winter is removed from the dwelling-places, and then after seventeen in the number of nights, according to hearsay, after spring had come to town, to people's villages, the warrior, the Saviour's thegn, the famous Mathias, suffered death. (23–9a)

Likewise, after three and two nights, its coming, its first day, is widely known to people everywhere, to peasants and nobles, except when the bissextile day should be added every fourth year; then it comes forth among us to town one night later, decorated with hoar-frost and hail-showers, March the fierce, *Hlyda* the great, comes over the middle-earth. (29b–37a)

Then after eleven nights, the saint, noble Gregory, famous in Britain, hastened into God's protection. (37b–40a)

Likewise, Benedict, after nine nights, sought the Saviour; vigorous and

Menologium

  embe nigon niht þæs nergend sohte,
  heard and higestrang, þæne heriað wel
  in gewritum wise, wealdendes þeow
  rincas regolfæste. Swylce eac rimcræftige
45 on þa ylcan tiid emniht healdað,
  forðan wealdend God worhte æt frymðe
  on þy sylfan dæge sunnan and monan.
    Hwæt ymb feower niht fæder onsende,
  þæs þe emnihte eorlas healdað,
50 heahengel his, se hælo abead
  Marian mycle, þæt heo meotod sceolde
  cennan, kyninga betst, swa hit gecyðed wearð
  geond middangeard; wæs þæt mære wyrd
  folcum gefræge! Swylce emb feower and þreo
55 nihtgerimes þætte nergend sent
  Aprelis monað, on þam oftust cymð
  seo mære tiid mannum to frofre,
  drihtnes ærist; þænne dream gerist
  wel wide gehwær, swa se witega sang:
60 'Þis is se dæg þæne drihten us
  wisfæst worhte, wera cneorissum,
  eallum eorðwarum eadigum to blisse.'
  Ne magon we þa tide be getale healdan
  dagena rimes, ne drihtnes stige
65 on heofenas up, forþan hi hwearfað aa
  wisra gewyrdum, ac sceal wintrum frod
  on circule cræfte findan
  halige dagas. Sculan we hwæðere gyt
  martira | gemynd ma areccan,   113r
70 wrecan wordum forð, wisse gesingan,
  þæt embe nihgontyne niht [and fifum]
  þæs þe Eastermonað to us cymeð,
  þæt man reliquias ræran onginneð,
  halige gehyrste; þæt is healic dæg,
75 bentiid bremu. Swylce in burh raþe
  [embe syx niht þæs], smicere on gearwum,
  wudum and wyrtum cymeð wlitig scriðan
  Þrymilce on tun; þearfe bringeð
  Maius micle geond menigeo gehwær.

65b hi] he
71b and fifum] Not in MS; see Commentary
76a embe syx niht þæs] Not in MS; see Commentary
78a Þrymilce] þrymlice

Menologium

brave, servant of the Ruler, whom wise men, people adhering to the monastic rules, highly praise in books. (40b–4a)

Likewise, those skilled in reckoning hold the equinox at the same time, since Ruler God created, in the beginning, the sun and the moon on this very day. (44b–7)

How the Father, four nights after people hold the equinox, sent his archangel! Who made a great salutation to Mary that she would give birth to the Lord, the best of kings, as it was made known throughout the middle-earth; that was a great event known to people! (48–54a)

Likewise it is after four and three in the number of nights that the Saviour sends the month of April, in which the great feast, the Resurrection of the Lord, most often comes to humankind as consolation. Then, jubilation is appropriate far and wide in all directions, as the prophet sang, 'This is the day which the wise Lord wrought as the bliss of all humankind, of all the blessed earth-dwellers'. We cannot hold the feast (of Easter) nor the Lord's Ascension up into heaven by reckoning the number of days, because they always change according to the rules of the wise, so the advanced in learning must skilfully find these holy days in the cycle (of the movable feasts). (54b–68a)

Yet hereafter we must further recount the commemorations of martyrs, recite forth by words, and certainly sing that it is after nineteen and five nights after *Eastermonað* comes to us that man raises up relics, the holy treasures; that is a high day, the great Rogation Day. (68b–75a)

Likewise, after six nights, beautiful *Þrymylce* comes gliding quickly into the citadel, into town, elegantly clad in adornments, woods and plants; May brings much of what is needed among a multitude of people everywhere. (75b–9)

Menologium

80 Swa þi ylcan dæge   æþele geferan,
    Philippus and Iacob,   feorh agefan,
    modige magoþegnas   for meotudes lufan.
    And þæs embe twa niht   þætte tæhte God
    Elenan eadigre   æþelust beama,
85 on þam þrowode   þeoden engla
    for manna lufan,   meotud on galgan
    be fæder leafe.   Swylce ymb fyrst wucan
    butan anre niht   þætte yldum bringð
    sigelbeorhte dagas   sumor to tune,
90 wearme gewyderu.   Þænne wangas hraðe
    blostmum blowað;   swylce blis astihð
    geond middangeard   manigra hada
    cwicera cynna,   cyninge lof secgað
    mænifealdlice,   mærne bremað,
95 ælmihtigne.   Þæs emb eahta and nigon
    dogera rimes   þætte drihten nam
    in oðer leoht   Agustinus,
    bliðne on breostum,   þæs þe he on Brytene her
    eaðmode him   eorlas funde
100 to Godes willan,   swa him se gleawa bebead
    Gregorius.   Ne hyrde ic guman awyrn
    ænigne ær   æfre bringan
    ofer sealtne mere   selran lare,
    bisceop bremran.   Nu on Brytene rest
105 on Cantwarum,   cynestole neah,
    mynstre mærum.   Þænne monað bringð
    ymb twa and *feower*   tiida lange,
    Ærra Liða,   us to tune,
    Iunius on geard,   on þam gim astihð
110 on heofenas up   hyhst on geare,
    tungla torhtast,   and of tille agrynt, |
    to sete sigeð.   Wyle syððan leng   113v
    grund behealdan   and gangan lator
    ofer foldan wang   fægerust *l[e]ohta*,
115 woruldgesceafta.   Þænne wuldres þegn
    ymb þreotyne,   þeodnes dyrling,
    Iohannes in geardagan   wearð acenned
    tyn nihtum eac.   We þa tiid healdað

81a Iacob] Iacob:, of which O'Brien O'Keeffe suggests the reading *Iacobus*; see Commentary
91b blis] A later hand adds a long *s* at the end, turning it into *bliss*
107a feower] þreo; see Commentary
114a l[e]ohta] lohta with *e* added above *o* by a later hand

Menologium

So also on the same day, noble comrades, Philip and James, brave thegns, gave up their lives for the love of God. (80–2)

And it is after two nights that God showed to blessed Helena the noblest of crosses, on which the Lord of angels, the Creator on the gallows, suffered for the love of men, by his Father's leave. (83–7a)

Likewise it is after a week but a night that summer brings to town among people sun-bright days and warm weathers. Then fields quickly flourish with blossoms; thus bliss of many ranks of living things arises throughout the middle-earth, and they repeatedly express praise to the King, extol the great Almighty. (87b–95a)

Then it is after eight and nine in the number of days that the Lord took Augustine, the one peaceful at heart, into the other light, after he had, here in Britain, found people obedient to him, to God's will, as the prudent Gregory had ordered him. I have never heard of anyone anywhere bringing over the salt sea a better doctrine, and of a more famous bishop. Now he rests in Britain among the Kentish people near the principal city (of Kent and) the famous minster. (95b–106a)

Then after two and four days, the (next) month, *Ærra Liða*, *June*, brings long (daytime) hours to town, to our enclosure, during which the gem, the brightest of stars, ascends into heaven above, highest in the year, and descends from its standing-place, sinks to its setting. Then the fairest of lights and of things in this world wishes to behold the ground longer and go more slowly over the earth. (106b–15a)

Then, after thirteen and ten nights, the thegn of heaven, the Lord's darling, John (the Baptist) was born in the days of old. We celebrate the feast with great respect at the summer solstice. (115b–19)

Menologium

    on midne sumor   mycles on æþelum.
120   Wide is geweorðod,   swa þæt wel gerist,
    haligra tid   geond hæleða bearn,
    Petrus and Paulus.   Hwæt þa apostolas,
    þeodenholde,   þrowedon on Rome
    ofer midne sumor,   miccle gewisse
125   furðor fif nihtum,   folcbealo þrealic,
    mærne martyrdom;   hæfdon mænige ær
    wundra geworhte   geond wærþeoda,
    swylce hi æfter þam   unrim fremedon
    swutelra and gesynra   þurh sunu meotudes,
130   ealdorþegnas.   Þænne ædre cymð
    emb twa niht þæs   tidlice us
    Iulius monað,   on þam Iacobus
    ymb feower niht   feorh gesealde
    ond twentigum,   trum in breostum,
135   frod and fæstræd   folca lareow,
    Zebedes afera.   And þæs symle scriþ
    ymb seofon niht þæs   sumere gebrihted
    Weodmonað on tun,   *welhwær* bringeð
    Agustus   yrmenþeodum
140   hlafmæssan dæg.   Swa þæs hærfest cymð
    ymbe oðer swylc   butan anre wanan,
    wlitig, wæstmum hladen;   wela byð geywed
    fægere on foldan.   Þænne forð gewat
    ymb þreo niht þæs   þeodne getrywe
145   þurh martyrdom,   mære diacon,
    Laurentius;   hæfð nu lif wið þan
    mid wuldorfæder   weorca to leane.
    Swylce þæs ymb fif niht   fægerust mægða,
    wifa wuldor,   sohte weroda God
150   for suna sibbe,   sigefæstne ham
    [on] neorxnawange; | hæfde nergend þa   114r
    fægere fostorlean   fæmnan forgolden
    ece to ealdre.   Þænne ealling byð
    ymb tyn niht þæs   tiid geweorðad
155   Bartholomeus   in Brytene her,
    wyrd welþungen.   Swylce eac wide byð

128a hi] hi turned into *hy* by a later hand
134a ond] on
138b welhwær] wel hwæt
151a on] Not in MS
156a wyrd] wyrð

Menologium

In such a manner as is quite appropriate, the feast of the holy ones, Peter and Paul, is widely celebrated among children of men. What a severe torment in public, great martyrdom, the apostles faithful to their Lord suffered in Rome, exactly five nights after midsummer! The chief thegns had formerly worked many wonders among people, and also after that performed countless distinct and evident signs through the son of God. (120–30a)

Then at once comes timely to us after two nights the month of July, in which after four and twenty nights, James, firm at heart, the wise and steadfast teacher of people, Zebedee's child, gave up his life. (130b–6a)

And then after seven nights, the summer-glorified *Weodmonað* always comes to town; everywhere August brings to mighty people Lammas Day. (136b–40a)

Then autumn comes after another such period but lacking one day, beautiful and laden with fruits. Prosperity is revealed beautifully on earth. (140b–3a) Then departed forth, after three nights, the one loyal to the Lord, the famous deacon Laurence, through martyrdom; in return for this, he is now given a life with the heavenly Father as a reward for his deeds. (143b–7)

Likewise after five nights, the fairest of maidens, the glory of women, went to the God of hosts, the victorious home of paradise, for the love of her son. Then the Saviour beautifully gave a reward for his fostering to the Lady for ever and ever. (148–53a)

Then always after ten nights, the feast of Bartholomew, the honourable event, is celebrated here in Britain. (153b–6a)

Likewise after four nights, the death of a nobleman is widely revealed

Menologium

   eorlum geypped æþelinges deað
   ymb feower niht, se þe fægere iu
   mid wætere oferwearp wuldres cynebearn,
160 wiga weorðlice. Be him wealdend cwæð
   þæt nan mærra man geond middangeard
   betux wife and were wurde acenned.
   Ond þæs ymbe þreo niht geond þeoda feala
   þætte Haligmonð, heleþum geþinged,
165 fereð to folce, swa hit foregleawe,
   ealde uþwitan, æror fundan,
   Septembres fær, and þy seofoþan dæg
   þæt acenned wearð cwena selost,
   drihtnes modor. Þænne dagena worn
170 ymbe þreotyne þegn unforcuð,
   godspelles gleaw, gast onsende
   Matheus his to metodsceafte
   in ecne gefean. Þænne ealling cymð
   ymb þreo niht þæs þeodum wide
175 emnihtes dæg, ylda bearnum.
    Hwæt we weorðiað wide geond eorðan
   heahengles tiid on hærfeste,
   Michaheles, swa þæt menigo wat,
   fif nihtum ufor þæs þe folcum byð,
180 eorlum geywed emnihtes dæg.
   And þæs embe twa niht þæt se teoða monð
   on folc fereð, frode geþeahte,
   October on tun us to genihte,
   Winterfylleð, swa hine wide cigð
185 igbuende Engle and Seaxe,
   weras mid wifum. Swylce wigena tiid
   ymb twentig þæs twegra healdað
   and *seofon* nihtum samod ætgædere
   on anne dæg. We þa æþelingas
190 fyrn gefrunan þæt hy foremære,
   Simon | and Iudas, symble wæron,   114v
   drihtne dyre; forþon hi dom hlutan,
   eadigne upweg. And þæs ofstum bringð
   embe feower niht, folce genihtsum,
195 Blotmonað on tun, beornum to wiste,
   Nouembris, niða bearnum
   eadignesse, swa nan oðer na deð
   monað maran miltse drihtnes.

188a seofon] fif; see Commentary

Menologium

to men, of the fighter who in the past fittingly and worthily sprinkled the royal Child of heaven with water. Regarding him, the Ruler said that no greater man, throughout the middle-earth, had ever been born between woman and man. (156b–62)

And it is after three nights, among many people, that *Haligmonað* comes to the folk as arranged for people, as the prudent, ancient scholars formerly found it, the coming of September; and it is on the seventh day that the best of women, the Lord's mother, was born. (163–9a)

Then after a number of days, after thirteen days, the reputable thegn skilled in (writing) the Gospel, Matthew, sent out his spirit, at the appointed destiny, into the eternal joy. (169b–73a)

Then after three nights, the day of the (autumnal) equinox always comes widely to people, to children of men. (173b–5)

How widely throughout the earth we celebrate the feast of the Archangel, of Michael, in autumn, as a multitude (of people) know, five nights after the day of equinox is revealed to people, to men! (176–80)

And it is after two nights that the tenth month comes to the folk in accordance with the wise scheme; October comes to town for our abundance, or *Winterfylleð*, as the island-dwelling Angles and Saxons, men as well as women, widely call it. (181–6a)

Likewise after twenty and seven nights, people hold the feast of two warriors together on one day. About these noblemen, renowned Simon and Jude, we formerly learned that they had always been dear to the Lord; therefore they won the glory, the blessed ascension. (186b–93a)

And then after four nights, *Blotmonað*, November, abundant for the nation, speedily brings to town, as sustenance for the people, as bounty for the children of men, as no other month does more through the mercy of the Lord. (193b–8)

Menologium

      And þy ylcan dæge   ealra we healdað
200   sancta symbel   þara þe sið oððe ær
      worhtan in worulde   willan drihtnes.
      Syþþan wintres dæg   wide gangeð
      on syx nihtum,   sigelbeortne genimð
      hærfest mid herige   hrimes and snawes,
205   forste gefeterad,   be frean hæse,
      þæt us wunian ne mot   wangas grene,
      foldan frætuwe.   Þæs ymb feower niht
      þætte Martinus   mære geleorde,
      wer womma leas,   wealdend sohte,
210   upengla weard.   Þænne embe eahta niht
      and feowerum   þætte fan Gode
      besenctun on sægrund   sigefæstne wer,
      on brime haran,   þe iu beorna *fela*
      Clementes oft   clypiað to þearfe.
215   And þæs embe seofon niht,   sigedrihtne l[e]of,
      æþele Andreas   up on roderum
      his gast ageaf   on Godes wære,
      fus on forðweg.   Þænne folcum bringð
      morgen to mannum   monað to tune,
220   Decembris   drihta bearnum,
      Ærra Iula.   Swylce emb eahta and twelf
      nihtgerimes   þætte nergend sylf
      þristhydigum   Thomase forgeaf
      wið earfeðum   ece rice,
225   bealdum beornwigan   bletsunga his.
      Þænne emb feower niht   þætte fæder engla
      his sunu sende   on þas sidan gesceaft
      folcum to frofre.   Nu ge findan magon
      haligra *tiida*   þe man healdan sceal,
230   swa bebugeð gebod   geond Brytenricu
      Sexna kyninges   on þas sylfan tiid. |

211b fan Gode] fangode
213b fela] felda
215b leof] lof
229a tiida] tiid

Menologium

And on the same day, we hold the feast of all saints who ever worked God's will in the world. (199–201)

Afterwards the winter's day widely comes in six nights, and seizes, by the Lord's command, the sun-bright autumn with a troop of rime and snow fettered with frost, so that the green fields, the ornaments of the earth, cannot remain with us. (202–7a)

Then it is after four nights that the famous Martin departed; the flawless man went to the Ruler, the Guardian of the heavenly angels. (207b–10a)

Then it is after eight and four nights that people hostile to God drowned the victorious man on the seabed, in the grey sea, to whom many men often pray, in advance (of his feast), to Clement, as is needed. (210b–14)

And then after seven nights, the man dear to the victorious Lord, noble Andrew, delivered into God's protection up in heaven his own spirit eager to go forth. (215–18a)
Then the month of December, *Ærra Iula*, brings the next morning to town, to nations, to people, to children of men. (218b–21a)

Likewise it is after eight and twelve in the number of nights that the Saviour himself gave to bold-minded Thomas, to the brave warrior – in return for hardship – the eternal kingdom, his blessings. (221b–5)

Then it is after four nights that the Father of angels sent His son to this spacious world for the consolation of nations. (226–8a)
Now you can find the feasts of the saints that should be observed as far as the command of the king of the Saxons extends over the spacious kingdoms of Britain at this very time. (228b–31)

Menologium

Commentary

The abbreviated titles and/or the calendar numbers in parentheses at the end of each note for the feast day indicate which feast is mentioned in which works and/or calendars. Calendar numbers correspond to those listed in Appendix 5. They are underlined when the feast in question is marked as a high feast, whereas they are in parentheses if it is a later addition probably made before 1100 (additions made after 1100 are ignored).

1–2a. The Nativity of Christ on 25 December. The feast coincided with the winter solstice, the mid-point of winter, under the original Julian calendar and Christmas was often called *midwinter, middewinter, middanwinter, middewintres mæssedæg, middes wintres mæssedæg*, etc. until the end of the Old English period. Christmas was generally known as the beginning of the Christian year in Anglo-Saxon England and on the Continent (cf. the complaint by Bede about the popular way of conceiving the Christian year in *DTR* 30). Thus martyrologies and liturgical works often begin with Christmas as in *Martyrologium Hieronymianum, Old English Martyrology*, and Ælfric's *Catholic Homilies*. The poet, as well as the compiler of the prose *Menologium*, also follows this tradition. The Metrical Calendar by Eugenius Vulgarius also begins with Christmas, although Latin metrical calendars usually begin with 1 January. In many cases, the year also begins with 25 December in the Anglo-Saxon Chronicle. Imelmann (pp. 43–4) claims that the *Menologium* is influenced by the Gregorian Sacramentary, simply because both begin with Christmas, but this is untenable. For a general introduction to the beginning of the year in medieval Europe, see Cheney and Jones, ed., *A Handbook of Dates*, pp. 8–12, while for the beginning of the year in Anglo-Saxon England, see ÆCHom I 6.129–40. See also Harrison, 'The Beginning of the Year', and Godden, 'New Year's Day'. For the beginning of the year in the Anglo-Saxon Chronicle, see Poole, 'The Beginning of the Year'; Beaven, 'The Beginning of the Year'; Hodgkin, 'The Beginning of the Year'; Whitelock, 'On the Commencement of the Year'; and Swanton, *The Anglo-Saxon Chronicle*, pp. xv–xvi.
1. In the manuscript, the first line of the poem is mostly written in capital letters. The initial C is a huge capital decorated with an image of an eagle, which seems to symbolise Christ himself.
1b. *cyninga wuldor* 'the glory of kings'. This is a kenning for Christ attested eleven more times in Old English poems. Cf. *wifa wuldor* 'the glory of women' referring to Mary in line 149b.
3b–4. The feast of the Circumcision of Christ on 1 January is represented by the reference to the naming of Christ on his eighth day. By adopting the phrase *on þy eahteoðan dæg* 'on the eighth day', the poet fails to follow the way of counting days otherwise consistently followed in the poem; according to his usual way of counting days, it should be on the seventh rather than the eighth day. Thus Dobbie (p. lxiii) and Grimaldi (p. 42) consider that the

half-line involves an interpretational difficulty. As Dobbie writes, the alliteration confirms that *eahteoðan* is correct, but his conjecture is unlikely: that it may be either that 'the poet was wrong in his counting, or that we are really to take December 24th, the vigil of the Nativity, as the date indicated in ll. 1–3a'. As rightly suggested by Greeson, *on þy eahteoðan dæg* is intended to mean 'on the octave day' of Christmas ('Two Old English Observance Poems', p. 256). See also the *DOE*, s.v. *eahteoða*, definition 1.a.i. Here the poet adopts a conventional expression regarding the Circumcision; according to the Old Testament, a male child needed to be circumcised and named eight days after his birth (Genesis 17.12; 21.4), and Christ was circumcised and named Jesus (*Hælend* in Old English) on his eighth day as narrated in Luke 2.21, whose Old English translation reads as follows: *Æfter þam þe ehta dagas gefyllede wæron þæt ðæt cild emsnyden wære. His nama wæs hælend* (*West Saxon Gospels*, Luke 2:21) 'After eight days were completed, that child was circumcised. His name was *Hælend*'. For further details, see Karasawa, 'A Note'. For the endingless locative (dative) singular form *dæg*, see Hogg and Fulk, p. 17, §2.18. The usual locative/dative singular form with the ending, *dæge*, is also used in 47a, 80a and 199a. (MCY, MCH, MCR, ÆCHom I, *OEM*, Calendars 1, 4, 6–9, 11–13, 14–16, 17–21, 22, 23, 24, 25, 27)

5–9a. The first day/month of the Roman year. The liturgical year began with 25 December, while the Roman year begins with 1 January. The poet marks the beginning of the former by starting the poem with 25 December, while he refers to the beginning of the latter as *foreweard gear* (6b) 'the beginning of the year' (cf. *þone forman dæig on geare* 'the first day in the year' in the *Old English Martyrology* referring to 25 December). The poet's references to *kalend* (7a) 'the first day of the (Roman) month', *folc mycel* (9b) 'great folk, i.e. the Romans' and *Ianuarius* (10a) 'January, the first month of the Roman year' emphasise its Roman origin. For the beginning of the year in Anglo-Saxon England, see the note for lines 1–2a.

5b–6a. *side herigeas, folc unmæte* 'vast multitudes, innumerable people' refers to the Anglo-Saxons. The same combination of these phrases in the same order appears in *Andreas* 652b–3a. Of the two phrases, the latter is attested only in these lines in the *Menologium* and *Andreas*, while the former is a formula attested in several poems.

7. *se kalend us cymeð geþincged*. Hickes, Fox, Grein, and Earle read *kalendus* rather than *kalend us* (though Grein corrects his earlier reading to *kalend us* in his 'Zur Textkritik'). Perhaps this is because *us* was considered to be redundant, since there is another *us* in the next line; Imelmann and Fritsche even omit the first *us* in their texts. However, the *us* in question is the dative of interest, and is used with *geþincged*, to mean '(as) arranged for us' (by the Romans). As *geþincged*, as well as the Latin loan-word *kalend*, implies, the poet is talking about the Roman year arranged by the Romans. See also notes for lines 5–9a and 9b–10.

8b. *us to tune*. Since there is another *us* in the previous line, Wülker regards the one in this half-line as redundant (*Bibliothek*, p. 283). However, they function differently as seen in the note for line 7. The *us* in line 8b is the possessive dative, the whole half-line meaning 'to our town'. The literal meaning of the phrase '(the first day of the month comes) to our town' or 'to town among us' seems odd to our modern eyes, but it should be understood more generally to mean 'to us English people, to England, etc.'. The same half-line appears in 34b and 108b. It has sometimes been pointed out that this is one of the earliest examples of the phrase 'to town'. See, for instance, Dobbie, ed., *The Anglo-Saxon Minor Poems*, p. 170, and Greeson, 'Two Old English Observance Poems', p. 258. For this and other similar phrases, see also Stanley, 'The Prose *Menologium* and the Verse *Menologium*', pp. 256–7.

9a. *forma monað*. Latin and Old English month-names are, in most cases, used together in the *Menologium*, but here January is called *forma monað* 'the first month' rather than *Æfterra Iula*, the Old English month-name corresponding to January. This is probably because *Æfterra Iula* sounds somewhat inappropriate for the first month and/or the beginning of the year because of its first element *æfterra* 'latter'. The only other Latin month-name used alone is *Iulius* (132a), whose Old English counterpart is *Æfterra Liða*. The names of *Æfterra Iula* and *Æfterra Liða* can be easily inferred from the names of the previous months, *Ærra Iula* and *Ærra Liða*, which may be another reason why these month-names are omitted. For the use of Latin and Old English month-names, see Appendix 9.

9b–10. *folc mycel Ianuarius gerum heton*. As Wülker suggests, the phrase *folc mycel* 'great folk' refers to the Romans (p. 283). The poet attributes to them the origin of the month-name *Ianuarius* and that of the year consisting of twelve months which he superimposes upon the liturgical year. A similar but more clear-cut attribution of a Latin month-name to the Romans is found in the *Seasons for Fasting* 49–50. When they are used in Old English writings, the Latin origin or the foreign nature of the Latin month-names is often mentioned or implied, and the poet also follows this tradition. See also the instances in the *Old English Martyrology*, where Latin month-names are nearly always mentioned as Latin words. For the use of the Latin nominative ending *-us* for the accusative case in Old English writings, see Baker, 'The Inflection of Latin Nouns'. As in this case, moreover, nominative forms are often used for the objective complements of verbs of calling and naming. Numerous examples are listed, for instance, in Grein, Holthausen and Köhler, *Sprachschatz*, s.v. *hatan*.

11. *And þæs embe fif niht þætte* 'And then [it is] after five nights that ...' involves an elliptical construction frequently appearing in this poem. For details, see the Introduction. See also Fritsche, p. 26, and Mitchell, *Old English Syntax* II, p. 23, §1973. Imelmann and Fritsche often change the word order of this sort of phrase as in *And embe fif niht þæs, þætte* (11a), but such a change is unnecessary. Similar instances are found in lines 23a, 83a, 148a, 163a, 181a, 215a.

11–15a. The feast of Epiphany, or *twelfta dæg* (13a) 'Twelfth Day', on 6 January. Various manifestations of Christ's divinity were celebrated on the feast of Epiphany, especially the baptism, the miracle at Cana, and the visit of the Magi (see, for instance, the entry for the Epiphany in *OEM* and the two homilies for the feast in ÆCHom I and ÆCHom II). In this poem, on the other

Commentary

hand, Christ's baptism alone is mentioned. Holthausen would emend *twelfta* (13a) to *twelftan* ('C. Plummer', p. 239), but the emendation is unnecessary. As seen above in the note for lines 9b–10, a noun in its nominative form is very often used as an objective complement with a verb of calling or naming. (MCY, MCH, MCR, ÆCHom I, ÆCHom II, *OEM*, Calendars 1, 4–9, 11–13, 14–16, 17–22, 23, 24, 25, 26, 27)

13b. *tireadige*. The parasite vowel -*i*- in the adjectival suffix -*ig* is metrically necessary here. Hutcheson's corpus covering 13,044 lines, approximately 40% of the extant Old English poetic corpus, contains only four instances where adjectival -*ig* before an inflectional ending beginning with a vowel is metrically necessary, i.e., *Elene* 377b, *Exodus* 50a, *Judith* 229a and 245a. See Hutcheson, *Old English Poetic Metre*, p. 64. The *Menologium*, which is not included in his corpus, adds three instances (13b, 68a and 223a) and the frequency seems high.

14b–15a. *on Brytene, in foldan her* 'in Britain, here in this land'. Often referring to Britain, as well as to 'this land', 'our town', etc., the poet emphasises the domestic perspective of the poem. The word *Bryten* is used five times in the poem, and the frequency is exceptionally high. It never occurs more than once in other Old English poems: *Guthlac A* 175a, *Guthlac B* 883b, *Metres of Boethius*, Metre 20, 99a, *Battle of Brunanburh* 71b, *Death of Edgar* 14a, *Seasons for Fasting* 56b and *Aldhelm* 5a.

15b–19a. The beginning of February. *Solmonað* (16a) is the Old English name for February. Cf. Old Norse *sólmánuðr* 'sun-month, i.e. the third month in the summer'. Its etymology is not certain, but its first element has often been connected either with Old English *sōl* 'sun' or *sol* 'mire, mud'. Bede writes about the month as follows: *Solmonath potest dici mensis placentarum quas in eo diis suis offerebant* (*DTR* 15) '*Solmonath* can be called the month of cakes which they used to offer to their gods'. For its etymology, see Kluge, 'Zu altenglischen Dichtungen', p. 479; Weinhold, *Die deutsche Monatsnamen*, p. 56; Oberle, *Überreste germanischen Heidentums*, p. 46; and Schneider, 'The OE. Names of the Months', p. 264.

16b. The word *sigan* more often means 'to sink, descend' but it also means 'to advance, move, go' as it does here. Hart (*Learning and Culture* II.1, p. 189), trying to show a close connection between the *Menologium* and Byrhtferth's *Enchiridion*, claims that the latter meaning is unique in these two works, which is not the case. See, for instance, Grein, Holthausen and Köhler, *Sprachschatz*, p. 609, s.v. *sigan*.

17b–19a. A passage very similar in both meaning and structure is found in lines 165b–7a. Together with lines 9b–10, the poet mentions the ancient foreign origin of the Latin month-name and the Roman month-system. The word *ægleawe* 'learned in the laws (of reckoning)' implies the existence of learned computistical rules behind the course of the year. Although Greeson (p. 262) regards *Februarius* as an adjective modifying *fær* and the *DOE* follows this under the heading of *februarius*, it is, as paralleled by the phrase *Septembres fær* (167a), a noun in the genitive as Cosijn suggests ('Anglosaxonica', p. 443). The Latin ending -*us* is often used as a genitive singular ending in Old English writings.

Menologium

See p. 60 above. See also Baker and Lapidge, ed., *Byrhtferth's Enchiridion*, pp. cii–civ; and Baker, 'The Inflection of Latin Nouns'.

19b–22. The Presentation of Jesus at the Temple (2 February). The feast is referred to simply as *Marian mæssan* (20) 'Mary's feast'. The feast is also known as the Purification of the Virgin and the Meeting of the Lord, as it is often called *Purificatio Sancte Marie* 'Purification of St Mary' or *Ypapanti Domini* 'the Meeting of the Lord' in Anglo-Saxon calendars. For the event underlying the feast, see Luke 2.22–40. Here only the presentation of Jesus at the temple is mentioned without any references to Mary's ritual purification, as is also the case with MCY 9 and MCR 22: *Et quartas nonas Christus templo offerebatur* 'and on 2 February, Christ was offered to the temple'. (PM, MCY, MCH, MCR, ÆCHom I, Calendars 4, 5, 6, 7, 8, 9, 11–13, 14–16, 17–24, 25, 26, 27)

21a. *cyninges modor*. This phrase is attested otherwise only in prose works on history, where it always refers to a mother of an actual king, never Mary. Cf. *drihtnes modor* in line 169a, which is also used otherwise exclusively in prose.

23–4a. The beginning of spring on 7 February. Bede says that spring begins with 7 February in the Greek and Roman tradition (*DTR* 35), while Isidore of Seville, giving the date 22 February, follows a different tradition in his *DNR* 7.5. Anglo-Saxon calendars and computistical works such as Byrhtferth's *Enchiridion* (see II.1.394–7), as well as the prose and the verse *Menologium*, follow the former tradition.

24b–9a. The feast of St Mathias the Apostle (d. c. 80) on 24 February. The phrase *nergendes þegen* (26b) 'the Saviour's thegn' reflects his identity as an apostle, although he was chosen as an apostle after the Crucifixion and accordingly not by Christ himself but by the other eleven apostles to replace Judas Iscariot (see Acts 1.12–26). Cf. *ealdorþegnas* 'chief thegns' used for SS Peter and Paul in line 130a and *þegn unforcuð* 'honourable thegn' for St Matthew in line 170a. There are various accounts of the life and death of St Mathias and nothing certain is known. He is not mentioned in ÆCHom, *OEM*, or the *Fates of the Apostles*. (PM, MCY, MCH, MCR, Calendars 4–7, 9, 11, 12, 13–15, 16–22, 23, 24, 25–7)

25b. *swylt þrowade*. MS *swylc þrowade*. As Wülker (p. 284) notes, Sievers points out that *c* in *swylc* in the manuscript is added by a later hand over the erasure of original *t* (Sievers, 'Collationen angelsächsischer Gedichte').

26a. *nihtgerimes*. This word, meaning 'in the number of nights', is attested only in the adverbial genitive, and is used mostly in the on-verse with only one exception in *Genesis A* 1193b.

28–9a. The beginning of spring, which is indirectly mentioned as a time of removal of winter in lines 23–4a, is more directly mentioned here with the word *lencten* (28a) 'spring'. Lent, occurring in springtime, is a shortened form of Lenten (< OE *lencten*), originally meaning 'the season of spring'.

29b–37a. The beginning of March with the digression on the bissextile day in the leap year. The month is mentioned as *Martius reðe* (36b) 'fierce March' and *Hlyda healic* (37a) 'great *Hlyda*'. For the month-names and the adjecties used with them, see below.

Commentary

30a. *ymb III and twa*. In most cases, numerals indicating the number of days between two consecutive entries are used with a substantive such as *niht* or *nihtgerimes*, but they may be used without one as in this line and in line 107a.

30b. *gewelhwær*. Bouterwek emends to *wel gehwær* and Rositzke follows this, whereas Imelmann and Fritsche emend to *welgehwær*. However, there is no need of emendation since the word *gewelhwær* 'everywhere' is attested elsewhere (especially in Wulfstan's works) and presents no major problem from the semantic and metrical viewpoints.

31a. *his cyme, kalend*. These words are often interpreted as follows: *kalend* '(the first day of) the month' is the subject of the sentence, while *his cyme* is in the instrumental, meaning 'by its coming'. Dobbie, although admitting the obscurity of the meaning and construction, says this is the only possible interpretation (p. 171), and Greeson (p. 263) and Jones (p. 177) follow this. However, it seems more reasonable to consider that *his cyme* and *kalend* are appositive with each other in the nominative, both as the subject of the sentence, meaning 'its coming, the first day of the month'.

31b. *ceorlum and eorlum*. The phrase *ceorlum and eorlum*, a class-conscious expression meaning 'to peasants and nobles', is attested nowhere else, but is reminiscent of such phrases used in legal texts as *ge ceorle ge eorle* (Alfred 4.2), *ge eorl ge ceorl* (*Geþyncðo* 1), and *ægðer ge eorlisce ge ceorlisce* (VI Æthelstan, prologue) 'both peasants and nobles'. In the *Menologium*, this is the only instance of the word *eorl* used with this meaning; in the other places (lines 49b, 99b, 157a, and 180a), it simply means 'man' without any higher-class connotation.

32–4. The digression on the bissextile day. The intercalary day was inserted on the sixth calends of March (i.e. 24 February), and the day was doubled in leap years as reflected in the Latin term *bissextus* meaning 'twice sixth'; there were a first and a second sixth calends of March in leap years. According to Byrhtferth of Ramsey, perhaps a younger contemporary of the *Menologium* poet, the feast of St Mathias, falling on 24 February, was held on the second sixth calends of March in leap years, i.e. 25 February according to the modern calendar (see ByrEnch II.1.116–20). A note in Old English or Latin to the same effect is sometimes found at the foot of Anglo-Saxon calendar pages for February as in calendars 12, 19, 23 and 26. If we follow what Byrhtferth and these notes say, the feast of St Mathias rather than the calends of March comes one day later than usual in leap years, whereas the *Menologium* poet puts it the other way around. Hart tries to identify the poet with Byrhtferth (*Learning and Culture* II.1, pp. 192–3), but their treatments of the bissextile day are different.

32a. *bises* 'the bissextile day'. This is a *hapax legomenon*, and judging from its phonological features, may well be a very early loan-word from Latin (*bisextus* > *bisext > *bisest > *bises*). For the sound changes, see Campbell §417 and §537. In computistical prose works, a newly borrowed *bissextus* is used.

36b. *Martius reðe*. Together with *hrime gehyrsted, hagolscurum* (35) 'decorated with hoar-frost and hail-showers', *reðe* 'fierce' represents the still cold weather of the month. *Maxims II* also refers to spring as a rimy cold season in line

Menologium

6: *lencten hrimigost (he byð longest ceald)* 'spring is rimiest; it is cold the longest'. The word *reðe* in this context reminds us of the first element of the Old English name for March, *(h)reð(e)monað*, though Bede in *DTR* 15 explains that *Hredmonath a dea illorum Hreda, cui in illo sacrificabant, nominatur* 'Hredmonath is named after their goddess Hreda, to whom they used to offer a sacrifice during the month'. On the top left margin of the manuscript page, there is a memorandum by a later hand reading *[A]libi hrædmonað*, in an alternative Old English spelling.

37a. *Hlyda healic.* Although Fox (p. 15) and Hart (p. 201) fail to recognise it as a month-name, *Hlyda* is one of the Old English month-names for March as attested in ÆCHom I 6.150 and in *Leechdom* III 152.9, 250.5 and 228.21. While most of the Old English month-names became obsolete during the Middle English period, it survived, according to the *OED*2 (s.v. Lide), until the seventeenth century or even later. (*Hlyda* > Lide should not be confused with *Liða* 'June/July', which is related to *liðe* 'gentle, soft' > lithe. See also the note for lines 106b–15a.) Bouterwek (p. 7) translates the phrase as *mensis strepens* 'resounding month', based on its etymology, which is perhaps related to *hlud* 'loud'; he seems to regard *healic* as emphasising the meaning 'loud'. Greeson (p. 198) translates it as 'proud Hlyda', Malone ('Old English Calendar Poem', p. 194) 'haughty Hlyda' and Jones (p. 177) 'the excellent month of *Hlyda*', but none explains why the month is 'proud', 'haughty', 'excellent' etc. The following words by Byrhtferth on the month of March may provide the reason: *Ðeah ealle þa monðas synd mid mislicre blisse and wurðscipe geglengde, þeah is Martius swyðost* (ByrEnch II.1.232–3) 'Though all the months are adorned with various bliss and honour, March is the greatest'. This is because the most important events happen(ed) in March; and indeed Byrhtferth writes much longer on March than on any other month in this part of the book. From the computistical point of view, the vernal equinox, the key day in reckoning the date of Easter, is by far the most important, and in the month there are also some key days necessary for the right calculation of the date of Easter. March is also very important from the cosmogonical point of view, since it was said to be the month in which God created the world. The *Menologium* poet also refers to the Creation of the sun and the moon as an event which occurred in this month in lines 46–7. 25 March is also very important not only because it is Annunciation Day but because it was the day the angels had been created, Christ had suffered but had arisen from death, and God's spirit had come to mankind (see ByrEnch II.1.231–91). Thus March is full of important events and this may be why the poet uses the adjective *healic* 'high, elevated, great' for the month.

37b–40a. The feast of St Gregory the Great on 12 March. As a pope (reigned 590–604), he sent St Augustine to evangelise the Anglo-Saxons in 596, which the poet mentions in lines 100b–1a, and because of this he came to be revered highly among the Anglo-Saxons; the earliest life of Gregory, *Vita Gregorii*, is written by an anonymous author of Whitby in the early eighth century, while his *Dialogues* and *Regula pastoralis* were translated into Old English at the court of King Alfred. His feast is one of those most frequently marked as a high feast in extant Anglo-Saxon calendars (for details see Appendix 6). For the role he played in the evangelisation of England, see *HE* I.23–33, II.1, etc. (PM, MCY, MCH, MCR, ÆCHom II, *OEM*, Calendars 1, 4–7, 8, 9, 11, 12, 13–15, 16–25, 27)

37b. The scribe fails to place a *punctus* at the end of 37b and editors suggest two different readings as regards where line 37b ends. Grein, Wülker, Imelmann, Fritsche, Rositzke, Dobbie, Greeson, Hart and Jones place *þæs* at the end of 37b, whereas Hickes, Fox, Ebeling, Bouterwek, Plummer, Grimaldi and O'Brien O'Keeffe place it at the beginning of 38a. From the metrical point of view, the former seems more plausible, since the latter allows in the off-verse the light verse of the metrical pattern xxxSx, which usually appears in the on-verse and is extremely rare in the off-verse. See Bliss, *The Metre of* Beowulf, p. 122; and Hutcheson, *Old English Poetic Metre*, p. 289.

38b–9. *scynde ... in Godes wære* 'hurried into God's protection'. The verb *scyndan* 'to hurry, hasten' is used in relation to death in *Juliana* 489: *of flæschoman fæge scyndan* 'those doomed to die hastened forth from their bodies'. God's protection is often mentioned in relation to death in Old English poetry: *feran on Frean wære* (*Beowulf* 27) 'go into the protection of the Lord'; *on ðæs Waldendes wære geþolian* (*Beowulf* 3109) 'to abide in the protection of the Ruler'; *in Godes wære ... ferde* (*Guthlac A* 690b–1a) 'went into God's protection'. Cf. also *his gast ageaf on Godes wære* 'delivered his soul into God's protection' in line 217.

39a. *Gregorius*. This half-line consists only of this name. The same half-line, appearing again in line 101a, is otherwise attested only in the *Metrical Preface to the Pastoral Care* 6a. See also the note for line 97b.

40b–4a. The feast of St Benedict of Nursia (*c.* 480–*c.* 547), the founder of western monasticism. Although his feast falls on 11 July in the current Roman missal, he is traditionally said to have died at Monte Cassino on 21 March, and his feast used to be celebrated on this day. Since 21 March often falls within Lent, however, the Benedictines have long celebrated his feast on 11 July, the day his relics were transferred to Fleury in France in the latter half of the seventh century. (PM, MCY, MCH, MCR, ÆCHom II, *OEM*, Calendars 1, 4–9, 11, 12, 13–16, 17–21, 22, 23, 24, 25, 27)

41a. In the manuscript, the scribe fills in a *punctus* between *niht* and *þæs*, thereby indicating his reading that the on-verse ends at *niht*. Hickes, Ebeling, Rositzke and O'Brien O'Keeffe follow this in their editions. This makes the off-verse metrically problematic and therefore it seems more plausible that *þæs* forms part of the on-verse despite the scribe's punctuation. The same use of accented *þæs* at the end of the on-verse is found in lines 131a, 137a, 144a, 174a, 154a and 187a. Reconstructed line 76a also includes this use of *þæs*.

43b. Holthausen would emend *þeow* to *þeos* (nom., pl., m.) 'those', considering it to be parallel to *rincas* (44a) ('C. W. M. Grein', p. 226). As pointed out by Dobbie (p. 171) and followed by Greeson (p. 264), however, the manuscript reading makes good sense and there is no need of emendation. Here *þeow* is

Menologium

in the accusative singular, parallel to *þæne* (42b), and is the antecedent placed inside the relative clause. For a similar instance, see the note for line 214a.

44a. The word *regolfæste* is a *hapax legomenon*. The reference to *rincas regolfæste* 'people adhering to monastic rules', i.e. monks, praising St Benedict may allude to the Benedictine monastic revival in Anglo-Saxon England, which began under the abbotship of Dunstan at Glastonbury (appointed between 940 and 946). The movement especially flourished after 963, the year of the consecration of Æthelwold as bishop of Winchester, who had been a colleague of Dunstan's at Glastonbury during the 940s and early 950s. For the potential allusion, see Imelmann, pp. 52–3, and Fulk, *A History of Old English Meter*, p. 261. Bredehoft suggests a very close connection between Æthelwold and the verse *Menologium*. See Bredehoft, *Authors*, pp. 126–30.

44b–5. A passage on the vernal equinox on 21 March. With the word *rimcræftige* (44b) '(people) skilled in reckoning', otherwise attested only in Byrhtferth's *Enchiridion*, the poet may intend to reveal the educated/learned nature of the date 21 March; as regards the solstices and the equinoxes, he always follows the popular dates based on the original Julian calendar except for the case of the vernal equinox here in this passage, where he adopts the official/learned date based on the revised Julian calendar. Similarly, the word *rimcræft* 'reckoning' is connected with computistical education in the *Death of Edgar* 6a. For the explanations of the dates of the solstices and the equinoxes by Anglo-Saxon computists, see *DTR* 30, *DTA* 236–92 and ByrEnch II.1.232–346. See also pp. 36–7 above.

46–7. The creation of the sun and the moon. According to Genesis 1.14–19, God created the sun, the moon and the stars on the fourth day of creation and, traditionally, it was considered to be the day of the vernal equinox, when the sun rises directly in the east and sets directly in the west. Thus, as in this passage, the vernal equinox, as a day revealing the date of the first day of creation, is often connected with Biblical cosmogony. See *DTR* 6, *DTA* 76–92 and ByrEnch II.1.263–71. See also the *Old English Martyrology*, under 21 March 'The Fourth Day of Creation'. The first quarter of this poem ends with this passage, and the scribe makes this clear by placing a *punctus versus* after the last word of line 47, i.e. *monan*, and leaving the rest of the line (fol. 112v12) blank.

48–54a. The Annunciation to the Blessed Virgin Mary on 25 March. According to Luke 1.26–39, the angel Gabriel appeared to Mary to foretell the birth of Christ. The date of the event is not recorded in the Bible except that it is said to have been in the sixth month of Elizabeth's pregnancy with John the Baptist (Luke 1.26), but the feast is celebrated on 25 March, exactly nine months before Christmas. Gabriel is not named but is mentioned as *heahengel* (50a) 'archangel' (the same word is also used for Michael the Archangel in line 177a). Gabriel is not called archangel in the Bible but is often so called in Old English prose works including Ælfric's homilies and the *Old English Martyrology* as well as in apocryphal and deuteronomical books. This passage opens the second quarter of the poem and the word *hwæt*, a pronoun introducing an exclamative clause, which is often used at the beginning of a poem or speech, is used at the beginning. In this poem, it always marks the beginnings of quarters (in lines 48a, 122b and 176a). The scribe starts the word with a huge red capital in the margin, visually marking the beginning of a new quarter. In this context, the exclamative *hwæt* should be understood as used with a 'null adverb' which perhaps means something like 'judiciously, justly, graciously, etc'. For the use of *hwæt* plus a 'null predicate' receiving its value from the context, see Walkden, 'The Status of *hwæt* in Old English', p. 480. (PM, MCY, MCH, MCR, ÆCHom I, *OEM*, Calendars <u>4–7</u>, 8, <u>9</u>, <u>11</u>, <u>12</u>, 13–16, <u>17–22</u>, 23, <u>24</u>, 25, 27)

49a. *emnihte.* Besides the word form *emniht* as in line 45b, the form with final *e*, *emnihte*, is sporadically used in its nominative/accusative singular form as in this line. Both forms are used also in PMH. Here at the beginning of the second quarter, the poet refers to the vernal equinox for the second time in order to restart counting the number of days. In the same way, the poet always refers to the solstice or the equinox twice, just before and after the section boundaries. This produces a somewhat similar effect to that created by anadiplosis.

50b. *hælo abead.* Although *hælo* itself means health, luck, salvation etc., and Greeson (p. 324) and Jones (p. 177) actually translate it as 'salvation', the set phrase as a whole, referring to the salutation (*salutatio* in Luke 1.29 in the Vulgate) made to Mary by Gabriel, means 'saluted, made a salutation' in this context without any reference to good luck, salvation etc. It is used with this meaning also in *Beowulf* 2418a, to which Klaeber (*Beowulf*, p. 212), as well as Fulk, Bjork and Niles (*Beowulf*, p. 244), notes that the phrase 'carries no reference to good luck ... but means, quite in general, "saluted"'. In *Christ A* 202b, a similar phrase *hælo gebodade* is used with the same meaning referring also to the Annunciation, which was called *Marian bodungdæg* (*bodung* < *bodian* 'to tell, announce') in Old English. Cf. the following passage from the *Old English Martyrology* under March 25: *com Gabrihel ærest to Sancta Marian mid Godes ærende* 'Gabriel came first to Saint Mary with God's message' (saying that she is going to bear Christ). Although saluting words tend literally to mean something like 'good luck/health to you', as in the case of *wes þu hal* (e.g. *Beowulf* 407a), they must have often been used simply as words of salutation with no deep significance, as actually happened, for instance, to the address at parting 'God be with ye', which was later contracted as good-bye reflecting the complete loss of its original meaning. Similarly, the phrase *hælo abeodan*, though sometimes retaining its literal meaning as in *Beowulf* 653b, also came to mean 'to salute' with the literal meaning of *hælo* submerged.

53b–4a. *wæs þæt mære wyrd.* The word *wyrd* here means 'event', as in the following very similar words referring to the Deluge in *Genesis A* 1399b: *þæt is mæro wyrd* 'that is a famous event'. Cf. also *ymb þa mæran wyrd* 'about the famous event' (*Elene* 1063b); *Þæt wæs egeslic wyrd!* 'that was a fearful event' (*Dream of the Rood* 74b); and *wyrd seo mære* 'the notorious fate' (*The Wanderer* 100b).

54b–68a. The beginning of April and the Easter digression. After briefly mentioning the beginning of April, the poet, instead of giving some information about the month itself, begins to give an explanation of the movable nature of

Easter and Ascension Day. The poet inserts the Easter digression here at the beginning of the month, because April is called *Eastermonað* 'Easter-month' in Old English, as he mentions immediately after the digression. Its digressional nature is reflected in the fact that the poet himself clearly says that the movable feasts are outside the scope of the poem (63–8a). This also explains why he disregards only here in this digression the otherwise consistently followed order of time. For details see the note for lines 64b–5a.

56a. *Aprelis monað.* Imelmann and Fritsche emend *monað* to *monð*, which is possible considering the poet's use of the unconventional word form *monð* for metrical purposes in lines 164a and 181b but is not necessary. Probably they emend in order to avoid the metrical structure requiring double alliteration, in which this line is lacking; but the use of a proper name justifies the anomaly and I retain the original reading (cf. the case of *Iulius monað* in line 132a). For the suspension of mandatory double alliteration due to the use of a proper name, see, for instance, Bredehoft, *Early English Metre*, p. 31. The Old English equivalent of April, *Eastermonað*, is mentioned sixteen lines below in line 72a, which is exceptionally remote from its Latin equivalent, and this is probably due to the insertion of the Easter digression. For details, see the note for line 72a.

56b–7a. *Seo mære tiid* 'the great feast' refers to Easter. The poet says it 'most often' comes in April since it can be held in March, its earliest possible date being 22 March. Similarly, Byrhtferth writes Easter is 'often' held in April: *On þissum monðe oft byð seo Easterlice tid gehealden* (ByrEnch II.1.302) 'Easter is often held in this month'. For the metrical use of the unconventional word form *cymð*, see p. 67 above.

58b. *þænne dream gerist.* In this context, *dream* seems to mean 'jubilation, celebration' (see the *DOE*, s.v. *drēam*, definition 1.b.i), probably with an implication of 'singing of psalms' (see the *DOE*, s.v. *drēam*, definition 3.a.i.); a passage from a psalm actually follows. The word tends to be connected with jubilation, singing, noise of praise or of some musical instrument in prose works, glosses and glossaries, whereas in poetry it more often refers to festive, communal or heavenly joy. Here in this context, the word seems to have a meaning much closer to those mainly found in prose works, glosses and glossaries. For the semantic range of *dream*, see Schlenk, 'Studien zum Gebrauch von Dream'; Ostheeren, *Studien zum Begriff der 'Freude'*; Karasawa, 'An Aspect of OE Joy Term *Dream*'; and Karasawa, 'Christian Influence on OE *dream*'.

59b. *Se witega*, literally 'the wise man', means 'the prophet' or 'the psalmist' in this context, since a quotation from a psalm follows. Ælfric uses the same word in the same context: *Be ðam dæge cwæð se witega* ... (ÆCHom II 16.209) 'About the day (of Easter), the prophet says ...'. Also in the same context, Byrhtferth, writing in Latin, uses *propheta* 'prophet': *de qua propheta ait insignis* ... (ByrEnch IV.1.202) 'about which the renowned prophet declares ...'.

60–2. As first pointed out by Bouterwek (p. 23), the poet quotes a passage from the *Metrical Psalms*, Psalm 117.22. See also Dobbie, p. lxv. As Bredehoft writes (*Authors*, p. 113), the poet changes the unfamiliar phrase *eallum eorðtudrum*

Commentary

including a *hapax legomenon* to a more formulaic expression *eallum eorðwarum* attested in *Andreas* 568a and *Christ B* 723a. The corresponding Latin passage, *Hęc est dies quam fecit Dominus* 'this is the day which the Lord made' is quoted by Ælfric and Byrhtferth in relation to the Resurrection in ÆCHom II 16.209–11 and ByrEnch IV.1.202–3. In the same place, Ælfric also translates it into Old English: *Þes is se dæg þe drihten worhte* 'this is the day which the Lord made'. Hart, unaware of the passage in ÆCHom II, writes that '[n]owhere else in the sources of the period [apart from the *Menologium* and Byrhtferth's *Enchiridion*] have I found this text quoted in relation to the Resurrection', and regards it as a strong clue to identifying the *Menologium* poet with Byrhtferth (pp. 184–5). With another instance in a contemporary work by a different author, however, the case does not seem as convincing as Hart claims.

63–8a. The poet mentions the movable nature of Easter Day and Ascension Day, and places them outside the scope of the poem, saying that *Ne magon we þa tide be getale healdan dagena rimes, ne drihtnes stige on heofenas up* (63–5a) 'We can hold neither the feast (of Easter) nor the Lord's Ascension up into heaven by reckoning of the number of days'. These words contrast with the concluding remark at the end of the poem, *Nu ge findan magon, haligra tiida þe man healdan sceal* ... (228b–9) 'Now you can find the holy days which people must hold ...'.

64b–5a. *drihtnes stige on heofenas up* 'the Lord's Ascension up into heaven' refers to Ascension Day, celebrated on Thursday forty days after Easter. The phrase *drihtnes stige* is attested nowhere else. For the Ascension, the word *upstige* is more common (chiefly used in prose works but found three times in *Christ B* 615a, 655a, 711a), and the phrase *drihtnes upstige* is attested five times (all in prose works); but *upstige* would cause metrical difficulties here and the poet seems to have modified it to attain a standard metrical pattern. For the poet's flexiblility in modifying word forms for metrical purposes, see also pp. 66–8 above. Although Ascension Day, whose earliest possible date is 30 April, always comes after the Major Rogation (25 April), the poet mentions the former first and then the latter. The poet's disregard for the order of the feasts, which otherwise he strictly respects, reveals that the two movable feasts in the digressional passage are not regarded as regular entries in the poem.

65b. *forþan hi hwearfað aa.* MS *he* has often been emended to either *hi* as in the present text or *þe*. The problem is whether *he* can be regarded as a nominative plural form of the third person personal pronoun *he/heo*. Grein, Dobbie and Jones change it to *þe* to form the set phrase *forðan þe*, regarding the subject of the subordinate clause as unexpressed. In this poem, however, the conjunctive *forðan* is otherwise always used without *þe* and is always followed by the subject of the subordinate clause as in 21b and 46a. Bouterwek changes the unusual spelling *he* to *hi*, and Wülker, Greeson, Grimaldi and Hart follow this. Fox and Imelmann, as well as the editors of (semi-)diplomatic editions, retain the manuscript *he*, which is not totally impossible but seems less plausible; this use of *he* is attested only a few times in the mid-tenth-century Royal Psalter

Menologium

Glosses compiled in Winchester. See Campbell, pp. 288–9, §703 and Hogg and Fulk, p. 200, § 5.17n6.

66a. *wisra gewyrdum* 'according to the rules of the wise men'. This phrase alludes to the computistical background lying behind the calculation of the date of Easter. The meaning of *gewyrde* in this context is obscure, but Dobbie (p. 171) and Greeson (p. 266) follow BT, s.v. *gewyrde*, where it is defined as meaning 'rule'. Bouterwek translates it as *decretis* 'by decisions or principles' (p. 8), while Jones 'according to the ordinances' (p. 179).

66b. *wintrum frod*. This is a formulaic phrase attested in *Genesis A* 2355a, *Andreas* 506b, and *Beowulf* 1724a, 2114a, where it is always associated with old age and means 'advanced in years, old'. On the other hand, it is associated more with sagacity than with old age in this context. Here it may mean 'advanced in learning', or perhaps 'advanced both in years and learning', reflecting the two closely associated meanings of *frod*, i.e. 'wise' and 'old'.

67a. *on circule* 'in the cycle (of the dates of movable feasts)'. The word *circul* may mean 'table for the movable feast' here as in ByrEnch III.2. As regards the cycle and the table of movable feasts, see for instance, 'De circulis terminorum' in ByrEnch III.2, to which tables epitomising the cycle are attached. The word *circul* was a computistical technical term; it occurs about seventy-five times, mainly in ByrEnch and other computistical works, while it is attested nowhere else in Old English poems.

68b–75a. The Major Rogation falling on 25 April. Although it is only very sparingly that the Major Rogation is marked as an important feast in Anglo-Saxon calendars, it is mentioned as a regular entry both in the prose and the verse *Menologium*. As reflected in one of the terms for the feast, *gangdæg*, it was a day of *relicgong* 'relic procession', when people formed ceremonial processions raising relics, as is implied in lines 73–4a. On that day, people visited relics and prayed for God's protection, good weather, bountiful harvest and their health, as recorded in the *Old English Martyrology*, under 25 April 'Rogation Day'. For the celebration of the Major Rogation in Anglo-Saxon England, see also Canon 16 'De diebus Lætaniorum' laid down at the council at Clovesho in 747, which is edited in Haddan and Stubbs, eds., *Councils and Ecclesiastical Documents* III, p. 368. See also Hill, 'The *Litaniae maiores*', and Jones, ed., *Old English Shorter Poems*, p. 409. The custom of holding a procession on the Major Rogation is ultimately based on the ancient Roman *Robigalia*. This custom was Christianised and brought to the Anglo-Saxons, possibly supplanting some heathen festival including a procession like the festival of Nerthus recorded in *Germania* 40 or that of Freyr in *Flateyjarbók* (though the latter is a festival in autumn). See Chaney, *The Cult of Kingship*, p. 59. (*OEM*, Calendars 4, 6, 7, 8, (9), 11, 12, 13, 14, 15, 16, 18, 19, 20, 22, 24, 25, 27; it is treated as if it were a computistical entry in calendars 8, 11, 13, 14, 15, 19, 24, 25)

68b–9a. With the words *hwæðere gyt* 'yet hereafter', the poet marks his return to the main topic, i.e. immovable feasts, after a lengthy digression on the movable feasts. A later hand inserts a *punctus elevatus* after *hwæðere* marking the end of the off-verse. Fox follows this and places *gyt* at the beginning of the next

Commentary

line. Judged from the metrical point of view, however, *gyt* should be placed at the end of 68b. If not, 68b is scanned as xxxSx, which is never attested in off-verse. See Bliss, *The Metre of* Beowulf, p. 123; and Hutcheson, *Old English Poetic Metre*, p. 289. See also the note for line 37b. *We* seems to refer to the poet himself and this is an example of the so-called editorial 'we' (or plural of modesty) in Old English.

70b. *wisse*. This is a problematic word scarcely attested elsewhere but is retained in the present text. CH does not recognise it, while BT, regarding it as a variant of *gewisse* 'certainly', tentatively defines it as 'certainly' with a question mark. Greeson (pp. 201 and 338) and Jones (p. 179) follow the latter. Bouterwek emends to *wise*, and considers it to mean *carmine* 'by song', which Grimaldi (pp. 22–3 and 53) follows. CH, defining it as 'melody', also seems to follow this under the heading of *wise*; however, it seems that he was unable to find the meaning anywhere else since, just after the definition, he specifically refers to its occurrence here in this poem as '*Men* 70'. Grein also emends to *wise* ('Zur Textkritik', p. 422), while Grein, Holthausen and Köhler give a brief comment '*auch cantus, Gesangesweise, Melodie*' at the very end of definition 4 under the heading of *wise*, but do not cite any example, not even mentioning the potential example in the *Menologium* (*Sprachschatz*, p. 806, s.v. *wise*). Thus, even if we take *wisse* as an alternative spelling for *wise* meaning 'song, melody, etc.', the situation does not seem to become any better. This may well be why Dobbie suggests that 'we might read *wise* as the adverb, "wisely"' (p. 171). Alongside *gewiss* 'certain, certainty', the word form without the prefix *ge-* is attested twice as a gloss for Latin *profecto* 'assuredly, undoubtedly' in glosses to Aldhelm's *De laude virginitatis* (at AldV 1 1102 and AldV 13.1 1051). Along with *gewisslice*, moreover, *wisslice* 'certainly' is also attested, twice – in the *Metrical Psalter*, Psalm 58.13, and in 'The Temptation of Christ' in *Old English Homilies from MS Bodley 343*. Thus *wisse* may be regarded as a variant of *gewisse* 'certainly', which the poet uses in line 124b (Sweet recognises the word form without the prefix in his *Student's Dictionary*, p. 208, s. v. *gewiss, wiss*). The use of the rare word form may be explained from the metrical point of view; *gewisse* would yield a rare metrical pattern in this half-line while the poet occasionally uses non-standard/irregular word forms for the sake of attaining standard metre. Cf. the use of the nonce word *stige* in line 64b. For details, see pp. 66–8 above.

71a. *þæt*. Based on similar examples in lines 11a, 19b, 23a, 83a, 95b, 163,a 181a, 187a, and 207b, Holthausen would emend it to the adverbial *þæs* ('C. Plummer', pp. 239–40), and Imelmann follows this in his text. As Dobbie (p. 171) and Greeson (pp. 267–8) point out, however, such an emendation is unnecessary. It should be considered that *þæt* 'that' works as a subordinating conjunction used with *gesingan* 'to sing'. There is another conjunction *þæt* at the beginning of 73a, but, as Dobbie notes, the redundant use of it is not unparalleled (p. 171).

71–2. Although Fox and Wülker retain the manuscript reading, the original text corresponding to line 71 is too short and is certainly defective, and therefore Bouterwek places two asterisks after *niht*. Based on lines 26a, 55a and 222a, Grein, Imelmann and Fritsche read *nihtgerimes* instead of *niht*, but as first pointed out by Henel (*Studien*, pp. 79–80), nineteen (*nihgontyne*) days are insufficient to attain the right date of the next feast; *and fifum* best fits here, as followed by Rositzke, Dobbie, Greeson, Grimaldi, O'Brien O'Keeffe, Hart and Jones. Stanley claims that the incorrect *nihgontyne* must have come into existence because the scribe mistakenly took the Roman numeral *xxiiii* for *xuiiii* ('The Prose *Menologium* and the Verse *Menologium*', p. 260), which is implausible since the number *xxiiii* (i.e. *feower ond twentige*) does not fit in here from the viewpoints of metre and alliteration. If the line had originally read **þæt embe feower niht furðum twentige*, as Stanley suggests, then the number, separated in two half-lines, cannot have been written down in the Roman numeral. As regards the odd spelling *nihgontyne*, Stanley conjectures that 'the scribe was going to write *niht*, but a number came first' ('The Prose *Menologium* and the Verse *Menologium*', p. 260).

72a. *Eastermonað* 'Easter-month' is the Old English month-name for April. This is the only instance in the *Menologium* where an Old English month-name is placed far from its Latin correspondent, in different sentences. When restarting the calculation of the number of days after the lengthy digression on Easter and Ascension Day, the poet needed to refer to the beginning of April again as the starting point of calculation. He does not repeat the Latin month-name, taking advantage of having two different kinds of month-names. This instance, together with the cases of January and July, may suggest that the vernacular month-names are not always used as glosses for their Latin equivalents. According to Bede, *Eastermonað* is named after a pagan goddess *Eostre*: *Eosturmonath, qui nunc paschalis mensis interpretatur, quondam a dea illorum quae Eostre vocabatur et cui in illo festa celebrabant nomen habuit* (*DTR* 15) '*Eosturmonath*, which is interpreted now as the Paschal month, once had a name after their goddess who was called *Eostre* and whom they used to celebrate in that feast'.

73a. *reliquias* (< L *reliquiae*) 'relics' is a later, learned Latin loan-word attested nowhere else in Old English poems other than in the much later *Durham* 19b. It is rephrased in the vernacular as *halige gehyrste* 'holy treasures' in line 74a.

74a. *halige gehyrste*. Bouterwek emends it to *halig[r]a gehyrste*, and Fox and Grein to *haliga gehyrste*, but there is no need of emendation.

74b–5a. *þæt is healic dæg, bentiid bremu* 'that is a high day, the famous Major Rogation'. The word *bentiid* is a *hapax legomenon*, consisting of *ben* 'prayer' and *tid* 'time'. Despite the definition in CH (s.v. *bentid*) and Greeson's translation 'Rogation Days' (p. 201), it obviously means 'the Rogation Day', referring, in this case, to the Major Rogation on 25 April. The feast is called *micelra bena dæg* 'the day of the Greater Litany', translating the Latin name *Letania maiora* in the *Old English Martyrology* (under 25 April), while it is referred to as *ænlipiga gangdæg*, literally 'solitary procession day', in the prose *Menologium* ('solitary' in contrast with the Minor Rogations consisting of three days). There are also some other Old English terms for the Rogation Day such as *beddæg, gebeddæg, bendæg*, none of which is attested widely.

75b–9. The beginning of May. As reflected in the words *smicere on gearwum* (76b) 'elegantly in adornments' and *wlitig* (77b) 'beautiful', May was considered beautiful and elegant because of its fruitfulness symbolically manifested by many green leaves and flowers flourishing in this month. Byrhtferth writes: *he wynsumlice blowe and blædnyssa fægere geyppe* (ByrEnch II.1.312–13) 'it [May] joyfully flourishes and reveals its fruitfulness beauteously'. Cf. the reference to blossoms in lines 90b–1a describing the beginning of summer.

76a. *[embe syx niht þæs].* The words revealing the number of days from the previous entry to the beginning of May are lacking in the manuscript. Although Hickes and Fox do not notice any defect here, *smicere on gearwum* (76b) is, as noticed by the other editors, not long enough for a long-line, and is isolated in the original text from the viewpoints of metre and alliteration. Bouterwek, Wülker and Plummer are aware of the defect but do not insert anything other than asterisks or dots to fill the gap. Grein inserts *smylte and smeðe* 'mild and soft' (as line 76a), but later he suggests *þæs embe siex nieht* 'then after six nights' ('Zur Textkritik', p. 422). As regards the spelling of the numeral (as well as that of the word for night), the late West-Saxon form *syx* suggested by Imelmann and followed by Fritsche, Greeson and O'Brien O'Keeffe is more plausible than the early West-Saxon or Kentish form *siex* suggested by Grein and adopted by Dobbie, Grimaldi and Jones; the former appears in 203a while the latter is not used in the poem. A later punctuator fails to notice any defect here and his way of using punctuation marks is confused from here to 78b.

77a. *wudum and wyrtum*. *Wudu* literally means 'woods, trees', but in this context, it synecdochically implies exuberant leaves of trees, which constitute, together with *wyrtum* 'plants', the elegant *gearwum* (76b) 'adornments' of the season.

78a. *Þrymilce*. In the manuscript, it is spelt as *þrymlice*, which means 'gloriously'. The manuscript reading makes good sense and Fox, Bouterwek, Grein, Earle and Wülker retain it. Plummer and Rositzke also retain the original reading but, at the same time, suggest a reading *þrymilce* in a footnote, pointing out the note on the margin by a later hand: *Alibi þrymylce monað May*. Imelmann, Dobbie, Greeson, Grimaldi, Hart and Jones emend to *þrymilce* 'three-milk', the Old English month-name for May. From the semantic, grammatical and metrical points of view, there seems to be no problem with the manuscript reading, but still it seems reasonable to adopt the emendation, since when referring to a month the poet usually gives both Latin and Old English month-names (with two explicable exceptions); there are three other, very similar, passages in the poem (i.e. lines 138a–9a, 183a–4a, and 195a–6a), where either a Latin or an Old English month-name is followed by *on tun* and its Old English or Latin correspondent is referred to in the next line just as in this case, whereas the poet never places an adverb in front of the phrase *on tun*. Bede explains the etymology of the month-name as follows: *Thrimilchi dicebatur quod tribus vicibus in eo per diem pecora mulgerentur; talis enim erat quondam ubertas britanniae vel germaniae, de qua in britanniam nation intravit anglorum* 'it used to be called *Thrimilchi* because in that month cows were milked three times a day, since such was the fertility of Britain or Germania, from which the nation of the Angles migrated to Britain' (*DTR* 15). Nearly the same thing is said at the beginning of May in the *Old English Martyrology*. Thus May was

Menologium

considered to be a highly fertile month and the poet also describes it as such by his use of words such as *smicere on gearwum* (76b) and *wlitig* (77b) as well as with the statement in lines 78–9.

79a. *micle*, the accusative singular feminine form of *micel* 'much', modifies *þearfe* 'need' in 78b.

79b. *geond*. In the manuscript, as retained in Plummer, a punctuation mark is placed just after *geond*, showing that the scribe considers the on-verse of this line to end here. Rositzke follows this in his text. Other editors, however, consider the first half of this line to end at *micle* and include *geond* in the second half. The preposition *geond* and its object *menigeo* should be in the same hemistich as in all other similar instances.

80–2. The feast of SS Philip the Apostle and James, the son of Alphaeus, who are referred to as *Philippus and Iacob* (81a). Although St Philip alone is mentioned under 1 May in the *Old English Martyrology* and the two saints are treated separately in the *Fates of the Apostles* 37b–41 and 70–74 respectively, these two saints are always referred to together in the extant Anglo-Saxon calendars against 1 May. Despite the reading *Iacobus* suggested by O'Brien O'Keeffe based on the abbreviation in the manuscript, the name *Iacob* must have been originally without the Latin ending (unlike the case of *Iacobus* in line 132b), because the ending causes a metrical problem. The word form *Iacobus* is, in fact, uncommon in poetry, used only once in the aforementioned place in this poem for the sake of creating a metrical half-line. For details, see Karasawa, 'Some Problems'. (PM, MCY, MCH, MCR, ÆCHom II, Calendars 1, 4, 5, 6, 7–9, 11–12, 13–16, 17–21, 22, 23, 24, 25, 26)

82b. *for meotudes lufan* 'for the love of God'. *Meotudes* is the objective genitive. Cf. *for manna lufan* 'for the love of men' in 86a. Cf. also *þurh modlufan meotudes* 'through the love of God' in *Christ C* 1261; and *byrnende lufan metodes on mode* 'the love of God burning in the heart' in the *Death of Edgar* 20b–1a.

83–7a. The Invention of the True Cross on 3 May, celebrating the supposed discovery of the True Cross in Jerusalem by St Helena, the mother of Emperor Constantine the Great. The event was first mentioned in Ambrose's *De obitu Theodosii*. The legend of the finding of the True Cross, the earliest version of which is, according to Bodden, likely to be a Syriac version, was established by the end of the fourth century or the beginning of the fifth century (*The Old English Finding of the True Cross*, p. 30), but the feast on 3 May is first attested in the seventh century in Gaul (Blackburn and Holford-Strevens, *The Oxford Companion*, p. 194). Cynewulf's *Elene*, the prose *Finding of the True Cross*, and ÆCHom II.18 record the legend in Old English. For further information, see Bodden, *The Old English Finding of the True Cross*; and also Morris, *Legends of the Holy Rood*. (PM, MCH, MCR, ÆCHom II, OEM, Calendars (3), 4, 5, 6, 7, 8–11, 12, 13–17, 18, 19, 20, 21, 22–5, 27)

83b. The combination *God + tæhte* is attested in poetry only here. Ælfric uses it several times, while Wulfstan and other prose writers usually use *God + betæhte*. Cf. *frea/metod tæhte* in *Genesis A* 2874b and 2886b.

84a. *Elenan eadigre*. The adjective *eadig* 'blessed', as well as compounds

Commentary

including it, is often used for St Helena, as in *Elene* 605a and 619a (cf. *seo eadhreðige* in *Elene* 266), and in many prose works, as in *seo eadige Helena, þære eadigan cwene* (both in Ælfric's works), *seo eadige cwen* (used four times in the *Finding of the True Cross*) etc.

84b. The phrase *æþelust beama* 'the noblest of trees', referring to the True Cross, is attested nowhere else. Cf. *þone æðelan beam* (*Elene* 1073b) 'the noble tree'. Cf. also *beama beorhtost* 'the brightest of trees' in *Exodus* 249a, *Dream of the Rood* 6a and *Guthlac B* 1309a, and *mærost beama* 'the most famous of trees' in *Elene* 1012b, 1224b.

86a. *for manna lufan*. The same phrase is attested six times only in prose works including the *Vercelli Homilies*, Homily 25, where it is used in the same context related to the crucifixion of Christ. Cf. *for meotudes lufan* in line 82b.

86b. *meotud on galgan*. Both *meotud* and *galgan* display non-West Saxon phonological features, but both may be attributed to the poet's use of poetic koine. Cf. *god on galgan* 'God on the cross' in *Christ and Satan* 548a; and *godbearn on galgan* 'God's son on the cross' in *Elene* 719a.

87a. *be fæder leafe*. Cf. *be frean hæse* in 205b. The phrasing *be ... leafe* is otherwise never attested in poetry, while it is often used in prose works. Cf. *be Cristes/Godes leafe* in Ælfric's homilies. Cf. also *be mines fæder leafe* in the *Apollonius of Tyre*.

87b–90a. The beginning of summer on 9 May, six days after the Invention of the True Cross. In the prose *Menologium*, summer is also said to begin six days after the feast, whereas the date of the feast is expressed as *VI nihtum ær sumeres cyme* 'six nights before the coming of summer' in *Elene* 1227. The beginning of summer is listed against 9 May in many Anglo-Saxon calendars. For the date of the beginning of summer, see also ByrEnch II.1.314–15 and II.1.400–1, and the *Old English Martyrology*, under 9 May.

89a. *sigelbeorht* 'sun-bright', used twice in this poem, is otherwise attested only once in the *Judgement Day II* 117a.

89b. *sumor*. The scribe capitalises the initial of this word, perhaps reflecting its importance as a temporal indicator constituting a subdivision of the poem. However, his capitalisation is inconsistent as no other seasons are capitalised; the initial is decapitalised in the text, as has usually been done by editors of the poem.

90b–1a. Cf. the passage on May in Byrhtferth's *Enchiridion* quoted in the note for line 76b.

91b. *blis*. A later hand, adding a long *s*, makes it *bliss*, which is unnecessary. The combination *blis + (a)stigan* is attested nowhere else.

93b. The unique combination of *cyninge + lof + secgan* 'to express praise to the King' is introduced for the sake of alliteration; *drihtne/Gode + lof + secgan* with virtually the same meaning is more common, attested in *Andreas* 1006a, *Guthlac A* 527b, 613b–4a, as well as in some prose works.

95b–106a. The feast of St Augustine, the first archbishop of Canterbury (reigned 597–604x609), falling on 26 May. St Augustine, the 'apostle of the English', is the only 'English' saint mentioned in the poem. Mentioning his successful

Menologium

missionary activity in Britain and his burial in Canterbury, the poet spends more than ten lines on the saint, which is scarcely paralleled by any other saints in the poem. This may well reflect the domestic perspective of the poem as a whole (see the note for lines 14b–15a). For further information about the saint, see *HE* I.23–33 and II.2–3. (PM, MCH, MCR, *OEM*, Calendars 4, 5, 6, 7, 8, 9, 10, 11, 12, 13–16, 17, 18, 19, 20, 21, 22, 23, 24, 25, 27)

97a. *oðer leoht.* Presupposing 'this light' to represent the life in this world, *leoht* in this phrase seems to mean 'life, world, etc.' as more commonly attested in Old Saxon texts, where the phrase *thit lioht* 'this light, i.e. this world', as well as *ôðar lioht* 'other light, i.e. the other world', is attested. See, for instance, Sehrt, *Vollständiges Wörterbuch*, pp. 342–3, s.v. *lioht*. The phrase *oðer leoht* in the same sense is attested once more in the *Death of Edgar* 2b. Cf. *leoht* used in expressions for heaven and for death: *swegles leoht* 'light of heaven' (*Christ and Satan* 28b; *Guthlac A* 486b), *wuldres leoht* 'light of heaven' (*Christ and Satan* 140b, 251b, 447b, 555, 616b, 648b; *Fates of the Apostles* 61b; *Guthlac A* 8b), *dryhtnes liht* 'the Lord's light' (*Christ and Satan* 68b; *Guthlac A* 583b), *Godes leoht geceas* 'chose God's light, i.e. died' (*Beowulf* 2469), *se wuldres dæl of licfæte in godes leoht sigorlean sohte* 'the heavenly part (comes) out of the body to seek the victorious reward in God's light' (*Guthlac B* 1368b–70a). *Leoht* in the following expression for hell also means 'life, world' probably under the influence of Old Saxon: *forþon he heo on wyrse leoht under eorðan neoðan, ællmihtig god, sette sigelease* (*Genesis B* 310b–12a) 'therefore He, Almighty God, set them defeated in a worse world, under the ground below'. See Doane, ed., *The Saxon Genesis*, p. 379, s.v. *lēoht*[1].

97b. *Agustinus.* The same half-line occurs only once more in the *Metrical Preface to the Pastoral Care* 1b. See also the note for line 39a.

99b. *funde.* The regular preterite third person singular form of *findan* is *fand*, but here the word form *funde* is used to attain a sufficiently long half-line. The metrical use of *funde* instead of *fand* sporadically occurs in Old English poetry as in *Beowulf* 1415b and 1486b.

101b. *guman awyrn.* The manuscript reading is retained, although various emendations have been suggested by editors. Grein emends to *gumena fyrn* 'of men long ago', while Bouterwek *gummanna wyrn* 'hominum admonitionem'. Grein ('Zur Textkritik', p. 422), Wülker, Fritsche, Dobbie, O'Brien O'Keeffe, Hart and Jones emend to *a fyrn* 'ever before'. Rositzke, Greeson and Grimaldi retain the manuscript reading, while Imelmann slightly modifies the spelling of *awyrn* to *awern*. According to Campbell, p. 281, §680, *awyrn*, together with *ahwærgen* or *ahwergen*, is a semantically generalized version of *hwergen* 'somewhere' through the addition of the prefix *a-*. The *DOE* (s.v. *ā-hwergen*) recognises *awyrn*, as well as *owern* attested only once in a version of Old English Bede, as a variant spelling of *ahwergen*, and so does CH (s.v. *āwyrn*). The loss of *h* is paralleled, for instance, by *ahwær/awar/awer/ower* 'anywhere', while the contraction as in *ahwergen/a(h)wern* is also paralleled, for instance, by *æghwergen/æghwern* 'everywhere'. The change of vowel spellings/sounds from

Commentary

e to *y* or *i* is not unparalleled, as in *æmerge/æmyrge* 'embers', and *ærmergen/ærmyrgen* 'early morning'.

105b–6a. *cynestole neah, mynstre mærum* 'near the principal city, the famous cathedral'. These words specify the burial place of St Augustine of Canterbury; the preposition *neah* governs both *cynestole* and *mynstre mærum*. The word *cynestol* literally means 'royal seat, throne' but here it figuratively means 'the principal city or capital where the royal seat is located', referring to the city of Canterbury (see the *DOE*, s.v. *cynestōl*, definition 1.b.). The *mynstre mærum* 'the famous minster' refers to the cathedral church at Canterbury (i.e., not the monastery of St Augustine). According to Bede, Augustine was originally buried in St Augustine's abbey (*HE* II.3) built *non longe ab ipsa civitate ad orientem* (*HE* I.33) 'not far from the city [of Canterbury], to the east'; thus the poet says that he was buried near the city of Canterbury. The phrase *mære mynster*, used nowhere else in poetry, is attested once in ÆLS (in 'Passion of St. Denis and his Companions' 332) and five times in the Anglo-Saxon Chronicle under 948 (D), 1055 (C, D) and 1086 (twice in E). The phrase refers to Canterbury cathedral in the last instance. Jones, translating the phrases as 'in a famous monastery, near his throne' (p. 181), takes *cynestol* and *mynstre mærum* as referring to the cathedra in the cathedral and to St Augustine's abbey respectively, which may also be possible if the use of locative dative (with *on* in either 104b or 105a?) for the latter is justifiable.

106b–15a. The beginning of June. Along with *Iunius* 'June', the name *Ærra Liða* (108a) is used for June. The indigenous month of *Liða* seems originally to have covered June and July and accordingly, June is called *Ærra Liða* 'former *Liða*', while July is *Æfterra Liða* 'latter *Liða*'. The latter is not mentioned in this poem, probably because it can easily be inferred from the former. Similarly, *Æfterra Iula* 'latter *Iula*, i.e. January' is not mentioned. For the use of the month-names in the *Menologium*, see Appendix 9. According to Bede, the month is so called in Old English because: *Lida dicitur blandus sive navigabilis quod in utroque illo mense et blanda sit serenitas aurarum et navigari soleant aequora* (*DTR* 15) '*Lida* is said to be amiable and navigable since, in both of these months [i.e. June and July], the serenity of winds is pleasant and people are accustomed to navigating on plain surfaces of the sea'. The *Old English Martyrology* basically follows this at the beginning of the month of June, saying: *Se monað is nemned on Læden Iunius, ond on ure geþeode se Ærra Liða, forðon seo lyft bið þonne smylte ond ða windas. Ond monnum bið ðonne gewunelic, ðæt hi liðað ðonne on sæs bryme* 'The month is named in Latin *Iunius*, and in our language the *Ærra Liða*, because the air and the winds then are mild. And it was then customary to men that they sail over the waves of the sea'. Thus Bede and the martyrologist etymologically connect the month-name *Liða* (also spelt *Lida*) with *liðe* 'gentle, soft', *liðan* 'to travel, sail', *lid* 'ship', *lida* 'sailor', etc.

106b–9a. Despite the readings of Fox (p. 27), Bouterwek (p. 10), Wülker (p. 288) and Dobbie (p. 172), where either or both of the month-names are taken to be in the accusative, *monað*, *Ærra Liða* and *Iunius* are all in the nominative, and they are said to bring *tiida lange* 'long days, long daytime hours', since the summer solstice is in June and the month has the longest daytime hours in the year. For the reading of this passage, see Kock, *Jubilee*, p. 55, which Dobbie (p. 172) seems to misunderstand, as is pointed out by Greeson (p. 271).

107a. *ymb twa and feower* 'after two and four'. The numerals are used without a substantive, as is also the case in line 30a. The manuscript text reads *ymb twa ⁊ þreo* 'after two and three' and Hickes, Fox, Ebeling, Bouterwek, Grein, Earle, Wülker, Rositzke, Plummer and O'Brien O'Keeffe retain it in their texts. As first pointed out by Piper, however, there are six days, not five, from the previous feast to 1 June according to the method of counting days followed by the poet (*Kalendarien und Martyrologien*, p. 56). Accordingly, Imelmann, Fritsche, Dobbie, Greeson, Grimaldi, Hart and Jones change *þreo* to *feower*, which I follow.

109b. The sun is sometimes represented as a gem of heaven in Old English kennings for the sun, such as *heofones gim* (*Beowulf* 2072b, *Phoenix* 183a, *Guthlac B* 1212b), *swegles gim* (*Phoenix* 208b, *Metres of Boethius*, Metre 22, 23b), and *wuldres gim* (*Phoenix* 117b, 516a, *Andreas* 1268b), all meaning roughly the same, 'gem of heaven'.

111a. The phrase for the sun, *tungla torhtast* 'the brightest of stars', is attested nowhere else. Hickes, Fox, Ebeling, Wülker and O'Brien O'Keeffe read *torhtast*, while the other editors *torhtust*. The manuscript presents *a* rather than *u*: as O'Brien O'Keeffe says 'the *a* is clear' (p. 6, n. 34). Although the scribe otherwise consistently uses the superlative suffix -*ust* in this poem as in *oftust* (56b), *æþelust* (84b) and *fægerust* (114b, 148b), both -*ust* and -*ast* are possible as superlative endings developed from PGmc *-ōsta* (> OE -*ast*, -*ust* > -*ost*). See Hogg and Fulk, p. 176, § 4.63. See also p. 57 above.

111b. *of tille agrynt* 'descends from its standing-place'. The word *agrynt* (< *agryndan* '(of the sun) to descend, go down') is a *hapax legomenon*, but a form without the prefix *a*-, *gryndan* '(of the sun) to set, sink' (< POE **grundjan*) is attested in its present participle form only once, as a gloss for Latin *descendens*. Its etymological relationship with OE *grund* (ModE ground) elucidates its special connection with the setting of the sun.

114a. *foldan wang*. This phrase itself is attested nowhere else, but compare *foldwong* 'earthly plain, earth' attested in *Christ C* 974a and *Guthlac B* 1326a.

114b. *leohta*. The scribe spelt the word *lohta*, while a later hand corrects the scribal mistake by adding *e* above *o*.

115b–19. The Nativity of John the Baptist and the summer solstice, which coincide with each other on 24 June. The official date of the summer solstice based on the revised Julian calendar is 20 June, as Byrhtferth writes in the following passage: *and on .xii. kalendas Iulius bið sunstede, þæt ys on Lyden solstitium and on Englisc midsumor* (ByrEnch II.1.320–1) 'and on June the 20th is the solstice, that is in Latin *solstitium* and in English *midsumor*'. The poet, on the other hand, follows the original Julian calendar, where the day falls on 24 June, the mid-point of summer. Although the summer solstice is listed against 20 June in many Anglo-Saxon calendars, there are also some listing it against 24 June. Both versions of the prose *Menologium*, as well as the *Old*

Commentary

English Martyrology, also follow the original Julian calendar as regards the date of the summer solstice. Hart tries to attribute the poem to Byrhtferth of Ramsey (*Learning and Culture* II.1, pp. 192–3), but Byrhtferth always follows the official dates of the solstices and the equinoxes, whereas the poet follows the unofficial, popular dates except for the vernal equinox. See also the note to line 175a. According to Luke 1.36, Elizabeth, the mother of St John the Baptist, was already six months pregnant at the time of the Annunciation to the Blessed Virgin Mary, which is exactly nine months before Christmas. Thus the Nativity of St John the Baptist is traditionally celebrated on 24 June, three months after the Annunciation. For the symbolical meaning sometimes perceived behind the coincidence between the Nativity of St John the Baptist and the summer solstice, see *DTR* 30 and pp. 36–7 above. (PM, MCY, MCH, MCR, ÆCHom I, *OEM*, Calendars 1, 3, 4, 5–7, 8, 9, 10, 11, 12, 13–16, 17–20, (21), 22–5, 27)

116a. *ymb þreotyne* 'after thirteen'. This phrase is followed by *tyn nihtum eac* 'also ten nights' in line 118a, and accordingly the date mentioned here is twenty-three days after the beginning of June, that is, 24 June.

116b. *þeodnes dyrling* 'the Lord's darling', referring to John the Baptist. This phrase itself is attested only once, here in this poem, but phrases of very similar meaning are attested widely such as *cristes dyrling*, *dryhtnes dyrling*, *godes dyrling* 'Christ's, the Lord's or God's darling'. See the *DOE*, s.v. *dyrling*, definition 1.a.i. As regards the use of the phrase here, Bouterwek writes 'cognomen, quo Evangelista gaudebat ..., ad Baptistam transfertur' (p. 28). Dobbie also seems to consider that phrases meaning 'the Lord's darling' are especially intended for St John the Evangelist rather than the Baptist: 'Iohannes] That is, John the Baptist (June 24th), not John the Apostle, in spite of the phrase *þeodnes dyrling*, l. 116b, and such biblical passages as John xiii.23, xix.26, etc.' (p. 172). Greeson regards the use of the phrase as an obvious error of the poet, and even tries to find its potential source (pp. 272–3). These views notwithstanding, the use of phrases meaning 'the Lord's, God's or Christ's darling' is not limited to John the Apostle as far as the Old English literary tradition is concerned. According to my calculation based on the *DOEC*, one or other of these phrases are used for John the Apostle five times (in ÆCHom I 4, ÆCHom 2, HomS 22, HomS 33, HomS 44), but, at the same time, they are also used for King David once (CP), for St Maur once (ÆLS (Maur)), for St Benedict twice (ÆCHom II 11, GD 2 (C)), for St Nicholas three times (LS 29 (Nicholas)), and for St Egidius seven times (LS 9 (Giles)). There are some other instances where they are used for unnamed people (e.g. HomS 40.1 (Nap 49), HomS 40.3 (McCabeVercHom 10)). It is true that they are most widely attested for John the Apostle, but they are not exclusively for him. Thus there seems to be no reason why we should consider that the use of *þeodnes dyrling* for John the Baptist is unusual or erroneous, just because his name is, unlike the other cases, the same as John the Apostle's. See also Jones, ed., *Old English Shorter Poems*, p. 410.

117a. *in geardagan* 'in the days of old'. This is a formulaic phrase, but here it is in a later form, *geardagan* (< *geardagum*), which is attested nowhere else.

117b. *wearð acenned*. This half-line does not contain any alliterating word

Menologium

probably due to textual corruptions. For suggestions of emendations and/or modifications by various scholars, see pp. 65–6 above.

119b. *mycles on æþelum*. The meaning of the word *æþelum* here is not clear and several different interpretations are suggested. Grein, Holthausen and Köhler (*Sprachschatz*, p. 154, s.v. *eðel, œðel, œðel*), BT (s.v. *œðel*), Greeson (p. 314), Grimaldi (p. 27) and Hart (p. 207) take it as the noun *eþel* or its variant *æþel* but this is less plausible. The meaning 'one's own country, homeland, etc.' does not fit in this context especially when it is in the plural as in this half-line; the poet generally conceives Britain and the Anglo-Saxons living there as a unity, which means they share a homeland from the poet's point of view (but see also the note for line 230b). Cf. the word *tun* always used in the singular in the phrases *us to tune* 'to our town' and *on tun* 'into town'. Greeson mistakenly regards the *æþelum* here as the dative singular form (pp. 204 and 314), by which he seems (perhaps unconsciously) to follow a more plausible understanding of the context. The noun *eþel/æþel* is, moreover, never attested in its dative plural form. Bouterwek, on the other hand, takes *æþelum* as the dative plural form of the noun *æþelu* 'noble race, people', translating it as 'nobilibus' (p. 11). Hickes, Fox and Kock (*Jubilee*, p. 309) follow the same reading but take it in a neutral meaning 'hominibus', 'nations' and 'men', respectively. Malone also regards it as the same word, but with a different meaning 'kindreds' ('The Old English Calendar Poem', p. 196). The interpretation 'we (Anglo-Saxons) hold the feast ... among (noble) people', however, seems less apt since '(noble) people', referring to the same people as 'we', are redundant and makes the sentence clumsy. The word *æþelu* in this context should be understood as suggested in the *DOE*, where the half-line in question is cited under the heading of *æþelu*, definition 1, 'nobility, excellence'; with the preposition *on*, it forms an adverbial phrase 'nobly, splendidly' (though attested only here), which is emphasised by *mycles* 'greatly'. Jones follows this, translating it as 'with great dignity' (p. 183).

120–30a. The feast of SS Peter and Paul on 29 June observed in honour of their martyrdom in Rome. In the verse *Menologium*, as well as in many Anglo-Saxon calendars, the feast of these saints is listed against 29 June, the date of the translation of their relics, originally based an eastern tradition (Blackburn and Holford-Strevens, *The Oxford Companion*, p. 270). Following the Roman tradition, on the other hand, the prose *Menologium*, as well as a few Anglo-Saxon calendars, lists the saints separately against 29 and 30 June respectively. St Paul is not included in the Twelve Apostles but was an apostle, and is often referred to as such in Anglo-Saxon calendars. He is also mentioned in the *Fates of the Apostles* 11b–15. (MCY, MCH, MCR, ÆCHom I, *OEM*, Calendars 1, 4–6, 8, 10, 11, 13–16, 17, 19–24, (25), 27)

120a. *Wide*. In the manuscript, there is a large blank space before *wide*, and the scribe begins the word with a huge red capital, marking the beginning of the third division of the poem/year. As discussed in the Introduction, the poet divides the poem into four sections in accordance with the division of the solar year, which is reflected in the poet's wording as well as in the scribal sectioning. Some editors disregard the clear sign of pause in the manuscript, but there are no major problems in the manuscript reading and there seems no reason not to follow the original text.

122b. *Hwæt*. The word *hwæt*, a pronoun introducing an exclamative clause, often marks the beginnings of poems, speeches, sections etc., as in lines 48a and 176a in this poem. Here it marks the beginning of the third quarter of the poem, although it is not placed at the very beginning of the new quarter at 120a. Here the poet does not simply begin the new section by the pronoun as in the other cases but adds another sentence before it. By doing this, it seems, he consciously or unconsciously avoids the otherwise monotonous way of dividing the poem always beginning a new section with the pronoun *hwæt*. In this case, the poet introduces a sort of hysteron proteron, placing a concluding remark first with the introductory sentence, at the beginning of which is used the pronoun *hwæt*, placed in the second place. A similar use of *hwæt* is found, for instance, in *Beowulf* 2247–9a, where the last survivor gives his conclusion first, which is not repeated at the end of the speech, before starting his actual lamentation introduced by the pronoun *hwæt*.

122b. *þa apostolas*. The word *apostol* is a late Latin loan-word used sparingly in Old English poetry. Generally, Latin loan-words transferred the main stress to the first syllable in Old English, but this did not happen in a few words, whose first syllable was left unaccented and sometimes even lost. The word *apostol(us)* is one example of such late Latin loan-words, and indeed, the form *postol* without the original first syllable is attested. For details, see Campbell, pp. 206 and 215–17, §§516, 546 and 548. Thus it always alliterates on *p* in the extant Old English poems, as here in this line as well as in *Andreas* 1651a and the *Fates of the Apostles* 14b.

123a. *þeodenholde*. In the manuscript, it is spelt as *þeoden holde*, and Grein, Wülker and Rositske follow this, while Hickes, Fox, Ebeling and Bouterwek slightly modify the spelling to *ðeoden holde*. However, as Greeson rightly points out, such a reading is problematic; if *þeoden* means 'the Lord', it should be in the dative singular form, *þeodne*, while, if it is intended to refer to *þa apostolas* (122b), it should be in the nominative plural form, *þeodnas* (p. 275). Imelmann and Fritsche actually emend to *þeodne holde*. If we take it as a compound *þeodenhold*, however, there is no need of emendation; it can be understood as a nominative plural form of the compound, used in apposition with *þa apostolas* (122b). The same compound is attested in *Genesis A* 2042b, *Exodus* 87a, 182b and *Andreas* 384a.

124a. *ofer midne sumor*. Grein makes an incomprehensible mistake here, printing *vinter* instead of *sumor*.

124b–5a. Hickes translates the phrase *miccle gewisse* as 'magna cum celebritate' (p. 205), while Fox has 'much celebrated' (p. 29). Despite their interpretations, the half-line should be taken as an adverbial phrase meaning 'quite certainly', as is done by Bouterwek (p. 11), Greeson (p. 205) and Jones (p. 183). Wülker (p. 289) also agrees with Bouterwek's interpretation. Greeson (p. 205) and Jones (p. 183) consider that the adverbial phrase modifies *þrowedon* (123b), but it seems more likely to modify *furðor fif nihtum* (125a), in a similar way as the synonymous adverb *gewislice* in the following passage modifies *on XII kalendas aprilis*: *Ac ealle ða Easternan ⁊ Egyptiscan þe selost cunnon on gerimcræfte tealdon þæt seo lenctenlice emniht is gewislice on duodecima kalendas aprilis, þæt is on Sancte Benedictes mæssedæg* (*DTA* 238–41) 'but all the Eastern people and the Egyptians who are best skilled in computus calculated that the vernal equinox is certainly on 21 March, that is, on the feast of St Benedict'. See also Malone, 'The Old English Calendar Poem', p. 196.

125b. *folcbealo.* This is a *hapax legomenon*, meaning 'great torment in public'. In this case, it refers to the public executions imposed upon SS Peter and Paul. See the *DOE*, s.v. *folcbealu*. Bouterwek emends it to *feorhbealo* 'deadly evil, violent death', attested five times in poetry, but the original compound seems to make sense.

126a. The word *martyrdom*, consisting of the late Latin loan-word *martyr* and the vernacular suffix *-dom*, is rarely used in Old English poems; other than the two instances in the *Menologium* (126a and 145a), it is attested only once more in *Resignation* 81b, where it is used with the verb *adreogan* 'to suffer' in a unique sense 'suffering'. The examples in the *Menologium*, on the other hand, are the only instances in poetic works, where it is used in the ecclesiastical sense 'martyrdom'. In the prose works, it is used in this sense often with the verb *þrowian* 'to suffer' as is the case with this line. For the use of *martyrdom* in *Resignation* and other Old English works, see Malmberg, *Resignation*, p. 26.

127b. *wærþeoda.* The spelling *wær-* (< *wer-*) contains a hypercorrective *æ*, which often occurs in Kentish texts. See Fulk, *A History of Old English Meter*, pp. 284–7, § 335 (5).

128a. *hi.* In the manuscript, *hi* is changed to a clumsy *hy* by a later hand. Both spellings are possible and are used in the poem. I follow the original reading here.

130a. *ealdorþegnas.* Together with *ealdorapostol* 'prince of the Apostles' and *apostola ealdormann* 'chief of the Apostles', which are Old English translations of the traditional epithet for St Peter, *princeps apostolorum* 'prince of the apostles', the compound *ealdorþegn* 'chief retainer' is also used twice for St Peter in the *Vercelli Homilies*. Since SS Peter and Paul, sharing the same day as their feast, are closely associated with each other, these phrases are sometimes used not only for Peter but also for Peter and Paul. See the *DOE*, s.v. *ealdor-þegn*, *ealdor-apostol*, and *ealdor-mann* definition I.C.2.

130b–2a. The beginning of July. Only the month-name of Latin origin, *Iulius monað* (132a), is used for July. For the absence of its Old English counterpart, see the note for line 9a.

132b–6a. The feast of St James the Great on 25 July. For the name of the saint, the form with the Latin ending, *Iacobus,* is used here, although the form without the ending, *Iacob*, is otherwise always used in poetry. Here the poet adds the Latin ending for metrical purposes. For details, see p. 67. The saint is a son of Zebedee and a brother of St John the Apostle. He is referred to as a son of Zebedee here, while he is mentioned as a brother of St John in the prose *Menologium*, MCY and the *Fates of the Apostles* 33b–7a. Executed at the behest of Herod (reigned 41–4), he is considered to be the first among the apostles to have been martyred, and is the only apostle whose death is recorded in the New Testament (Acts 12.1–2). (PM, MCY, MCH, MCR, ÆCHom II, *OEM*, Calendars 1, <u>2</u>, <u>4–7</u>, 8, <u>9–13</u>, 14–16, <u>17–19</u>, 20, <u>21–5</u>, 27)

133a–4b. *ymb feower niht ... ond twentigum*. The manuscript text has *on* rather than *ond*. Grein, adopting *on*, suggests emendation of *twentigum* to *tintregum* 'torture' though with a question mark (p. 4). This is untenable since the emendation yields an incorrect number of days while the original has the right number. O'Brien O'Keeffe follows the original without furnishing any comments. There are two examples in PMC, where *ymb-* and *on*-phrases are combined to indicate the location of a feast; but these prepositional phrases are connected by the conjunction *ond*, which is lacking in the passage in question. Imelmann and Fritsche emend *on* to *eac*, which is too radical but theoretically possible on the basis of the example in lines 116a–18a (they also change the original *ond* to *eac* in lines 188a and 211a, but these are unnecessary emendations). Bouterwek and Wülker emend *on* to *ond* and many later editors including Dobbie follow them; the preposition *ymb* governs both *feower niht* (in the accusative) and *twentigum* (in the dative) and the preposition *ond* connects the two. Syntactically and graphically, this seems most plausible, and is adopted in the present text. We can find two, structurally similar examples in lines 187a–8a and 210b–11a. See also p. 58.

136a. *Zebedes afera* 'Zebedee's son', referring to St James the Great. The form *afera* is a non-Mercian form without the influence of guttural umlaut. As far as poetic works are concerned, the use of the Mercian form *eafora/eafera* is much more frequent. However, in the *Battle of Brunanburh* (7a, 52b) and in the *Capture of the Five Boroughs* in the A and C manuscripts of the Anglo-Saxon Chronicle, the latter of which contains the *Menologium*, the non-Mercian form is used. The initial *z* alliterates with *s* in the next half-line. There are only two other instances of alliteration on *z/s* in Old English poems, in *Riddle 40* 68 and the *Metrical Psalms* 82.9, 2.

136b–40a. The beginning of August and Lammas Day. The Old English name for August is *Weodmonað* (138a), which literally means 'weed-month'. Bede explains its origin as follows: *Vveodmonath mensis zizaniorum quod ea tunc maxime abundent* (*DTR* 15) '*Vveodmonath* is a month of weeds since they most greatly thrive then'. The author of *Old English Martyrology* also follows this in his explanation of the month of August: *Ond on ure geþeode we nemnaþ þone monaþ Weodmonaþ, forþon þe hi on þam monþe mæst geweaxaþ* 'and in our language, we name the month *Weodmonaþ*, because they [weeds] most greatly grow in this month'. The first of August was known as *hlafmæssan dæg* 'Lammas Day' as mentioned in line 140a. This is a unique English harvest festival, in which loaves of bread made from the first ripe corn were consecrated. As the poet says at the end of the poem (228b–31), he lists feasts and festivals observed especially in Britain rather than in the Western Church in general, and his reference to Lammas is in line with this statement.

137b. *sumere gebrihted* 'glorified by summer'. *Sumere* is in the instrumental

Menologium

dative. Translating it as 'lucid summer' as the subject of the sentence, Fox (p. 31) considers it in the nominative, which is impossible without emendations. Although Grein follows the manuscript reading, he later suggests emendation of *sumere* to *smicere* 'elegantly, finely' ('Zur Textkritik', p. 422), following Bouterwek. Imelmann and Fritsche follow this in their texts. However, the original text makes good sense and such an emendation is unnecessary. Although the past participle *gebrihted* here is often translated literally as 'brightened' as in Malone ('The Old English Calendar Poem', p. 197), Greeson (p. 206) and Jones (p. 183) and the season may actually be described as bright (cf. *sigelbeorhtne* 'sun-bright' used for autumn in line 203b), it may figuratively mean 'glorified' here, reflecting the abundance and plenty of the month. When describing the same season, Byrhtferth mentions its abundance but not its brightness: *And ymbe fiftyne niht Agustus sihð to mannum mid genihtsumum hærfeste, and autumnus (þæt is hærfesttima) cymð to mancynne binnan seofon nihta fyrste* (ByrEnch II 1.330–3) 'And after five nights, August comes to men with abundant harvest-time, and *autumnus* (that is harvest-time) comes to mankind in a period of seven nights'. See also the note for lines 142a and 142b–3a. For the meaning of *gebrihtan* 'to glorify', see the *DOE*, s.v. *ge-beorhtian, ge-byrhtan*, definition 4, and also *beorhtian, byrhtan*, definition 3.

138b. *welhwær*. In the manuscript, it is written as *wel hwæt*. Although Hickes, Fox, Bouterwek, Grein, Wülker, Imelmann and Fritsche retain the manuscript reading, it is, as pointed out by Dobbie (p. 173) and Greeson (pp. 276–7), difficult to understand the passage as it stands in the original; in fact, neither Hickes nor Fox translates the word/phrase in their translations. Grammatically, *welhwæt* 'everything' may be regarded as the object of the verb, but, as Dobbie notes, contextually it is unlikely that it is placed in apposition with another object, *hlafmæssan dæg* (140a) 'Lammas Day' (p. 173). Bouterwek, on the other hand, translates it as 'bene en' (p. 12), taking *hwæt* as an interjection meaning 'lo'. However, the interjection, which is actually a pronoun according to Walkden's recent study 'The Status of *hwæt* in Old English', is not attested as accompanied by any word except in two cases where it is preceded by an interjection *eala* added to emphasise the exclamatory function of *hwæt* (*Christ and Satan* 315a and *Meters of Boethius* 4.25). The word *hwæt* or the phrase *eala hwæt* is always used at the beginning of a sentence or clause and at the beginning of an on- or off-verse, whereas the *hwæt* in question is not. Moreover, it is never followed directly by a verb as here except in the *Soul and Body I, II* (22a), where it is followed by a verb because an interrogative sentence follows. In these respects, Bouterwek's reading is untenable. Since the manuscript reading does not seem to make sense, I adopt the emendation *welhwær* 'everywhere', following Dobbie, Greeson, Grimaldi, O'Brien O'Keeffe, Hart and Jones.

139a. *Agustus* is not long enough for a half-line, and Holthausen would add *fær* or *monð* after it, based on the examples such as *Februarius fær* (18a) and *Aprelis monað* (56a) ('C. W. M. Grein', p. 226). There are, however, other similar examples in the poem, i.e. *Nouembris* (196a) and *Decembris* (220a), and, as suggested by Dobbie (p. 173), the addition is not necessary.

139b. *yrmenþeodum* 'mighty people', referring to the Anglo-Saxons, is a *hapax legomenon*. Cf. *eormencynn* (*Beowulf* 1957a, *Fortunes of Men* 96b) 'immense race, human race' and *eormenstrynd* (*Solomon and Saturn* 331a) 'immense race, mighty generation'.

140b–2a. The beginning of autumn on 7 August. In most of the Anglo-Saxon calendars, it is listed against 7 August. The abundance and plenty of the season is suggested by the words *wlitig, wæstmum hladen* (142a) 'beautiful, laden with abundances'. Cf. also *sumere gebrihted* (137b) 'glorified by summer' and Byrhtferth's words quoted in the note for line 137b.

142b–3a. *wela bið geywed fægere on foldan* 'prosperity is revealed beautifully on earth'. Along with 137b and 142a, this passage expresses the abundance and plenty of the season. Hickes, Fox and Grein have *geyped* instead of *geywed*. Sievers also prefers *geyped* ('Zur Rhythmik', p. 517). They mean more or less the same and either is equally possible, and the letters *p* and wynn can look quite similar, but in this case, it looks much more like wynn, and most of the later editors print *geywed* here. Fox, Bouterwek and Greeson take *fægere* as an adjective, but it is more likely to be an adverb, the half-line having the same construction as *smicere on gearwum* (76b) 'beautifully in adornments'.

143b–7. The feast of St Laurence of Rome on 10 August. St Laurence is one of those who died in the persecution of Valerian in 258. Among the victims of this persecution were Pope Sixtus II and six other deacons, but St Laurence has been one of the most honoured martyrs of the Roman Church since the fourth century; hence he is mentioned as a *mære diacon* (145b) 'famous deacon'. (PM, MCY, MCH, MCR, ÆCHom I, *OEM*, Calendars 1, 2, 4–12, 13–16, 17–25, 27)

146b. *wið þan*. In the manuscript, these words are written as they stand in the present text, while Dobbie, O'Brien O'Keeffe, Hart and Jones combine them into one word as *wiðþan*, which is attested nowhere else. The phrase consists of the preposition *wið* 'in return for' and *þan* (< *þam* < *þæm*), a late West Saxon, masculine, dative, singular form of the demonstrative *se*, referring to *martyrdom* (145a). For the word form *þan*, see Brunner, *Altenglische Grammatik*, p. 151, §187 and p. 262, §337.

146b–7. As Imelmann points out in *Das altenglishe Menologium*, p. 45, these lines are quite similar to the *Fates of the Apostles* 73b–4: *Hafað nu ece lif* ‖ *mid wuldorcining, | wiges to leane* '(St James) has the eternal life now with the heavenly King as a reward for his battle'.

148–53a. The Assumption of the Virgin Mary into heaven on 15 August. This is the third of the four Marian feasts mentioned in the poem. The origin of the feast, as well as the date of Mary's death, is unknown, but it is said to have been celebrated in Rome on 15 August at least from the sixth century. For further details, see Holwek, 'The Feast of Assumption', pp. 6–7. (PM, MCY, MCH, MCR, ÆCHom I, ÆCHom II, *OEM*, Calendars 4, 5, 6, 7, 8, 9–13, 14, 15, 16–25, 27)

148b. *fægerust mægða* 'the most beautiful of maidens', referring to Mary. The superlative *fægerust* is sometimes used to represent the ultimate beauty or fairness of God, Christ, the sun, the phoenix etc. in prose works, but it is never used in poetic works other than in the *Menologium*, in which it is also used for the sun in line 114b. The superlative is otherwise never used for Mary either. Thus the wording, though ordinary at first glance, is rather peculiar.

149a. *wifa wuldor* 'glory of women'. This is a kenning used for Mary and is attested nowhere else. Cf. *cyninga wuldor* 'glory of kings', a kenning for Christ used in line 1b and in many other Old English poems. Cf. also other kennings for Mary such as *ealra femna wyn* (*A Prayer* 46a) 'joy of all women' and *wifa wynn* (*Christ* 71a) 'joy of women'.

150a. *for suna sibbe* 'for the love of her son'. Cf. *for meotudes lufan* (82b) and *for manna lufan* (86a).

150b–1a. *sigefæstne ham on neorxnawange* 'victorious home in Paradise'. The phrase *sigefæstne ham* is attested nowhere else. The preposition *on* is lacking in the manuscript, as if *neorxnawange* were in the locative dative meaning 'in Paradise'. The use of locative dative is, however, unusual in Old English and emendation seems necessary. Wülker emends *neorxnawange* to *neorxnawang* so as to make it assume the accusative singular form, but this causes a metrical problem; due to the omission of the final syllable, the half-line becomes too short. Bouterwek, Grein, Holthausen ('C. W. M. Grein', p. 226) and Greeson emend it to the genitive singular form *neorxnawanges*, which depends on *sigefæstne ham*. Cf. *þam halgan ham heofona rices* 'the holy home of the heavenly kingdom' in *Andreas* 1683; *neorxnawanges eðle* 'homeland of paradise' (*Vercelli Homilies*, Homily 11, line 47). Dobbie, Grimaldi, O'Brien O'Keeffe, Hart, and Jones, on the other hand, add *on* and read: *sigefæstne ham on neorxnawange*, which is comparable with *hyhtlicra ham in heofonrice* 'pleasant home in the heavenly kingdom' in *Christ and Satan* 215. The last two readings seem both possible, meaning more or less the same, but I follow Dobbie and others in order to retain the original word form.

152a. *fostorlean* 'reward for fostering'. Greeson (p. 279) quotes the following passage from Paulus Diaconus' homily 45 in *In Assumptione sanctae Mariae* as reflecting the underlying commonplace idea of *fostorlean* that Mary is said to have received here: *Dignum erat ut familiarius hanc amaret, copiosius remuneraret, quae singularius atque accentius omni rationali creatura ipsum dilexerat* (*PL* 95, 1491) 'It was fitting that he should love more familiarly and award more abundantly the one who had loved him more specially and intensely than any other rational creature'. Greeson (pp. 278–9) also claims that the word *fostorlean* may well be a loan-translation of the Latin phrase *nutricii merces* 'reward for a rearer' as is indicated in BT s.v. *fostor-lean, foster-lean*. However, the word is attested elsewhere, where it is unlikely to be a loan-word: *Æfter ðam is witanne, hwam ðæt fosterlean gebyrige; weddige se brydguma eft þæs; 7 hit aborgian his frynd* (*Be wifmannes beweddunge* 2) 'After that is to know to whom that foster-reward should belong; the bridegroom afterwards should make a vow and his relatives give a pledge for it'. It is also used in the Latin version of this text: *Postea sciendum est, cui fosterleanum pertineat; uadiet hoc bridguma, et plegient amici sui* ('De sponsalibus' in *Quadripartitus*). Thus

Commentary

it seems probable that the word existed as a native legal term, which the poet adopts to a religious context.

153a. *ece to ealdre* 'for ever and ever'. Both *ece* and *to ealdre* mean 'always, ever, for ever', and they are combined to emphasise the meaning. The same half-line is attested three more times in *Christ B* 690a, *Juliana* 646a and *Phoenix* 594a. Of these three poems, the first two are Cynewulfian poems, under whose influence the third may have been composed. Cf. also *a / awa / æfre to ealdre* 'for ever and ever'. See the *DOE*, s.v. *ealdor*, definition 2.b.

153b–6a. The feast of St Bartholomew on 25 August. The feast is celebrated on 24 August, but in Anglo-Saxon England, the majority of people seem to have celebrated it on the 25th as the *Menologium* poet says. This feast is also said to fall on 25 August in *OEM*, ÆCHom (I.31) and PM. Most of the extant Anglo-Saxon calendars also list it against 25 August. According to Felix's *Vita sancti Guthlaci*, moreover, Guthlac reached Crowland on 25 August or St Bartholomew's feast: *Deinde peracto itinere, die octava kalendarum Septembrium, quo sancti Bartholomaei sollemnitas celebrari solet* ... 'Then the journey being finished on 25 August, on which St Bartholomew's feast is customarily celebrated'. See also Godden, *Ælfric's Catholic Homilies: Introduction, Commentary and Glossary*, p. 258. On the other hand, the feast is always listed against the 24th in the English Benedictine calendars which were compiled after 1100 and are edited in Wormald, *English Benedictine Kalendars* I and II. (PM, MCY, MCH, MCR, ÆCHom I, *OEM*, Calendars 1, 2, 4, 5, 6, 7, 8, 9, 12, 13–15, 16–20, 22, 24, 25, 27; MCH and calendar 25 list it against 24 August)

153b. *ealling*. The word *ealling* usually means 'all the time, continually, ever, etc.', but in the *Menologium* (153b and 173b), it means 'every time, on every occasion', referring to a recurring cycle of time (see the *DOE*, s.v. *ealling*, definitions 1 and 2). It is otherwise always used in prose works, although a similar adverb *eallunga/eallinga* 'altogether, entirely, completely, etc.' is used in several poems.

156a. *wyrd welþungen*. MS. *wyrð wel þungen*. Without any inflectional ending, the original *wyrð* 'honoured' does not seem to make sense in this context, as Dobbie notes that '*wyrð* ... does not mean anything unless it is an error for *wyrðe* "worthy"' (p. 173). Ebeling, Grein, Imelmann Fritsche, Dobbie, Greeson, Grimaldi, O'Brien O'Keeffe, Hart and Jones emend it to *wyrd*, taking the phrase *wyrd welþungen* 'honoured event' in apposition with *tiid ... Bartholomeus* (154b–5a) 'Bartholomew's feast', and I follow this reading. The word *welþungen* is otherwise attested only once in *Beowulf* 1927a.

156b–60a. The Decollation of St John the Baptist on 29 August. The saint is referred to only as an *æþeling* (157b) 'noble man' and is not named here. One reason why his name is not mentioned may be that it has already been mentioned in 117a (the poet also avoids using the same vernacular month-names twice in the cases of *Iula* and *Liða*). The omission of his name is made possible by the statement that this *æþeling* is he who baptised Christ (158b–60a), which clearly identifies the saint. Thus the poet sometimes presupposes the audience's knowledge and keeps some basic information unsaid. The compiler of the prose

Menologium also sometimes does similar things; he never mentions Christ and St John the Baptist's names when he refers to Christmas and the nativity of the saint, which are mentioned as *middes wintres/sumeres mæssedæg* 'the feast at midwinter/midsummer' (whereas he mentions St John the Baptist's name when referring to his Decollation). (PM, MCY, MCH, MCR, ÆCHom I, *OEM*, Calendars 1, 2, 4–7, 8, 9, 10, 11, 12, 13–15, 16–19, 20, 21, 22, 23, 24, 25, 27)

158b–60a. John the Baptist baptised Jesus in the River Jordan. See Mark 1.4–9. Neither the river nor its name is mentioned but it is simply said that John *mid wætere oferwearp wuldres cynebearn* 'sprinkled with water the royal child of heaven'. The word *cynebearn*, literally meaning 'royal child', is sometimes used specifically for Christ as in *Andreas* 566a and the *Lord's Prayer II* 117a (see the *DOE*, s.v. *cyne-bearn*, definition 1.a). Cf. expressions for God as king, such as *wuldorcyning* 'heavenly or glorious king', *se heofonlica cyning* 'the heavenly king', *se soþa cyning* 'the true king', etc.

160b–2. These lines are based on Matthew 11.11: *Non surrexit inter natos mulierum maior Iohanne Baptista* 'No one arose among the sons of women greater than John the Baptist'. Ælfric translates the passage as follows: *Betwux wifa bearnum ne aras nan mærra man; ðonne is iohannes se fulluhtere* (ÆCHom I.25.103–4) 'among the children of women, no one has arisen greater than John the Baptist is'. Similarly, in the *West-Saxon Gospels* it is said: *Soþlice ic eow secge ne aras betwyx wifa bearnum mara iohanne fulwihtere* (Matthew 11.11) 'Truly, I tell you that among children of women, no one has arisen greater than John the Baptist'. A similar statement is found also in the *Old English Martyrology* (under 24 June, St John the Baptist): *þes Johannes wæs mara þonne ænig oðer man buton Criste; ealle heahfæderas ond godes witga he up oferhlifað, ond ealle þa apostolas ond martyras he foregongeð ond æghwelcne þara þe wæs of were ond of wife acenned* 'This John was greater than any other man except Christ. All the patriarchs and God's prophets he surpasses, and all the apostles and martyrs he precedes, and each of those who were born from man and woman.' As in the verse *Menologium*, the *Old English Martyrology* mentions 'man and woman', while the passage from the Bible and others mention women alone.

163–7a. The beginning of September. *Haligmonð* (164a), literally meaning 'Holy-month', is an Old English name for September. The form *-monð* instead of the regular *monað* is adopted for metrical purposes (for the same use of it, see line 181b). Bede very briefly mentions this month-name: *Halegmonath mensis sacrorum* (*DTR* 15) '*Haligmonath* is the month of religious rituals'. The origin of the name is explained in the following passage from the *Old English Martyrology* (September): *Se monaþ hatte on Leden Septembris, ond on ure geþeode Haligmonaþ, forþon þe ure yldran, þa þa hi hæþene wæron, on þam monþe hi guldon hiora deofolgeldum* 'The month is called in Latin *Septembris* and in our language *Haligmonaþ*, because our ancestors, when they were heathen, in this month, sacrificed to their devil-idols'. These records suggest that the month-name is related to the heathen harvest festivals, which are often said to have been held around the autumnal equinox in the latter half of

Commentary

September. See Chaney, *The Cult of Kingship*, p. 242; and Wilson, *Anglo-Saxon Paganism*, p. 36. According to Ælfric's *Grammar* XVIII, September was also called *hærfestmonoð* 'harvest-month' (see *Aelfrics Grammatik und Glossar*, p. 43).

164b. *heleþum*. Fox and Bouterwek emend to *hæleðum*, while Grein emends to *häleðum*, but the original spelling, possibly reflecting a phonological feature of Kentish, is attested elsewhere and the emendation is not necessary. See Campbell, p. 122, §288; and Hogg, pp. 203–5, §§5.189–5.191. See also p. 56 above.

165b–7a. This passage is comparable with lines 17b–19a, where the ancient, foreign origin of the Latin month-name *Februarius*, which is used with *fær*, is made clear by the reference to ancient (Roman) scholars and by the use of the adverb *geo* (17b) 'formerly' plus a verb in the past tense. As Dobbie rightly suggests, *fær* means 'journey, movement' in both lines 18a and 167a, and is not a variant form of *fæger* 'beautiful, fair' (p. 171) as Grein, Holthausen and Köhler (*Sprachschatz*, p. 174, s.v. *fær*) and Wülker (p. 291) suggest. In both cases, what the ancient scholars discovered is not (the notion of) a month itself but its 'movement, journey', that is, when it begins and ends. Months are often said to 'come' (rather than 'begin') and the verb *faran* 'go, travel', related to *fær*, is used to describe the coming of a month three times, in lines 35b, 165a, 182a.

167b–9a. The Nativity of St Mary the Virgin. This is the last of the four Marian feasts venerated in the Roman church, all of which are mentioned in the poem. Mary's birth is not recorded in the Bible but is traditionally celebrated on 8 September, nine months after her Immaculate Conception on 8 December. Cf. the cases with the dates of the Annunciation and the Nativity of John the Baptist explained in the notes for lines 48–54a and 115b–19. (PM, MCY, MCH, MCR, OEM, Calendars 1, 4, 5, 6, 7, 8, 9, 11–13, 14–16, 17–25, 27; calendar 1 lists it against 9 September)

167b. *and þy seofoþan dæg* 'and on the seventh day (counting from 1 September)' i.e. on the 8th of September, rather than 'on the seventh (of September)'. Besides the exceptional case of line 3b, where a different counting principle is followed, this is the only instance where the poet uses an ordinal number to refer to the number of days from one entry to the next.

168b. *cwena selost* 'the best of women', a phrase used for St Mary the Virgin, is attested nowhere else, although the word *cwen* is often used in her epithets both in poetry and in prose, such as *seo clæneste cwen* (*Christ A* 276) 'the purest woman', *seo halige cwen* (ÆCHom I.30.262) 'the holy woman', *ða ealra femna cwen* (HomS 40.1 12) 'the queen of all women', etc.

169a. *drihtnes modor* 'the Lord's mother', a phrase for Mary, is attested otherwise only in prose works. Similar expressions such as *Cristes/Godes/ Hælendes modor* are also found only in prose. Cf. *cyninges modor* in line 21a.

169b–73a. The feast of St Matthew the Apostle and Evangelist on 21 September. The phrases used for him here, *þegn unforcuð* (170b) 'honorable thegn' and *godspelles gleaw* (171a) 'skilful in (writing) the Gospel', present his identity

Menologium

as an apostle and evangelist respectively. Neither phrase is attested anywhere else, although as regards the former, similar phrases are recorded: *eorl unforcuð* in *Andreas* 475a, 1263a, *unforcuð eorl* in the *Battle of Maldon* 51, and *frean unforcuð* in *Riddle 62* 2b. (PM, MCY, MCH, MCR, ÆCHom II, *OEM*, Calendars 1, 2, 4–7, 8, 9, 11, 12, 13–16, 17–19, 20, 21, 22, 23, 24, 25, 27)

169b–70a. As Dobbie suggests '*ymbe* goes with both *dagena worn* and *þreotyne*' (p. 173), these lines should be understood as meaning 'after a number of days, thirteen'.

172b. *to metodsceafte* 'at the appointed destiny (or destined time)'. The same phrase is used in *Beowulf* 2815b and *Christ C* 887b. Cf. *to gescæphwile* 'at the appointed time' in *Beowulf* 26b. For the meaning of the phrase, see Mackie, 'Notes', p. 96.

173b–5. The autumnal equinox. The poet, listing the autumnal equinox under 24 September, follows the unofficial/popular date as he also does regarding the solstices. The official date was 20 September, as, for instance, Byrhtferth says that *he gewurðode oððe geendebyrde þa twelf | monðas on twam emnihtum, þa synd gesette on .xii. kalendas Aprilis and on .xii. kalendas Octobris* (ByrEnch I 1.94–7) 'He [God] adorned or ordered the twelve months with two equinoxes, which are set on March 21 and on September 20' and that *seo emniht byð þæræfter on .xii. kalendas Octobris* (ByrEnch II 1.342–3) 'the equinox is thereafter on 20 September'. Along with the official date, however, the unofficial date also persisted in Anglo-Saxon England partly because it was unimportant, having nothing to do with the calculation of the date of Easter. Bede writes that the vernal equinox is 21 March but he does not specify the dates of the other three solar turning points, saying that *specialiter adnotatur, caeteros quoque tres temporum articulos putamus aliquanto priusquam vulgaria scripta continent esse notandos* 'we think the other three divisions of the seasons should be noted as somewhat earlier than (the dates) mentioned in popular writings'. Wallis comments on this passage that 'Bede is not interested in fixing the dates of the autumn equinox or the solstices, as they are of no computistical consequence' (*Bede: The Reckoning of Time*, p. 88n270). Thus the popular date of the autumnal equinox persisted or coexisted with the official one. It is listed against 24 September in the majority of Anglo-Saxon calendars, and the *Menologium* poet and the compiler of the prose *Menologium* also follow this tradition. See Appendix 8.

175b. *ylda bearnum* 'to children of men'. This is a common poetic formula widely attested. This is the end of the third section and a *punctus versus*, which tends to be used for a longer pause, is placed after this phrase.

176–80. The feast of St Michael the Archangel on 29 September. The name of the Archangel appears nowhere else in the extant Old English poems. The veneration of the saint, which is said to have been originated in Phrygia, was quite widespread and there was a variety of dates for his feast. The *Menologium* poet follows the same tradition that all the extant Anglo-Saxon calendars follow. The earliest records of the date 29 September are found in the seventh-century Gelasian Sacramentary and then in the eighth-century Gregorian Sacramentary.

Commentary

See Holwek, 'Michael the Archangel', p. 276. This passage, beginning with the pronoun *hwæt* (176a) introducing an exclamative clause, opens the last quarter of the poem. For the use of the pronoun in this poem, see the note for lines 48–54a. (PM, MCY, MCH, MCR, *OEM*, Calendars (1), 2, 4–9, 11, 12, 13–16, 17–22, 23, 24, 25, 27)

178b. *menigo*. Hickes, Fox and Grein emend to *manigo*, which is unnecessary. Grein later retracts this reading in his 'Zur Textkritik', p. 422.

179a. The third quarter ends with a reference to the autumnal equinox, and the first feast in the fourth quarter is located in terms of the same equinox. Thus the autumnal equinox is mentioned for the second time here at the beginning of the fourth section. The poet always mentions the solar turning points twice, just before and after each section boundary. Hickes, Fox and Grein read *geyped* 'revealed' rather than *geywed*, as they also do in 142b (see the note for lines 142b–3a). This is possible, but the manuscript clearly has *geywed*.

181–6a. The beginning of October. The month is called *se teoða monð* 'the tenth month' before its Latin and Old English names are mentioned. Cf. *forma monað* (9a) for January. The unconventional word form *monð* is used to attain a metrical half-line. See p. 67 above and the note for 164a. *Winterfylleð* (184a), used in apposition to *se teoða monð* and *October* (183b), is the Old English month-name for October. Bede explains its etymology as follows: *Unde et mensem quo hiemalia tempora incipiebant vvinterfilleth appellabant, composito nomine ab hieme et plenilunio quia videlicet a plenilunio eiusdem mensis hiems sortiretur initium* (*DTR* 15) 'And thus they named the month in which the winter season used to begin *Winterfilleth*, a composite name consisting of 'winter' and 'full moon' obviously because winter began on the full moon of that month'. Schneider, following Bede, writes that the month-name reflects that winter began in this month among pre-Christian Anglo-Saxons ('The OE. Names of the Months', p. 272). Among Christian Anglo-Saxons, on the other hand, winter began on 7 November, as the *Menologium* (202–3a), as well as many of the Anglo-Saxon calendars, confirms. In the *Old English Martyrology*, in which the author, usually following Bede, gives some explanations of the vernacular month-names, *Winterfylleð* is used without any further comment, which may be because of the contradiction between the etymology/meaning of the month-name and the actual custom.

182b. *frode geþeahte* 'in accordance with the wise scheme'. The phrase implies the learned nature of calendrical matters. Cf. lines 18b–19a and 165b–6a.

183b. *us to genihte* 'for our abundance'. Since October comes just after the harvest (and perhaps also after the harvest festival in the latter half of September mentioned in the note for 164a), it is an abundant month. November is also said to be abundant in lines 194b–5a.

184b. *cigð*. The manuscript reads *cigð*, while Bouterwek, Grein, Wülker, Dobbie and Hart emend to *cigað*, the third-person, present, plural form, since the subject of the sentence is in the plural. On the other hand, Hickes, Fox, Imelmann, Greeson, O'Brien O'Keeffe and Jones retain the manuscript reading. Holthausen points out that, while *cigð* presents a metrical half-line, *cigað* does not and is unacceptable as an emendation ('C. W. M. Grein', p. 226). He also points out that, when preceding a plural subject, a verb sometimes stands in the singular. Stanley would also rather retain the manuscript reading ('The Prose *Menologium* and the Verse *Menologium*', p. 261). Since there is another similar instance in line 206a, where *mot* is used with a plural subject following it, I adopt the manuscript reading. Mitchell suggests that *cigð* here should be attributed to scribal weakening of plural forms through the stages *cigað* > *cigeð*, but together with the instance of *mot*, which Mitchell claims should be emended to *moton* (Mitchell, *Old English Syntax* I, pp. 636–7, §§ 1522–3), this may be regarded as an instance of the poet's use of an unconventional/non-standard word form in order to attain a metrical half-line. Similar modifications of word forms to suit the metrical requirement are also observed in 88b, 106b, 164a, 181b, 193b and 218b. For further details, see p. 68 above and Karasawa, 'Some Problems'.

185. *igbuende Engle and Seaxe* 'the island-dwelling Angles and Saxons'. The reference to Angles and Saxons together is rare in poetry, attested only twice elsewhere – in the *Battle of Brunanburh* 70a and the *Death of Edward* 11a. The use of the rare expression may reflect the poet's emphasis on his domestic perspective, which is also perceived in the frequent references to 'us' Anglo-Saxons and to Britain. See the note for lines 14b–15a. The use of the vernacular month-names also emphasises the domestic perspective, which is especially clear here in this context (lines 184–6a), where it is said that the Anglo-Saxons call the month *Winterfylleð* (rather than *October*).

186a. *weras mid wifum*, literally 'men with women', i.e. 'men as well as women'. The phrase is attested only once more in *Genesis A* 1738a, while *weras mid wifum 7 cildum* is used in the *Numbers* XVI.31.

186b–93a. The feast of SS Simon and Jude on 28 October. Traditionally, they are said to have been martyred together in Beirut about AD 65, and they are venerated together in the Western Church on 28 October. Jude is also known as Thaddeus, as he is called in the prose *Menologium*. (PM, MCY, MCH, ÆCHom II, *OEM*, Calendars 1, 2, 4–7, 8, 9, 11, 12, 13–15, 16–19, 20, 21–4, 25, 27)

187a–8a. The manuscript has *fif* but emendation to *seofon* is necessary in order to attain the right number of days, although Hickes, Fox, Ebeling, Grein, Wülker, Earle, Rositzke, Plummer and O'Brien O'Keeffe retain the original reading. The emendation is supported by the test of alliteration: *fif* does not alliterate with any word, whereas *seofon* alliterates with *samod* in the off-verse. Rositzke (p. 8) and Plummer (p. 279), though retaining the original reading, admit the necessity of the emendation in their footnotes. In his note, on the other hand, Fox (p. 62) suggests replacing *fif* with *eahta*, but this violates the way of counting days followed by the poet in this poem, nor is it appropriate from the viewpoint of alliteration.

192b–3a. *dom hlutan, eadigne upweg* 'won glory, blessed ascension'. As Sweet notes '*w. g., i.*' (*Student's Dictionary*, p. 90, s.v. *hlēotan*), the verb *hleotan* is more often used with genitive or instrumental (dative) objects as in *domes hleotan* (*Guthlac B* 972b, *Rune Poem* 3b), *leana hleotan* (*Juliana* 622b) and *leanum hleotan* (*Christ B* 783b), but its use with accusative objects is also sporadically

Commentary

attested, as in this passage as well as in *Þæs ðu gife hleotest, haligne hyht on heofonþrymme* 'Therefore you win a favour, holy exultation in heavenly glory' (*Andreas* 480b–1). The phrase *eadigne upweg* 'blessed ascension' is attested nowhere else, with a possible exception in *Christ A* 20a, if one reads *eadga[n] upwegas* 'blessed ways to heaven' as suggested by Krapp and Dobbie (*The Exeter Book*, p. 247). The phrase may be based on expressions for the ascension of a blessed soul to heaven, such as *Ða wæs Guðlaces gæst gelæded eadig on upweg* (*Guthlac B* 1305–6a) 'Then Guthlac's soul was led blessed on the upward way' (see also *Andreas* 829–30).

193b–8. The beginning of November. The abundance and prosperity of the month is emphasised by *genihtsum* (194b) 'abundance', *wiste* (195b) 'abundance, plenty, sustenance', and *eadignesse* (197a) 'prosperity', and it is even said that no other month brings greater prosperity (197a–8a). This may be partly because the month is not long after the harvest season (see the notes for lines 164a and 183b), and also because of the 'sacrifice' or slaughter of livestock taking place in this month as suggested by the vernacular month-name *Blotmonað*, literally meaning 'sacrifice-month'. Bede explains its etymology as follows: *Blodmonath mensis immolationum quod in eo pecora quae occisuri erant diis suis voverent* (*DTR* 15) '*Blodmonath* is the month of sacrifices because in it they offered to their gods cattle which were to be slaughtered'. Similarly, the month-name is explained as follows in the *Old English Martyrology* (November): *Se monoð is nemned on Læden Novembres, ond on ure geðeode Blodmonað, forðon ure yldran, ða hy hæðenne wæron, on ðam monðe hy bleoton a, þæt is þæt hy betæhton ond benæmdon hyra deofolgyldum ða neat þa ðe hy woldon syllan* 'The month is named in Latin *Novembres* and in our language *Blodmonað*, because our ancestors, when they were heathen, always sacrificed in this month. That is, they dedicated and assigned to their idols the cattle that they would give.' Sacrifices taking place in this month are said to have been made not only for religious purposes but also for more practical reasons. Chaney, for instance, writes that they sacrificed the cattle which could not be maintained during the winter (*The Cult of Kingship*, pp. 57 and 239), while Wilson mentions, in terms of the vernacular month-name, 'the annual autumnal slaughter of quantities of livestock to provide food for the people during the winter' (*Anglo-Saxon Paganism*, p. 36).

193b. *ofstum* 'hastily, speedily'. Bouterwek emends to *ofetum*, translating it as 'fructibus' (dative plural form of *ofet* 'fruit'), which is not necessary, as the dative plural form of *ofost* 'haste, speed', *of(e)stum*, is widely attested chiefly in poetry, whereas the word form *ofetum* is never attested.

196a. *Nouembris* 'November'. This half-line, consisting of only three syllables, is defective from the viewpoint of traditional Old English poetic metre. However, there are two other similar instances in the poem: *Agustus* 139a and *Decembris* 220a.

198b. *miltse drihtnes* 'through the mercy of the Lord'. This phrase of seemingly very common meaning is attested nowhere else in poetry. It is otherwise attested only in the following passage in the *Life of St Nicholas*: *ge sculon biddan*

Menologium

anrædlice ures drihtnes miltse her wiðinnen 'you should earnestly bid our Lord's mercy here from within'. However, the phrase with virtually the same meaning, *Godes miltse*, is attested both in prose and verse. Cf. also *metodes miltsa* in *Exodus* 530a.

199b–201. All Saints' Day, or *ealra ... sancta symbel* 'the feast of all saints' (199b–200a), on 1 November. The scribe uses a capital for the initial of *sancta*, which I decapitalise. The phrase *ealra haligra/halgena tid/mæsse* is much more commonly used for the feast, but the poet adopts the Latin loan-word for the sake of alliteration. Neither the half-line *sancta symbel* nor the combination *ealra sancta* is attested elsewhere. (PM, MCY, MCH, MCR, ÆCHom I, *OEM*, Calendars 4, 5, 6, 7–9, 11, 12, 13–16, 17–25, 27)

200b. *sið oððe ær*, literally 'after or before', means 'at any time, ever'. The same phrase is also attested in *Elene* 974b and Conf 4 18.71. Cf. *ær oððe sið* (e.g. *Christ C* 893a; *Riddle 60* 8a) and *ær oððe æfter* (e.g. WHom 5 38) used with the same meaning. See the *DOE* s.v. *ær*, definition I.A.4.b.

201b. *willan drihtnes* 'will of the Lord'. The usual word order is *drihtnes willan*, but the poet adopts the inverted word order, which is otherwise scarcely attested, for the sake of alliteration.

202–7a. The beginning of winter, i.e. *wintres dæg* (202a) 'winter's day' on 7 November. It is listed against 7 November in Anglo-Saxon calendars, and the prose *Menologium* also follows this. The *Old English Martyrology* also says that *On ðone seofeþan dæg þæs monðes bið wintres <fruma>* (7 November) 'On the seventh day of the month (of November) is the beginning of winter'. Byrhtferth does not mention the date of the beginning of winter in his *Enchiridion* II.1, where he mentions the beginnings of the other three seasons (ll. 392–416).

203b–4b. *sigelbeortne genimð hærfest mid herige hrimes and snawes*. Winter's day 'seizes the sun-bright autumn with a troop of rime and snow'. The adjective *sigelbeorht*, also used for summer days (89a), describes pleasant autumn, which comes to an end with the beginning of cold winter bringing rime and snow. The combination of rime and snow occurs only once more in poetry, in the *Wanderer* 48a, while that of frost and snow is more common both in poetry and prose. See, for instance, *Daniel* 377b, *Azarias* 104a, *Phoenix* 14b, 248b.

205a. *forste gefeterad* 'fettered with frost'. Frost is sometimes conceived metaphorically as a fetter as in the phrase *forstes fetre* 'a fetter of frost' in *Maxims I* 75a. See also the *Seafarer* 8b–10a, where the narrator says his feet are *forste gebunden caldum clommum* 'bound with frost, cold fetters'.

205b. *be frean hæse* 'by the Lord's command'. Cf. *be fæder leafe* in line 87a. Just as the prosperity of the season is brought by *miltse drihtnes* (198b) 'the mercy of the Lord', the beginning of winter to end glorious autumn (203b–4b) is also attributed to God.

206a. *mot*. Grein first emended it to *moton*, considering the concord with the plural subjects (*wangas grene* (206b) 'green fields' and *foldan frætuwe* (207a) 'ornaments of the earth'), and Dobbie, Greeson, O'Brien O'Keeffe, Hart and Jones follow this. Mitchell is also of this opinion (Mitchell, *Old English Syntax* I, p. 637, §1524). However, together with Hickes, Fox, Wülker, Imelmann,

Commentary

Fritsche and Grimaldi, I retain the manuscript reading for the same reason that I gave for the retention of *cigð* (see the note for line 184b). As Sievers rightly argues ('Zur Rhythmik', p. 517), *moton* causes a metrical problem, while *mot* does not; just as in the case of *cigð*, the poet seems to have placed a premium upon standard metre at the cost of grammatical word form. As Dobbie rightly points out (p. 174), we need to be consistent at any rate in emending or retaining the original text at lines 184b and 206a. See also Stanley, 'The Prose *Menologium* and the Verse *Menologium*', p. 261; and Karasawa, 'Some Problems'.

206b. *wangas grene* 'green fields'. The phrase is more often attested in its ordinary word order *grena wong/grene wongas*, as in *Genesis A* 1657b, *Guthlac A* 477a, 746a, *Riddle 12* 2a, *Riddle 66* 5a. The poet adopts the inverted word order for the sake of alliteration, as also found in *Riddle 40* 51b, 83b. Magennis writes that '[t]he notion of the ideal landscape being green ... occurs with formulaic regularity in Old English religious poetry' (*Images of Community*, p. 147). Here in this context, *wangas grene* also represents a landscape of an ideal season, which is described as *sigelbeortne ... hærfest* 'sun-bright autumn' (203b–4a).

207a. *foldan frætuwe* 'ornaments of land'. Green leaves of trees and plants are regarded as ornaments of the land. Cf. *smicere on gearwum, wudum and wyrtum* (76b–7a) 'elegantly (clad) in adornments, leaves and plants', describing the month of May. The same phrase occurs only in the *Phoenix* 257a. Cf. *wæstmum stod folde gefrætwod* 'the ground stood adorned with plants (or fruits)' in *Genesis A* 215a. Cf. also *ond gefrætwade foldan sceatas leomum ond leafum* (*Beowulf* 95–6a) 'and adorned the corners of the field with branches and leaves'.

207b–10a. The feast of St Martin on 11 November. St Martin (*c*. 316–97) was a bishop of Tours and his shrine there was a popular place for pilgrims to visit on the way to Santiago de Compostela. Alcuin served as abbot of the abbey of Saint-Martin at Tours from 796 to his death in 804, and wrote a life of St Martin based on Sulpicius Severus' *Vita S. Martini*. Ælfric, based on Alcuin, also wrote a homily for the feast, which is contained in the second series of his *Catholic Homilies* (XXVIII 'Depositio sancti Martini episcopi'). For a potential source of the popularity of his feast in Anglo-Saxon England, see Chaney, *The Cult of Kingship*, p. 58. (PM, MCY, MCH, MCR, ÆCHom II, OEM, Calendars (1), 4–7, 8, 9, 11, 12, 13–16, 17–22, 23, 24, 25, 27)

209a. *wer womma leas* 'a man devoid of flaws'. The same phrase is attested only in *Daniel* 282a, but the phrase *womma leas* 'devoid of flaws' is a formula attested widely – in *Christ A* 188a, *Christ C* 1451a, 1464a, the *Judgement Day I* 94a and the *Seasons for Fasting* 170b.

210b–14. The feast of St Clement of Rome on 23 November. He was the fourth pope and reigned from 92 to 99. According to one tradition, he was, under the Roman emperor Trajan (reigned 98–117), imprisoned and eventually put to death by being thrown into the sea with an anchor, as is roughly followed by the *Menologium* poet. The *Old English Martyrology* (under 23 November, 'Pope Clement I') also says: *Þa het he hym gebyndan anne ancran on hys sweoran ond hyne forsendan on sæ* 'then he ordered them to fasten an anchor on his neck and throw him into the sea'. See also the note for lines 212–13a. (PM, MCY, MCH, MCR, ÆCHom I, *OEM*, Calendars 1, 4, 5–7, 8, 9, 11, 12, 13–16, 18, 19, 20, 21, 22, 23, 24, 25, 27)

211b. *fan Gode*. MS *fangode*. Hickes, Fox, Grein, Earle and Plummer retain the manuscript reading. If we follow their reading, *fangode* should be understood as the past participle of **fangian*, which is attested only once in the form of the past participle *gefangod* 'joined, fastened' (see the *DOE*, s.v. *gefangod*). If this is the case, *fangode* seems to describe how St Clement was killed (see the previous note). The problem is the ending -*e*; *fangode* in this context should be in the accusative singular masculine, and the theoretically possible forms are *fangod* (when indeclinable), *fangodne* (when following the strong declension), and *fangodan* (when following the weak declension). Probably with this grammatical difficulty in mind, Grein regards *fangode* as the (plural) subject of the sentence (p. 6), but as he himself admits, it does not seem to make sense in this context. Bouterwek emends it to *feogande* and glosses it as *osores* 'haters', which is semantically possible but seems to be too radical a change, and nobody follows it. Grein later suggests that *fangode* should be regarded as a phrase consisting of two words, i.e. *fan gode* ('Zur Textkritik', p. 422), and Wülker, Imelmann, Fritsche, Dobbie, Greeson, Grimaldi, O'Brien O'Keeffe, Hart and Jones follow this. The word *fan* has usually been regarded as a nominative plural masculine form of *fah* 'hostile', functioning as the subject of the sentence. Although Greeson notes that this is not decisive, since the form *fan* is attested only here (p. 284), it may well be a contracted form of *fah* formed through the process of **fahan/fagan* > **fa-an* > *fan*, as the word form *fane* formed through a very similar process is attested in *Beowulf* 2655a. For the loss of /x/, see Campbell, p. 186, §461 and pp. 264–5, §643(2); and Hogg, pp. 271–5, §§7.45–7.51. The *DOE* (s.v. *fā*), on the other hand, regards it as a nominative plural form of the noun *fa* 'foe, enemy'. It is attested nowhere else but the form with the prefix *ge-*, *gefa* 'foe, enemy', is attested nine times. The problem of the latter reading is, as the *DOE* itself admits, that the noun requires the genitive rather than dative form of *God*, so that the whole phrase would mean 'God's enemies'. It is true that the former reading may also be somewhat problematic in that the adjective is without a demonstrative, expected from the weak declension it follows, but this occasionally occurs even in such a traditional poem as *Beowulf*, and may not be too problematic. Thus, following many editors, I read *fan Gode* taking it to mean 'those hostile to God'. Cf. *drihtne dyre* (192a) 'dear to the Lord' and *sigedrihtne leof* (215b) 'dear to the glorious Lord'.

212a–13a. St Clement was drowned, as narrated, for instance, in *Passio S. Clementis*, Bede's *Martyrologium*, the *Old English Martyrology* (quoted above), the homily on the nativity of St Clement in the first series of Ælfric's *Catholic Homilies* I.37 and his *Lives of Saints* 31. Lapidge conjectures that the *Menologium* poet 'perhaps got it from Bede, or directly from the *passio*' ('The Saintly Life', p. 251). Ælfric uses the phrase *on sægrunde* (in the dative) when referring to St Clement's drowning both in *Catholic Homilies* (I.37.250) and in *Lives of Saints* (31.899) and these are the only instances of the phrase used in Old English writings apart from *on sægrund* (in the accusative) in the *Menologium*. Thus the phrase *on sægrund(e)* is attested always in the same context. The indicative preterite plural ending *-un* instead of *-on* is used in *besenctun*. Theoretically, *-un* (< Gmc *-*un* < IE *-*nt*) is the older form of *-on*, and as Campbell (pp. 301–3, §735) and Hogg and Fulk (p. 225, §6.22) note, is attested in early Mercian glossaries and the Vespasian Psalter glosses. However, it is plausible that its use here is a result of fusion and/or confusion of unaccented back vowels in late texts rather than that it indicates the quite early origin of the poem.

213b–14b. *iu ... clypiað*. Grein emends *iu* to *nu* 'now'. This seems to be because it goes better with the verb *clypiað* in the present tense. Malone seems to avoid translating the adverb ('The Old English Calendar Poem', p. 198), while Hickes translates it as 'utique' (p. 207). Visser, on the other hand, suggests a need for the emendation of *clypiað* to *clypodon* (*An Historical Syntax* II, p. 738, §792). As reflected in these emendations and interpretations, the combination of *iu* and *clypiað* has often been considered problematic; *iu* usually means 'formerly, before' and is used with a verb in the past rather than present tense. In the discussion on the use of *ær* 'formerly, before' with a verb in the present tense, Mitchell explains that the use of *iu* here is of a similar nature (Mitchell, *Old English Syntax* I, p. 241, §622). He writes that 'the present tense *clypiað* probably certifies that the writer is viewing the appeal to Clement as something which is to precede the coming of his feast day rather than as something which preceded his death.'

213b. *beorna fela* 'many (of) men'. MS *beorna felda*. Hickes, Fox, Earle and Plummer follow the manuscript reading; Hickes translates the passage as 'invocant homines, in agrorum beneficium', while Fox 'formerly men invoked for benefit of the field'. These interpretations are interesting in terms of the homily on the nativity of St Clement in ÆCHom I.37.75–82, where the saint is said to have rescued people from a famine by finding a plentiful wellspring. As Greeson points out (p. 285), however, their interpretations are grammatically problematic, since they take *beorna* as the nominative plural form, which it is not; their interpretations require an emendation to *beornas*. Many editors, on the other hand, emend *felda* to *fela* 'many', so that the phrase would mean 'many (of) men'. Both of the aforementioned suggestions may be possible, but the former gives a rather restrictive, though interesting, interpretation, whereas the latter yields a phrase of more generally applicable sense (though never attested elsewhere). Since St Clement, even in the homily mentioned above, is not regarded as a saint worshipped especially in connection with the fertility of the land, it seems more plausible to consider that he is said to be invoked for the alleviation of hardship in general rather than of famine or crop failure alone. Later in the same homily, in fact, Ælfric also writes that people suffering from various kinds of afflictions such as illness, blindness, diabolic possession, etc. seek Clement's sepulchre on his feast (ÆCHom I.37.123–7). Thus I emend *felda* to *fela*, as Stanley also would ('The Prose *Menologium* and the Verse *Menologium*', p. 261).

214a. *Clementes*. The word form is supposed to be an accusative singular form,

Menologium

although its ordinary form in Latin is *Clementem*, which is attested elsewhere in Old English writings. Although its nominative singular form in Latin is *Clemens*, which is also attested elsewhere, the form *Clementes*, which is usually used as a genitive singular form, is also used as its nominative singular form as attested in the *Old English Martyrology* (23 November, 'Pope Clement I'). Since the *Menologium* poet uses Latin nominative singular forms also as the accusative, as in *Agustinus* (97b) and *Ianuarius* (10a), the word form *Clementes* can also be used as its accusative singular form. *Clementes*, earlier referred to as *sigefæstne wer* (212b), which is the antecedent of the relative *þe*, is another antecedent placed inside the relative clause. For a similar instance, see the note for line 43b.

215–18a. The feast of St Andrew the Apostle on 30 November. The saint is the brother of St Peter and is said to have been martyred at Patras in Achaea in 60. He was buried there but most of his relics were later translated to Constantinople about 375. There is a poetic account of his life in Old English, *Andreas*, while Ælfric writes a homily for the feast in ÆCHom I. The saint is also briefly mentioned in the *Fates of the Apostles* 16–22. (PM, MCY, MCH, MCR, ÆCHom I, OEM, Calendars 1, 4, 5–9, 11, 12, 13–16, 17–22, 23, 24, 25, 27)

215b. *sigedrihtne leof*. MS *sige drihtne lof*. Hickes and Fox retain the manuscript reading, translating the phrase as 'in gloriæ domini honorem', and '*A* glory to *his* Lord', respectively. Hickes's interpretation is problematic from the grammatical point of view, while Fox's is grammatical but it seems unusual for the word *lof* 'praise, glory' to represent a person (in this context St Andrew mentioned in the next line). Earle (p. xxxiv) also retains the manuscript reading, while Plummer emends to *sige drihtne l[e]of*. These editors, whether or not they emend the original *lof*, print *sige drihtne* as two words, but *sigedrihten* 'glorious Lord' is a common poetic compound and should be printed as one word. Bouterwek, Grein, Wülker, Imelmann, Fritsche, Dobbie, Greeson, Grimaldi, O'Brien O'Keeffe, Hart and Jones emend to *sigedrihtne leof* 'dear to the glorious Lord'. Cf. *drihtne dyre* (192a) 'dear to the Lord'; and *fan Gode* (211b) '(those) hostile to God'.

217. The expression *his gast ageaf* and the like is quite common in prose works, while it is used only sparingly in poetry. As far as I can find, it is otherwise used only once in *Andreas* 1416: *ic gast minne agifan mote ... on þines sylfes hand* 'I could deliver my soul into your own hand'. Cf. also *Þonne he gast ofgifeð* (*Metrical Psalms* 102.15, 1) 'then he gave up (his) soul'. A somewhat similar expression for death is used in lines 38b–9. For phrases similar to *on Godes wære* used in expressions for death, see the note for line 38b–9.

218a. *fus on forðweg* 'eager for the onward way' is a poetic expression often used for the soul of a dying/dead person, for instance, in *Exodus* 129a and *Guthlac B* 945a. See the *DOE* s.v. *forþ-weg*. O'Brien O'Keeffe, printing *forð weg*, regards it as a phrase, but it should be taken as a compound. Cf. *fus forðweges* 'eager for the onward way' in *Riddle 30a/30b* 3a.

218b–21a. The beginning of December. The month was called *Ærra Iula* 'the former Yule', in the vernacular; December and January shared the name *Iula* (*Giuli, Geola*) and *Ærra* 'former' or *Æfterra* 'latter' was added to distinguish the two. As regards its origin, Bede writes: *Menses giuli a conversione solis in*

Commentary

auctum diei ... nomen accipiunt (*DTR* 15) 'The months of *Giuli* get their name from the sun's turning point at which the day began to increase'. In this context, *morgen* 'morning' means 'the next morning' (see BT, s.v. *morgen* definition II). It is also sometimes used in this meaning in the prose *Menologium* as in *and þæs ymbe ane wucan and ymbe ane niht bið Sancte Cuthberhtes mæsse, and on morgen Sancte Benedictus and emnihte* 'And after a week and a day is St Cuthbert's feast, and in the next morning, St Benedict's (feast) and the (vernal) equinox'. It is true that it sounds more natural to say that the next morning brings the month of December, in which case *morgen* (219a) is the subject and *monað* (219b), *Decembris* (220a), and *Ærra Iula* (221a) are the objects. Fox (p. 43), Bouterwek (p. 16), Malone ('The Old English Calendar Poem', p. 199), Greeson (p. 285) and Jones (p. 189) follow this reading. Yet *Ærra Iula* is in the nominative form and as Kock suggests, this must be one of the subjects of the sentence, paralleled with *monað* and *Decembris* (*Jubilee*, p. 55). Similar parallelism is found in lines 106b–9a, where *Ærra Liða* is paralleled with *monað* and *Iunius*. At the same time, the structure of the sentence is very similar to that of lines 88b–9, where the object of the sentence whose main verb is *bringð* is placed immediately after the verb in the next half-line and the subject plus *to tune* follows this in the next half-line. It is also noteworthy that in the *Menologium* a month, as the subject of a sentence, is sometimes said to bring something, as in the cases of May (78b–9), June (106b–9a), August (138b–40a) and November (193b–7a), while a month is never said to be brought by something. In other cases, months are usually said to come by themselves (*cymð* (7b, 72b, 77b, 130b), *sigeð* (16b), *færð* (35b), *scriþ* (136b), *fereð* (165a, 182a)), with an exception where it is said that *nergend sent Aprelis monað* (55b–6a) 'the Saviour sends the month of April'. Thus the passage means that the month of December brings the next morning, which is a slightly circumlocutory way of saying that December begins next morning. Mensel suggests that *morgen* here may figuratively allude to the coming of Christ ('On the Principles of Artistic Order', p. 53), in which case *morgen* seems to be more appropriate to be brought by the month of December than the other way around; December comes first and near the end of it the Nativity.

220a. *Decembris*. It is not impossible to consider that *Decembris* in the genitive depends on *monað* in the previous half-line. However, it seems more plausible that *Decembris* is an abbreviated form of *mensis Decembris* and is virtually in the nominative, paralleled with *Ærra Iula* (221a). The form *Decembris* is attested as a nominative form in Old English writings, as in the following passage from the *Old English Martyrology* (December): *Se monað ys nemned on Leden Decembris, and on ure geþeode se Ærra Geola* 'The month is named in Latin *Decembris* and in our language the *Ærra Geola*'.

221b–5. The feast of St Thomas the Apostle falling on 21 December. He is said to have gone on missionary journeys as far as India, where he was martyred. No details about his life and death are given in the *Menologium*, while his missionary work and martyrdom in India are mentioned in the *Old English*

Martyrology as well as in the *Fates of the Apostles* 50–62. (PM, MCY, MCH, MCR, *OEM*, Calendars 1, 4, 5–7, 8, 9, 11, 12, 13–16, 17–22, 23, 24, 25, 27)

224a. *wið earfeðum* 'in return for hardship (he experienced)'. The preposition *wið* is used in the same meaning in 146b. The same phrase is attested twice in *Guthlac A* in 457a and 556a.

224b. *ece rice* 'the eternal kingdom'. This phrase seems to be a slightly modified version of *þæt/his ece rice*, which is attested only in prose. The poet modifies it for metrical purposes.

225a. The word *beornwiga* is a *hapax legomenon*. Thomas is mentioned as a bold warrior perhaps because of legends regarding his missionary journeys even to India. In the *Fates of the Apostles*, he is mentioned as *collenferð* 'bold-hearted, courageous' (54a), and is said to have ventured to India *priste* 'boldly' (50b).

226–8a. The Nativity of Christ on 25 December. Christmas is also mentioned at the very beginning of the poem. It is mentioned for the second time here at the end of the poem, which is probably for the same reason as it is also mentioned twice at the beginning and the end in the prose *Menologium*. For details, see p. 28. (PM, MCY, MCH, MCR, ÆCHom I, ÆCHom II, *OEM*, Calendars 1, 4–9, 11, 12, 13, 14, 15, 16–25, 27)

226b. *fæder engla* 'Father of angels'. This is a common poetic phrase for God, attested in various poems including *Andreas* (2x), *Elene*, *Guthlac B*, *Phoenix* (2x), *Juliana* and the *Metres of Boethius* (3x).

227b. *þas sidan gesceaft* 'this spacious creation' is a common poetic phrase for the world. Exactly the same phrase is used in *Genesis A* 675a, *Christ A* 59b, 239b, 356b, and the *Metres of Boethius*, Metre 11, 63b while its variants are also numerously attested.

228b–31. The concluding remark, in which the poet, saying that 'now you can locate the (immovable) feasts of the holy saints', specifies the main target of the poem as the feasts of the saints. Cf. lines 63–8a, where movable feasts are excluded from the scope of the poem.

229a. *haligra tiida* 'feasts of the holy'. MS *haligra tiid*. Hickes, Fox, Bouterwek, Grein, Wülker and Imelmann follow the manuscript reading, while Dobbie, Greeson, Grimaldi, O'Brien O'Keeffe, Hart and Jones emend it to *haligra tiida*. As far as the interpretation of the phrase is concerned, however, all the editors seem to agree that *tiid(a)* is in the accusative plural. Cosijn takes *tiid* as a possible neuter plural form of *tid* ('Anglosaxonica', p. 443), while Sievers (*Angelsächsische Grammatik*, pp. 140–1, §269n5) and Brunner (*Altenglische Grammatik*, pp. 217–18, §269n5) comment that in Northumbrian *tid* (and similar long-stem feminine nouns) can appear as neuter nouns. However, the poem is written in late West Saxon and the few Northumbrian features in it are to be attributed to the use of poetic koine. The poet otherwise never uses the word *tid* as a neuter noun; as Dobbie notes 'the noun *tid* is not elsewhere found as a neuter' (p. 174). Thus the emendation seems necessary. The same phrase in the singular, *haligra tid*, appears in line 121a, while it is otherwise attested only in prose works.

230a. *swa bebugeð gebod*. Bouterwek starts a new sentence here, regarding *swa* as an adverb corresponding to Latin *sic*. Probably he follows the scribe,

Commentary

who uses a capital for the initial of *swa* as if indicating the beginning of a new sentence. In this context, however, it seems more suitable to take *swa* as a conjunction. Regarding the exact meaning of *swa* in this context, various opinions have been expressed: Hickes takes it as meaning 'quemadmodum' (p. 207), Greeson 'because' (p. 212), Fox (p. 45) and Malone ('The Old English Calendar Poem', p. 199) 'as', while Jones has 'wherever' (p. 189). Imelmann suggests the king's command mentioned here may be V Æthelred issued in 1008, where strict observance of important feasts is regulated (pp. 39–40 and 53). However, the absence of reference to the feast of St Edward the Martyr suggests that the poem was composed before the promulgation of V Æthelred; its strict observance is independently regulated in clause 16 of V Æthelred, while other feasts are mentioned collectively in clauses 14–15. If the poet composed the poem under the influence of V Æthelred, it seems less likely for him openly to neglect to follow it; in fact, nearly all the calendars compiled after 1008 mark the feast as an important feast. Perhaps the passage, meaning 'as far as the command (of the king of Saxons) extends', does not refer to any specific law or king but means generally 'under the rule of the Anglo-Saxon king' or 'in Anglo-Saxon England'. At any rate, this passage emphasises the domestic perspective of the poem repeatedly displayed throughout (see also the next note).

230b. *geond Brytenricu* means either 'over the spacious kingdoms' or 'over the kingdoms of Britain' (see the *DOE*, s.v. *bryten-rīce*). The origin of the element *bryten-* (also attested as a word in *Christ and Satan* 686a) is not clear, and it is not totally certain with which meaning it is used here. The word *brytenrice* is used in the former meaning in *Azarias* 107b. Cf. also *brytengrundas* 'spacious lands' in *Christ A* 357a and *brytenwongas* 'spacious plains' in *Christ A* 380b. On the other hand, *Breotenrice,* a variant which is not recognised in the *DOE*, is attested in *Durham* 1b and in the Old English Bede (chapter 5), in both of which it means the kingdom of Britain. In *Durham* 1b, moreover, it is used in the same phrase *geond Breotenrice* (but in the singular). Regardless of its origin, the element *bryten* seems to evoke Britain in this context of the *Menologium* because the domestic perspective is emphasised by the reference to the Saxon king and because the word *Bryten* is used exceptionally frequently in this poem (see the note for lines 14b–15a). Thus I adopt the spelling *Brytenricu* but translate it as 'the spacious kingdoms of Britain', having both meanings in mind. It is used in the plural, perhaps because of the awareness that kingdoms once existed in England, which later came to be ruled by a single (West Saxon) king, or perhaps because of the influence from similar expressions always attested in the plural such as *geond woruldricu* (*Metrical Psalms* 113.9) 'over the kingdoms in the world' and *geond ealle eorðricu* (Deuteronomy 28.25) 'over all the earthly kingdoms' (the latter is a translation of *per omnia regna terræ* 'through all the kingdoms of the world'). For the use of the phrase, see O'Donnell, 'The Old English *Durham*', pp. 154–5.

231b. *on þas sylfan tiid.* Liebermann considers that this prepositional phrase means 'concerning these same feast-days' which depends on *gebod* 'command'

Menologium

('Zum angelsächsischen Menologium', p. 99). Yet his reading, requiring the emendation of *tiid* to *tiida*, is less plausible. The phrase *(on) þa(s) sylfan tiid* seems to be a variant of *on þa(s) ilcan tid* meaning '(at) the/this same or very time' attested three more times in Old English poems in the *Menologium* 5a, *Genesis A* 2393b, and *Christ C* 1148b, as Hickes (p. 207), Fox (p. 45), Bouterwek (p. 17), Imelmann (p. 39), Sokoll ('R. Imelmann', p. 315), Malone ('The Old English Calendar Poem', p. 199) and Jones (p. 189) seem to believe. Greeson also follows basically the same reading, translating it as 'unto this very time' (p. 212). Hickes (p. 207) and Sokoll ('R. Imelmann', p. 315) take the phrase as depending on *healdan sceal*, but it seems more likely that it is included in the subordinate clause beginning with *swa bebugeð* ... (230a).

Appendix 1
The Prose *Menologium*

The following text is based chiefly on PMH with some modifications and additions based on PMC. Italics mark emendations. Abbreviations, including the Tironian sign, are expanded without notice, while Roman numerals are retained as they are in the manuscript. The overall layout, word division, capitalisation and punctuation follow modern convention.

Appendix 1

ᵃDE DIEBUS FESSTISᵃ

Ærestᵇ fromᶜ middan wintra biðᵈ to Sancta Marian mæssan .v. wucanᵉ and .iiii. niht.

And ðæsᶠ on .v. nihtumᵍ gæð lengtenʰ on tun.

And þæs ymbe twa wucanⁱ and ymbe *.iii.* ʲ niht biðᵏ Sancte Mathiasˡ mæsse.

And ðæsᵐ ymbe twa ⁿwucan and twaⁿ nihtᵒ biðᵖ Sancte Gregorius mæsse.

5   And ᑫþæs ymbe ane wucanᑫ and ymbe aneʳ niht bið Sancte ˢCuthberhtes mæsseˢ, ᵗand on morgen Sancteᵗ Benedictus ᵘand emnihteᵘ.

And ðæsᵛ on ʷfeower nihtumʷ biðˣ Sancta Marian mæsse.ʸ⁻ʸ

And ðæsᶻ ymbe ᵃfeower wucanᵃ and ymbe þreoᵇ niht biðᶜ se ænlipiga gangdæg.

And ðæsᵈ ymbe .vi. niht biðᵉ Sancte Philippus mæsse ᶠand Iacobusᶠ.

10 And ᵍðæs ymbe twa niht biðᵍ Inuentio Sancte Crucis.

And ðæsʰ ymbe .vi.ⁱ niht gæð sumerʲ on tun.

And ðæsᵏ ymbe ˡtwa wucanˡ and ymbe .iii.ᵐ niht biðⁿ Sancte Augustinusᵒ mæsse.

And ᵖðæs ymbe .iiii. wucan and ymbe ane niht biðᵖ middes sumeres mæssedæg ᑫ[and þær is fæsten to]ᑫ.

15 And ðæsʳ ymbe .v.ˢ niht biðᵗ Sancte Petres mæssedæg, and on morgenᵘ Sancte Paules ᵛ[and þær is fæsten to]ᵛ.

And ʷðæs ymbe .iii. wucanʷ and ymbe *.iiii.*ˣ niht biðʸ Sancte Iacobusᶻ mæsse, Iohannes broðor ᵃ[and þær is fæsten to]ᵃ.

And ðæsᵇ ymbe ane ᶜwucan bið Hlafmæssandægᶜ.

20 And ðæs ymbe .vi.ᵈ niht gæð hærfestᵉ on tun.

And ðæsᶠ ymbe .iii. niht biðᵍ Sancte Laurentius mæsseʰ ⁱ[and þær is fæsten to]ⁱ.

And ðæsʲ ymbe .v. niht ᵏbið *Sancta*ᵏ Marian mæsse ˡ[and þær is fæsten to]ˡ.

And ðæsᵐ ymbe .x.ⁿ niht biðᵒ Sancte Bartholomeus mæsse ᵖ[and þar is fæsten to]ᵖ.

And ᑫðæs ymbeᑫ .iiii. ʳniht biðʳ Sancte Iohannes mæsse Baptistanˢ.

ᵃ⁻ᵃ Not in C | ᵇ Not in C | ᶜ fram C | ᵈ byð C | ᵉ ucan C | ᶠ þæs | ᵍ nihton C | ʰ lencgten C | ⁱ ucan C | ʲ .iiii. H | ᵏ byð C | ˡ Mathianes C | ᵐ þæs C | ⁿ⁻ⁿ *added above the line probably by the same hand* H; ucan and on twam C | ᵒ nihton | ᵖ byð C | ᑫ⁻ᑫ on þæs on twam ucan C | ʳ .i. C | ˢ⁻ˢ Cuðberhtes mæssedæg C | ᵗ⁻ᵗ and þæs on mergen Sanctus C | ᵘ⁻ᵘ Not in C | ᵛ þæs C | ʷ⁻ʷ .iiii. nihton C | ˣ byð C | ʸ⁻ʸ and byð emnihtesdæg C | ᶻ þæs C | ᵃ⁻ᵃ .iiii. ucan C | ᵇ .iii. C | ᶜ byð C | ᵈ þæs C | ᵉ byð C | ᶠ⁻ᶠ and sancte Iacobes C | ᵍ⁻ᵍ þonne on twa nihton C | ʰ þæs C | ⁱ syx C | ʲ sumor C | ᵏ þæs C | ˡ⁻ˡ .ii. ucan C | ᵐ twa C | ⁿ byð C | ᵒ Agustinus C | ᵖ þæs on .iiii. ucan and on anre nihte byð C | ᑫ⁻ᑫ Not in H | ʳ þæs C | ˢ fif C | ᵗ Not in C | ᵘ *After* morgen C *has* þæs | ᵛ⁻ᵛ Not in H | ʷ⁻ʷ þæs ymbe þreo ucan C | ˣ .v. CH | ʸ byð C | ᶻ Iacobes C | ᵃ⁻ᵃ Not in H | ᵇ þæs C | ᶜ⁻ᶜ ucan byð hlafmæssedæg C | ᵈ syx C | ᵉ hærefest C | ᶠ þæs C | ᵍ byð C | ʰ mæssedæg C | ⁱ⁻ⁱ Not in H | ʲ þæs C | ᵏ⁻ᵏ Sancta C; bið Sancte H | ˡ⁻ˡ Not in H | ᵐ þæs C | ⁿ tyn C | ᵒ byð C | ᵖ⁻ᵖ Not in H | ᑫ⁻ᑫ þæs on C | ʳ⁻ʳ nihton byð C | ˢ Not in C |

Prose Menologium

In the following translation, words in parentheses are of supplementary and/or explanatory nature added by the translator and not in the original text.

On Feast Days

First from the midwinter (i.e. the winter equinox and Christmas) to St Mary's feast (i.e. the Purification) is five weeks and four nights.
And then in five nights spring comes to town.
And then after two weeks and three days is St Mathias's feast.
And then after two weeks and two days is St Gregory's feast.
And then after a week and a day is St Cuthbert's feast,
and on the next morning, St Benedict and the (vernal) equinox.
And then in four days is St Mary's feast (i.e. Annunciation Day).
And then after four weeks and three days is the Major Rogation.
And then after six days is SS Phillip and James's feast.
And then after two days is the Invention of the Cross.
And then after six days, summer comes to town.
And then after two weeks and three days is St Augustine's feast.
And then after four weeks and a day is midsummer's feast (i.e. the feast of St John the Baptist coinciding with the unofficial summer solstice) [and there is a fast day before it].
And then after five days is St Peter's feast-day,
And in the next morning St Paul's [and there is a fast day before it].
And then after three weeks and four days is St James's feast, John's brother [and there is a fast day before it].
And then after a week is Lammas Day.
And then after six days, autumn comes to town.
And then after three days is St Laurence's feast [and there is a fast day before it].
And then after five days is St Mary's feast (i.e. the Assumption) [and there is a fast day before it].
And then after ten days is St Bartholomew's feast [and there is a fast day before it].
And then after four days is St John the Baptist's feast.

Appendix 1

25　And ðæs^t ymbe .x.^{u} niht bið^v Sancta Marian mæsse^w.
　　And ðæs^x ymbe *.xiii.*^{y} niht bið^z Sancte Matheus mæssedæg ^{a}[and þar is fæsten to]^a.
　　And ðæs^b ymbe .iii.^{c} niht bið^d eminiht^e.
　　And ðæs^f ymbe .v. niht bið^g Sancte Michaheles^h mæssedæg.
　　And ðæs ymbe .iiii. wucan^i and ymbe^j ane niht ^{k}bið Sancte Simones^k mæsse and
30　Taddeus ^{l}[and þar is fæsten to]^l.
　　And ^{m}ðæs ymbe^m .iiii. nihtum bið^n ealra halgena^o mæssedæg ^{p}[and þær is fæsten to]^p.
　　And ðæs^q ymbe .vi. niht gæð winter on tun.
　　And ðæs ymbe .iiii. niht ^{r}bið [Sancte]^r Martinus mæsse.
　　And ðæs^s ymbe .xii. ^{t}niht bið Sancte Clementes^t mæsse.
35　And ðæs ymbe *.vii.*^{u} niht bið^v Sancte Andreas mæsse^w ^{x}[and þar is fæsten to]^x.
　　And ðæs^y ymbe .iii. ^{z}wucan bið *Sancte*^{z}Thomas mæsse^a ^{b}[and þar is fæsten to]^b.
　　And ðæs^c ymbe .iiii. niht bið^d middes wintres mæssedæg.

---

^{t} þæs C | ^{u} tyn C | ^{v} byð C | ^{w} mæssedæg C | ^{x} þæs C | ^{y} .xii. H; feowertyne C | ^{z} byð C | $^{a-a}$ Not in H | ^{b} þæs C | ^{c} .iiii. C | ^{d} Not in C | ^{e} emnihtesdæg C | ^{f} þæs C | ^{g} byð C | ^{h} Michaeles C | ^{i} ucan C | ^{j} ymb C | $^{k-k}$ byð Simonis C | $^{l-l}$ Not in H | $^{m-m}$ þæs on C | ^{n} byð C | ^{o} haligra C | $^{p-p}$ Not in H | ^{q} þæs C | $^{r-r}$ byð Sancte C; bið H | ^{s} þæs C | $^{t-t}$ byð Climentes C | ^{u} .vi. H | ^{v} byð C | ^{w} mæssedæg C | $^{x-x}$ Not in H | ^{y} þæs C | $^{z-z}$ wucan bið Sanctae H; ucan byð C | ^{a} mæssedæg C | $^{b-b}$ Not in H | ^{c} þæs C | ^{d} byð C |

Prose Menologium

And then after ten days is St Mary's feast (i.e. the Nativity).
And then after thirteen days is St Matthew's feast-day [and there is a fast day before it].
And then after three days is the (autumnal) equinox.
And then after five days is St Michael's feast-day.
And then after four weeks and a day is SS Simon and Jude's feast [and there is a fast day before it].
And then after four days is All Saints' Day [and there is a fast day before it].

And then after six days, winter comes to town.
And then after four days is St Martin's feast.
And then after twelve days is St Clement's feast.
And then after seven days is St Andrew's feast [and there is a fast day before it].
And then after three weeks is St Thomas's feast [and there is a fast day before it].
And then after four days is the midwinter's feast-day (i.e. Christmas coinciding with the unofficial winter solstice).

Appendix 1

Commentary

The title 'DE DIEBUS FESSTIS', is found only in PMH, where the preceding text is entitled 'DE DIEBUS MALIS', whereas PMC has no title. 'DE DIEBUS MALIS', a note on the twenty-four Egyptian Days or unlucky days, is edited, together with its variants, in Henel, 'Altenglischer Mönchsaberglaube', and in Chardonnens, *Anglo-Saxon Prognostics*, pp. 370–2.

1. *wucan*. This word form is always used in PMH, while a later form *ucan* is consistently used in PMC.

2. *nihtum*. This word form is always used in PMH, while a corrupt form *nihton* is used in PMC with only one exception in line 31.

3. *Mathias*. The form in PMC, *Mathianes*, is otherwise attested nowhere else in Old English writings.

5. *þæs ymbe ane wucan*. The corresponding part in PMC is *on þæs on twam ucan*, where the scribe seems confused, possibly under the influence of the *on twam* in the previous line.

6. *emnihte* 'equinox'. Following the revised Julian calendar, the vernal equinox coincides with the feast of St Benedict (21 March) in PMH, while it coincides with Annunciation Day (25 March) in PMC, which follows the original Julian calendar. Thus the words *and byð emnihtesdæg* 'and is the equinox day' come just after *Sancta Marian mæsse* 'the feast of St Mary' in PMC.

9. *Iacobus*. PMC has *Sancte Iacobes,* while the word *Sancte* is lacking in PMH. Probably this is not a mistake, since the same thing happens when the feast of SS Simon and Jude is mentioned in line 30. *Iacobus* is the genitive form with the word *mæsse* omitted after it; here PMC has the word form with the Old English genitive ending, *Iacobes*. In PMC, some words are erased after *Iacobes*. They are undecipherable, but is it possible that they are *(mæsse) Iohannes broðor*, which is appropriate if used for his namesake St James the Less?

10. *ðæs ymbe twa niht bið*. PMC has *þonne on twa nihton*. As in this line, PMC occasionally omits the verb *bið* as in lines 15, 22, 27, while it is never omitted in PMH. PMC more often uses *on* in place of *ymbe* than PMH.

14. Fast days are never mentioned in PMH, and the references to them seem to be later additions to the original prose *Menologium*. For details, see pp. 29–30.

17. Both PMH and PMC have *.v.* instead of the right number *.iv.* This is the only shortcoming regarding the number of days that is shared by the two variants.

24. *Baptistan*. The epithet of St John the Baptist, which is only found in PMH, is abbreviated as *bapt* in the manuscript and Henel expands it as *baptistae*, adding the Latin ending *-ae*, which is possible. Here I added the genitive singular ending of Old English weak noun *-an*, since the form *baptistan* (gen sing) is attested once in the *Blickling Homilies*, while the form *baptistae* is attested only in Latin passages.

26. *.xiii.* PMH has *.xii.* while PMC has *feowertyne*; each is erroneous in a different way.

30. *Taddeus* is another name of St Jude the Apostle. For the omission of the

Prose Menologium

word *Sancte* before *Taddeus*, see the note for line 9 above. PMC omits *Sancte* before *Simones* too.

31. *ealra halgena mæssedæg*. PMC has *ealra haligra mæssedæg*. Both readings are possible; the latter is attested at least once in the Anglo-Saxon Chronicle (A, 900), while the former is much more common.

Appendix 2
Metrical Calendar of York

The following are the only two English manuscripts preserving the text of the Metrical Calendar of York, which I shall call V and Tr respectively:

V : British Library, MS Cotton Vespasian B.vi, fol. 104r–v (s. ix in);
Tr : Cambridge, Trinity College Library O.2.24, fols. 87v–9r (s. xii in).

The following edition is based chiefly on V with emendations and additions based on Tr. As regards the first fifteen lines, however, they are based on Tr as these lines are missing from V. Apart from the two manuscripts, I also consulted the editions included in the ePL and Wilmart, 'Un témoin anglo-saxon du calendrier métrique d'York', to which I shall refer as PL and W respectively. The words in square brackets are those added based on Tr, while emendations are marked by italics. Abbreviations are expanded without notice. Word division, punctuation and capitalisation follow modern convention. Line numbers are inserted on the left hand side of the page, while folio numbers are inserted on the right hand side. The end of a manuscript page is indicated in the text by |.

[Prima dies Iani est qua circumciditur *agnus*.   Tr fol. 88r
Octauas idus colitur theophania Christi.
Deserti quartas primus capit accola Paulus.
Sex decimas Antonius obtinet aeque kalendas.
5   Tres decimas Sebastianus tenuisse refertur.
Bis senas meritis mundo fulgentibus Agnes,

Martyrio undecimas et Anastasius memoratur.
Prima dies Februi est iam qua patitur Policarpus,
Et quartas nonas Christus templo offerebatur.
10 Nonarumque *diem* festum celebramus Agathae,
Atque Ualentini sedenis *sorte kalendis*.

1 agnus] Not in V; annus Tr; emended PL W
2 Octauas] Not in V; Octabas Tr; emended PL W
4 Sex decimas] Not in V; Sedecimas Tr; emended W
9 Et] Not in V; A Tr; emended PL W
10 diem] Not in V; die Tr; emended PL W
11 sorte] Not in V; porte Tr; forte PL; sorte W
11 kalendis] Not in V; Kalende Tr; emended PL W

Metrical Calendar of York

The following is an English translation based on the edited text. The numbers in the brackets on the left hand side of the page reveal the date of each feast.

(1 Jan)   The first day of January is when the Lamb was circumcised.
(6)   The sixth is worshipped because of the theophany of Christ.
(10)   Paul, the first inhabitant of the desert, occupies the 10th.
(17)   Similarly, Anthony obtains the 17th.
(20)   Sebastian is said to have obtained the 20th.   5
(21)   Because of merits conspicuous to the world, Agnes is commemorated on 21st,
(22)   and through martyrdom Anastasius is commemorated on the 22nd.
(1 Feb)   The first day of February is just when Polycarp suffered.
(2)   And Christ was offered to the temple on the 2nd.
(5)   We celebrate Agatha's feast day on the 5th,   10
(14)   and also Valentine's is assigned to the 14th.

Appendix 2

      Sic Iuliana et bis septenas ornat honore,
      Ac senas merito Mathias uirtute dicabat.
      Hinc idus *Martis* quartas Gregorius aurat.
15   Cuthbertus denas tenuit ternasque kalendas,]
      Bis senis sanctus post quem sequitur Benedictus.   V fol. 104r
      Octauis merito gaudet conceptio Christi.
      Atque Georgius hinc euectus ad astra uolauit
      Carnifices nonis Maiae uincente kalendis.
20   Ecgberhtus digna uirtutum laude [choruscus,
      Astriferum octauis ueneranter scandit] Olympum.
      Quoque die praesul penetrauit Uilfridus alma
      Angelico gaudens uectus trans culmina coetu. |
      Uilfridus et ternis superam penetrauit in aulam   Tr fol. 88v
25   Tempore posterior, morum non flore secundus.
      Iacobus seruus domini pius atque Philippus
      Mirifico Maias uenerantur honore kalendas.
      Bis binis sequitur Pancratius idibus insons.
      Ter quinis Marcus meruit pausare kalendis.
30   Iunius in nonis mundo miratur ademtam
      Et summis Tatberhti animam trans *sidera* uectam.
      Atque die uincens *eadem* Bonifatius hostes
      Martyrio fortis bellator ad astra recessit.
      Inque suis quadris Barnaban idibus aequat.
35   *Geruasius* denis patitur ternisque kalendis
      Protasius simul in regnumque *perenne* uocati.
      Estque Iohannes bis quadris baptista colendus
      Natalis pulchre feste plaudente corona.
      Martyrio et Paulus senis ouat atque Iohannes.
40   Doctores Petrus et Paulus ternis sociantur
      Maxima quos palma clarat sibi lumina mundus.

13 merito] Not in V; meriti PL W
14 Martis] martias Tr; emended PL W
19 Carnifices] Carnifes V; emended PL W
19 Maiae] maie Tr; emended PL W
19 uincente] uincenti Tr; emended PL W
20 Ecgberhtus] Egberhtus Tr
21 octauis] octouis Tr; emended PL W
21 Olympum] olimphum Tr; emended PL W
24 et] Not in V; in Tr; emended W
27 Maias] maius Tr
31 trans sidera] transidera V; trans sydera Tr
32 eadem] eandem V
35 Geruasius] Gerbasius V Cf. Octauas/Octabas in line 2.
36 perenne] perenna V

Metrical Calendar of York

(16) And then Juliana decorates the 16th with honour,
(24) and also, Mathias deservedly made the 24th a holy day by his virtue.
(12 Mar) Here Gregory gilds the 12th of March.
(20) Cuthbert obtained the 20th, 15
(21) after whom St Benedict follows on the 21st.
(25) Christ's conception rightly enjoys the 25th.
(23 Apr) And George was taken from hence and flew to the stars,
      by overcoming executioners, on the 23rd.
(24) Ecgberht, shining with due praise for his virtue, 20
      dutifully ascended starry Olympus on the 24th.
(24) On the same day, Wilfrid the Bishop reached heaven,
      rejoicing in being borne by the angelic host through the delightful heights.
(29) And Wilfrid, on the 29th, went into the heavenly court,
      following him in time, but second to none in the flower of his virtues. 25
(1 May) James, the pious servant of the Lord, and also Philip
      are worshipped with great honour on the first of May.
(12) The innocent Pancras followed on the 12th.
(18) On the 18th, Mark deserved to rest.
(5 Jun) June, on its fifth day, worships Tatberht's soul 30
      taken away from the world and carried through the heavens.
(5)   And on this same day, Boniface the mighty warrior,
      victorious over his enemies, departed to heaven through martyrdom.
(10) (June) treats Barnabas in the same way on the 10th.
(19) Gervasius suffered on the 19th, 35
(19) as did Protasius, and both were summoned to the eternal kingdom.
(24) And John the Baptist is to be revered on the 24th,
      on this feast of his beautiful birth, in the glory of his crown.[1]
(26) And through martyrdom, Paul rejoices on the 26th, and so does John.
(29) The teachers Peter and Paul are associated (with each other) on the 29th, 40
      illustrious men whom the world illuminates with the greatest honour.

---

[1] The line could also be interpreted as 'his nativity, by people by beautiful, festive applauding'.

Appendix 2

     Iulius in quadris bis gaudet ferre kalendis
     Iacobum fratremque Iohannis more colendum.
     Sanctificant Abdo et Sennis ternos uenerando.
45 Augustus Xystum octauis tenet idibus aptum.
     Bis binis uictor superat Laurentius hostes. |
     Sancta Dei genetrix senas ter constat adire   Tr fol. 89r
     Angelicos uecta inter coetus uirgo kalendas.
     Octonos sanctus sortitur Bartholomeus.
50 [Bis b]inis passus colitur b[aptista Ioh]annes. |
     Idus Septembris senas dedicabat honore   V fol. 104v
     Quis meruit nasci felix iam uirgo Maria.
     Octauas decimas Cornelius inde kalendas
     Consecrauit et Cyprianus ordine digno.
55 Eufemia ac sex decimas tenet intemerata.
     Undecimas capit et Matheus doctor amoenus,
     Mauricius decimas tenet martyr cum milibus [una].
     Quintanas sortitur Cosmas sibi cum Damiano.
     Michahelis ternas templi dedicatio sacrat.
60 At bonus pridias micat interpres Hieronymus.
     Sextas Octembris nonas Bosa optat habere
     Sollemnes terris summo qui gaudet Olympo.
     At gemini quinis Haeuualdi sorte coluntur.
     Paulinus senas metet idus iure magister.
65 Doctor ter quinis Lucas succurrere kalendis.
     Simonis quinis et Iudas uota feramus.
     Multiplici *rutilet* gemma ceu in fronte Nouember
     Cunctorum fulget sanctorum laude decorus.
     Martinus *ternis* scandit super idibus astra.

44 ternos uenerando] uenerando kalendis Tr
45 Xystum] syxtum Tr
48 coetus] coetos V, Tr; emended PL W
49 Ontonos] Octauos Tr
49 sortitur] potitur Tr Cf. sorte/porte in line 11.
50 The manuscript leaf of V is damaged here and several characters are lost, but they are preserved in Tr.
52 Idus] Idibus Tr
54 consecrauit] consecrabis Tr; consecrat PL W
61 Octembris] octobris Tr
61 nonas] sonnas Tr
62 Sollemnes] Sollemnis V; Solennis Tr; emended Pl
62 summo] sumno Tr
63 Haeuualdi] heaualdi Tr
65 succurrere] succurre Tr
65 kalendis] kalendas Tr
67 rutilet] rutulet V
69 ternis] toronis V; turonis Tr; emended PL W
69 super] nam Tr

Metrical Calendar of York

(25 Jul)	On July 25th, a happy day,
	James, the brother of John, is celebrated in the usual way.
(30)	Abdon and Sennen consecrate the 30th by venerating it.
(6 Aug)	Appropriately, August has its sixth day as the feast of Sixtus. 45
(10)	On the 10th, the victor Laurence overcomes enemies.
(15)	The holy Mother of God, it is agreed, has her feast on the 15th,
	the day on which the Virgin was carried to the angelic hosts.
(25)	St Bartholomew is put on the 25th.
(29)	On the 29th, the martyr, John the Baptist, is worshipped. 50
(8 Sept)	The Blessed Virgin Mary gave honour to the 8th of September,
	the day on which she was born.
(14)	Cornelius then made the 14th holy,
(14)	and did Cyprian in the appropriate order.
(16)	The chaste Eufemia obtains the 16th. 55
(21)	And the delightful teacher Matthew occupies the 21st.
(22)	Maurice the martyr together with thousands (of others) obtains the 22nd.
(27)	Cosmas is put on the 27th, along with Damian.
(29)	The dedication of the Temple of Michael makes the 29th holy.
(30)	And the good translator Jerome sparkles on the day before (the 1st of Oct). 60
(2 Oct)	Bosa, who is venerated on earth, as he rejoices on the heights of Olympus,
	wishes to have the 2nd of October solemn.
(3)	And it falls to the twin Ewalds to be worshipped on the 3rd.
(10)	The master Paulinus rightly marks out the 10th.
(18)	Luke the teacher is to be remembered on the 18th. 65
(28)	Let us pay reverence to Simon and Jude on the 28th.
(1 Nov)	As a jewel worn on the brow sparkles time and again, so November
	at its beginning is resplendent with the praise given to all the saints.
(11)	Martin ascended above the stars on the 11th.

Appendix 2

70   Quindecimis uitam finiuit Tecla kalendis. |
       Caecilia astra merito decimis cum laude migrauit.   Tr fol. 89v
       Clementis laeti ueneramur festa nouenis.
       Octauis Crysogonus ouat uitalibus armis.
       Andreas pridias iuste ueneratur ab orbe.
75   Tres decimas adiit iam Ignatius aeque kalendis.
       Bis senis caelum coepit conscendere Thomas.
       Octauis Dominus natus de Uirgine casta.
       Martyrio Stephanus septenis alma petiuit.
       Bis ternis euangelicus scriptor penetrauit
80   Angelico uectus tutamine uirgo Iohannes.
       Martyrio *tenera* prostrantur milia quinis.
       Siluestrem pridias celebramus ab orbe uerendum.

70 Quindecimis] Quindecimas Tr
71 migrauit] migrabat V
75 Tres decimas] Tredecimas Tr
75 iam Ignatius] Ignatius iam Tr
81 tenera] teneran V; tenerant Tr; emended PL W
82 Siluestrem] Silvestrum Tr

Metrical Calendar of York

(17)   Thecla finished her life on the 17th.   70
(22)   Cecilia deservedly left for heaven with praise on the 22nd.
(23)   We happily venerate Clement's feast on the 23rd.
(24)   Chrysogonus in his mighty armour rejoices on the 24th.
(30)   Andrew is properly venerated round the world the day before (the 1st of Dec).
(20 Dec) On the 20th (of Dec), similarly, Ignatius departed.   75
(21)   Thomas began to ascend to heaven on the 21st.
(25)   The Lord was born from the immaculate Virgin on the 25th.
(26)   Through martyrdom, Stephen sought his reward on the 26th.
(27)   On the 27th, the evangelist reached heaven,
         the innocent John, borne by the protection of the angels.   80
(28)   Through martyrdom, thousands of infants were overthrown on the 28th.
(31)   We celebrate the Reverend Silvester, who is to be honoured throughout the world on the day before (the 1st of Jan).

Appendix 2

Commentary

In parentheses at the end of each entry, it is indicated which feast is mentioned in which works and/or calendars. For more information about the notations adopted there, see the note at the beginning of the Commentary to the verse *Menologium*. As regards the feasts mentioned in the verse *Menologium*, see also the Commentary to the poem.

1. The feast of the Circumcision of Jesus on 1 January. Latin metrical calendars, following the framework of the Roman year beginning with New Year's Day, usually begin with this feast, whereas the first entry of the prose and the verse *Menologium*, following a different scheme, is Christmas on 25 December. The Circumcision alone is mentioned here, while the verse *Menologium* mentions only the naming of Christ on his eighth day. (VM, MCH, MCR, ÆCHom I, *OEM*, Calendars 1, 4, 6–9, 11–13, 14–16, 17–21, 22, 23, 24, 25, 27)
2. The Epiphany on 6 January. (VM, MCH, MCR, ÆCHom I, ÆCHom II, *OEM*, Calendars 1, 4–9, 11–13, 14–16, 17–22, 23, 24, 25, 26, 27)
3. The feast of St Paul of Thebes on 10 January. According to *Vita Pauli primi eremitae* by St Jerome, St Paul fled from the Decian or Valerian persecution (*c.* 250–*c.*260) into the Theban desert when he was still quite young and lived in a cave until he was 113. As reflected in the phrase *deserti ... primus ... accola* 'the first inhabitant of the desert', he is regarded as the first Christian hermit and is known as St Paul the First Hermit or of the Desert. Anglo-Saxon calendars often refer to him as *Sancti Pauli primi heremite* 'St Paul the first hermit' (MCH, *OEM*, Calendars 4, 6, 7, 9, 11–15, 17–25, 27)
4. The feast of St Anthony the Great on 17 January. He was an Egyptian ascetic who went into the wilderness *c.* 270–1. Together with St Paul of Thebes mentioned in the previous line, he is one of the earliest Christian ascetic hermits and is the best known among the Desert Fathers. There is a well known life of the saint by Athanasius of Alexandria (d. 373) (MCH, MCR, *OEM*, Calendars 1, 4, 6, 7, 9, 11–25, 27)
5. The feast of St Sebastian on 20 January. He was martyred during the persecution of Diocletian c. 288. (MCH, MCR, *OEM*, Calendars 1, 4–9, 11, 12, 13–20, 21, 22–7)
6. The feast of St Agnes of Rome on 21 January. Suffering in her early teens *c.* 304, she was one of the most highly venerated virgin martyrs, and is quite often referred to as *Sancte Agnetis uirginis* 'St Agnes the virgin' in Anglo-Saxon calendars. The words *meritis mundo fulgentibus* 'merits conspicuous to the world' may refer to her virginity and faith unshaken even under torture. (MCH, MCR, *OEM*, Calendars (1), 4–9, 11, 12, 13–27)
7. The feast of St Anastasius of Persia (d. 628) on 22 January. The feast of St Vincent on the same day, which is marked as a high feast in calendars 11 and 20, is much more frequently listed in Anglo-Saxon calendars, while the feast of St

Anastasius is listed less frequently and is never marked as a high feast. (MCH, *OEM*, Calendars 4, 6, 7, 13, 27)

8. The feast of St Polycarp on 1 February. He was a bishop of Smyrna and was martyred in the mid second century. His feast is included only very sparingly in Anglo-Saxon calendars, whereas the feast of St Brigid on the same day is much more frequently listed. MCH mentions Brigid rather than Polycarp, while MCR lists both. (MCR, Calendars 1, 4, 6, 13)

9. The Presentation of Jesus at the Temple on 2 February. The presentation of Jesus alone is mentioned here (based on Luke 2.22), as well as in the verse *Menologium* 21b–2. (VM, PM, MCH, MCR, ÆCHom I, Calendars 4, 5, 6, 7, 8, 9, 11–13, 14–16, 17–24, 25, 26, 27)

10. The feast of St Agatha of Sicily on 5 February. Together with St Agnes, who is mentioned in line 6, Agatha was one of the most highly venerated virgin martyrs, suffering *c.* 251. Her identity as a virgin is almost always mentioned in Anglo-Saxon calendars listing this saint. (MCH, MCR, Calendars 1, 4–9, 11, 12, 13–20, 21, 22–7)

11. The feast of St Valentine on 14 February. Nothing certain is known about this saint. (MCH, MCR, Calendars (1), 4–9, 12, 13, 15–25, 27)

12. The feast of St Juliana of Nicomedia on 16 February. She is said to have been martyred during the Diocletian persecution in the early fourth century. There is an Old English poetic account of her martyrdom, *Juliana*, which is attributed to Cynewulf and is uniquely preserved in the Exeter Book. (MCH, MCR, Calendars 1, 6–9, 11–25, 27)

13. The feast of St Mathias (d. *c.* 80) on 24 February. According to the Acts of the Apostles 1.12–26, he was chosen as an apostle by the eleven apostles to replace Judas Iscariot. PL and W emend *merito* to *meriti*. (VM, PM, MCH, MCR, Calendars 4–7, 9, 11, 12, 13–15, 16–22, 23, 24, 25–7)

14. The feast of St Gregory the Great (*c.* 540–604) on 12 March. He was highly venerated as their apostle by the Anglo-Saxons, as is noted in the Commentary to the verse *Menologium* lines 37b–40a. However, as well as many other major saints, he is treated only very briefly in this poem, while more words tend to be appropriated for minor Northumbrian saints, as in the cases of Egbert (20–1), Wilfrid I (22–3), Wilfrid II (24–5), Tatberht (30–1) and Bosa (61–2), some of whom are never mentioned in the extant Anglo-Saxon calendars. (VM, PM, MCH, MCR, ÆCHom II, *OEM*, Calendars 1, 4–7, 8, 9, 11, 12, 13–15, 16–25, 27)

15. The feast of St Cuthbert (d. 687) on 20 March. This is the first of the eight feasts of Northumbrian saints mentioned in this poem. Among those saints, he is the only one widely venerated and is mentioned in both MCH and MCR. He is also mentioned in the prose *Menologium* but not in the verse. Blair writes that the saint 'occurs in many late Anglo-Saxon litanies' and 'the cult is prominent in the later medieval Scandinavian liturgical sources' ('A Handlist of Anglo-Saxon Saints', p. 521). His life is recorded by Bede both in prose and verse, while an anonymous monk also wrote his life in prose. See Colgrave, *Two Lives*. See also

Appendix 2

HE IV.27–32. (PM, MCH, MCR, ÆCHom II, *OEM*, Calendars 1, 4, 6, 7, 8, 9, 11, 12, 13, 14–16, 17–21, 22, 23, 24, 25, 27)

16. The feast of St Benedict of Nursia (*c.* 480–*c.* 547) on 21 March. (VM, PM, MCH, MCR, ÆCHom II, *OEM*, Calendars 1, 4–9, 11, 12, 13–16, 17–21, 22, 23, 24, 25, 27)

17. The feast of the Annunciation on 25 March. (VM, PM, MCH, MCR, ÆCHom I, *OEM*, Calendars 4–7, 8, 9, 11, 12, 13–16, 17–22, 23, 24, 25, 27)

18–19. The feast of St George (d. 303) on 23 April. The phrase *Carnifices ... uincente* 'by overcoming executioners' may reflect the fact that St George was a soldier in the Roman army and was venerated as a military saint. The tale about his fight with the dragon seems of later origin, dating back only to the age of the Crusades. (MCH, MCR, *OEM*, Calendars 4–9, 11–16, 17, 18, 19, 20–5, 27)

20–1. The feast of St Egbert of Ripon (d. 729) on 24 April. This is the second of the eight feasts of Northumbrian saints mentioned in this poem. The saint is known to have sent St Willibrord, St Wigbert and others to Friesland to convert the pagans there. His feast is never mentioned in the extant Anglo-Saxon calendars, MCH, MCR or *OEM*, but is known from Bede's *HE* III.27, V.9, 22, and Æthelwulf's *De Abbatibus* 113–82.

22–3. The feast of St Wilfrid I of York (d. 709–10) on 24 April. This is the third of the eight feasts of Northumbrian saints mentioned in this poem. The saint is known to have advocated the Roman liturgical tradition at the synod of Whitby in 664. Though appointed as bishop of Northumbria in the same year, he was a controversial figure. He acquired many enemies, including Abbess Hild of Whitby and King Ecgfrith, by the latter of whom he was expelled from his see in 678, was later imprisoned and was eventually exiled. After his return to Northumbria on the authority of King Aldfrith, he was again expelled by the same king in 691. According to Blair, the saint 'occurs in five late Anglo-Saxon litanies' ('A Handlist of Anglo-Saxon Saints', pp. 559–60). His life is recorded in Bede, *HE* III.25, Eddius Stephanus,*Vita S. Wilfridi*, Frithegod of Canterbury, *Breviloquium vitae Wilfridi*, and Eadmer, *Vita S. Wilfridi*. (*OEM*, Calendars 4, 6, 12, 16, 18, 22)

24–5. The feast of St Wilfrid II of York on 29 April. This is the fourth of the eight feasts of Northumbrian saints mentioned in this poem. The phrase *Tempore posterior* 'following in time' shows that Wilfrid II (reigned 714?–32, d. 745–6) is a later bishop than his namesake Wilfrid I (d. 709–10) mentioned in line 22. According to Lapidge, Wilfrid II 'was ... remembered with great affection at York', and 'in particular, Alcuin in his poem on the saints of York devoted an extensive account to his benefactions' ('Wilfrid II'). The words *morum non flore secundus* 'second to none in the flower of his virtues' may reflect such high esteem of him in York. His feast is never mentioned in the extant Anglo-Saxon calendars, MCH, MCR or *OEM*. See *HE* IV.23, and Alcuin, *The Bishops, Kings and Saints of York* 94–8.

26–7. The feast of SS James (d. *c.* 62) and Philip (d. *c.* 80) on 1 May. These saints are both apostles and their identity as such is expressed by the phrase used for the former, *seruus domini pius* 'the pious servant of the Lord'. Cf. the phrase used for them, *modige magoþegnas* 'brave thegns (of the Lord)', in the verse *Menologium* 82a. Cf. also *nergendes þegen* 'the Saviour's thegn' used for Mathias the Apostle in the verse *Menologium* 26b. As here and in the prose and the verse *Menologium*, these saints are nearly always mentioned together in the extant Anglo-Saxon calendars, while Philip alone is mentioned in the *Old English Martyrology*. (VM, PM, MCH, MCR, ÆCHom II, Calendars 1, 4, 5, 6, 7–9, 11–12, 13–16, 17–21, 22, 23, 24, 25, 26)

28. The feast of St Pancras of Rome (d. 304) on 12 May. He is mentioned as *insons* 'guiltless, innocent' perhaps because he is said to have been only fourteen years old when he was beheaded for his faith. (MCH, *OEM*, Calendars 1, 3–18, 20–25, 27)

29. The feast of St Mark the Evangelist on 18 May. The usual date of the feast is 25 April as in calendars 6, 8, (9), 11, 12, 13–15, 16, 17, 18–20, 21–25, but it is listed against 18 May in several Anglo-Saxon calendars. MCY follows the latter tradition. (Calendars 3, 6, 7, 9, 25, 27)

30–1. The feast of St Tatberht on 5 June. This is the fifth of the eight feasts of the Northumbrian saints mentioned in this poem. He was the successor of Wilfrid I as abbot of Ripon in the early eighth century. His feast is never mentioned in the extant Anglo-Saxon calendars, MCH, MCR or *OEM*. His name is mentioned in the *Chronicle of Hugh Candidus* 55.

32–3. The feast of St Boniface (*c.* 675–754) on 5 June. Born and educated in Wessex, he is known to have evangelised Germany and have become the first archbishop of Mainz. He was martyred with fifty-two other missionaries in the Netherlands in 754. The words *uincens ... hostes ... fortis bellator* 'a mighty warrior victorious over enemies' may reflect his brave and successful missionary works among pagans on the Continent. He is known as the author of *Ars grammatica*, *Ars metrica* and twenty *enigmata*, while many of his letters are extant. The earliest life of St Boniface was written by an Anglo-Saxon priest Willibald in the latter half of the eighth century. (Calendars (3), 4, 6, 7, 9–25, 27)

34. The feast of St Barnabas on 10 June. In the extant Anglo-Saxon calendars, his feast is listed more often against 11 June, as in calendars 3, 9, (10), 11, 12, 14–16, 17, 18–20, 21, 22–25, 27. (MCH, *OEM*, Calendars 4, 6?, 13)

35–6. The feast of SS Gervasius and Protasius on 19 June. These two saints, suffering on the same day probably in the second century, are said to be twins, whose parents were also martyrs. The date of 19 June is that of the translation of their relics rather than of their deaths. (MCH, MCR, *OEM*, Calendars (1), 3–5, 7–25, 27)

37–8. The Nativity of St John the Baptist on 24 June. Line 38 could also be interpreted as 'his Nativity, by people by beautiful, festive applauding'. (VM, PM, MCH, MCR, ÆCHom I, *OEM*, Calendars 1, 3, 4, 5–7, 8, 9, 10, 11, 12, 13–16, 17–20, (21), 22–5, 27)

39. The feast of SS John and Paul on 26 June. They are Roman martyrs, and not apostles. (MCH, MCR, *OEM*, Calendars 1, 4–11, 13–15, 16, 17, 18–25, 27)

40–1. The feast of SS Peter the Apostle and Paul the Apostle on 29 June. The

Appendix 2

word *Doctores* 'teachers' (of the gospel of Christ) reflects the saints' identity as apostles. St Paul mentions himself as a *praedicator* 'herald', *apostolus* 'apostle' and *doctor gentium* 'teacher of the people' in I Timothy 2.7. SS Peter and Paul were two of the most important figures in the Apostolic Age and this may be why it is said *Maxima quos palma clarat sibi lumina mundus* 'the world illuminates the illustrious men with the greatest honour'. (VM, MCH, MCR, ÆCHom I, *OEM*, Calendars 1, 4–6, 8, 10, 11, 13–16, 17, 19–24, (25), 27)

42–3. The feast of St James the Great on 25 July. He was the son of Zebedee and a brother of St John the Apostle. Here, as well as in the prose *Menologium*, he is mentioned as a brother of St John, whereas he is referred to as a son of Zebedee in the verse *Menologium* 136a. (VM, PM, MCH, MCR, ÆCHom II, *OEM*, Calendars 1, 2, 4–7, 8, 9–13, 14–16, 17–19, 20, 21–25, 27)

44. The feast of SS Abdon and Sennen on 30 July. They are said to be Persian martyrs who suffered *c*. 250, but not much is known about them. (MCH, MCR, *OEM*, Calendars (1), 4–16, 17, 18–25, 27; calendar 4 lists it against 31 July)

45. The feast of St Sixtus II on 6 August. He was a pope when he was martyred with six deacons during the Valerian persecution in 258. (MCH, MCR, *OEM*, Calendars 1, 2, 4–25, 27)

46. The feast of St Laurence of Rome on 10 August. He was ordained a deacon under Pope Sixtus II mentioned in the previous line, and was martyred a few days later than the pope and other six deacons in the Valerian persecution in 258. (VM, PM, MCH, MCR, ÆCHom I, *OEM*, Calendars 1, 2, 4–12, 13–16, 17–25, 27)

47–8. The Assumption of the Virgin Mary on 15 August. (VM, PM, MCH, MCR, ÆCHom I, ÆCHom II, *OEM*, Calendars 4, 5, 6, 7, 8, 9–13, 14, 15, 16–25, 27)

49. The feast of St Bartholomew the Apostle on 25 August. (VM, PM, MCH, MCR, ÆCHom I, *OEM*, Calendars 1, 2, 4, 5, 6, 7, 8, 9, 12, 13–15, 16–20, 22, 24, 25, 27; MCH and calendar 25 list it against 24 August)

50. The Decollation of St John the Baptist on 29 August. The word *passus* '(the one who) suffered' implies his martyrdom on this day. The nativity of the same saint is referred to in lines 37–8. (VM, PM, MCH, MCR, ÆCHom I, *OEM*, Calendars 1, 2, 4–7, 8, 9, 10, 11, 12, 13–15, 16–19, 20, 21, 22, 23, 24, 25, 27)

51–2. The Nativity of the Virgin Mary on 8 September. (VM, PM, MCH, MCR, *OEM*, Calendars 1, 4, 5, 6, 7, 8, 9, 11–13, 14–16, 17–25, 27; calendar 1 lists it against 9 September)

53–4. The feast of SS Cornelius and Cyprian on 14 September. Cornelius (d. 253) and Cyprian (d. 258) share the same day as their feast, but the former died five years earlier than the latter; the phrase *ordine digno* 'the appropriate order' seems to refer to the order of their deaths. They actually died on different days, although St Jerome writes they 'suffered on the same day in different years' (see Chapman, 'Pope Cornelius'). PL and W emend *consecrauit* to *consecrat* and add *simul* after *Cyprianus*, in which case, *ordine digno* may mean differently. (MCH, *OEM*, Calendars 1, 2, 5–9, 11, 12, 14, 15, 17–25)

55. The feast of St Euphemia on 16 September. She was martyred in the early fourth century. Her identity as a consecrated virgin is reflected in the word *intemerata* 'chaste'. (MCH, *OEM*, Calendars 1, 4–8, 11–18, 19, 20–25)

56. The feast of St Matthew the Apostle and Evangelist on 21 September. The phrase *doctor amoenus* 'the delightful teacher' seems to reflect his identity as an apostle and evangelist. Cf. the case of SS Peter and Paul mentioned as *doctores* 'teachers' in line 40, and that of St Luke the Evangelist mentioned as a *doctor* in line 65. Cf. also the case of St John the Evangelist, for whom the word *euangelicus* 'evangelist' is used in line 79. (VM, PM, MCH, MCR, ÆCHom II, *OEM*, Calendars 1, 2, 4–7, 8, 9, 11, 12, 13–16, 17–19, 20, 21, 22, 23, 24, 25, 27)

57. The feast of St Maurice on 22 September. He was a leader of the Theban Legion. It is said that he did not follow the order of Emperor Maximilian to attack Christians and was persecuted and martyred with 6666 members of the legion in 287. Some Anglo-Saxon calendars list the feast in such a manner as follows: *Sancti Mauricii cum sociis. vi millibus. DC. LXVI* 'St Maurice with 6666 companions'. Thus the phrase *cum milibus* 'with thousands (of people)' refers roughly to the number of those martyred with him. (MCH, MCR, *OEM*, Calendars 1, 2, 4–9, 11–18, 19, 20–25)

58. The feast of SS Cosmas and Damian on 27 September. They were twins and were martyred together in *c*. 287, during the persecution under Diocletian. Cf. SS Gervasius and Protasius mentioned in lines 35–6. (MCH, MCR, *OEM*, Calendars 1, 2, 4–9, 11–25, 27)

59. The feast of St Michael the Archangel on 29 September. The feast is known as the Dedication of St Michael's Church, which is here referred to as *Michahelis ... templi dedicatio* 'the dedication of the Temple of Michael'. In Anglo-Saxon calendars, the feast is often mentioned as *Dedicatio Sancti Michahelis archangeli* 'the Dedication of St Michael the Archangel', *Dedicatio ecclesie Michaelis* 'the Dedication of St Michael's church', *Dedicatio Basilice sancti Michaelis* 'the Dedication of St Michael's Basilica', etc. (VM, PM, MCH, MCR, *OEM*, Calendars (1), 2, 4–9, 11, 12, 13–16, 17–22, 23, 24, 25, 27)

60. The feast of St Jerome on 30 September. He is best known as the translator of the Bible and is referred to as a *bonus ... interpres* 'good translator'. PL and W emend *At* to *Atque*. Cf. *At* in line 63, which they retain. (MCH, MCR, *OEM*, Calendars (1), 2, 4–9, 11, 12, 13–15, 17–20, 21, 22, 23–25, 27)

61–2. The feast of St Bosa of York (d. 706) on 2 October. This is the sixth of the eight feasts of the Northumbrian saints mentioned in this poem. Educated at Whitby under Abbess Hild, he was later appointed bishop of York. This feast is never mentioned in the extant Anglo-Saxon calendars, MCH, MCR or *OEM*, and Blair writes that '*MCY* seems to be the only evidence for a pre-Conquest cult' of the saint ('A Handlist of Anglo-Saxon Saints', p. 518).

63. The feast of the two Hewalds on 3 October. The two Hewalds are Northumbrian saints and are distinguished as Hewald the Black and Hewald the Fair. They engaged in missionary works in Germany and were martyred there *c*. 692. Blair writes that their 'careers were abroad' and their 'shrines and cult sites were outside England', and omits them from his 'Handlist' ('A Handlist of

Appendix 2

Anglo-Saxon Saints', p. 495). Their feast is mentioned only very sparingly in Anglo-Saxon calendars. (*OEM*, Calendars 25, 27)

64. The feast of St Paulinus of York (d. 644) on 10 October. This is the last of the eight feasts of the Northumbrian saints mentioned in this poem. Italian by birth, he was sent to Kent to support Augustine by Gregory I in 601. Consecrated the first bishop of York in 625, he went to Northumbria, where he converted King Edwin and others. For his life, see *HE* II.9–20, III.1, 14 (MCH, Calendars 4, 6, 7, 9, 13–19, 21–24)

65. The feast of St Luke the Evangelist on 18 October. As in the case of St Matthew in line 56, his identity as an evangelist may be reflected in the word *doctor* 'teacher'. Cf. the case of St John the Evangelist, for whom the word *euangelicus* 'evangelist' is used in line 79. Cf. also the case of SS Peter and Paul, who are referred to as *doctores* 'teachers' in line 40. (MCH, MCR, *OEM*, Calendars 1, 2, 4, (6), 7–9, 11, 12, 13–16, 17, 18–25, 27; MCH lists it against 17 October)

66. The feast of SS Simon and Jude on 28 October. Juxtaposed with *Simonis*, *Iudas* seems intended as a genitive form as it often happens in Old English texts. See the section treating the declensions of foreign words in the *Menologium* above. PL and W emend *Iudas* to *Iudae*. (VM, PM, MCH, ÆCHom II, *OEM*, Calendars 1, 2, 4–7, 8, 9, 11, 12, 13–15, 16–19, 20, 21–24, 25, 27)

67–8. All Saints' Day on 1 November. (VM, PM, MCH, MCR, ÆCHom I, *OEM*, Calendars 4, 5, 6, 7–9, 11, 12, 13–16, 17–25, 27)

69. The feast of St Martin of Tours (*c.* 316–97) on 11 November. (VM, PM, MCH, MCR, ÆCHom II, *OEM*, Calendars (1), 4–7, 8, 9, 11, 12, 13–16, 17–22, 23, 24, 25, 27)

70. The feast of St Thecla on 17 November. As a first-century virgin martyr, she is always mentioned as a virgin in the few Anglo-Saxon calendars listing her. (Calendars (1), 4, 6, 7, 13, 22)

71. The feast of St Cecilia on 22 November. She is a second-century virgin saint and is nearly always mentioned as such in Anglo-Saxon calendars listing her. (MCH, MCR, *OEM*, Calendars 1, 4–9, 11, 12, 13–25, 27)

72. The feast of St Clement on 23 November. (VM, PM, MCH, MCR, ÆCHom I, *OEM*, Calendars 1, 4, 5–7, 8, 9, 11, 12, 13–16, 18, 19, 20, 21, 22, 23, 24, 25, 27)

73. The feast of St Chrysogonus on 24 November. He was martyred in the Roman city of Aquileia probably in the early fourth century and was buried and venerated there. (MCH, MCR, *OEM*, Calendars (1), 4–7, 9, 11–25, 27)

74. The feast of St Andrew the Apostle on 30 November. (VM, PM, MCH, MCR, ÆCHom I, *OEM*, Calendars 1, 4, 5–9, 11, 12, 13–16, 17–22, 23, 24, 25, 27)

75. The feast of St Ignatius on 20 December. This feast is listed only very sparingly in Anglo-Saxon calendars. (Calendars 1, 6, (19))

76. The feast of St Thomas on 21 December. (VM, PM, MCH, MCR, *OEM*, Calendars 1, 4, 5–7, 8, 9, 11, 12, 13–16, 17–22, 23, 24, 25, 27)

Metrical Calendar of York

77. The Nativity of Christ on 25 December. (VM, PM, MCH, MCR, ÆCHom I, ÆCHom II, *OEM*, Calendars 1, 4–9, 11, 12, 13, 14, 15, 16–25, 27)

78. The feast of St Stephen on 26 December. He was martyred in Jerusalem *c.* 43 and is traditionally known as the first Christian martyr. (MCH, MCR, ÆCHom I, ÆCHom II, *OEM*, Calendars 1, 4–7, 8, 9, 11, 12, 13–15, 16–19, 20, 21, 22, 23, 24, 25, 27)

79–80. The feast of St John the Apostle and Evangelist on 27 December. He is the son of Zebedee and the brother of St James the Great mentioned in lines 42–3. (MCH, MCR, ÆCHom I, *OEM*, Calendars 1, 4–7, 8, 9, 11, 12, 13–15, 16–18, 19, 20–22, 23, 24, 25, 27)

81. Holy Innocents' Day on 28 December. The feast commemorates those young male children killed at the behest of Herod the Great (reigned 37 BC–4 BC). For the account of the massacre, see Matthew 2.16–18. Some Anglo-Saxon calendars refer to them as *Sanctorum cxliiii milia innocentum* '144,000 holy innocents'. (MCH, ÆCHom I, *OEM*, Calendars 1, 4–7, 8, 9, 11, 12, 13–16, 17–19, 20, 21, 22, 23, 24, 25, 27)

82. The feast of St Silvester I (reigned 314–35) on 31 December. He was the pope when the first Council of Nicaea was held in 325, but not much is known about him. (MCH, MCR, *OEM*, Calendars 1, 4, 5, 6–9, 12–20, 21, 22–5, 27)

Appendix 3
Félire Adamnáin

Félire Adamnáin, since it was first regarded by Hennig as an Old Irish counterpart of the *Menologium*, has sometimes been compared with the poem, although as I have discussed above, the two seem to have little in common. I include it here in an appendix since neither its text nor English translation is readily accessible, which may have hindered due comparison. The following text and English translation are both based on M. E. Byrne's published in *Eriu* 1 (1904), pp. 225-8, with some changes in the overall layout.

    Incipit feleire Adamnain dia math*air* hic.

1   Noimh nac ceithre raithe   dutracht lim a nguidhe
     Romsaerat ar phiana   noimh na bliadhna huile.

2   Naoimh ind erraigh errdairc   lim do deoin Dé daltait
     Im Brighit noigh niodhaim   im Grighair im Pattraicc.

3   Naimh int samraidh tirim   impa ata mo baile
     On tírsa co tíssa   co hÍssa m*a*c Maire.

4   Naimh ind foghmair álainn   ailim drong nad dichéol
     Co tísat im gaire   im Maire is im Michéol.

5   Naimh in geimridh guidim   lium fri drongu demhna
     Im Iosa na nionat   in spirat naemh nemhdha.

6   In feilire naemhsa   bias ag sruithibh sáeraibh
     Cipsa lia do randaib   nocha lia do naemhaibh.

7   Aitcim naoim in talman   aitchim aingle ile
     Aitchim Dia fodeine   fo eirge is fo lighe
     Cia denar cia therar   co trebhar tir nimhe.

Félire Adamnáin

Here begins *the Saints' Calendar of Adamnan* to his mother.

1. The saints of the four seasons, I long to pray to them, may they save me from torments, the saints of the whole year!

2. The saints of the glorious spring-time, may they be with me by the will of God's fosterling, together with Brigid, a maiden pure, with Gregory and Patrick.

3. The saints of the dry summer, about them is my poetic frenzy, that I may come from this land to Jesus, Son of Mary.

4. The saints of the beauteous autumn, — I call upon a company not inharmonious, that they may come near me, together with Mary and Michael.

5. The saints of the winter I pray to, may they be with me against the throngs of demons, around Jesus of the mansions, the holy, heavenly spirit.

6. This saints' calendar [*i.e.*, the calendar of Oengus], which noble sages will have, though more numerous in verses, it is not more numerous in saints.

7. I beseech the saints of the earth, I beseech all the angels, I beseech God Himself, both rising and lying down, whate'er I do or whate'er I say, that I may inhabit the heavenly land.

Appendix 4
Enlaith betha

The Old Irish poem *Enlaith betha*, probably of ninth-century origin, is a poem narrating the yearly cyclic activities of some birds and animals and includes the 'theme of the praise of the Creator by Nature'.[1] Hennig regards it, together with *Félire Adamnáin*, as an Old Irish counterpart of the *Menologium*,[2] and it has sometimes been compared with the poem. The following text and English translation are based on Best and Lawlor's edition in *The Martyrology of Tallaght*, pp. 94–7. The commentary to the English translation is mine. A new translation is available in Riordan (2014), pp. 19–20.

    E(nlaith) betha brig cen tair
       is ar fálti frisin gréin.
    Hi n*oi*n enair cipsi uair.
       congair a sluaig din chaill chéir.

5   I n-*ocht calaind* ap*r*eil áin
    tecait fainnli f*r*ia nglan dail
    t*r*aig ardd (i   ) (c)id (n)osceil
    i n-*ocht calaind* octimb*i*r.

    I feil Ruadain rád cen dis
10   [is] and oslaicther a nglais
    hi *sechtmad déc calaind* mái
       dogair in chúi din chaill chaiss.

    Hi n*oi*n iúil anait eoin
       (do chantain) ch(iui)l lith lathi
15   conait chet bí
    do Mail Ruain o Thamlacti.

    Hi feil Ciarain m*ei*c in tsaer
       tecait giugraind dar fairge uair
    I feil Ciprian condelgg n-oll
20   (geis)id da(m) (do)nd din rái réid.

---

[1] Greeson, 'Two Old English Observance Poems', p. 102.
[2] Hennig, 'The Irish Counterparts'.

Enlaith betha

The birds of the world, power without ill,
    'tis to welcome the sun.
On January's nones, whatever hour it be,
the cry of the host from the dark wood.

On the eighth of the calends of noble April
the swallows come on their pure tryst
. . . . . , what hides them?
on the eighth of the calends of October.

On the festival of Rúadán, no petty saying,
their fetters are then unloosed.
On the seventeenth of the calends of May
the cuckoo calls from the pleasant wood.

On the nones of July the birds cease
to sing the music of holydays
. . . .
for Máel Rúain from Tamlachta.

On the festival of Cíarán, son of the wright,
wild geese come over the cold sea.
On the festival of Cyprian, a great counsel,
the brown stag bells from the ruddy field.

Appendix 4

Tri fichit c*et* mbl*iadna* mbán
 amser in domuin cen len.
memais trethan dar ca*ch* n-airm
 i ndeud aidchi im gairm na n-én. E.

25 (At)nagat co*m*bi*n*ni cheóil
 ind eoin fri rig nime nél
ic admolad ind rig reil
 coistid cleir na n-én do chéin. E.

Enlaith betha

Three score hundred fair years,
the world's age, without sorrow,
the ocean will burst over every place
at the end of the night, at the call of the birds.

Melodious music the birds perform
to the king of the heaven of clouds,
praising the radiant king.
Hark from afar to the choir of the birds.

Appendix 4

Commentary

3. January's nones is 5 January, the day before Epiphany.

4. The wood is dark (*din chaill chéir* 'the dark wood') because it is before the 'coming' of Christ on the next day (i.e. the Epiphany), who seems to be compared to the sun in this stanza. Cf. *din chaill chaiss* 'the pleasant wood' in the third stanza.

5. The eighth of the calends of noble April is 25 March, or Annunciation Day, on which the vernal equinox falls, according to the original Julian calendar. April is said to be *áin* 'noble' probably because it is the month in which Easter is most often held. No other month-names in this poem are modified by any adjective.

8. The eighth of the calends of October is 24 September, or the day of the conception of St John the Baptist, on which the autumnal equinox falls, according to the original Julian calendar.

9. The festival of Rúadán falls on 15 April.

11. The seventeenth of the calends of May is 15 April.

12. The cuckoo was the bird of summer, which is also the case among the Anglo-Saxons and the Norse. E.g., *sumeres weard* in *The Seafarer* 54a and the passage in *Guthlac A* 742–5. See also Alcuin's *Versus de cuculo* and *Conflictus versis et hiemis*. Cf. also *gaukmanuðr* 'cuckoo-month', a name of the first summer month covering from mid-April to mid-May mentioned in Snorri's *Skáldskaparmál*. Cf. also *gaukmessa* 'cuckoo-mass' referring to the first of May. As regards the cuckoo in Old English poetry and some other related literary traditions, see Gordon, ed., *The Seafarer*, pp. 17–18.

12. Cf. *din chaill chéir* 'the dark wood' in the first stanza.

13. The nones of July is 7 July.

16. The feast of St Máel Rúain falls on 7 July, which is referred to at the beginning of this stanza.

17. The festival of Cíarán falls on 9 September.

19. The festival of Cyprian falls on 14 September.

Appendix 5
List of Anglo-Saxon Calendars

The following information, as well as the classification numbers, of the twenty-seven extant Anglo-Saxon calendars is based chiefly on Rushforth, *Saints in English Kalendars before A.D. 1100*, and partly on Gneuss, *Handlist*. The following list contains: the manuscript and folio numbers; date; probable place of origin; catalogue number in Ker, *Catalogue*, Gneuss, *Handlist* and/or Lapidge, *Anglo-Saxon Litanies*; editions available if any. If the item is edited in Wormald, *English Kalendars before A.D. 1100*, its classification number in the edition is given with the editor's name, as in Wormald 3. A brief comment regarding the relationship with other calendars may be added at the end of each item, based on the aforementioned book(s) by Rushforth and/or Wormald.

1. Paris, Bibliothèque Nationale, latin 10837, 34v–40r; early eighth century; Echternach; Gneuss 897; Wilson, *The Calendar of St Willibrord*.
2. Hauzenstein near Regensburg, Gräflich Walderdorffsche Bibliothek, s.n.; mid eighth century; Northumbria; Gneuss 791; Siffrin, 'Das Walderdorffer Kalenderfragment'. It is a fragment consisting of the entries for July to October.
3. Munich, Hauptstaatsarchiv, Raritäten-Selekt 108; eighth century; Northumbria or some Continental house with Insular connections; Gneuss 855.5; Lowe, *Codices Latini Antiquiores*, vol. 9, p. 1236, Bauerreis, 'Ein angelsächsisches Kalenderfragment', and Gamber, *Das Bonifatius-Sakramentar*. It is a fragment consisting of the entries for 3–20 May and 4–24 June.
4. Oxford, Bodleian Library, Digby 63 (S.C. 1664), 40r–45v; *c.* 867? or 892?; Northumbria? (manuscript *c.* 1000), probably at the Old Minster, Winchester; Ker 319, Gneuss 611; Wormald 1.
5. Oxford, Bodleian Library, Junius 27 (S.C. 5139), 2r–7v; 920s; Winchester or Canterbury?; Ker 335, Gneuss 641; Dumville, *Liturgy and the Ecclesiastical History*, pp. 1–38. It may share a source with two New Minster calendars, i.e., calendars 14 and 23, while it is similar to calendar 9 in the choice of high-grade feasts.
6. Salisbury, Cathedral Library, 150, 3r–8v; 969–987; Sherborne? or Shaftesbury?; Ker 379, Gneuss 740, Lapidge XLIII; Wormald 2. Wormald links the text of this calendar with that of no. 16.
7. Oxford, Bodleian Library, Bodley 579 (S.C. 2675), 39r–44v; 979–987; Glastonbury? or Canterbury?; Ker 315, Gneuss 585, Lapidge XXIX; Wormald 4; Warren, *The Leofric Missal*, pp. 23–34; Orchard, *The Leofric*

Appendix 5

Missal II, pp. 57–68. According to Wormald, the text of this calendar is at the centre of a group consisting of calendars 7, 9, 13 and 27. Digitised images of the manuscript are available online at http://image.ox.ac.uk/show?collection=bodleian&manuscript=msbodl579.
8. Paris, Bibliothèque Nationale, latin 7299, 3v–9r; late tenth century; England (with additions and alterations at Fleury in the eleventh century); Gneuss 888.
9. London, British Library, Additional 37517, 2r–3r; late tenth or early eleventh century (988–1008); Christ Church, Canterbury; Ker 129, Gneuss 291, Lapidge X; Wormald 5. It is closely related to no. 7, while, according to Wormald, it belongs to a group also consisting of calendars 13 and 27.
10. Paris, Bibliothèque Nationale, latin 10062, 162r–3v; early eleventh century; Christ Church, Canterbury; Gneuss 895; Ebersperger, *Die angelsächsischen Handschriften,* no. 21, pp. 85, 118–28. It is a fragment consisting of the entries for May to August.
11. London, British Library, Arundel 155, 2r–7v; 1012–1023; Christ Church, Canterbury; Ker 135, Gneuss 306, Lapidge XIII; Wormald 13.
12. Rouen, Bibliothèque Municipale, Y.6 (274), 6r–11v; early eleventh century; Peterborough? or Canterbury?; Ker 377, Gneuss 921, Lapidge XL, Wormald 15; Wilson, *The Missal of Robert of Jumièges,* pp. 9–20. Wormald links it with no. 22.
13. Cambridge, University Library, Kk.v.32 (2074), 50r–55v; 1012–1030 (1021 or 1022?); Canterbury; Ker 26, Gneuss 26; Wormald 6. Wormald links it with nos. 7, 9 and 27.
14. London, British Library, Cotton Titus D.xxvii, 3r–8v; second quarter of the eleventh century; New Minster, Winchester; Ker 202, Gneuss 380, Lapidge XXI; Wormald 9. It is closely related to no. 15.
15. Cambridge, Trinity College, R.15.32 (945), pp. 15–26; 1035/36; Ker 90, Gneuss 186; Wormald 10. It is closely related to no. 14.
16. London, British Library, Cotton Nero A.ii, 3r–8v; 1029–46; Leominster; Ker 157, Gneuss 342, Lapidge XVI; Wormald 3; Gasquet and Bishop, *The Bosworth Psalter,* pp. 165–71; Muir, *A Pre-conquest English Prayer-book,* pp. 3–14. Wormald links the text of this calendar with that of no. 6.
17. Oxford, Bodleian Library, Douce 296 (S.C. 21870), 1r–6v; mid eleventh century; Crowland; Gneuss 617, Lapidge XXXII; Wormald 20.
18. Rome, Vatican Library, Reg. Lat. 12, 7r–12v; 1030s? mid eleventh century, probably the third quarter? before 1064?; Christ Church, Canterbury, for the use of Bury St Edmunds; Gneuss 912, Lapidge XLV; Wormald 19.
19. Cambridge, Corpus Christi College, 422, pp. 29–40; middle of the eleventh century, *c.* 1061–63?; New Minster, Winchester for the use of Sherborne?; Ker 70B, Gneuss 111, Lapidge VIII; Wormald 14.
20. Cambridge, Corpus Christi College, 9, pp. 3–14; 1032–1062?; Worcester?; Ker 29, Gneuss 36; Wormald 18.
21. Cambridge, Corpus Christi College, 391, pp. 3–14; third quarter of the eleventh century; Worcester; Ker 67, Gneuss 104, Lapidge VI; Wormald 17.

22. Oxford, Bodleian Library, Hatton 113 (S.C. 5210), iii r–viii v; 1064–1095; Evesham? or Worcester; Ker 331, Gneuss 637; Wormald 16. Wormald links it with no. 12.
23. London, British Library, Cotton Vitellius E.xviii, 2r–7v; mid eleventh century (around 1031? or 1062?); New Minster, Winchester; Ker 224, Gneuss 407; Wormald 12. It is similar to calendars 14, 15 and 24.
24. London, British Library, Arundel 60, 2r–7v; 1060–1087; New Minster, Winchester; Ker 134, Gneuss 304, Lapidge XII; Wormald 11. It is very similar to calendars 14 and 23.
25. London, British Library, Cotton Vitellius A.xviii, 3r–8v; second half of the eleventh century; south-west England (Canterbury, Sherborne, Winchester, Glastonbury?); Gneuss 400; Wormald 8.
26. London, British Library, Egerton 3314, 18v–30r; late eleventh century or early twelfth (1073–1076?); Christ Church, Canterbury; Gneuss 411. Rushforth writes that 'the names of saints ... were filled in only in the tables for January and February' (p. 52).
27. London, British Library, Cotton Vitellius A.xii, 65v–71r; late eleventh century; Salisbury; Gneuss 398; Wormald 7. The text of this calendar is very similar to that of no. 7, and Wormald groups it with calendars 7, 9 and 13.

Appendix 6
Immovable Feasts Marked in Anglo-Saxon Calendars

Many Anglo-Saxon calendars mark important immovable feasts by the sign of the cross, the letter F,[1] by capital and/or coloured letters, or by a metrical entry. The following table lists which calendars mark which feasts in which manners. The number in the leftmost column corresponds to the classification number of the extant Anglo-Saxon calendars indicated in Appendix 5 above. I exclude calendars 1, 14 and 15, since they do not mark any feast,[2] while I also exclude calendars 2, 3, 10 and 26, since they are highly fragmentary (for details, see Appendix 5 above). I shall use the following symbols, letters and their combinations to indicate the manners of marking in each calendar:

†	marking by the sign of the cross
†c	marking by the sign of the cross and coloured letters
†C	marking by the sign of the cross and capital letters
†cC	marking by the sign of the cross and coloured capital letters
c	marking by coloured letters
C	marking by capital letters
F	marking by the letter F
FC	marking by the letter F and capital letters
FcC	marking by the letter F and coloured capital letters
M	marking by a metrical entry

At the bottom of each page, there are three rows indicating whether or not each feast is mentioned in the prose *Menologium* (PM), the verse *Menologium* (VM) and the 'Metrical Calendar of York' (MCY), the oldest and shortest of Latin metrical calendars. The feasts in square brackets are not marked in any calendar but are included in the table because they are mentioned either in the prose and the verse *Menologium* or in the MCY. The prose and the verse *Menologium*, whose entries are very similar, cover most of the feasts frequently marked while excluding all the feasts marked only sparingly with two exceptions (for details,

---

[1] I exclude feasts marked by the letter S, which seems to mark less important feasts than those marked by the letter F. See Warren, *The Leofric Missal*, p. xlv; and Rushforth, *Saints in English Kalendars*, p. 25. Regarding calendar 12, where higher feasts and second-class ones seem to be distinguished by different letter styles, I follow the criterion shown in Wilson, ed., *The Missal of Robert of Jumièges*, p. xxii.

[2] Calendar 14 marks Ascension (5 May) by the letter F, which may not be authentic as Wormald prints 'F(?)' in his edition of the calendar. See Wormald, *English Kalendars*, p. 118.

Immovable Feasts

see the Introduction above). On the other hand, MCY, while excluding several feasts very frequently marked, includes many feasts marked only sparingly and also several of those never marked. The close affinity in the choice of entries between the prose and the verse *Menologium* may reveal their close relationship, while the large difference observed in the MCY reflects that it differs not only in its scope but also in its purpose and nature. It is also noteworthy that the set of important feasts in calendar 7 is very close to the sets of entries of the prose and the verse *Menologium*.

In the following table, I shall use the following abbreviations:

Ap	Apostle
Aps	Apostles
Bapt	Baptist
Conv	Conversion
Decoll	Decollation
Ded	Dedication
Ev	Evangelist
Inv	Invention
Mart	Martyr
Nat	Nativity
Oct	Octave
Ord	Ordination
Tr	Translation
Ttl	Total

Appendix 6

Calendar number	Circumcision (1 Jan)	Epiphany (6 Jan)	Wulfsige (8 Jan)	Hadrian (9 Jan)	Tr of Judoc (9 Jan)	Oct of Epiphany (13 Jan)	[Paul the Hermit (10 Jan)]	[Anthony the Great (17 Jan)]	Fabian (20 Jan)	Sebastian (20 Jan)	[Agnes (21 Jan)]	Vincent (22 Jan)
4	†	†										
5		M										
6	†	†										
7	FC	FC										
8	C	cC										
9	FC	FC		F								
11	C	C										C
12	cC	cC										
13	C	†c										
16												
17	cC	cC										
18	cC	cC										
19	C	FC	FC		FC	C						
20	C	C			C							C
21	C	cC			C				C	C		
22		cC										
23	C											
24	†cC	†cC			†							
25												
27	C											
Ttl	16	16	1	1	4	1	0	0	1	1	0	2
PM	-	-	-	-	-	-	-	-	-	-	-	-
VM	+	+	-	-	-	-	-	-	-	-	-	-
MCY	+	+	-	-	-	-	+	+	-	+	+	-

Immovable Feasts

Calendar number	[Anastasius of Persia (22 Jan)]	Tr of Hiurmin (24 Jan)	Conv of Paul (25 Jan)	[Polycarp (1 Feb)]	Purification (2 Feb)	Wærburga (3 Feb)	Agatha of Sicily (5 Feb)	[Valentine (14 Feb)]	Devil Left Lord (15 Feb)	Tr of Botulph (15 Feb)	[Juliana (16 Feb)]
4					†						
5					M						
6											
7					FC						
8											
9					FC						
11			C		C						
12					cC						
13			†		†cC				c		
16											
17					cC						
18		cC	C		cC					cC	
19			C		FC						
20					C						
21			C		†C	(C)	C				
22					C	C					
23					C						
24					†C						
25											
27									cC		
Ttl	0	1	5	0	15	2	1	0	2	1	0
PM	-	-	-	-	+	-	-	-	-	-	-
VM	-	-	-	-	+	-	-	-	-	-	-
MCY	+	-	-	+	+	-	+	+	-	-	+

Appendix 6

Calendar number	Chair of St Peter (22 Feb)	Mathias Ap (24 Feb)	Oswald (28 Feb)	Felix (8 March)	Gregory (12 March)	Edward Mart (17/18 March)	Cuthbert (20 March)	Benedict of Nursia (21 March)	Annunciation (25 March)	Resurrection (27 March)	Tr of Edmund (30 March)	Tr of Edmund (31 March)
4		†			†		†	†	†			
5		M			M			M	M			
6		†			†		†	†	†			
7		FC			FC		FC	FC	FC			
8							C		C			
9		FC			FC	F	FC	FC	F			
11		C			C	C		C	C			
12		cC			cC	cC	cC	cC	cC	cC		
13						†						
16	c	c			c							
17	C	cC			cC	cC	cC	cC	cC			
18	C	cC		cC	cC	C	cC	cC	C	C	cC	cC
19	FC	FC			FC	FC	FC	FC	FC			
20	C	C			C	C	C	C	C	C		
21	C	C	†C		C	C	C	C	C	C		
22		C	C		C				C	C		
23					C				C			
24		†C			†C	C	†C	†C	†C	C		
25					†							
27												
Ttl	6	15	2	1	17	9	12	14	15	7	1	1
PM	-	+	-	-	+	-	+	+	+	-	-	-
VM	-	+	-	-	+	-	-	+	+	-	-	-
MCY	-	+	-	-	+	-	+	+	+	-	-	-

Immovable Feasts

Calendar number	Guthlac (11 April)	Tr of Oswald (15 April)	Ælfheah (19 April)	Rufus (19 April)	George (23 April)	Wilfrid I of York (24 April)	[Ecgberht of Ripon (24 April)]	Major Rogation (25 April)	Mark Ev (25 April)	[Wilfrid II of York (29 April)]	Philip and James Aps (1 May)
4						†					†
5											
6											†
7	FC							FC			FC
8											
9	FC										
11											C
12											cC
13											
16									c		
17	cC				C				C		cC
18								cC			cC
19			F		FC						FC
20			C								C
21		C	†C								C
22		C	C								
23											
24											†C
25			†	†							†
27											
Ttl	3	2	5	1	2	1	0	2	2	0	12
PM	-	-	-	-	-	-	-	+	-	-	+
VM	-	-	-	-	-	-	-	+	-	-	+
MCY	-	-	-	-	+	+	+	-	-	+	+

Appendix 6

Calendar number	Invention of the Cross (3 May)	Alexander and Eventius (3 May)	Ascension (4/5 May)	John of Beverley (7 May)	Tr of Martin (11 May)	[Pancras (12 May)]	[Mark Ev (18 May)]	Dunstan (19 May)	Potentiana (19 May)	Augustine of Canterbury (26 May)	Bede (26 May)	[Tatberht of Ripon (5 June)]
4	†			†						†		
5	M									M		
6	†									†		
7	FC									FC		
8												
9	FC							FC		FC		
11								C				
12	cC									cC		
13			cC									
16			c									
17								cC		cC		
18	C							†C				
19	FC	C	cC					FC	FC	F	F	
20			C		c					C	C	
21	C							C		C		
22												
23												
24								C		†C		
25	†							†	†	†		
27												
Ttl	10	1	4	1	1	0	0	8	2	12	2	0
PM	+	-	-	-	-	-	-	-	-	+	-	-
VM	+	-	-	-	-	-	-	-	-	+	-	-
MCY	-	-	-	-	-	+	+	-	-	-	-	+

Immovable Feasts

Calendar number	[Boniface (5 June)]	Barnabas (11 June)	Basilius (14 June)	Eadburga (15 June)	Vitus (15 June)	Botulph (17 June)	[Gervasius and Protasius (19 June)]	James Ap (22 June)	Alban (22 June)	Æthelthryth (23 June)	Nat of John Bapt (24 June)
4								†	†		
5											M
6								†	†	†	†
7											FC
8											
9									F		FC
11											C
12											cC
13				†	†						
16											
17		C	C	C		C			C	C	cC
18						C				C	cC
19											FC
20											C
21		C									†(C)
22											C
23											C
24				†							†cC
25											†
27											
Ttl	0	2	1	3	1	2	0	2	4	3	15
PM	-	-	-	-	-	-	-	-	-	-	+
VM	-	-	-	-	-	-	-	-	-	-	+
MCY	+	+	-	-	-	-	+	-	-	-	+

Appendix 6

Calendar number	John and Paul (26 June)	Peter and Paul Aps (29 June)	Peter Ap (29 June)	Paul Ap (30 June)	Swithun (2 July)	Tr & Ord of Martin of Tours (4 July)	Grimbald (8 July)	Ælfgifu (10 July)	Tr of Benedict of Nursia (11 July)	Tr of Swithun (15 July)	Kenelm (17 July)	Margaret of Antioch (20 July)
4		†		†								
5		M										
6		†		†	†							
7			FC	FC								
8		C		C					C			
9			FC	FC								
11		C		C					C			
12			cC	cC								
13											C	
16		†										
17	C	cC		cC	C	C			cC			cC
18			cC	cC	cC				C			
19		FC		FC	C		C		C			
20		C		C								
21		†C		†C	†C				C	C	†	
22		C			C				C		C	
23		C										
24		†cC		†cC		†		†				
25			†?	†								
27								C				
Ttl	1	13	5	14	5	3	1	2	7	1	3	1
PM	-	-	+	+	-	-	-	-	-	-	-	-
VM	-	+	-	-	-	-	-	-	-	-	-	-
MCY	+	+	-	-	-	-	-	-	-	-	-	-

Immovable Feasts

Calendar number	Mary Magdalen (22 July)	Christina (24 July)	James the Greater, Ap (25 July)	Christopher (25 July)	Abdon and Sennes (30 July)	St Peter's Chains (1 Aug)	Maccabees (1 Aug)	[Lammas Day (1 Aug)]	Inv of Stephen (3 Aug)	Oswald (5 Aug)	[Pope Sixtus II (6 Aug)]
4			†							†	
5			M								
6			†	†							
7			FC								
8											
9			FC								
11			C								
12			cC								
13			†				†				
16											
17	C	C	cC		C				C	C	
18			c	c		C					
19	C		FC			FC	FC				
20											
21			C							C	
22			C							C	
23			C	C							
24			†C								
25			†	†							
27											
Ttl	2	1	16	4	1	2	2	0	1	4	0
PM	-	-	+	-	-	-	-	+	-	-	-
VM	-	-	+	-	-	-	-	+	-	-	-
MCY	-	-	+	-	+	-	-	-	-	-	+

Appendix 6

Calendar number	Laurence (10 Aug)	Assumption (15 Aug)	Oct of Laurence (17 Aug)	Credan (19 Aug)	Audoen (24 Aug)	Bartholomew Ap (24/25 Aug)	Augustine of Hippo (28 Aug)	Decoll of John Bapt (29 Aug)	Sabina (29 Aug)	Tr of Guthlac (30 Aug)	Tr of Cuthbert (4 Sept)
4	†	†				†		†			
5	M	M						M			
6	†							†			
7	FC	FC				FC		FC			
8	C										
9	FC	FC				FC		FC			
11	C	C									
12	cC	cC				cC		cC			
13		c									
16		†				†		†			
17	cC	cC			C	cC	C	C		C	
18	cC	cC				cC		C			
19	FC	FC	C			F		FC			C
20	C	C				C					
21	C	C						C			
22	C	cC	C	C		C		C			C
23	C	C							C		
24	†C	†cC				C		C			
25	†	†			†	†					
27		C									
Ttl	17	18	2	1	2	12	1	13	1	1	2
PM	+	+	-	-	-	+	-	+	-	-	-
VM	+	+	-	-	-	+	-	+	-	-	-
MCY	+	+	-	-	-	+	-	+	-	-	-

Immovable Feasts

Calendar number	Tr of Birinus (4 Sept)	Nat of Mary (8 Sept)	Hadrian (8 Sept)	Tr of Ecgwine (10 Sept)	Holy Cross Day (14 Sept)	[Cornelius & Cyprian (14 Sept)]	Euphemia (16 Sept)	Geminianus (16 Sept)	Matthew Ap (21 Sept)	Maurice (22 Sept)	[Cosmas & Damian (27 Sept)]
4		†							†		
5		M							M		
6									†		
7		FC							FC		
8											
9		FC							FC		
11		C							C		
12		cC							cC		
13		cC			†						
16											
17		cC							cC		
18		cC							c		
19		FC	FC				FC	FC	FC	C	
20		C									
21	C	†C							C		
22		cC	c	cC					C		
23		C									
24		†cC							†cC		
25		†	†						†		
27		C									
Ttl	1	17	3	1	1	0	1	1	14	1	0
PM	-	+	-	-	-	-	-	-	+	-	-
VM	-	+	-	-	-	-	-	-	+	-	-
MCY	-	+	-	-	-	+	+	-	+	+	+

175

Appendix 6

Calendar number	Michael the Archangel (29 Sept)	Jerome (30 Sept)	[Bosa of York (2 Oct)]	[Two Hewalds (3 Oct)]	Pope Mark (7 Oct)	Osgytha (7 Oct)	Dionisius (9 Oct)	[Paulinus of York (10 Oct)]	Tr of Ecgwine (10 Oct)	Tr of Æthelthryth (17 Oct)	Luke Ev (18 Oct)	Justus (18 Oct)
4	†											
5	M											
6	†											
7	FC											
8	C											
9	FC											
11	C											
12	cC											
13												
16												
17	cC				C						C	C
18	cC						C			cC		
19	FC											
20	C											
21	C	†										
22	cC	†C				C			C			
23												
24	†cC											
25	†											
27												
Ttl	16	2	0	0	1	1	1	0	1	1	1	1
PM	+	-	-	-	-	-	-	-	-	-	-	-
VM	+	-	-	-	-	-	-	-	-	-	-	-
MCY	+	+	+	+	-	-	-	+	-	-	+	-

Immovable Feasts

Calendar number	Ded of Mary & Edmund (18 Oct)	Simon and Jude Aps (28 Oct)	Ord of Swithun (30 Oct)	All Saints' Day (1 Nov)	Caesarius (1 Nov)	Eustachius (2 Nov)	Martin of Tours (11 Nov)	Menna (11 Nov)	Bricius (13 Nov)	Tecla (17 Nov)	Edmund Mart (20 Nov)	[Caecilia (22 Nov)]
4		†		†			†					
5		M					M					
6		†					†	†				
7		FC		FC			FC					
8				C								
9		FC		FC			FC					
11		C		C			C					
12		cC		cC			cC					
13												
16		†										
17		cC		cC			cC		C		C	
18	cC	cC		cC		C	cC		†C		cC	
19		FC		FC			FC	FC				
20				C			C	C				
21		C		†C			†C	C				
22		C	C	C			C			c		
23		C		C								
24		†cC		†cC			†cC	†cC				
25				†	†		†	†				
27				cC								
Ttl	1	15	1	16	1	1	15	4	4	1	2	0
PM	-	+	-	+	-	-	+	-	-	-	-	-
VM	-	+	-	+	-	-	+	-	-	-	-	-
MCY	-	+	-	+	-	-	+	-	-	+	-	+

Appendix 6

Calendar number	Clement (23 Nov)	Felicitas (23 Nov)	[Chrysogonus (24 Nov)]	Andrew Ap (30 Nov)	Tr of Benedict (4 Dec)	Nicholas (6 Dec)	Oct of Andrew Ap (7 Dec)	Conception of Mary (8 Dec)	Judoc (13 Dec)	Lucy and Judoc (13 Dec)	[Ignatius of Antioch (20 Dec)]
4	†			†							
5	M			M							
6	†			†							
7	FC			FC							
8				C	C						
9	FC			FC							
11	C			C							
12	cC			cC							
13											
16											
17				cC	C	C	C				
18	†C			cC							
19	FC			FC							
20				C							
21	†C			†C				C	C		
22				C	C	C					
23											
24	†C			†cC		cC				†	
25	†	†		†							
27											
Ttl	12	1	0	16	3	3	1	1	1	1	0
PM	+	-	-	+	-	-	-	-	-	-	-
VM	+	-	-	+	-	-	-	-	-	-	-
MCY	+	-	+	+	-	-	-	-	-	-	+

Immovable Feasts

Calendar number	Thomas Ap (21 Dec)	Christmas (25 Dec)	Anastasia (25 Dec)	Stephen the First Mart (26 Dec)	John Ap and Ev (27 Dec)	Holy Innocents (28 Dec)	Ecgwine (30 Dec)	Silvester I (31 Dec)	Total
4	†	†		†	†	†			36
5	M	M		M	M	M		M	27
6	†	†		†	†	†			33
7	FC	FcC		FcC	FcC	FcC			34
8		C							13
9	FC	FcC	Fc	FcC	F	FcC			37
11	C	cC		cC	cC	cC			32
12	cC	cC		cC	cC	cC			34
13		cC	cC						17
16		†		†	†				13
17	cC	cC		cC	cC	cC	C		63
18	†cC	cC		cC	cC	cC			54
19	FC	FC		FC		C			54
20	C	C			C		C		35
21	C	cC		C	cC	C		C	56
22	C	cC	c	cC	cC	cC	cC		45
23		C							15
24	†C	†cC		†cC	†cC	†cC			41
25	†	†C		†	†	†			33
27		cC		cC	cC	cC			10
Ttl	15	20	3	16	16	15	3	2	
PM	+	+	-	-	-	-	-	-	29
VM	+	+	-	-	-	-	-	-	29
MCY	+	+	-	+	+	+	-	+	65

Appendix 7
Vigils in Anglo-Saxon Calendars

The following table reveals which vigils are listed in which calendars. Parentheses mean later additions. The bottom row shows which vigils are mentioned in PMC. Grey cells mean the absence of references to the corresponding feasts in PMC.

Calendar number	V of Epiphany (1/5)	V of Purification (2/1)	V of Mathias (2/23)	V of John Bapt (6/23)	V of Peter & Paul (6/28)	V of Paul (6/29)	V of James (7/24)	V of Laurence (8/9)	V of Assumption (8/14)	V of Bartholomew (8/24)	V of Nat of Mary (9/7)	V of Matthew (9/20)	V of Simon & Jude (10/27)	V of All Saints' Day (10/31)	V of Andrew (11/29)	V of Thomas (12/20)	V of Christmas (12/24)	Total
4	-	-	-	+	+	-	-	+	-	-	-	-	+	-	+	-	+	6
5	-	-	-	+	+	-	-	+	-	-	-	-	-	-	+	-	-	4
6	+	-	-	+	+	-	-	+	-	-	-	-	+	+	+	-	+	8
7	-	-	-	+	+	-	-	+	-	-	-	+	+	+	+	-	+	8
8	+	-	-	+	+	-	-	+	+	-	-	-	-	-	-	-	-	5
9	-	-	-	+	+	-	-	+	+	-	-	+	+	-	+	-	+	8
11	-	-	-	+	+	-	-	+	+	-	-	+	+	+	+	-	+	9
12	-	-	-	+	+	-	-	+	-	+	+	+	+	+	+	-	-	9
13	-	-	-	+	+	-	-	+	+	-	-	+	+	-	+	-	+	8
14	-	-	-	+	+	-	+	+	+	+	+	+	+	-	+	-	+	11
15	-	-	-	+	+	-	+	+	+	+	-	+	+	+	+	-	+	11
16	-	-	-	-	-	-	-	+	+	-	-	+	+	+	+	-	-	6
17	-	+	+	+	+	-	+	+	+	+	-	+	+	-	+	+	+	13
18	-	-	-	+	+	-	-	+	+	+	-	+	+	+	+	+	-	10
19	-	-	-	+	+	-	+	+	+	-	-	-	+	+	+	+	+	10
20	-	-	-	+	+	-	+	+	-	+	+	+	+	-	+	+	+	11
21	-	+	-	+	+	-	+	+	+	(+)	-	+	+	+	+	+	+	13
22	+	+	+	+	+	-	+	+	+	+	+	+	+	+	+	+	+	16
23	-	-	-	+	+	-	-	+	+	-	-	+	+	+	+	+	+	10
24	-	-	-	+	+	-	+	+	+	-	+	+	+	+	+	+	+	12
25	-	-	-	+	+	-	+	+	+	+	-	+	+	+	+	+	+	12
27	-	-	-	+	+	-	+	+	-	+	-	+	+	+	+	+	+	11
Ttl	3	3	2	21	21	0	11	23	16	11	5	18	21	15	22	11	17	
PM		-	-		+	+	+	+	+	-	+	+	+	+	+	+	-	10

Appendix 8
Dates of the Solar Turning Points in Anglo-Saxon Calendars

Calendar number	Vernal Equinox				Summer Solstice		Autumnal Equinox			Winter Solstice	
	21 March	22 March	24 March	25 March	20 June	24 June	20 Sept	21 Sept	24 Sept	21 Dec	25 Dec
4	-	-	+	-	+	-	-	-	+	+	-
5	+	-	-	-	-	-	-	-	+	+	-
6	-	-	-	+	+	-	-	-	+	+	-
7	-	-	-	+	-	+	-	-	+	-	+
8	-	-	-	-	+	+	-	-	-	-	-
9	+	-	-	-	+	+	-	-	+	-	+
11	+	-	-	+	+	-	-	-	+	+	-
12	+	-	-	-	+	-	-	-	+	-	-
13	+	-	-	-	-	-	-	-	+	-	-
14	+	-	-	-	+	-	+	-	-	+	-
15	+	-	-	-	+	-	+	-	-	+	-
16	-	-	-	-	+	+	-	+	-	+	-
17	+	-	-	-	-	-	-	+	+	-	-
18	+	-	-	-	+	-	-	-	+	-	-
19	+	-	-	+	+	+	+	-	+	+	+
20	+	-	-	-	-	-	-	+	-	-	-
21	-	-	-	-	-	-	-	+	+	-	-
22	+	-	-	-	+	-	+	-	-	+	-
23	+	-	-	-	+	+	-	+	+	-	+
24	+	-	-	-	+	-	+	-	-	-	-
25	+	-	-	-	-	-	-	-	-	-	-
27	-	+	-	-	-	+	-	-	+	-	+
Ttl	15	1	1	4	14	7	5	5	14	9	5
PM	+	-	-	-	-	+	-	-	+	-	+
VM	+	-	-	-	-	+	-	-	+	-	+

Appendix 9
Latin and Old English Month-Names in the Old English Written Tradition and in the Verse *Menologium*

The verse *Menologium* presents one of the few instances of heavy use of Old English month-names, and Imelmann summarises a brief history of English month-names in his edition of the poem.[1] Together with Chapter 15 of Bede's *De temporum ratione*, where the origins of the vernacular month-names are explained, the poem is also sometimes mentioned in studies related to Old English month-names.[2] However, the background of the dual use of Latin and Old English month-names in the poem has not been examined, which is why I shall discuss the issue here in an appendix. The issue has much to do with how the two sets of month-names were conceived and used in Old English writings in late Anglo-Saxon England, and therefore, I shall first survey the use of Latin and Old English month-names in the Old English written tradition.

The issue is also interesting since it is related to the problem of the replacement of the vernacular month-names by the Latin ones in Old English. It seems worth examining since our knowledge about the issue is limited. It is not known when Latin month-names replaced vernacular ones; some suggest that the replacement had already been completed by the time of Bede,[3] but as I shall argue below, written evidence suggests otherwise, and the native terms were still current at the end of the tenth century, when the *Menologium* was composed, and even in the eleventh century. As we shall see, Latin month-names, as learned terms, first began to be used among literate people, while vernacular ones seem to have lingered especially in colloquial contexts among the less learned at least until the first half of the eleventh century, since they are used as glosses for their Latin equivalents in the eleventh-century calendar in Cambridge, Corpus Christi College, MS 422.[4] The dual use of month-names in the verse *Menologium* may also have something to do with the difference in vocabulary between the learned and the less learned. Yet before drawing any conclusion, it is necessary to know

---

[1] Imelmann, *Das altenglische Menologium*, pp. 45–52.
[2] See, for instance, Weinhold, *Die deutsche Monatsnamen*; and Schneider, 'The OE. Names of the Months', pp. 260–75.
[3] See, for instance, Page, 'Anglo-Saxon Paganism', p. 128; Wallis, *Bede: The Reckoning of Time*, p. 287; and Blake, ed., *Ælfric's De Temporibus Anni*, p. 113.
[4] The manuscript contains the prose *Menologium*. For further information about the manuscript, its contents and its intended users, see pp. 26–7 above.

how these two sets of month-names coexisted or were segregated from each other in the latter half of the tenth century.

Latin and Vernacular Month-Names in the Old English Written Tradition: An Overview

Throughout the Old English corpus, the Latin month-names are much more frequently used than the vernacular ones.[5] One of the earliest examples of a Latin month-name used in Old English writings is recorded in Cynewulf's *Elene*, probably composed in the early ninth century: *on maius monað* (1228a) 'in the month of May'.[6] In the *Old English Martyrology* composed in the ninth century,[7] all the Latin month-names but February are used.[8] They are also used in the Alfredian Bede (8x) and Boethius (1x), and in the *Leechbook* (1x), which is said to have been composed a little later than the time of King Alfred. Latin month-names are then found in the probably tenth-century *Herbarium Apuleii* (8x), the *Old English Benedictine Rule* (2x) translated after 960, the *Death of Edgar* (1x) recorded in the Anglo-Saxon Chronicle under the year 975, the late tenth-century verse *Menologium* (12x), Ælfric's *De temporibus anni*, *Catholic Homilies*, *Lives of Saints* and others (7x in total) composed in the late tenth century, the *Seasons for Fasting* (3x) composed around 1000, Byrhtferth's *Enchiridion* (some 166x) in the early eleventh century, various versions of the Anglo-Saxon Chronicle (5x), and various other minor works (some 179x in total).[9] Thus the Latin month-names are attested frequently and extensively in

---

5   Hereafter I shall consider the month-names used for purposes other than dating in the Roman reckoning, unless otherwise stated. This could be justified by the fact that Latin month-names used for the Roman reckoning, together with *kalendas*, *nonas* and *idus*, are always declined in accordance with Latin grammar (unless of course they are abbreviated), while when used for other purposes they usually follow various other ways of declension, most of which were invented for Latin loan-words in an attempt to integrate them into the Old English vocabulary. Thus Latin month-names used in the Roman reckoning and those used for other purposes were treated quite differently. As regards the various ways of declension, see Baker and Lapidge, ed., *Byrhtferth's Enchiridion*, pp. cii–cv; Baker, 'The Inflection of Latin Nouns', pp. 187–206.
6   The word *monað* is abbreviated as *kł* in the manuscript. For details, see Sisam, *Studies*, pp. 14–15; and Gradon, ed., *Cynewulf's 'Elene'*, p. 70.
7   For its date, see Rauer, *The Old English Martyrology*, pp. 1–4.
8   The period from 25 January to 27 February is not recorded in any manuscript containing the work, which is why February is not used in this work. See Rauer, *The Old English Martyrology*, pp. 18–19 and also the table on page 23. See also Herzfeld, *An Old English Martyrology*, p. 32. On the other hand, the end of February is recorded, where its Old English counterpart, *Solmonað*, is used; the martyrologist always uses vernacular month-names when referring to a month for the second time. For details, see below.
9   I.e. BenR, BenRW, Comp 1.2.3, Comp 1.2.4, Comp 1.5, Comp 1.6, Comp 3.1, Comp 7, Comp 11.1.2, Comp11.2, Comp 11.3, Comp 12.1.2, Comp 12.2, Days 1.1, Days 1.2, Days 3.1, Days 3.2, Days 3.3, Days 4, Days 5.1, Days 5.2, Days 5.3, Days 5.4, Days 6, HomU 35.2, HomU 36, Med 3, LS 16, LS 23, Alexander's Letter to Aristotle, Prognostics, Gospel

Appendix 9

various writings in the vernacular from relatively early times to the late Old English period. According to my calculation, they occur some 412 times in all.

On the other hand, the number of attestations of the vernacular month-names is much smaller. The earliest extant instance of a vernacular month-name is said to be found in the preface to the Wihtræd's law promulgated in 696, in which the word *rugern* is used. This is a *hapax legomenon* and its meaning is not clear, but it is often considered to mean 'the month of the rye harvest', i.e. August.[10] The references to the Old English month-names in Bede's *De temporum ratione*, written around 725, are well known and probably the second oldest instances, but they are recorded in Latin passages and accordingly irrelevant for our purpose here. Vernacular month-names are also found in the *Old English Martyrology* (21x), *Leechbook* (1x), the verse *Menologium* (10x[11]), Ælfric's *Catholic Homilies* (1x), some glosses and glossaries, some tables juxtaposing the two sets of month-names (47x),[12] and various other minor works recorded in eleventh- or twelfth-century manuscripts (7x).[13]

The *Old English Martyrology* presents interesting examples of Latin and vernacular month-names, which may reflect their positions in Old English writings in the ninth century. At the beginning of each month, the martyrologist gives brief explanations of the month based seemingly on Bede's in *De temporum ratione*, as in the following example:

> On ðæm þriddan monðe on geare bið an ond þrittig daga. Ond se monð is nemned on Læden Martius, ond on ure geþeode Hredmonað.[14]
>
> (The Beginning of March)
>
> In the third month in the year there are one and thirty days, and the month is named in Latin *Martius* and in our language *Hredmonað*.

---

of Nicodemus, *Gerefa*, etc. As regards the title of these works, I basically followed the *DOE* short titles. In some cases, I indicate titles by which the text is better known.

[10] See Liebermann, ed., *Die Gesetze* III, p. 25; and Attenborough, ed., *The Laws of the Earliest English Kings*, p. 180. See also CH, under the heading of *rugern*. On the other hand, Whitelock considers it to mean September (Whitelock, *English Historical Documents*, p. 362, n. 1).

[11] I exclude *forma monað* (9a) used for January, regarding it as a phrase meaning 'the first month' rather than a month-name. I also exclude *se teoða monð* (181b) 'the tenth month' for the same reason.

[12] I.e., the table in ByrEnch (11x), OccGl 88 (i.e. the calendar glosses in CCCC 422) (11x), OccGl 95.2 (24x), and *Ælfric's Grammar* (1x). In Byrhtferth's *Enchiridion*, Old English month-names are indicated in a table juxtaposing Latin and Old English month-names, where all but the term for May appear. The term for May seems mistakenly to have dropped out. In addition, the term for November is mistakenly mentioned as *haligmonað*, which corresponds to September. The right term for November is *blotmonað*. See Baker and Lapidge, eds., *Byrhtferth's Enchiridion*, p. 24. A pair, i.e. *augustus-weodmonað*, does not appear in *OccGl 95.2*. *Ælfric's Grammar* includes only one pair, *september-hærfestmonað*.

[13] I.e., Days 3.2 (2x), Days 5.3 (2x), Days 6 (2x), and Notes 10.2 (1x).

[14] All the quotations of the *Old English Martyrology* are based on Rauer, ed., *The Old English Martyrology*. My translation.

It is noteworthy that in this kind of introductory passage Latin month-names are always used with the phrase *on Læden* 'in Latin' (except for the case of January), while vernacular ones are always used with *on ure geþeode* 'in our language'. Similarly, Latin, Greek and/or Hebrew counterparts of some important word or phrase are often indicated in this work, as in the following example:

> Se nama wæs on Iudisc Ihesus, ond on Grecisc Soter, ond on Læden Saluator, ond on ure geðeode Hælend. (1 January: Octave of Christ and Mary)

> The name was *Ihesus* in Hebrew, *Soter* in Greek, *Salvator* in Latin, and *Hælend* in our language.

The phrase *on Læden* used with the Latin month-names seems to be of basically the same nature, indicating the foreign nature of the month-names. This is supported by the fact that when the month-names are mentioned for the second time at the end of each month, only the Old English ones are mentioned, as in the following instance:

> Ðonne se Hreðmonað bið agan, þonne bið seo niht twelf tida lang, ond se dæg þæt ilce. (The End of March)

> When the *Hreðmonað* has passed, then the night is twelve hours long and the day the same.

Thus in the *Old English Martyrology*, vernacular month-names are predominant, while Latin ones are treated as foreign words rather than words integrated fully into Old English vocabulary. It seems probable, therefore, that they had not yet replaced vernacular ones by the second half of the ninth century, when the *Old English Martyrology* was probably composed.

A similar example is found in a more or less contemporary work, the *Leechbook*, which is considered to have been composed around the time of King Alfred:[15]

> Eft ifig croppena on þam monðe gegaderod þe we hatað ianuarius on læden and on englisc se æftera geola fif and XX. and pipores eac swa gegnid þonne mid þy selestan wine and gehæte sele þam seocan men neahtnestigum drincan.[16]
> (*Leechbook* 214.18–22)

> Again gather ivy of five and twenty bunches in the month which we call *ianuarius* in Latin and in English the *æftera geola*, and of pepper as much, rub then with the best wine, and heat (it and) give (it) to the sick man to drink after a night's fasting.

---

[15] As regards the date of composition, see Fulk and Cain, *A History of Old English Literature*, p. 156. See also Greenfield and Calder, *A New Critical History of Old English Literature*, p. 117; Anderson, *The Literature of the Anglo-Saxons*, p. 295; and Pollington, *Leechcraft*, p. 71.

[16] This passage is quoted from Cockayne, ed., *Leechdoms* II, p. 214. My translation.

This is the only instance of month-names in this work. Here again, the Latin month-name is used with the phrase *on Læden* 'in Latin' and the vernacular one with *on englisc* 'in English'.

These instances reveal that until near the end of the ninth century vernacular month-names were still among the living vocabulary of written Old English, while Latin ones were not yet so highly integrated as to replace the native ones. At the same time, however, the fact that not only vernacular month-names but also Latin ones are mentioned (especially in the *Leechbook*) may well suggest the gradual rise of the latter, which may well have triggered the gradual decline of the former in the following centuries, as observed in the statistical data above.

From the tenth century onwards, Latin month-names are usually used alone independently of their vernacular counterparts, except for the cases of glosses, glossaries, and tables juxtaposing Old English and Latin month-names, and their Latin origin is rarely mentioned, which may well reflect the high degree of their integration into the Old English written vocabulary. Roughly speaking, therefore, Latin month-names became predominant in the tenth century, while vernacular ones continued to be used from time to time but sparingly. The question of how long the Old English month-names were used or when their replacement was completed is addressed in the next section.

Latin and Old English Month-Names in the Latter Half of the Tenth Century and Later

The overview outlined in the previous section chiefly reflects the situation in written Old English among the literate Anglo-Saxons. If we pay closer attention to the actual texts as we shall do here, however, we notice that the issue has another aspect; the use of Latin month-names seems to have been confined to a learned few, while the majority of people seem to have continued using in their spoken Old English the traditional, vernacular terms until a rather late period. If we take such a situation into consideration, it seems probable that the replacement was never completed in the Anglo-Saxon period, or even if it was, only in the latest period.

The difference in the use of the names for the months between the learned and others in the late Anglo-Saxon period is tellingly expressed in the following passage from Ælfric's *Catholic Homilies*:

> Nu heold þæt hebreisce folc þone forman geares dægi on lenctenlicere emnihte for þan ðe on þam dæge wurdon gearlice tida gesette; Se eahtateoða dæg þæs monðes þe we hatað martius þone ge hatað hlyda wæs se forma dæg þyssere worulde;[17] (ÆHom I.229.146–50)

---

[17] This passage is quoted from Clemoes, ed., *Ælfric's Catholic Homilies: The First Series, Text*, p. 229. My translation.

Now the Hebrew people hold the first day of the year on the vernal equinox because yearly times were set on the day. The eighteenth day of the month which we call *Martius*, and which you call *Hlyda*, was the first day of this world.'

We refers to the learned people represented by Ælfric, while *ge* refers to the readers/audience. As Ælfric himself reveals in the Old English preface to the first series of his *Catholic Homilies*, from which the passage is quoted, the work was intended for unlearned people who did not know Latin.[18] Thus this passage reveals that while Latin month-names were used among the learned, vernacular ones were still predominant among the unlearned at the close of the tenth century.

The following passage from the *Death of Edgar* recorded under the year 975 in the A, B and C manuscripts of the Anglo-Saxon Chronicle also reveals that the Latin month-names were still learned terms in the late tenth century, when the poem seems to have been composed:

> Nemnað leoda bearn
> men on moldan   þæne monað gehwær
> in ðisse eðeltyrf   þa þe ær wæran
> on rimcræfte   rihte getogene
> Iulius monoð   þæt se geonga gewat
> on þone eahteðan dæg   Eadgar of life
> beorna beahgyfa.[19]   (*Death of Edgar* 4b–10a)

Children of men, people on earth, who had been rightly educated in computus, call the month everywhere in this fatherland, the month of July, when the young Edgar, ring-giver of people, departed from life on the eighth day.

The statement '(those) who had been rightly educated in computus' implies that those without such education did not know or use the Latin month-name, which may well indicate that there was another set of month-names for the unlearned. The connection between the Latin month-names and education in computus (*rimcræft*), clearly stated here, is also important for our later discussion concerning the use of the Latin month-names in the *Menologium*, which is contemporary with this poem.

In the *Seasons for Fasting*, also probably more or less contemporary with the *Death of Edgar*,[20] the Latin month-names are also treated differently from ordinary, vernacular words:

---

[18] As regards the audience of his homilies (at Cerne Abbas) in relation to the *Catholic Homilies*, see also Wilcox, ed., *Ælfric's Prefaces*, p. 12.

[19] The quotation is based on Dobbie, ed., *The Anglo-Saxon Minor Poems*. My translation.

[20] Regarding the date of composition of the *Seasons for Fasting*, Dobbie considers it to have been composed in 'middle or late tenth century', Sisam 'the two decades which fall on either side of the year 1000', Greeson, following Sisam, 980–1020, and Richards the early eleventh century. See Dobbie, ed., *The Anglo-Saxon Minor Poems*, p. xciv; Sisam,

Appendix 9

> We þæt forme sceolan fæsten heowan
> on þære ærestan wucan lengtenes,
> on þam monþe þe man Martius
> geond Romwara rice nemneð, ...[21] (*Seasons for Fasting* 47–50)

> We must have the first fast in the first week of Lent, in the month which is named *Martius* throughout the empire of the Romans.

The lines *on þam monþe | þe man Martius || geond Romwara | rice nemneð* 'in the month which is named *Martius* throughout the empire of the Romans' reveal the month-name's foreign origin and seem to be of similar nature to the phrase *on Læden* 'in Latin' in the *Old English Martyrology* and the *Leechbook*. The reference to its Roman origin may well imply that the Latin month-name was not the only possible choice as well as that it was of learned nature in Old English in comparison with its vernacular equivalent. For the poet and/or the intended audience, the Latin month-name was felt to be clearly different from ordinary, vernacular words.

The poet's special treatment of Latin month-names as observed when he uses them for the second and third time may also reflect their special status in Old English writings/poems at the time of composition:

> on þam monþe, þæs þe me þinceð,
> þe man Iunius gearum nemde. (*Seasons for Fasting* 61–2)

> in the month which, as it seems to me, was formerly named *Iunius*.

> on þam monþe, mine gefræge,
> þe man September *** genemneð. (*Seasons for Fasting* 69–70)

> in the month which, according to hearsay, is named *September*.

In these passages, their Roman origin is not directly mentioned unlike the case of the first instance,[22] but they are always accompanied with such phrases as *me þinceð* 'methinks' and *mine gefræge* 'according to hearsay, I hear'. It seems these phrases are comparable with Ælfric's *we hatað* 'we call' in contrast with *ge hatað* 'you call' and may well reflect the poet's awareness of their foreign and/or learned nature. Thus the instances in the *Seasons for Fasting* may also support what I have argued above based on the examples in Ælfric's *Catholic Homilies* and the *Death of Edgar*.

A dual use of Latin and Old English month-names similar to that in Ælfric's

---

Studies, p. 50; Greeson, 'Two Old English Observance Poems', pp. 28–38; and Richards, *The Old English Poem Seasons for Fasting*, p. 35.

[21] All the passages of the *Seasons for Fasting* are quoted from Dobbie, ed., *The Anglo-Saxon Minor Poems*. My translations.

[22] It is noteworthy that in the first instance, the Roman origin is clearly stated, in the second instance, the Roman origin is much more covertly implied by *man ... gearum nemde* 'man formerly named', while in the third instance the locally and temporally distant origin of the Latin month-names is not mentioned at all.

Catholic Homilies and the *Leechbook* is attested in three versions of basically the same work in manuscripts made in the eleventh century:[23]

> þæt is se forma dæg on martio on hlydan monðe 7 se feorða dæg ærþam þe he on weg fa(reð)[24] (Days 5.3)
>
> that is the first day in March, (that is) in *Hlydanmonað*, and the fourth day before it goes away.

It seems probable that the vernacular name is intended to help readers understand its Latin counterpart immediately preceding it. Interestingly, however, from the next sentence onwards, Latin names alone are used, as in the following passage:

> On þam oðrum monðe þe we aprilis hatað. s(e) teoþa dæg is deri(gendlic) and se endlyfta dæg ær his utgange. (Days 5.3)
>
> In the next month which we call April, the tenth day is noxious and also the eleventh day from its end.

Similarly, all the months from May to December and January and February are mentioned only by their Latin names. This seems to be because, even if readers do not understand Latin month-names, based on the first instance of March/ *Hlyda*, it is quite easy to understand which month each name refers to; since they are arranged in month order. Once you know from which month the list begins, you can readily perceive which month comes next. This arrangement is made clear by *oðrum* 'next' in the quotation above. The use of the phrase *we hatað* 'we call', which can function in a similar way to the same phrase in Ælfric's above-quoted passage from *Catholic Homilies*, is also noteworthy. The relative pronoun clause including *we hatað* is used to refer to April and May, but when referring to June, the author simply writes *On Iuniusmonðe* 'in the month of June' without using the relative pronoun clause but with the word *monað* 'month' added to the Latin month-name. Then from July on, the author uses Latin month-names with neither the relative pronoun clause nor the word *monað*.

---

[23] The three manuscripts in question are: British Library, MS Cotton Caligula A.xv (xi med.; xi/xii); British Library, MS Cotton Vitellius E.xviii (xii; xi med. or xi[3/4]); and British Library, MS Harley 3271 (xi[1]). As regards the dates of the manuscripts, those by Ker are placed first in the parentheses and then by Gneuss, except for the case of Harley 3271, on whose date they agree with each other). See Ker, *Catalogue*; and Gneuss, *Handlist*. These variant texts are called 'Tables of Lucky and Unlucky Days' in the *DOEC*, and they are numbered as Days 3.2, Days 5.3 and Days 6, respectively. These texts are printed in Chardonnens, *Anglo-Saxon Prognostics*, pp. 370–2; Cockayne, ed., *Leechdoms* III, pp. 152–4; Förster, 'Die altenglischen Verzeichnisse von Glücks- und Unglückstagen'; and Henel, 'Altenglischer Mönchsaberglaube'. Days 6, recorded in Harley 3271, is entitled *DE DIEBUS MALIS* and precedes the prose *Menologium*, which is entitled *DE DIEBUS FESSTIS*.

[24] All the quotations of Days 5.3 are based on the edition in Chardonnens, *Anglo-Saxon Prognostics*, p. 371. My translation.

Appendix 9

After a series of information about unlucky days in each month, however, the dual use of Latin and Old English month-names appears again as in the following passage:

> We gesetton on foreweardan on þyssere endebyrd(nesse þone) monað Martius. þe menn hatað hlyda for(þam he is angin æfter) rihtum getele ealles þæs geares. (Days 5.3)

> We set at the beginning of this series (of information) the month of March, which is called *Hlyda*, because it is the beginning according to the right reckoning of the year.

This passage explains why the list begins with March, instead of January.[25] Thus this is an additional explanation of the list and is located outside the series of information. This seems to be why the Latin month-name is redefined, since the serial way of understanding the list is not applicable here; the Old English month-name is used here for the same purpose as in the first instance mentioned above. The shift in the way of referencing the months in Days 5.3 may well betray the author's awareness that some readers may not be familiar with Latin month-names. Thus even in works recorded in eleventh-century manuscripts, Old English month-names are used as a brief and complementary explanation for less learned readers. This use of vernacular month-names may have been handed down from earlier versions merely through mechanical copying, but it is noteworthy that all three versions, which differ from one another in many details, unanimously present the same use of the month-names. This may reflect that Old English month-names were still widely used among less learned people in those days.

This is also supported by the fact that Old English month-names are used in some calendars in eleventh-century manuscripts: i.e. calendars 15, 17, 19, 23.[26] Among these, calendar 19 is especially noteworthy. This manuscript contains a version of the prose *Menologium* and, as we have seen above, is probably intended for students not far advanced in their studies. In the calendar, accordingly, glosses are sometimes added to Latin words and phrases, most of which are computistical terms such as the signs of the zodiac, the terms for the equinox and the solstice, etc. At the top of each month, there is a brief summary

---

[25] January is the beginning of the year according to the Julian calendar, while March 21 (the vernal equinox, when the sun and the moon were considered to have been created) or March 25 (the Annunciation) was an alternative date for the beginning of the year. The list follows the latter tradition and this passage explains that this is the right way of conceiving the course of the year.

[26] For details of these calendars and manuscripts containing them, see Appendix 5. See also Wormald, *English Kalendars before A.D. 1100*; Ker, *Catalogue*; Gneuss, *Handlist*; Gneuss and Lapidge, *Anglo-Saxon Manuscripts*; and Rushforth, *Saints in English Kalendars*.

of the month, in which a Latin month-name is used always with a gloss in the vernacular, as in the following instance:[27]

MAIUS ðrymylce HABET DIES . XXXI . LUNA . XXX .
Ðes monoð hæfð . xxxi . daga . se mona . xxx . nihta eald.[28]

This month has 31 days. The lunar month has 30 nights.

That this calendar is intended for students is made clear not only by the glosses for the Latin month-names and other computistical terms but also by the Old English translations furnished under the Latin passage, which is unusual in calendars. It seems reasonable to suppose that glosses for Latin month-names reveal that in those days less learned people knew vernacular month-names better than Latin ones, and that Latin ones were still learned terms more or less like terms for the zodiac signs, the equinox, the solstice, etc.

On the other hand, the references to Old English month-names in other Anglo-Saxon calendars preserved in eleventh-century manuscripts seem to be of a different nature. They do not seem to be intended as glosses but as additional information. For instance, at the head of each month in the calendar in Cotton Vitellius E xviii, there is a brief summary of the month like the following:

PRINCIPIUM IANI SANCIT TROPICUS CAPRICORNUS.
Iani prima dies et septima fine timetur.
Mensis giuli habet dies . xxxi . lunam . xxx .[29]

The tropic of Capricorn blesses the beginning of January.
The first day of January and the seventh day from its end are fearful.
The month of *giuli* has 31 days and 30 moons.

Here the Old English month-name *giuli* is used in the Latin passage. Since, in this calendar (and also in calendar 17), vernacular month-names are used instead of Latin ones in Latin passages, and since no Latin words are glossed in this calendar (and similarly in calendar 17), it is reasonable to consider that they are not intended as glosses; but it seems probable that they are used so as to follow a certain tradition often observed in computistical writings. The following passage found at the beginning of January in calendar 15 much more clearly presents the influence of this tradition:

HEbraice: Tebeth; Grece: Eidyneos; Aegyptiace: Thybi;
Principium iani sancit tropicus Capricornus.
Mensis giuli . habet dies . xxxi . luna . xxx .[30]

---

[27] As regards February, the Latin month-name and an Old English gloss are not preserved because of damage in the manuscript.
[28] This is quoted from Wormald, *English Kalendars before A.D. 1100*, p. 188. My translation.
[29] This is quoted from Wormald, *English Kalendars before A.D. 1100*, p. 156. My translation.
[30] This is quoted from Wormald, *English Kalendars before A.D. 1100*, p. 128. My translation.

Appendix 9

Hebrew: *Tebeth*; Greek: *Eidyneos*; Egyptian: *Thybi*.
The tropic of Capricorn blesses the beginning of January.
The month of *giuli* has 31 days and 30 moons.

Besides the vernacular name *giuli*, its Hebrew, Greek and Egyptian equivalents are indicated here. Textbooks of computus written in Anglo-Saxon England often contain this sort of catalogue of month-names in several languages. For instance, Bede's *De temporum ratione* contains the chapters on the Roman, Greek and Anglo-Saxon months (chapters 12, 14, 15, respectively), in which the Latin, Greek and Old English month-names are listed. In Byrhtferth's *Enchiridion* (I.2), there are tables indicating the Hebrew, Egyptian, Greek and Old English month-names.[31] Calendar 15 also follows this tradition. On the other hand, calendars 17 and 23, in which Old English month-names alone appear besides Latin ones, present an abbreviated version with the Hebrew, Greek and Egyptian equivalents omitted. Such an abbreviation might well seem a little too drastic, but a similar instance of a simplified version of a catalogue of month-names is actually extant elsewhere. An example is found in the introductory passages for each month in the *Old English Martyrology*, where the martyrologist mentions the vernacular and Latin month-names basically following Bede's explanation of the Old English month-names in *De temporum ratione* (chapter 15).

It is noteworthy that Old English names are clearly treated differently from the other foreign month-names in calendar 15. The Hebrew, Greek and Egyptian counterparts are placed at the top with the words indicating to which language they belong. On the other hand, vernacular ones are not placed in the row of foreign month-names and are abruptly used in Latin passages without any words identifying their origin. The reference to some sets of month-names reflect the tradition of cataloguing them in computistical books, but the familiarity of the vernacular month-names to the readers, as well as unfamiliarity of the foreign ones, can be perceived in the very different treatments of them. Thus vernacular month-names may well have been well known to people and still in use (mainly in the spoken language) in the eleventh century.

This is also supported by the evidence found in the tables of month-names in Byrhtferth's *Enchiridion* (I.2), where Hebrew, Egyptian and Greek month-names are glossed by their Latin equivalents, while Latin ones are glossed by their Old English equivalents, although the main purpose seems to be not so much glossing Latin ones as listing Old English month-names. Whatever the purpose, the vernacular names, 'glossing' the Latin ones, are placed after their Latin counterparts; while Latin ones glossing foreign names are always placed after their foreign equivalents.

All these instances lead us to the conclusion that vernacular month-names were still well known in the eleventh century, although they had been nearly replaced by their Latin equivalents in written Old English. Latin month-names

---

[31] See Baker and Lapidge, eds., *Byrhtferth's Enchiridion*, p. 24; and Crawford, ed., *Byrhtferth's Manual*, p. 22 and p. 24.

seem to have still been learned terms in the eleventh century, and to have been diffused chiefly among the learned, while the unlearned were unfamiliar with them, which must have helped the survival of the native names in spoken Old English even after their replacement by Latin names in the written language.

At the same time, however, it should also be noted that those instances in the eleventh-century calendars are the last attestations of many vernacular month-names; from the twelfth century onward, certain native month-names alone are attested. The survivors in the Middle English period are *yol* (< *geol*), *lide* (< *hlyda*), *efterliðe* (< *æfterra liða*) and *hervest month* (< *hærfestmonað*),[32] each of which is attested more than once in different works from different dates; it is probable that for some reason they outlived the others which became obsolete at an earlier stage in the Middle English period. The following instance from the so-called 'Note on Adam' recorded in British Library, MS Cotton Julius A.ii (s. xii med.)[33] may reflect varied degrees of replacement among different month-names:

> Þis syndon þa ðreo frigedagas þe man sceall fæsten on twelf monþum. Se æresta on hlydan, & se æftresta þe byð on iulius.[34] (Notes 10.2)
>
> There are three Fridays on which one must fast in the twelve months. The first (is) in *hlyda* (i.e. March), and the last is in July.

The vernacular name *hlyda* is used for March, whereas the Latin *iulius* is used for July. Together with the instances from Ælfric's *Catholic Homilies* I.229.146–50 and Days 5.3 (both quoted above), the use of *hlyda* here may reflect its strong persistence in later writings, while the use of *iulius* the subsidence of others. This may be supported by the following instance from *Seinte Marherete* composed in the early Middle English period (c. 1200):

> Þus þe eadi meiden, Margarete bi nome, i þe moneð þet ure ledene, þet is ald Englis, Efterliðe inempnet, t Iulium o Latin, o þe twen | tuðe dei deide wið tintrohe, ant wende from þes weanen to lif þet aa lesteð, to blisse bute balesið, to wunne buten euch wa.[35]
>
> (*Seinte Marherete* (based on Bodley 34), p. 52, ll. 31–35)
>
> Thus the blessed maiden, Margaret by name, in the month that our language, that is old English, names *Efterlið*, and *Iulius* in Latin, on the twentieth day

---

[32] The month-name *hærfestmonað* appears only once in Ælfric's *Grammar*, whereas *haligmonað* is more commonly attested for September.

[33] Ker indicates its date as 'xii med.', while Laing 'C12a2–b1'. See Ker, *Catalogue*, p. 202; and Laing, *Catalogue of Sources*, p. 77.

[34] The passage is quoted from Napier, 'Altenglische Kleinigkeiten'. My translation.

[35] The passage is quoted from Mack, *Seinte Marherete*. Page and line numbers in the edition are indicated. My translation. The two versions are recorded in the early thirteenth-century manuscripts: Oxford, Bodleian Library, Bodley 34 (C13a1); and London, British Library, Royal 17 A xxvii (C13a1 (c. 1220–1230)). As regards the dates of these manuscripts, I follow Laing, *Catalogue of Sources*. As regards Bodley 34, Dobson dates it to c. 1225. See Dobson, *The Origins*, p. 163.

Appendix 9

died in torment, and went from those woes to the life that lasts forever, to bliss without death, to joy without every woe'.

Although the vernacular month-name for July, *Efterlið*, is used as a term in *ure ledene* 'our language', it is also said to belong to *ald Englis* 'old English'; it was felt to be outdated in the early thirteenth century, and this may be why its Latin equivalent is also used here.[36] This may have much to do with why the author of 'Note on Adam', composed some decades earlier, prefers the Latin name for July, while he prefers the vernacular *hlyda* for March.

To sum up what has been discussed in this section: although Latin month-names seem to have nearly replaced their vernacular equivalents in written Old English by the end of the tenth century, this reflects only one aspect of the process of replacement. Various written evidence suggests that even in the mid eleventh century, vernacular names were still used and better known by unlearned people who used them in the spoken language. Many of the vernacular names seem to have become obsolete by the end of the eleventh century, but some of them survived into the Middle English period and later.

Latin and Old English Month-Names in the Verse Menologium

At the time of composition of the verse *Menologium*, Latin month-names were learned terms mainly known to and used by those who have learned at least the basic part of computus, as suggested in the contemporary poem *Death of Edgar* (quoted above), while Old English names were used among less learned people. The *Menologium* has often been supposed to be intended for unlearned people, perhaps for educational purposes. Thus it may be argued that the Old English month-names are intended primarily as glosses for their Lain counterparts, with which the intended readers may well have been unfamiliar; and in fact, the two kinds of month-names are often juxtaposed with each other. However, considering that the prime purpose of the poem is to reveal the right locations of important feasts, and that unlearned people were unfamiliar with Latin month-names, a question arises why, in the first place, the poet uses Latin month-names together with their vernacular equivalents. Even the latter alone would perfectly well suffice for the purpose, while the use of unfamiliar terms may have caused the audience unnecessary confusion and difficulties. Another difficulty arises when we notice that the use of Latin month-names sometimes causes metrical problems too (see lines 139a, 196a and 220a). It should be also noted that while all the Latin month-names are used, they are not always accompanied by their vernacular counterparts; two Old English names are not mentioned and another is used rather far away from its Latin equivalent. These

---

[36] In the quoted passage, the Latin name is referred to as a Latin term and has the Latin accusative singular ending *-um*. In the other version, it does not have the ending *-um* but *-us*, while its Latin origin is mentioned in the same way.

may suggest that Old English names are not intended purely as glosses for Latin ones but also have some other purposes. On the other hand, if we suppose that the poem is intended primarily for a more or less learned audience, then the question arises as to why the poet undertook to use Old English month-names, which seem to have been nearly replaced by Latin ones in written Old English by the time of composition.

With all these in mind, I shall argue in the following pages that there are two aspects behind the use of Old English month-names along with Latin ones in the *Menologium*; the first as glosses for Latin equivalents and the second based on a tradition of computistical writings. The usage of Latin and Old English month-names in this poem seems to reflect the purpose of the poet and the nature of the poem as well.

Special Treatments of Latin Month-Names[37]

The *Menologium* poet often seems to use Latin month-names with consideration for those who are unfamiliar with them, which suggests that the intended audience was less learned people. Thus the poet refers to an Old English month-name first and then its Latin equivalent so that it would be easier to understand the meaning of the latter, as in the following passage:

> Swylce in burh raþe
> [embe syx niht þæs,]   smicere on gearwum,
> wudum and wyrtum   cymeð wlitig scriðan
> *Þrymilce* on tun;   þearfe bringeð
> Maius micle   geond menigeo gehwær. (75b–9)

> Likewise, after six nights, beautiful *Þrymylce* comes gliding quickly into the citadel, into town, elegantly clad in adornments, woods and plants; May brings much of what is needed among a multitude of people everywhere.

Basically the same instances are found for June and November, where Latin names are used as variations as in this case, while those for February, August and September are also similar but in these cases Latin names are not used as variations of their vernacular equivalents.

When referring to a Latin month-name first, or when referring to a Latin month-name alone without its Old English equivalent, the poet takes steps to make its identity as a month-name as clear as possible (cf. the case of Days 5.3 discussed above). For instance:

> hrime gehyrsted   hagolscurum færð
> geond middangeard   Martius reðe,
> Hlyda healic. (35–7a)

---

[37] See also Karasawa, 'On the Usage'.

Appendix 9

decorated with hoar-frost and hail-showers, March the fierce, *Hlyda* the great, comes over the middle-earth.

This use of month-names is exceptional in this poem in that there is no other instance where two month-names are mentioned in two consecutive half-lines. Put immediately after its Latin equivalent, the vernacular name may well work as a gloss here.

Another way of clarifying the identity of a Latin month-name is found in the following passage:

> And þæs embe twa niht   þæt se teoða monð
> on folc fereð,   frode geþeahte,
> October on tun   us to genihte,
> Winterfylleð,   swa hine wide cigð
> igbuende   Engle and Seaxe,
> weras mid wifum. (181–6a)

> And it is after two nights that the tenth month comes to the folk in accordance with the wise scheme; October comes to town for our abundance, or *Winterfylleð*, as the island-dwelling Angles and Saxons, men as well as women, widely call it.

Here the Latin name *October* is mentioned before the vernacular *Winterfylleð* in the next line, but *October* is a variation of *se teoða monð* 'the tenth month' mentioned earlier and its meaning is readily understandable.[38]

The following passage presents a similar instance:

> Þænne folcum bringð
> morgen to mannum   monað to tune,
> Decembris   drihta bearnum,
> Ærra Iula. (218b–21a)

> Then the month of December, *Ærra Iula*, brings the next morning to town, to nations, to people, to children of men'.

Here the Latin *Decembris* is mentioned first, but it is preceded by the word *monað* 'month', making it clear that it is a month-name.

This way of identifying is also used when a Latin month-name alone is used as in the following instance:

> Swa þa sylfan tiid,   side herigeas,
> folc unmæte,   habbað foreweard gear,
> for þy se kalend us   cymeð geþincged
> on þam ylcan dæge   us to tune,
> forma monað.   Hine folc mycel
> Ianuarius   gerum heton. (5–10)

---

[38] It is noteworthy that the poet states that the Anglo-Saxons widely call (in the present tense) the month *Winterfylleð*, which provides another piece of evidence that reveals vernacular month-names were still in use in spoken Old English in the late tenth century.

> At the same time, vast multitudes, innumerable people, hold the beginning of the year, since the first day of the month, the first month, comes to town among us on the same day, as arranged for us. The great people formerly called it January.

For January, only its Latin name is used, but it is earlier mentioned as *forma monað* 'the first month' and its identity as a month-name is clear.

In other instances where a Latin month-name is used independently of its Old English equivalent, the Latin name is always used with the word *monað* 'month', as in the following instance:

> Swylce emb feower and þreo
> nihtgerimes þætte nergend sent
> Aprelis monað, on þam oftust cymð
> seo mære tiid mannum to frofre,
> drihtnes ærist; (54b–8a)

> Likewise it is after four and three in the number of nights that the Saviour sends the month of April, in which the great feast, the Resurrection of the Lord, most often comes to humankind as consolation'.

The Old English equivalent of April is mentioned in line 72a, after the Easter digression, which begins with this passage, and seems to be located rather far away from its Latin equivalent to function as a gloss. Used with the word *monað* 'month', however, *Aprelis* is readily understood as a month-name. The poet uses the same technique for July (i.e. *Iulius monað* (132a) 'the month of July'), for which the Latin name alone is used.

In this way, the poet seems to use Latin month-names with considerable care. This might well be, for one reason, because month-names are important in this poem for providing key dates for the readers to grasp the course of the year, but for another, and more fundamentally, because they were learned terms probably less familiar to the intended readers. As the poet himself says in lines 184–6a, people at the time of composition widely used the vernacular month-names, while he sometimes associates Latin month-names with Roman scholars or rules based on their calculations (as in lines 17b–19a and 181b–3a), implying their learned nature.[39] This also explains why in most cases Old English names are used together with Latin ones; they may have a function as aids for less learned people.

---

[39] Especially in the case of lines 181b–3a, the Latin *October* is associated with *frode geþeahte* (182b) 'the wise scheme', and this creates a clear contrast with the reference to its vernacular counterpart *Winterfylleð*, which is mentioned as a (common) month-name widely used by the Anglo-Saxons.

Appendix 9

The Tradition of Enumerating Various Month-Names in Computistical Works

What I have discussed in the previous section scarcely explains why the poet chooses to use two kinds of month-names together, and especially why he chooses to use Latin ones predominantly despite the fact that they seem to have been less familiar to his intended audience. In this section, we shall see another aspect of the use of Latin and Old English month-names.

In the *Menologium*, Latin month-names are predominant in that all of them are used, while only ten of their vernacular equivalents are mentioned. The two Old English names that are not mentioned are *Æfterra Iula* 'the latter *Iula*, i.e. January' and *Æfterra Liða* 'the latter *Liða*, i.e. July'. They may well have been skipped because they are, if necessary, easily reconstructed based on the names of the previous months, i.e. *Ærra Iula* 'the former *Iula*, i.e. December' and *Ærra Liða* 'the former *Liða*, i.e. June'. In the case of January, moreover, the month-name *Æfterra Iula* may be felt less appropriate, since *æfterra* 'latter' denotes following the preceding month but in the context in the poem it is the first month ahead of all the others; thus the poet calls it *forma monað* 'the first month' instead. The omission of *Æfterra Liða* may be also connected with this; the poet chooses to be consistent in omitting all the month-names beginning with *æfterra*. In addition to these, the name for April, *Aprelis*, is also used virtually on its own; *Eastermonað* in line 72a cannot be a gloss for *Aprelis monað* sixteen lines ahead in line 56a. These instances of January, April and July suggest that the vernacular names are not always regarded as necessary.

The peculiarities of the poet's use of month-names may be explained from the perspective of a tradition observed in computistical writings. In Anglo-Saxon textbooks of computus, as we have seen above, it was customary to consider the months in various calendars in various civilisations; Bede writes on the Roman, Greek and Anglo-Saxon months in his *De temporum ratione* (Chapters 12, 14 and 15), while Byrhtferth makes a list of the Hebrew, Egyptian, Greek, (Latin) and Old English month-names in his *Enchiridion* (I.2). This tradition is also sometimes taken over in calendars; calendar 15, for instance, lists the Hebrew, Greek, Egyptian, Latin and Old English month-names, and calendar 24 lists the Hebrew, Greek, Egyptian and Latin month-names, while calendars 17 and 23 list the Latin and Old English month-names.[40] The last two contain only two kinds of month-names and can be seen as abbreviated versions of the more extended ones. The *Old English Martyrology*, also containing brief comments on the Latin and Old English month-names at the beginning of each month, follows this latter tradition of the abbreviated indication of different month-names.

---

[40] Calendar 19 also contains the Roman and Anglo-Saxon names. However, in most cases, Old English month-names are used as glosses for their Latin equivalents and do not necessarily belong to this tradition.

If we suppose that the *Menologium* poet also follows this tradition, the peculiarities of the use of month-names in the poem can be explained to a considerable degree. The main month-names are the Latin ones since all of them are used, but the poet also uses most of the Old English names following this tradition of cataloguing different kinds of month-names. His is the abbreviated version as found in the two calendars mentioned above as well as in the *Old English Martyrology*. As a catalogue of Old English month-names, the poem contains virtually all the names; if we neglect the subdivision using *ærra* 'former' and *æfterra* 'latter', there are only ten month-names in Old English and they are all mentioned.[41] Thus, the question of the references to the vernacular month-names together with their Latin equivalents, and that of the omission of two of the Old English names, are both logically explained if we suppose that the poet follows the tradition in computistical writings of listing month-names in more than one language.

As far as the extant computistical works in Old English are concerned, Latin month-names are the standard terms, whereas Old English names are rarely used, mainly found in notes on Anglo-Saxon months and/or month-names. Together with such words as *bises* 'bissextile day', *circul* 'cycle', *emniht* 'equinox', *kalend* 'the first day of the month', etc., the Latin month-names were also learned terms at the time of composition of the *Menologium*, and the use of these computistical/learned words may reflect not only the poet's learning in computus but also the nature of the intended audience, who might be students who were (or needed to be) acquainted with the basics of computus. The poet's use of the Latin and Old English month-names may also follow a computistical tradition listing month-names in various languages. The poet combines this tradition with the use of Old English month-names as glosses for Latin ones as actually attested in calendar 19, which contains the prose *Menologium* and other computistical fragments probably intended for students not far advanced in their studies. Thus not only the fact that the prose and the verse *Menologium* are quite similar in nature, but also the similar treatment of Latin and Old English month-names observed in the calendar in this manuscript and in the verse *Menologium*, may point to a similar kind of audience/readers; they seem to be students acquainted with, or at least learning, the computistical basics, including Latin month-names, to a very similar degree.

---

[41] In the table of Latin and Old English month-names in ByrEnch I.2, the two are not distinguished by *ærra* and *æfterra*.

Glossary

Abbreviations

*	indicates a *hapax legomenon*	ptcl	particle
a	accusative	pers	person(al)
adj	adjective	pl	plural
adv	adverb	pr n	proper noun
anom	anomalous	pp	past participle
comp	comparative	prep	preposition
conj	conjunction	pres	present
d	dative	pret	preterite
def art	definite article	pron	pronoun
dem pron	demonstrative pronoun	pret-pres vb	preterite-present verb
f	feminine	rel	relative
g	genitive	s	singular
indec	indeclinable	subj	subjunctive
indic	indicative	str vb	strong verb (e.g., str vb^2 = strong verb of Class II)
i	instrumental		
indef pron	indefinite pronoun	superl	superlative
inf	infinitive	v	vocative
m	masculine	vb	verb
n	nominative or neuter	w	with (e.g., w d = with dative)
num	numeral		
ord	ordinal	wk vb	weak verb (e.g., wk vb^2 = weak verb of Class II)
part	participle		

aa adv *always, continuously* 65

abeodan str vb^2 *to announce, proclaim* (in the phrase **hælo abeodan** 'to salute') pret 3 sing **abead** 50

ac conj *but* 66

acennan wk vb^1 *to bring forth* pp **acenned** 117, 162, 168; **acennyd** 1

afera m *son, child* ns 136

aferian wk vb^1 *to remove, withdraw, depart* pp **afered** 23

*****agryndan** wk vb^1 *to descend* pres 3 sing **agrynt** 111

Agustinus m pr n *Augustine* as 97

Agustus m pr n *August* ns 139

agyfan str vb^5 *to give up, give, deliver* pret 3 sing **ageaf** 217; pret 3 pl **agefan** 81

an num *one* df **anre** 34, 88, 141; am **anne** 189; af **ane** 19

and conj *and* 11, 19, 24, 30, 31, 42, 47, 54, 71, 77, 81, 83, 95, 107, 111, 113, 122, 129, 135, 136, 162, 167, 181, 185, 188, 191, 193, 199, 204, 211, 215, 221; **ond** 134, 163

Andreas m pr n *Andrew* ns 216

apostol m *apostle, disciple* np **apostolas** 122

Aprelis m pr n *April* gs 56

Glossary

areccan wk vb¹ *to set forth, recount, explain* inf 69

astigan str vb¹ *to proceed, go, rise, ascend* pres 3 sing **astihð** 91, 109

awyrn (< **ahwergen**) adv *anywhere* 101

ædre adv *at once* 130

æfre adv *ever* 102

æfter prep (w d) *after* 25, 128

ægleaw adj *learned in the law* npm **ægleawe** 19

ælmihtig I m *the Almighty* ns 3; II adj *almighty* asm **ælmihtigne** 95

ænig adj *any* asm **ænigne** 102

ær adv *before, formerly* 102, 126, 200 (sið oððe ær *ever*)

ærist m *resurrection* ns 58

æror adv *before, formerly* 166

ærra adj *former, preceding* nsm 108, 221

æt prep (w d) *at* 46

ætgædere adv *together, at the same time* 188

æþele adj *noble, famous, glorious, devout, pious* nsm 38, 216; npm 80; superl asm **æþelust** 84; dpm **æþelum** 119

æþeling m *nobleman, prince* gs **æþelinges** 157; ap **æþelingas** 189

Bartholomeus m pr n *Bartholomew* gs 155

be prep (w d) *by, of, through, with, to, at* 63, 87, 160, 205

beald adj *bold, brave, strong* dsm **bealdum** 225

beam m *tree, cross* gp **beama** 84

bearn n *son, child* as **bearn** 22; dp **bearnum** 175, 196, 220; ap **bearn** 121

bebeodan str vb² *to require, bid* pret 3 sing **bebead** 100

bebugan str vb² *to reach, extend* pres 3 sing **bebugeð** 230

behealdan str vb⁷ *to behold, look at* inf 113

Benedictus m pr n *Benedict* ns 40

***bentid** f *prayer time, a Rogation Day* ns **bentiid** 75

gebeodan str vb² *to offer, give, grant* pp **geboden** 32

beon anom vb *to be* pres 3 sing **byð** 23, 142, 153, 156, 179; **is** 29, 60, 74, 120; pret 3 sing **wæs** 1, 53; pret 3 pl **wæron** 191

beorn m *man* gp **beorna** 213; dp **beornum** 195

***beornwiga** m *warrior, hero* ds **beornwigan** 225

besencan wk vb¹ *to cause to sink, drown* pret 3 pl **besenctun** 212

betst superl adj., *best* asm 52

betux prep (w d) *between, among* 162

bisceop m *bishop, high-priest* as 104

***bises** m *the bissextile day* ns 32

bletsung f *blessing, favour* ap **bletsunga** 225

bliss f *bliss, grace, favour* ns **blis** 91; ds **blisse** 62

bliðe adj *joyous, peaceful* asm **bliðne** 98

blostm mf *flower, blossom* dp **blostmum** 91

Blotmonað m pr n *'sacrifice-month', November* ns 195

blowan str vb⁷ *to flower, flourish, blossom* pres 3 pl **blowað** 91

gebod n *command* ns 230

breman wk vb¹ *to honour, extol* pres 3 pl **bremað** 94

breme adj *famous, noble* nsm 40, nsf **bremu** 75; comp asm **bremran** 104

breost n *breast, bosom* dp **breostum** 98, 134

gebrihtan wk vb¹ *to glorify, brighten* pp nsm **gebrihted** 137 [a metathesised form of **gebyrhtan**]

brim n *surf, flood, wave, sea* ds **brime** 213

bringan wk vb¹ *to bring, carry, offer* inf 102; pres 3 sing **bringð** 88, 106, 193, 218; **bringeð** 78, 138; pret 3 sing **brohte** 22

Bryten f pr n *Britain* ds **Brytene** 14, 40, 98, 104, 155

Brytenrice n pr n *spacious kingdom* ?, *kingdom of Britain* ? ap **Brytenricu** 230 [see *DOE*, s. v. *bryten-rice*;

Glossary

and O'Donnell 'The Old English *Durham*']
burh f *borough* as 75
butan prep (w d) *except, but* 17, 32, 88, 141
Cantware mpl pr n *Kentish people* dp **Cantwarum** 105
cennan wk vb¹ *to bring forth* inf 52
ceorl m *freeman of the lowest class, peasant* dp **ceorlum** 31
cigan wk vb¹ *to call, name* pres 3 sng **cigð** 184
circul m *cycle or table of a movable feast* ds **circule** 67
Clementes m pr n *Clement* as 214
clypian wk vb² *to call, invoke* pres 3 pl **clypiað** 214
cneoriss f *tribe, race* dp **cneorissum** 61
cræft m *skill* ds **cræfte** 67
Crist m pr n *Christ* ns 1; as 21
cuman str vb⁴ *to come, approach, arrive* pres 3 sing **cymeð** 7, 12, 33, 72, 77; **cymð** 56, 130, 140, 173
cuð adj *known, well known* nsm 29
cwen f *woman* gp **cwena** 168
cweðan str vb⁵ *to say* pret 3 sing **cwæð** 160
cwic adj *living* gpn **cwicera** 93
cyme m *coming, arrival* ns 31
cynebearn n *royal child, prince, i.e. Christ* as 159
cynestol m *chief city, royal-dwelling* ds **cynestole** 105
cyning m *king* gs **cyninges** 21; **kyninges** 231; gp **cyninga** 1; gp **kyninga** 52; ds **cyninge** 93
cynn n *race, kin, people* gp **cynna** 93
gecyðan wk vb¹ *to make known, reveal* pp **gecyðed** 52
dæg m *day* ns 60, 74, 175, 180, 202; ds **dæge** 8, 21; as 13, 140, 189; is 3, 167; is **dæge** 47, 80, 199; gp **dagena** 64, 169; ap **dagas** 68, 89
dead m *death* ns 157
Decembris m pr n *December* ns or gs 220
diacon m *deacon* ns 145
dogor mn *day* gp **dogera** 96

dom m *glory, honour* as 192
don anom vb *to do* pres 3 sing **deð** 197
dream m *delightful singing* ns 58
driht f *people* gp **drihta** 220
drihten m *the Lord, God* ns 60, 96; gs **drihtnes** 12, 58, 64, 169, 198, 201; ds **drihtne** 192
dyre adj *dear* npm 192
dyrling m *darling, favourite* ns 116
eac adv *also, likewise, moreover* 29, 44, 118, 156
eadig adj *blessed* dsf **eadigre** 84; asm **eadigne** 193; dpm **eadigum** 62
eadignes f *happiness, prosperity* as **eadignesse** 197
eahta num *eight* a 95, 221; af 210
eahteoða adj *eighth* (*in the phrase* se eahteoðan dæg *the octave*) ism **eahteoðan** 3
eald adj *ancient* npm **ealde** 19, 166
ealdor m *eternity* ds **ealdre** 153 (**to ealdre** 'forever')
ealdorþegn m *chief attendant, chief apostle* np **ealdorþegnas** 130
eall adj *all, every* gpm **ealra** 199; dpm **eallum** 62
ealling adv *always, every time* 153, 173
earfeðe n *hardship* dp **earfeðum** 224
Eastermonað m pr n *'Easter-month', April* ns 72
eaðmod adj *humble-minded, obedient* apm **eaðmode** 99
ece I adj *perpetual, eternal* nsm 3; gsm **eces** 12; asm **ecne** 173; asn **ece** 224; II adv *ever, evermore* 153
Elene f pr n *Helena* ds **Elenan** 84
emb(e) see **ymb(e)**
emniht(e) (<**efenniht**) f *equinox* as **emniht** 45, **emnihte** 49; gs **emnihtes** 175, 180
endleofon num *eleven* af **XI** 38
engel m *angel* gp **engla** 85, 226
Engle mp pr n *the Angles* np 185
eorl m *nobleman, man* np **eorlas** 49; dp **eorlum** 31, 157, 180; ap **eorlas** 99
eorðe f *earth* as **eorðan** 176

Glossary

eorðwaran mp *earth-dwellers* dp **earðwarum** 62
fæder m *Father* ns 48, 226; gs 87
fæger adj *fair, beautiful* superl ns **fægerust** 114, 148
fægere adv *fairly, beautifully, kindly, justly* 143, 152, 158
fæmne f *virgin, woman* ds **fæmnan** 152
fær n *journey, passage, movement* as 18, 167
fæstræd adj *firm, steadfast* nsm 135
fah adj *hostile* npm **fan** 211
faran str vb^6 *to set forth, go, travel* pres 3 sing **færð** 35; **fereð** 165, 182
gefea m *joy* as **gefean** 173
Februarius m pr n *February* gs 18
fela adj indec *many* as **feala** 163; np 213
feorh n *life* as 133; ap 81
feorða ord *fourth* dsm **feorðan** 33
feower num *four* df **feowerum** 211; af 15, 48, 54, 107, 133, 158, 194, 207, 226.
gefera m *comrade, fellow-disciple* np **geferan** 80
gefeterian wk vb^2 *to fetter, bind* pp **gefeterad** 205
fif num *five* df 125, 179; **fifum** 71; af 11, 23, 148
findan str vb^3 *to find* inf 67, 228; pret 3 sing **funde** 99; pret 3 pl **fundan** 166
folc n *folk, people, nation* ds **folce** 165, 194; as 182; np 6, 9; gp **folca** 135; dp **folcum** 54, 179, 218, 228
*****folcbealo** n *torment in public* as 125
folde wk f *land, country, field* gs **foldan** 114, 207; ds **foldan** 15, 143
for prep (w d/i.) *for, on account of, owing to* 82, 86, 150 (**for þy** *since, because*, 7)
foregleaw adj *very wise, prudent* npm **foregleawe** 165
foremære adj *illustrious, renowned, famous* npm 190
foreweard adj *beginning of* (**foreweard gear** *the beginning of a year*) asn 6

forgyfan str vb^5 *to give, grant* pret 3 sing **forgeaf** 223
forgyldan str vb^3 *to reward, give* pp **forgolden** 152
forma adj *first* nsm 9
forst m *frost* ds **forste** 205 [a metathesised form of **frost**]
forð adv *forth, forwards, further* 70, 143
forþan, forþon I conj *for, for (the reason) that, because* 21, 46, 65; II adv *therefore* 192
forðweg m *journey, departure* as 218 (**on forðweg** *away*)
fostorlean n *reward for fostering* as 152
gefræge I n *information through hearsay* is **gefræge** 27; II adj *well-known, celebrated* nsn **gefræge** 54
frætwe fp *treasures, ornaments* np **frætuwe** 207
frea m *lord* gs **frean** 205
fremman wk vb^1 *to perform, do* pret 3 pl **fremedon** 128
gefrignan str vb^3 *to hear of, learn about* pret 1 pl **gefrunan** 190
frod adj *wise, old* nsm 66, 135; dsf 182; npm **frode** 18
frofor f *consolation, help* ds **frofre** 57, 228
frymð m *beginning, foundation* ds **frymðe** 46
*****fulwihttid** f *baptismal-tide* ns 11
furðor adv *further, forwards, more, later* 33, 125
fus adj *ready to depart, eager for* asm 218
fyrn adv *once, formerly* 190
fyrst adj *first* asf 87
galga m *cross* ds **galgan** 86
gangan str vb^7 *to go, come* inf 113; pres 3 sing **gangeð** 202
gast m *soul* as 171, 217
ge pers pron *you* n 228
gear n *year* ds **geare** 33, 110; as 6; dp **gerum** 10 (adverbial dative, 'formerly').
geard m *yard, enclosure, land* as 109

Glossary

geardagas mp *days of old* dp **geardagan** 117
gearwe f *adornment* dp **gearwum** 76
geo (= **iu**) adv *once, formerly, before* 17
geond prep (w a) *throughout, through, over* 36, 53, 79, 92, 121, 127, 161, 163, 176, 230
gerum *see* **gear**
gesiþ m *retainer, man* np **gesiþas** 18
gim m *gem, the sun* ns 109
gleaw adj *prudent, wise* nsm wk **gleawa** 100; *learned in* (w g) nsm 171
God m *God* ns 46, 83; gs **Godes** 39, 100, 217; ds **Gode** 211; as 149
godspell n *gospel* gs **godspelles** 171
Gregorius m pr n *Gregory* ns 39, 101
grene adj *green* npm 206
grund m *ground, plain, land, earth* as 113
guma m *man* as **guman** 101
gyt adv *yet, still* 68
habban wk vb³ *to have* pres 3 sing **hæfð** 146; pres 3 pl **habbað** 6; pret 3 sing **hæfde** 28, 151; pret 3 pl **hæfdon** 126
had m *rank, order* gp **hada** 92
Hælend m *the Saviour, Jesus* as **Hælend** 4
hæleð m *man, warrior* np 14; gp **hæleða** 121; dp **heleþum** 164
hælo f (literally 'salvation, health, healing, etc.') in the phrase **hælo abeodan** *to salute* as 50
hærfest m *autumn, harvest-time* ns 140; ds **hærfeste** 177; as 204
hæs f *command* ds **hæse** 205
hagolscur m *hail-shower* dp **hagolscurum** 35
halga m *saint* ns 37
halig adj *holy* gp **haligra** 121, 229; apm **halige** 68; apf 74
Haligmonað m pr n *holy-month, September* ns **Haligmonð** 164
ham m *home, dwelling, region* as 150
har adj *hoary, grey, old* dsn **haran** 213
(ge)hatan str vb⁷ *to call, name* pres 3 pl **hatað** 14; pret 3 pl **heton** 10; pp **gehaten** 4
he pers pron *he* ns 33, 98; gs **his** 31, 50, 172, 217, 225, 227; ds **him** 99, 100, 160; as **hine** 9, 184
heah adj *high* superl **hyhst** nsm 110
heahengel m *archangel* gs **heahengles** 177; as 50
healdan str vb⁷ *to hold, celebrate* inf 63, 229; pres 1 pl **healdað** 20, 118, 187, 199; pres 3 pl **healdað** 45, 49
healic adj *exalted, great, excellent* nsm 37, 74
heard adj *strong, intense, vigorous* nsm 42
heaðurof adj *famed in war, brave* npm **heaðurofe** 14
heo pers pron *she* ns 21, 51
heofon m *heaven* ap **heofenas** 65, 110
heofonrice n *heavenly kingdom* gs **heofonrices** 4
her adv *here, in this place* 15, 98, 155
here m *multitude* ds **herige** 204; np **herigeas** 5
herian wk vb¹ *to praise, extol* pres 3 pl **heriað** 42
hi pers pron *they* npm 128, 192; **hy** 190; **he** 65
higestrang adj *mentally strong, brave* nsm 42
hit pron *it* ns 52; as 17, 165
hladan str vb⁶ *to lade, heap up* pp nsm **hladen** 142
hlafmæsse f *Lammas* gs **hlafmæssan** 140
hleotan str vb² *to obtain, win* pret 3 pl **hlutan** 192
Hlyda m pr n *March* ns 37
hraþe adv *immediately, promptly* 90; **raþe** 75
hrim m *rime, hoar-frost* gs **hrimes** 204; ds **hrime** 35
gehwær adv *everywhere* 59, 79
hwæt pron introducing an exclamative clause *what* 48, 122, 176
hwæðere adv *yet, still* 68
hweorfan str vb³ *to wander, move, change* pres 3 pl **hwearfað** 65

Glossary

hyran wk vb[1] *to hear* pret 1 sing **hyrde** 101
gehyrst f *ornament, decoration, treasure* ap **gehyrste** 74
gehyrstan wk vb[1] *to decorate, ornament* pp **gehyrsted** 35
Iacob m pr n *St James the Less* ns 81
Iacobus m *St James the Great* ns 132
Ianuarius m pr n *January* as 10
ic pers pron *I* ns 101; gs **mine** 27
igbuende adj *living on an island* np 185
in prep (w d or a) *in, into* 15, 39, 40, 43, 75, 97, 117, 134, 155, 173, 201
Iohannes m *John the Baptist* ns 117
iu adv *once, of old, before* 158, 213
Iudas m pr n *Jude* ns 191
Iula m pr n *Yule* (*in* Ærra **Iula** *December*) ns 221
Iulius m pr n *July* gs 132
Iunius m pr n *June* ns 109
kalend m *the first day of the month* ns 7, 31
kyning *see* **cyning**
lang adj *long* apf **lange** 107
lange adv *far, long* comp **leng** 112
lar f *learning, doctrine* as **lare** 103
lareow m *teacher, preacher* ns 135
lator adv comp *later, slower* 113
Laurentius m pr n *Laurence* ns 146
leaf f *leave, permission* ds **leafe** 87
lean n *reward, gift* ds **leane** 147
leas adj (w g) *without, devoid of* nsm 209
lencten m *spring* ns 28
leof m *beloved one* ns 215
leoht n *light, daylight; life, world* gp **leohta** 114; as 97
geleoran wk vb[1] *to depart, die* pret 3 sing **geleorde** 208
lif n *life* as 146
Liða m (*in* Ærra **Liða** *June*) ns 108
geliðan str vb[1] *to go, travel* pp **geliden** 28
lof n *praise* as 93
lufe f *love, affection, favour* ds **lufan** 82, 86
ma adv *further* 69

mægð f *maiden, virgin, woman* gp **mægða** 148
mænifealdlice adv *in many ways* 94
mære adj *famous, great* nsm 2, 27, 145, 208; nsn 53; nsf 57; dsn **mærum** 106; asm **mærne** 94, 126; comp nsm **mærra** 161
mæsse f *feast* as **mæssan** 20
magan pret-pres vb *can, be able to* pres 1 pl **magon** 63, 228
magoþegn m *young servant, retainer* np **magoþegnas** 82
Maius m pr n *May* ns 79
man indef pron *one, people* ns 73, 161, 229
manig adj *many* gpm **manigra** 92; apn **mænige** 126
mann m *man, mankind* gp **manna** 86; dp **mannum** 57, 219
Maria f pr n *Mary* gs **Marian** 20; ds **Marian** 51
Martinus m pr n *Martin* ns 208
martir m *martyr* gp **martira** 69
Martius m pr n *March* ns 36
martyrdom m *martyrdom* as 126, 145
Matheus m pr n *Matthew* ns 172
Mathias m pr n *Mathias* ns 27
menigo f *company, multitude, host* ns 178; as **menigeo** 79
meotud m *Creator, Christ* ns 86; gs **meotudes** 82, 129; as **meotod** 51
mere m *sea, ocean* as 103
metodsceaft f *destiny* ds **metodsceafte** 172
miccle adv *much* 124
micel adj *many, much, great* gs **mycles** 119 (in the adverbial genitive 'greatly'); asf **micle** 79; **mycle** 51; npn **mycel** 9; comp asf **maran** 198
Michahel m *Michael* gs **Michaheles** 178
mid prep (w d) *with* 147, 159, 186, 204
mid adj *mid, middle* asm **midne** 2, 119, 124
middangeard m *this world, earth* as 36, 53, 92, 161
milts f *mercy, favour* ds **miltse** 198
modig adj *bold, brave, high-souled* npm **modige** 82

Glossary

modor f *mother* ns 169; gs 21
mona m *moon* as **monan** 47
monað m *month* ns 9, 106, 132, 198, 219; ns **monð** 181; as 56
morgen m *the next morning, the next day* as 219
motan pret-pres vb *to be able to* pres 3 sing **mot** 206 (see the note on line 206a)
gemynd n *memory, remembrance* ap 69
mynster n *minster, cathedral* ds **mynstre** 106
na adv *never* 197
nan adj *no* nsm 161, 197
ne I adv *not, never* 63, 101, 206; II conj *nor* 64
neah prep (w d) *near* 105
neorxnawang m *paradise* ds **neorxnawange** 151
nergend m *Christ, the Saviour* ns 55, 151, 222; gs **nergendes** 26; as 41
nigon num *nine* af 41; am 95
nihgontyne num *nineteen* apf 71 (for the odd spelling, see the note for lines 71–2)
niht f *night* as 19; ds 34, 88; dp **nihtum** 17, 118, 125, 179, 188, 203; ap 11, 23, 38, 41, 48, 71, 76, 83, 131, 133, 137, 144, 148, 154, 158, 163, 174, 181, 194, 207, 210, 215, 226
geniht f *abundance* ds **genihte** 183
nihtgerim n *number of nights* gs **nihtgerimes** 26, 55, 222 (in the adverbial genitive 'in the number of nights')
genihtsum adj *abundant, abounding* nsm 194
(ge)niman str vb⁴ *hold, seize, take* pres 3 sing **genimð** 203; pret 3 sing **nam** 96
niðas mp *men* gp **niða** 196
Nouembris m pr n *November* ns 196
nu adv *now, at present* 104, 146, 228
October m *October* ns 183
of prep (w d) *from* 24, 111
ofer prep (w a) *over, after* 103, 114, 124

oferweorpan str vb³ *to sprinkle* pret 3 sing **oferwearp** 159
ofstum adv *speedily, hastily* 193
oft adv *often, frequently* 214; superl **oftust** 56
on prep (w d, i or a) *on, in, into, onto, to* 2, 3, 8, 14, 21, 28, 45, 47, 56, 65, 67, 76, 78, 85, 86, 98a, 98b, 104, 105, 109a, 109b, 110a, 110b, 119a, 119b, 123, 132, 138, 143, 151, 177, 182, 183, 189, 195, 203, 212, 213, 216, 217, 218, 227, 231
onginnan str vb³ *to begin* pres 3 sing **onginneð** 73 (here it is used periphrastically with a verb in inf to denote the simple action of it.)
onsendan wk vb¹ *to send out, send forth* pret 3 sing **onsende** 48, 171
oðer adj *another, other, next* nsm 197; asn 97, 141
oððe conj *or* 200
Paulus m pr n *Paul* gs 122
Petrus m pr n *Peter* gs 122
Philippus m pr n *Philip* ns 81
ræran wk vb¹ *to raise, lift up* inf 73
***regolfæst** adj *adhering to monastic rules, strict, rigid* npm **regolfæste** 44
reliquias mpl *relics of saints* ap 73
restan wk vb¹ *to rest* pres 3 sing **rest** 104
reðe adj *fierce, cruel, violent, severe* nsm 36
rice n *kingdom* as 224
rim n *number* gs **rimes** 64, 96
rimcræftig adj *skilled in reckoning* np **rimcræftige** 44
rinc m *man* np **rincas** 44
gerisan str vb¹ *to be fitting, be proper* pres 3 sing **gerist** 58, 120
rodor m *sky, heaven* dp **roderum** 216
Rom f *Rome* ds **Rome** 123
sægrund m *sea-bottom* as 212
samod adv *together, at the same time* 188
sanct m *saint* gp **sancta** 200
gesceaft f *what is created by God, the earth, the world* as 227

Glossary

scriðan str vb[1] *to go, move, glide* inf 77; pres 3 sing **scriþ** 136

sculan pret-pres vb *to be obliged, have to, must* pres 3 sing **sceal** 66, 229; pres 1 pl **sculan** 68; pret 3 sing **sceolde** 51

scyndan wk vb[1] *to hurry, hasten* pret 3 sing **scynde** 38

se I def art, dem pron, *the, that*; nsm 7, 24, 37, 59, 60, 100, 181; nsn **þæt** 53, 74, 120; nsf **seo** 57; npm **þa** 122; dsm **þam** 8, 21; **þan** 146; dpn **þam** 128; asn **þæt** 178; ism **þy** 3, 7, 47, 167, 199; **þi** 80; asf **þa** 5, 45, 63, 118; apm **þa** 189; II rel pron *who, whom, which, that*; nsm **se** 50, **se (þe)** 158; dsm **þam** 56, 85, 109; dsm **þam** 132; gpm **þara** 200; asm **þæne** 13, 42, 60

sealt adj *salt, briny* asm **sealtne** 103

Seaxe mp *the Saxons* np 185; gp **Sexna** 231

secan wk vb[1] *to seek, desire* pret 3 sing **sohte** 41, 149, 209

secgan wk vb[3] *to say, declare, recite* pres 3 pl **secgað** 93

sel adj *good, great* comp asf **selran** 103; superl ns **selost** 168

gesellan wk vb[1] *to give, give up* pret 3 sing **gesealde** 133

sendan wk vb[1] *to send* pres 3 sing **sent** 55; pret 3 sing **sende** 227

seofon num *seven* df 188; af 137, 215

seofontyne num *seventeen* d **seofontynum** 25

seofoþa *seventh* ism **seofoþan** 167

September m pr n *September* gs **Septembres** 167

set n *setting* ds **sete** 112

sibb f *love, peace* ds **sibbe** 150

sid adj *ample, wide, spacious* asf wk **sidan** 227; npm **side** 5

sigan str vb[1] *to approach, advance, move, go, set, sink* pres 3 sing **sigeð** 16, 112

sigedrihten m *victorious Lord, God* ds **sigedrihtne** 215

sigefæst adj *victorious, triumphant* asm **sigefæstne** 150, 212

sigelbeorht adj *sun-bright, brilliant* asm **sigelbeortne** 203; apm **sigelbeorhte** 89

Simon m pr n *Simon* ns 191

(ge)singan str vb[3] *to sing* inf **gesingan** 70; pret 3 sing **sang** 59

sið adv *afterwards* 200 (**sið oððe ær** *ever*)

smicere adv *beautifully, elegantly* 76

snaw m *snow* gs **snawes** 204

Solmonað m pr n *February* ns 16

***stige** m *ascent, ascension* as 64

sumor m *summer* ns 89; ds **sumere** 137; as 119, 124

sunna m *sun* as **sunnan** 47

sunu m *son* gs **suna** 150; as 129, 227

swa I adv *thus, just as* 5, 80, 140; II conj *as, like, as far as* 17, 52, 59, 100, 120, 165, 178, 184, 197, 230

swutol adj *distinct, evident, clear* gp **swutelra** 129

swylc pron *such a one*; as 141

swylce adv *thus, likewise, in like manner, moreover* 15, 29, 40, 44, 54, 75, 87, 91, 128, 148, 156, 186, 221

swylt m *death* as 25

sylf I pron *self* nsm 222; II adj *same* asf **sylfan** 5, 231; ism **sylfan** 47

symbel n *holy day, feast-day* as 200

symble adv *continuously, always* **symle** 136; **symble** 191

gesyne adj *visible, evident* gp **gesynra** 129

syððan adv *afterwards, then* 112, 202

syx num *six* df 203; af 76

tæcan wk vb[1] *to teach, show, instruct* pret 3 sing **tæhte** 83

getæl n *reckoning* ds **getale** 63

getellan wk vb[1] *to compute, count, calculate* pret 3 pl **getealdon** 17

tempel n *temple* ds **temple** 22

teoða ord *tenth* nsm 181

Thomas m pr n *Thomas* ds **Thomase** 223

tid f *time, hour, feast-day* ns 121; **tiid** 57, 154; as **tiid** 5, 45, 118, 177, 186, 231; **tide** 63; ap **tiida** 107, 229

tidlice adv *timely* 131

208

Glossary

till n *standing-place* ds **tille** 111
tireadig adj *glorious, famous* npm **tireadige** 13
to prep (w d) *to, into, for, as, according to* 8, 12, 16, 22, 29, 34, 57, 62, 72, 89, 100, 108, 112, 147, 153, 165, 172, 183, 195, 214, 219a, 219b, 228.
torht adj *bright, beautiful, splendid* superl ns **torhtust** 111
trum adj *firm, strong, vigorous* nsm 134
getrywe adj *faithful* nsm 144
tun m *enclosure, village, town* ds **tune** 8, 16, 34, 89, 108, 219; as 28, 78, 138, 183, 195
tungol n *star, planet* gp **tungla** 111
twa num *two* gpm **twegra** 187; df **twam** 17; af 30, 83, 107, 131, 181
twelf num *twelve* ap 221
twelfta ord *twelfth* asm 13
twentig num *twenty* dp **twentigum** 134; ap 187
tyn num *ten* df 118; af 154
þa adv *then, after that time* 24, 151
þænne (= **þonne**) I adv *then, thereafter* 23, 33, 37, 58, 90, 106, 115, 130, 143, 153, 169, 173, 210, 218, 226; II conj (w subj) *when* 32
þæs adv *thence, afterwards* 11, 19, 23, 38, 41, 76, 83, 95, 131, 136, 137, 140, 144, 148, 154, 163, 174, 181, 187, 193, 207, 215; in the phrase **þæs þe** *since* 28, 49, 72, 98, 179
þæt conj *that, so that, in order that* 20, 23, 51, 71, 73, 161, 168, 181, 190, 206
þætte conj *that, so that* 11, 16, 55, 83, 88, 96, 164, 208, 211, 222, 226
þe I indecl ptcl (in phrases such as **þeah þe, for þæm þe, þæs þe**) 28, 49, 72, 98, 179; II indecl rel pron 158, 200, 213, 229
geþeaht f *direction, thought, consideration* ds **geþeahte** 182
þearf f *what is needed, need, necessity* ds **þearfe** 214; as **þearfe** 78
þegn m *thegn, follower, servant, retainer* ns **þegen** 26; **þegn** 115, 170
þeod f *people, nation, region, country* gp **þeoda** 163; dp **þeodum** 30, 174
þeoden m *lord, ruler, prince* ns 2, 85; gs **þeodnes** 116; ds **þeodne** 144
þeodenhold adj *faithful to one's lord* npm **þeodenholde** 123
þeow m *servant* as 43
þes dem pron *this* nsm **þis** 60; asf **þas** 227, 231
geþingan wk vb¹ *to prescribe, determine, arrange* pp nsm **geþincged** 7; pp nsm **geþinged** 164
þrealic adj *severe, terrible* asn 125
þreo num *three* af 54, 144, 163, 174; **III** 30
þreotyne num *thirteen* d 116, 170
þristhydig adj *bold-minded, valorous* dsm **þristhydigum** 223
þrowian wk vb² *to die, suffer* pret 3 sing **þrowade** 25; **þrowode** 85; pret 3 pl **þrowedon** 123
Þrymilce n pr n *'three-milk (month)', May* ns 78
þurh prep (w a) *through, by* 129, 145
ufor adv *later* 34, 179
unforcuð adj *noble, honourable* nsm 170
unmæte adj *excessive, great, vast* npn 6
unrim n *countless number, large quantity* as 128
up adv *above, up, upwards* 65, 110, 216
upengel m *heavenly angel* gp **upengla** 210
upweg m *ascension* as 193
uþwita m *scholar* np **uþwitan** 166
wær f *keeping, protection* as **wære** 39, 217
wæstm m *product, fruit* dp **wæstmum** 142
wæter n *water* ds **wætere** 159
wana f *lacking, wanting* ds **wanan** 141
wang m *field* np **wangas** 90, 206; as 114
we pers pron *we* np 20, 63, 68, 118, 176, 189, 199; dp **us** 7, 8, 12, 34, 60, 72, 108, 131, 183, 206

Glossary

wealdend m *the Ruler, the Lord* ns 46, 160; gs **wealdendes** 22, 43; as 209

weard m *ward, guard, guardian* ns 4; as 210

wearm adj *warm* apn **wearme** 90

wel adv *well, quite, very* 42, 59, 120

wela m *prosperity, happiness* ns 142

(ge)welhwær adv *everywhere* **gewelhwær** 30; **welhwær** 138

welþungen adj *honoured* nsf 156

Weodmonað m pr n *'weed-month', August* ns 138

weorc n *work, deed* gp **weorca** 147

weorðan str vb³ *to become, get, be* (passive aux.) pres subj 3 sing **weorðe** 32; pret 3 sing **wearð** 52, 117, 168; pret subj 3 sing **wurde** 162

(ge)weorðian wk vb² *to honour, exalt, celebrate, praise* pres 1 pl **weorðiað** 176; pp **geweorðod** 120, **geweorðad** 154

weorðlice adv *worthily, splendidly, fitly* 160

wer m *man* ns 209; ds **were** 162; as 212; np **weras** 186; gp **wera** 61; dp **werum** 29

werod n *host, band* gp **weroda** 149

werðeod f *folk, people* ap **wærþeoda** 127 (for the spelling *wær-*, see the note for line 127b)

wic n *dwelling-place, village* dp **wicum** 24, 29

wide adv *widely, far and wide* 29, 59, 120, 156, 174, 176, 184, 202

wif n *woman, female* ds **wife** 162; gp **wifa** 149; dp **wifum** 186

wiga m *warrior, fighter* ns 160; gp **wigena** 186

wigend m *warrior, fighter* ns 24

willa m *will, determination* ds **willan** 100; as **willan** 201

willan anom vb *to wish* pres 3 sing **wyle** 112

winter m *winter, year* ns 24; gs **wintres** 202; as **winter** 2; dp **wintrum** 66

Winterfylleð m pr n *October* ns 184

wis adj *wise, learned* npm **wise** 43; gp **wisra** 66

wisfæst adj *wise* nsm 61

(ge)wiss n *certainty* ds (in the instrumental dative, meaning 'with certainty, certainly') **wisse** 70; **gewisse** 124

wist f *sustenance* ds **wiste** 195

witan pret-pres vb *to know* pres 3 sing **wat** 178

gewitan str vb¹ *to go depart, pass away* pret 3 sing **gewat** 143

witega m *wise man, prophet* ns **witega** 59

wið prep (w d) *in return for* 146, 224

wlitig adj *beautiful, fair* nsm 142; nsn 77

womm m *stain, disgrace, evil* gp **womma** 209

word n *word* dp **wordum** 70

worn m *a number, multitude* as 169

woruld f *world* ds **worulde** 201

woruldgesceaft f *things of this world* gp **woruldgesceafta** 115

wrecan str vb⁵ *to sing, recite, utter* inf 70

gewrit n *book, scripture, writing* dp **gewritum** 43

wucu f *week* as **wucan** 87; ap **wucan** 15

wudu m, *wood* dp **wudum** 77

wuldor n *glory, splendour, honour, miracle, wondrous thing, heaven* ns 1, 149; gs **wuldres** 115, 159

wuldorfæder m *Glorious* (or *Heavenly*) *Father* ds 147

wundor n *wonder* gp **wundra** 127

wunian wk vb² *to inhabit, dwell* inf 206

gewydere n *weather* ap **gewyderu** 90

(ge)wyrcan wk vb¹ *to make, build, perform, do* pret 3 sing **worhte** 46, 61; pret 3 pl **worhtan** 201; pp **geworhte** 127

wyrd n *event* ns 53, 156

gewyrde n *rule* dp **gewyrdum** 66

wyrt f *plant, herb* dp **wyrtum** 77

ylca pron *same* dsm **ylcan** 8; asf **ylcan** 45; ism **ylcan** 80, 199

Glossary

ylde mpl *men, people* gp **ylda** 175; dp **yldum** 88

ymb(e) prep (w a) *after, around* **ymb** 30, 48, 87, 107, 116, 133, 137, 141, 144, 148, 154, 158, 174, 187, 207; **ymbe** 163, 170; **emb** 15, 23, 38, 54, 95, 131, 221, 226; **embe** 11, 19, 41, 71, 76, 83, 181, 194, 210, 215

geyppan wk vb¹ *to bring out, display, reveal* pp **geypped** 157

*yrmenþeod f *mighty people* dp **yrmenþeodum** 139

geywan wk vb¹ *to show, reveal* pp **geywed** 142, 180

Zebede m pr n *Zebedee* gs **Zebedes** 136

Bibliography

Amodio, Mark C., *The Anglo-Saxon Literature Handbook* (Southern Gate, 2014).
Amos, Ashley Crandall, *Linguistic Means of Determining the Dates of Old English Literary Texts* (Cambridge, 1980).
Anderson, Earl R., 'The Seasons of the Year in Old English', *Anglo-Saxon England* 26 (1997), 231–63.
Anderson, George K., *The Literature of the Anglo-Saxons* (Oxford, 1957).
Anlezark, Daniel, ed. and trans., *The Old English Dialogues of Solomon and Saturn*, AST 7 (Cambridge, 2009).
Attenborough, F. L., ed., *The Laws of the Earliest English Kings* (Cambridge, 1922).
Baker, Peter S., 'OE Metrical Calendar', in *The Blackwell Encyclopaedia of Anglo-Saxon England*, ed. M. Lapidge et al. (Oxford, 1999), 312.
Baker, Peter S., 'The Inflection of Latin Nouns in Old English Texts', in *Words and Works: Studies in Medieval English Language and Literature in Honour of Fred C. Robinson*, ed. P. S. Baker and N. Howe (Toronto, 1998), 187–206.
Baker, P. S., and M. Lapidge, eds., *Byrhtferth's Enchiridion*, EETS ss 15 (Oxford, 1995).
Bately, Janet, ed., *The Old English Orosius*, EETS ss 6 (London, 1980).
Bauerreis, R., 'Ein angelsächsischen Kalenderfragment des bayrischen Hauptstaatsarchivs in München', *Studien und Mitteilungen zur Geschichte des Benediktinerordens und seiner Zweige* 51 (1933), 177–82.
Baxter, Stephen, 'MS C of the Anglo-Saxon Chronicle and the Politics of Mid-Eleventh-Century England', *EHR* 122 (2007), 1189–227.
Bazire, Joyce, and James E. Cross, eds., *Eleven Old English Rogationtide Homilies*, King's College London Medieval Studies 4 (1982; repr. London, 1989).
Beaven, M. L. R., 'The Beginning of the Year in the Alfredian Chronicle (866–87)', *EHR* 33 (1918), 328–42.
Best, R. I., and H. J. Lawlor, eds., *The Martyrology of Tallaght from the Book of Leinster and MS. 5100-4 in the Royal Library, Brussels*, HBS 68 (London, 1931).
Bethurum, D., ed., *The Homilies of Wulfstan* (New York, 1957).
Blackburn, Bonnie, and Leofranc Holford-Strevens, *The Oxford Companion to the Year: An Exploration of Calendar Customs and Time-Reckoning* (Oxford, 1999).
Blair, John, 'A Handlist of Anglo-Saxon Saints', in *Local Saints and Local Churches in the Early Medieval West*, ed. A. Thacker and R. Sharpe (Oxford, 2002), 495–565.
Blake, Martin, ed., *Ælfric's De Temporibus Anni*, AST 6 (Cambridge, 2009).
Bliss, A. J., *The Metre of Beowulf* (Oxford, 1958).
Bliss, A. J., *An Introduction to Old English Metre* (Oxford, 1962).
Bodden, Mary-Catherine, ed., *The Old English Finding of the True Cross* (Cambridge, 1987).
Bollard, J. K. 'The Cotton Maxims', *Neophilologus* 57.2 (1973), 179–87.
Bosworth, Joseph, and T. Northcote Toller, ed., *An Anglo-Saxon Dictionary Based on the Manuscript Collections*, 2 vols. (London, 1898).
Bouterwek, K. W., ed., *Calendcwide i.e. Menologium Ecclesiæ Anglo-Saxonicæ Poeticum* (Gütersloh, 1857).

Bibliography

Bredehoft, Thomas A., 'Ælfric and Late Old English Verse', *Anglo-Saxon England* 33 (2004), 77–107.
Bredehoft, Thomas A., *Early English Metre* (Toronto, 2005).
Bredehoft, Thomas A., *Authors, Audiences, and Old English Verse* (Toronto, 2009).
Bredehoft, Thomas A., '*The Battle of Brunanburh* in Old English Studies', in *The Battle of Brunanburh: A Case Book*, ed. M. Livingston (Exeter, 2011), 285–94.
Brook, G. L., *An Introduction to Old English* (Manchester, 1955).
Brunner, Karl, *Altenglische Grammatik nach der angelsächsischen Grammatik von Eduard Sievers*, 3rd and new ed. (Tübingen, 1965).
Byrne, M. E., 'Féilire Adamnáin', *Eriu* 1 (1904), 225–8.
Calder, D. G., and M. J. B. Allen, *Sources and Analogues of Old English Poetry: The Major Latin Sources in Translation* (Cambridge, 1976).
Campbell, Alistair, *Old English Grammar* (Oxford, 1959).
Campbell, Alistair, ed., *An Anglo-Saxon Dictionary Based on the Manuscript Collections of Joseph Bosworth: Enlarged Addenda and Corrigenda to the Supplement by T. Northcote Toller* (Oxford, 1972).
Cavill, Paul, *Maxims in Old English Poetry* (Cambridge, 1999).
Chaney, William A., *The Cult of Kingship in Anglo-Saxon England: The Transition from Paganism to Christianity* (Manchester, 1970).
Chapman, 'Pope Cornelius', in *The Catholic Encyclopedia*, vol. 4, ed. C. G. Herbermann et al. (London, 1908), pp. 375–6.
Chardonnens, László Sándor, 'London, British Library, Harley 3271: The Composition and Structure of an Eleventh-Century Anglo-Saxon Miscellany', in *Form and Content of Instruction in Anglo-Saxon England in the Light of Contemporary Manuscript Evidence*, ed. P. Lendinara, L. Lazzari and M. A. D'Aronco, Fédération Internationale des Instituts d'Études Médiévales, Textes et Études du Moyen Âge 39 (Turnhout, 2007), 3–34.
Chardonnens, László Sándor, *Anglo-Saxon Prognostics, 900–1100: Study and Texts*, Brill's Studies in Intellectual History 153, Brill's Texts and Sources in Intellectual History 3 (Leiden, 2007).
Cheney, C. R., and Michael Jones, ed., *A Handbook of Dates for Students of British History*, New ed. (Cambridge, 2000).
Clark Hall, J. R., ed., *A Concise Anglo-Saxon Dictionary*, 4th ed. with a supplement by Herbert D. Meritt (Cambridge, 1960).
Clemoes, Peter, ed., *Ælfric's Catholic Homilies: The First Series, Text*, EETS ss 17 (Oxford, 1997).
Cockayne, Oswald, ed., *Leechdoms, Wortcunning, and Starcraft of Early England Being a Collection of Documents, for the Most Part Never Before Printed, Illustrating the History of Science in This Country before the Norman Conquest*, 3 vols. (London, 1864–66).
Colgrave, B., ed., *Felix's Life of Saint Guthlac* (Cambridge, 1956).
Conner, Patrick W., ed., *The Anglo-Saxon Chronicle: A Collaborative Edition*, vol. 10: The Abingdon Chronicle, A.D. 956–1066 (MS. C, with Reference to BDE) (Cambridge, 1996).
Cosijn, P. J. 'Anglosaxonica', *Beitrage zur Geschichte der deutschen Sprache und Literatur* 19 (1894), 441–61.
Crawford, S. J., ed., *Byrhtferth's Manual (A.D. 1011) Now Edited for the First Time from MS. Ashmole 328 in the Bodleian Library*, vol. 1, EETS os 177 (1929; repr. London, 1966).

Bibliography

Doane, A. N., ed., *The Saxon Genesis: An Edition of the West Saxon Genesis B and the Old Saxon Vatican Genesis* (Madison, 1991).

Doane, A. N., ed., *Anglo-Saxon Manuscripts in Microfiche Facsimile*, vol. 10: Manuscripts Containing Works by Bede, the Anglo-Saxon Chronicle, and Other Texts, MRTS 253 (Tempe, 2003).

Dobbie, E. V. K., ed., *The Anglo-Saxon Minor Poems*, ASPR 6 (New York, 1942).

Dobson, Eric John, *The Origins of Ancrene Wisse* (Oxford, 1976).

Donoghue, Daniel, *Style in Old English Poetry: The Test of the Alliteration* (New Haven, 1987).

Dumville, David N., *Liturgy and the Ecclesiastical History of Late Anglo-Saxon England: Four Studies* (Woodbridge, 1992).

Earle, J., ed., *Two of the Saxon Chronicles Parallel with Supplementary Extracts from the Others* (Oxford, 1865).

Ebeling, F. W., *Angelsächsisches Lesebuch* (Leipzig, 1847).

Ebersperger, B. *Die angelsächsischen Handschriften in den Pariser Bibliotheken* (Heidelberg, 1999).

Elstob, Elizabeth, *An English-Saxon Homily on the Birth-day of St Gregory: Anciently Used in the English-Saxon Church Giving an Account of the Conversion of the English from Paganism to Christianity* (London: 1709).

Enkvist, Nils Erik, *The Seasons of the Year: Chapters on a Motif from Beowulf to the Shepherd's Calendar*, Societas Scientiarum Fennica, Commentationes Humanarum Litterarum XXII.4 (Helsingfors, 1957).

Evan, Peter D., 'Wordplay as Evidence for the Date of *Durham*', *MÆ* 82.2 (2013), 314–17.

Förster, Max, 'Die altenglischen Verzeichnisse von Glücks- und Unglückstagen', in *Studies in English Philology: A Miscellany in Honor of Frederick Klaeber*, ed. K. Malone and M. B. Ruud (Minneapolis, 1929), 258–77.

Fox, Samuel, *Menologium seu Calendarium Poeticum, ex Hickesiano Thesauro, or the Poetical Calendar of the Anglo-Saxons* (London, 1830).

Fritsche, Paul, *Darstellung der Syntax in dem altenglischen Menologium: Ein Beitrag zu einer altenglischen Syntax* (Berlin, 1907).

Fulk, R. D., *A History of Old English Meter* (Philadelphia, 1992).

Fulk, R. D., and C. M. Cain, *A History of Old English Literature* (Oxford, 2003).

Fulk, R. D., R. E. Bjork, and J. D. Niles, eds., *Klaeber's Beowulf and the Fight at Finnsburg*, 4th ed. (Toronto, 2008).

Gamber, K., *Das Bonifatius-Sakramentar und weiter frühe Liturgiebücher aus Regensburg*, Textus patristici et liturgici 12 (Regensburg, 1975).

Gasquet, F. A., and E. Bishop, *The Bosworth Psalter: An Account of a Manuscript Formerly Belonging to O. Turville-Petre, Esq., of Bosworth Hall, Now Additional MS. 37517 at the British Museum* (London, 1908).

Gneuss, Helmut, 'The Origin of Standard Old English and Æthelwold's School at Winchester', *Anglo-Saxon England* 1 (1972), 63–83.

Gneuss, Helmut, *Handlist of Anglo-Saxon Manuscripts: A List of Manuscripts and Manuscript Fragments Written or Owned in England up to 1100*, MRTS 241 (Tempe, 2001).

Gneuss, Helmut, and Michael Lapidge, *Anglo-Saxon Manuscripts: A Bibliographical Handlist of Manuscripts and Manuscript Fragments Written or Owned in England up to 1100* (Toronto, 2014).

Bibliography

Godden, Malcolm, ed., *Ælfric's Catholic Homilies: The Second Series, Text*, EETS ss 5 (London, 1979).

Godden, Malcolm. 'New Year's Day in Late Anglo-Saxon England', *NQ* 39 (1992), 148–50.

Godden, Malcolm, *Ælfric's Catholic Homilies: Introduction, Commentary and Glossary*, EETS ss 18 (Oxford, 2000).

Gordon, Ida, ed., *The Seafarer*, with a bibliography compiled by Mary Clayton (Exeter, 1996).

Gough, J. V., 'Some Old English Glosses', *Anglia* 92 (1974), 273–90.

Gradon, P. O. E., ed., *Cynewulf's 'Elene'*, revised ed. (Exeter, 1977).

Graham, Timothy and A. G. Watson, *The Recovery of the Past in Early Elizabethan England: Documents by John Bale and John Joscelyn from the Circle of Matthew Parker*, Cambridge Bibliographical Society Monograph 13 (Cambridge, 1998).

Greenfield, Stanley B., and Daniel G. Calder, *A New Critical History of Old English Literature* (New York, 1986).

Greenfield, Stanley B., and Richard Evert, '*Maxims II*: Gnome and Poem', in *Anglo-Saxon Poetry: Essays in Appreciation for John C. McGalliard*, ed. Lewis E. Nicholson and Dolores Warwick Frese (Notre Dame, 1975), 337–54.

Greenfield, Stanley B., and Fred C. Robinson, eds., *A Bibliography of Publications on Old English Literature to the End of 1972* (Toronto, 1980).

Greeson, Jr, H. St Clair, 'Two Old English Observance Poems: *Seasons for Fasting* and *The Menologium* – An Edition', diss., University of Oregon, 1970.

Grein, C. W. M., ed., *Bibliothek der angelsächsischen Poesie in kritisch bearbeiteten Texten und mit vollständigem Glossar*, II.2 (Göttingen, 1858).

Grein, Christian W. M., 'Zur Textkritik der angelsächsischen Dichter', *Germania* 10 (1865), 416–29.

Grein, Christian W. M., F. Holthausen, and J. J. Köhler, eds., *Sprachschatz der angelsächsischen Dichter*, new ed. (Heidelberg, 1974).

Gretsch, Mechthild, 'Winchester Vocabulary and Standard Old English: The Vernacular in Late Anglo-Saxon England', *Bulletin of the John Rylands University Library of Manchester* 83.1 (2001), 41–87.

Grimaldi, M., ed., *Il 'Menologio' poetico anglosassone: introduzione, edizione, traduzione, commento* (Naples, 1988).

Haddan, Arthur West, and William Stubbs, eds., *Councils and Ecclesiastical Documents Related to Great Britain and Ireland*, 3 vols. (Oxford, 1869–1873).

Hampson, R. T., ed., *Medii Aevi Kalendarium or Dates, Charters, and Customs of the Middle Ages with Kalendars from the Tenth to the Fifteenth Century and an Alphabetical Digest of Obsolete Names of Days Forming a Glossary of the Dates of the Middle Ages with Tables and Other Aids for Ascertaining Dates*, 2 vols. (London, 1841).

Hansen, Elaine Tuttle, 'Wisdom Literature in Old English Verse', diss., University of Washington, 1975.

Hansen, Elaine Tuttle, *The Solomon Complex: Reading Wisdom in Old English Poetry*, McMaster Old English Studies and Texts 5 (Toronto, 1988).

Harrison, Kenneth, 'The Beginning of the Year in England, c. 500–900', *Anglo-Saxon England* 2 (1973), 51–70.

Harrison, Kenneth, *The Framework of Anglo-Saxon History to A.D. 900* (Cambridge, 1976).

Hart, Cyril. *Learning and Culture in Late Anglo-Saxon England and the Influence of Ramsey Abbey on the Major English Monastic Schools: A Survey of the Development*

Bibliography

of *Mathematical, Medical, and Scientific Studies, in England before the Norman Conquest*, 2 vols in three books, Medieval Studies 17–18 (Lewiston, 2003).
Head, Pauline, 'Perpetual History in the Old English *Menologium*', in *The Medieval Chronicle: Proceedings of the 1st International Conference on the Medieval Chronicle, Driebergen/Utrecht 13–16 July 1996*, ed. Erik Kooper (Amsterdam, 1999), 155–62.
Henel, H., *Studien zum altenglischen Computus*, Beiträge zur englischen Philologie 26 (Leipzig, 1934).
Henel, H., 'Altenglischer Mönchsaberglaube', *Englische Studien* 69 (1934–35), 329–49.
Henel, Heinrich, ed., *Ælfric's De Temporibus Anni Edited from All the Known MSS. and Fragments*, EETS os 213 (London, 1942).
Hennig, John, 'The Irish Counterparts of the Anglo-Saxon *Menologium*', *Mediaeval Studies* 14 (1952), 98–106.
Hennig, John, 'A Critical Study of Hampson's Edition of the Metrical "Calendar" in Galba A. XVIII and Parallels', *Scriptorium* 8 (1954), 61–74.
Herzfeld, George, ed., *An Old English Martyrology Re-Edited from Manuscripts in the Libraries of the British Museum and of Corpus Christi College, Cambridge*, EETS os 116 (London, 1900).
Hickes, George, *Linguarum Vett. Septentrionalium Thesaurus Grammatico-Criticus et Archæologicus*, vol. 1, pt. 1. Institutiones Grammaticæ Anglo-Saxonicæ & Mæso-Gothicæ (Oxford, 1703).
Hill, David, 'Eleventh Century Labours of the Months in Prose and Pictures', *Landscape History* 20 (1998), 29–39.
Hill, Joyce, 'The *Litaniae maiores* and *minores* in Rome, Francia and Anglo-Saxon England', *Early Medieval Europe* 9 (2000), 211–46.
Hodgkin, R. H., 'The Beginning of the Year in the English Chronicle', *HER* 39 (1924), 497–510.
Hofstetter, Walter, 'Winchester and the Standardization of Old English Vocabulary', *Anglo-Saxon England* 17 (1988), 139–61.
Hogg, R. M., *A Grammar of Old English*, vol. 1: Phonology (Oxford, 1992).
Hogg, R. M., and R. D. Fulk, *A Grammar of Old English*, vol. 2: Morphology (Chichester, 2011).
Hollis, Stephanie, 'Scientific and Medical Writings', in *A Companion to Anglo-Saxon Literature*, ed. Phillip Pulsiano and Elaine Treharne (Oxford, 2001), 188–208.
Holthausen, F., 'C. Plummer, *Two of the Saxon Chronicles Parallel*', *Anglia Beiblatt* 3 (1893), 239–40.
Holthausen, F., 'C. W. M. Grein, *Bibliothek der angelsächsischen Poesie*', *Anglia Beiblatt* 5 (1894), 225–6.
Holweck, F. G., 'The Feast of Assumption', in *The Catholic Encyclopedia*, vol. 2, ed. C. G. Herbermann et al. (London: 1907), pp. 6–7.
Holweck, F. G., 'Michael the Archangel', in *The Catholic Encyclopedia*, vol. 10, ed. C. G. Herbermann et al. (London: 1911), pp. 275–7.
Howe, Nicholas, 'The Latin Encyclopedia Tradition and Old English Poetry', diss., Yale University, 1978.
Howe, Nicholas, *The Old English Catalogue Poems*, Anglistica 23 (Copenhagen, 1985).
Hutcheson, B. R. *Old English Poetic Metre* (Cambridge, 1995).
Imelmann, R., *Das altenglische Menologium* (Berlin, 1902).
Jackson, K. *Studies in Early Celtic Nature Poetry* (London, 1935).
Johnson, Samuel, *A Dictionary of the English Language* (1755; repr. London, 1979).

Bibliography

Jones, C. A., ed., *Old English Shorter Poems*, vol. 1: Religious and Didactic (Cambridge, MA, 2012).

Jones, C. W., ed., *Bedae Opera de Temporibus* (Cambridge, MA, 1943).

Jordan, Richard, *Eigentümlichkeiten des anglischen Wortschatzes: Eine wortgeographische Untersuchung mit etymologischen Anmerkungen*, Anglistische Forschungen 17 (Heidelberg, 1906).

Jorgensen, Alice, ed., *Reading the Anglo-Saxon Chronicle: Language, Literature, History*, Studies in the Early Middle Ages 23 (Turnhout, 2010).

Karasawa, Kazutomo, 'On the Usage of Latin Month-Names in *The Menologium*', *Sophia English Studies* 24 (1999), 69–87.

Karasawa, Kazutomo, 'An Aspect of OE Joy Term *Dream* in Comparison with *Wynn*', *Soundings* 24 (1999), 9–26.

Karasawa, Kazutomo, 'Christian Influence on OE *dream*: Pre-Christian and Christian Meanings', *Neophilologus* 87.2 (2003), 307–22.

Karasawa, Kazutomo, 'The Structure of the *Menologium* and Its Computistical Background', *Studies in English Literature* 84 (2007), 123–41.

Karasawa, Kazutomo, 'The Verse *Menologium*, the Prose *Menologium*, and Some Aspects of Computistical Education in Late Anglo-Saxon England – A New Edition', diss., Sophia University, Tokyo, 2007.

Karasawa, Kazutomo, 'A Note on the Old English Poem "Menologium" Line 3b *on þy eahteoðan dæg*', *NQ* ns 54.3 (2007), 211–15.

Karasawa, Kazutomo, 'Some Problems in the Editions of the *Menologium* with Special Reference to Lines 81a, 184b and 206a', *NQ* ns 56.4 (2009), 485–7.

Karasawa, Kazutomo, 'The Prose and the Verse *Menologium* in the Tradition of Elementary Computistical Education in Late Anglo-Saxon England', in *Secular Learning in Anglo-Saxon England*, ed. L. S. Chardonnens and B. Carella, Amsterdamer Beiträge zur älteren Germanistik 69 (Amsterdam, 2012), 119–43.

Karasawa, Kazutomo, 'Irish Influence upon the Old English Poem *Menologium* Reconsidered', forthcoming.

Karasawa, Kazutomo, 'Lexical Choice and Poetic Freedom in the Old English *Menologium*', forthcoming.

Kemble, John Mitchell, *The Saxons in England: A History of the English Commonwealth till the Period of the Norman Conquest*, 2 vols (London, 1876).

Ker, N. R., *Catalogue of Manuscripts Containing Anglo-Saxon* (Oxford, 1957).

Keynes, Simon, 'Manuscripts of the *Anglo–Saxon Chronicle*', in *The Cambridge History of the Book in Britain*, vol. 1. c.400–1100, ed. Richard Gameson (Cambridge, 2012), 537–52.

Klaeber, Frederick, ed., *Beowulf and the Fight at Finnsburg*, 3rd ed. with first and second supplements (Boston, 1950).

Kluge, Friedrich, 'Zu altenglischen Dichtungen', *Englische Studien* 8 (1885), 472–79.

Kock, Ernst A. *Jubilee Jaunts and Jottings: 250 Contributions to the Interpretation and Prosody of Old West Teutonic Alliterative Poetry* (Lund, 1918).

Kotzor, Günter, ed., *Das altenglische Martyrologium*, Bayerische Akademie der Wissenschaften, Philologisch-Historische Klasse Abhandlungen, Neu Folge 88, 2 vols (Munich, 1981).

Krapp, George Philip, ed., *The Paris Psalter and the Meters of Boethius*, ASPR 5 (New York, 1932).

Krapp, George Philip, and Elliot Van Kirk Dobbie, eds., *The Exeter Book*, ASPR 3 (New York, 1936).

Bibliography

Laing, M. *Catalogue of Sources for a Linguistic Atlas of Early Medieval English* (Cambridge, 1993).

Lapidge, Michael, 'A Tenth-Century Metrical Calendar from Ramsey', *Revue Bénédictine* 94 (1984), 326–69.

Lapidge, Michael, *Anglo-Saxon Litanies of the Saints*, HBS 106 (London, 1991).

Lapidge, Michael, 'The Saintly Life in Anglo-Saxon England', in *The Cambridge Companion to Old English Literature*, ed. M. Godden and M. Lapidge (Cambridge, 1991), 243–63.

Lapidge, Michael, *Anglo-Latin Literature 900–1066* (London, 1993).

Lapidge, Michael, 'Wilfrid II', in M. Lapidge, et al., *The Blackwell Encyclopaedia of Anglo-Saxon England* (Oxford, 1999), 476.

Lapidge, Michael, 'The Metrical Calendar in the "Pembroke Psalter-Hours"', *Analecta Bollandiana* 129 (2011), 325–87.

Larrington, Carolyne, *A Store of Common Sense: Gnomic Theme and Style in Old Icelandic and Old English Wisdom Poetry* (Oxford, 1993).

Liebermann, Felix, 'Zum angelsächsischen Menologium', *Archiv für das Studium der neueren Sprachen und Literaturen* 110 (1903), 98–9.

Liebermann, Felix, ed., *Die Gesetze der Angelsachsen*, 3 vols (1903–1916; repr. Tübingen, 1960).

Lowe, E. A., ed., *Codices Latini Antiquiores*, 11 vols and supplement (Oxford, 1934–71).

Mack, Frances M., ed., *Seinte Marherete þe Meiden ant Martyr Re–edited from MS. Bodley 34, Oxford MS. Royal 17A xxvii, British Museum*, EETS os 193 (London, 1934).

Mackie, W.S., 'Notes upon the Text and the Interpretation of "Beowulf", II'. *Modern Language Review* 36.1 (1941), 95–8.

Magennis, Hugh. *Images of Community in Old English Poetry*, CSASE 18 (Cambridge, 1996).

Malmberg, L., ed., *Resignation*, revised ed., Durham and St Andrews Medieval Texts 2 (Durham, 1982).

Malone, Kemp, 'The Old English Period (to 1100)', in *A Literary History of England I: The Middle Ages*, ed. K. Malone and A. C. Baugh, 2nd ed. (London, 1967), 3–105.

Malone, Kemp, 'The Old English Calendar Poem', in *Studies in Language, Literature, and Culture of the Middle Ages and Later*, ed. E. Bagby Atwood and A. A. Hill (Austin, 1969), 193–9.

McGurk, P., 'The Metrical Calendar of Hampson: A New Edition', *Analecta Bollandiana* 104 (1986), 79–125.

Mensel, William Langley, 'On the Principles of Artistic Order in Shorter Old English Poetry, and their Relevance to Critical Interpretation and Evaluation, with Illustrative Discussions of *Menologium, The Rune Poem, The Ruin, The Battle of Maldon*, and *The Battle of Brunanburh*', diss., University of Washington, 1974.

Meyvaert, Paul, 'A Metrical Calendar by Eugenius Vulgarius', *Analecta Bollandiana* 84 (1966), 349–77.

Minkova, Donka, *Alliteration and Sound Change in Early English*, Cambridge Studies in Linguistics 101 (Cambridge, 2003).

Mitchell, Bruce, *Old English Syntax*, 2 vols (Oxford, 1985).

Mohrbutter, A., 'Darstellung der Syntax in den vier echten Predigten des ags. Erzbischofs Wulfstan,' diss., University of Münster, 1885.

Moorman, Frederic W., *The Interpretation of Nature in English Poetry from Beowulf*

to Shakespeare, Quellen und Forschungen zur Sprach- und Culturgeschichte der germanischen Völker 95 (Strasbourg, 1905).
Morris, Richard, ed., *Legends of the Holy Rood*, EETS os 46 (London, 1871).
Muir, Bernard James, ed., *A Pre-Conquest English Prayer-Book (BL MSS Cotton Galba A.xiv and Nero A.ii (ff. 3–13))*, HBS 103 (Woodbridge, 1988).
Napier, Arthur S., 'Altenglische Kleinigkeiten', *Anglia* 11 (1889), 1–10.
Neville, Jennifer, 'The Seasons in Old English Poetry', in *La Ronde des saisons: les saisons dans la littérature et la société anglaises au Moyen Âge*, ed. Léo Carruthers, Cultures et Civilisations Médiévales 16 (Paris, 1998).
Neville, Jennifer, *Representations of the Natural World in Old English Poetry*, CSASE 27 (Cambridge, 1999).
Oberle, K. A., *Überreste germanischen Heidentums im Christentum oder die Wochentage, Monate und christlichen Feste etymologisch, mythologisch, symbolisch und historisch erklärt* (Baden Baden, 1883).
O'Brien O'Keeffe, Katherine, 'Reading the C-Text: The After-lives of London, British Library, Cotton Tiberius B. i.', in *Anglo-Saxon Manuscripts and their Heritage*, ed. P. Pulsiano, and E. M. Treharne (Aldershot, 1998), 137–60.
O'Brien O'Keeffe, Katherine, ed., *The Anglo-Saxon Chronicle: A Collaborative Edition*, vol. 5: MS. C (Cambridge, 2001).
O'Donnell, Thomas. 'The Old English *Durham*, the *Historia de sancto Cuthberto*, and the Unreformed in Late Anglo-Saxon Literature', *JEGP* 113.2 (2014), 131–55.
Orchard, Nicholas, ed., *The Leofric Missal*, 2 vols, HBS 113–14 (London, 2002).
Orel, Vladimir, *A Handbook of Germanic Etymology* (Leiden, 2003).
Ostheeren, Klaus, *Studien zum Begriff der 'Freude' und seinen Ausdrucksmitteln in altenglischen Texten (Poesie, Alfred, Aelfric)* (Heidelberg, 1964).
Page, R. I., 'Anglo-Saxon Paganism: The Evidence of Bede', in *Pagans and Christians: The Interplay between Christian Latin and Traditional Germanic Cultures in Early Medieval Europe: Proceedings of the Second Germania Latina Conference held at the University of Groningen May 1992*, Germania Latina 2, ed. T. Hofstra, L. A. J. R. Houwen and A. A. MacDonald (Groningen, 1995), 99–129.
Piper, Ferdinand, *Kalendarien und Martyrologien der Angelsachsen so wie das Martyrologium und der Computus der Herrad von Landsperg nebst Annalen der Jahre 1859 und 1860* (Berlin, 1862).
Plummer, Charles, ed., *Two of the Saxon Chronicles Parallel with Supplementary Extracts from the Others: A Revised Text*. 2 vols, reissued with a bibliographical note by Dorothy Whitelock (Oxford, 1952).
Pollington, Stephen, *Leechcraft: Early English Charms, Plantlore and Healing* (Frithgarth, 2000).
Pons, Emile, *Le Thème et le sentiment de la nature dans la poésie anglo-saxonne*, Publications de la Faculté des Lettres de l'Université de Strasbourg, fascicule 25 (Strasbourg, 1925).
Poole, R. L., 'The Beginning of the Year in the Anglo-Saxon Chronicles', *EHR* 19 (1901), 719–21.
Rask, Erasmus, *A Grammar of the Anglo-Saxon Tongue with a Praxis*, new ed. trans. B. Thorpe (Copenhagen, 1830).
Rauer, Christine, ed., *The Old English Martyrology: Edition, Translation and Commentary*, AST 10 (Cambridge, 2013).
Raw, Barbara C., *The Art and Background of Old English Poetry* (London, 1978).
Richards, Mary, 'Old Wine in a New Bottle: Recycled Instructional Materials in *Seasons*

for Fasting', in *The Old English Homily: Precedent, Practice, and Appropriation*, ed. Aaron J. Kleist, Studies in the Early Middle Ages 17 (Turnhout, 2007), 345–64.

Richards, Mary P., ed., *The Old English Poem Seasons for Fasting: A Critical Edition*, Medieval European Studies 15 (Morgantown, WV, 2014).

Riordan, Maurice, ed., *The Finest Music: An Anthology of Early Irish Lyrics* (London, 2014).

Robertson, A. J., ed., *The Laws of the Kings of England from Edmund to Henry I* (Cambridge, 1925).

Robinson, Fred C., 'Old English Literature in Its Most Immediate Context', in *Old English Literature in Context*, eds. John D. Niles (Cambridge, 1980).

Robinson, Fred C., and E. G. Stanley, ed., *Old English Verse Texts from Many Sources: A Comprehensive Collection* (Copenhagen, 1991).

Rositzke, H. A., *The C-Text of the Old English Chronicles*, Beiträge zur englischen Philologie 34 (Bochum-Langendreer, 1940).

Rushforth, Rebecca. *Saints in English Kalendars before A.D. 1100*, HBS 117 (London, 2008).

Schlenk, K. F., 'Studien zum Gebrauch von *Dream* in der angelsächsischen Poesie', diss., University of Marburg, 1950.

Schneider, Karl, 'The OE. Names of the Months', in *Sophia Lectures on Beowulf*, ed. Shoichi Watanabe, and Norio Tsuchiya (Tokyo, 1986), 260–75.

Schrader, B., *Studien zur Ælfricschen Syntax: Ein Beitrage zur ae Grammatik* (Jena, 1887).

Scragg, Donald, 'Manuscript Sources of Old English Prose', in *Working with Anglo-Saxon Manuscripts*, ed. Gale R. Owen-Crocker (Exeter, 2009), 61–87.

Sehrt, Edward H., *Vollständiges Wörterbuch zum Heliand und zur altsächsischen Genesis*, 2nd ed. (Göttingen, 1966).

Shepherd, Sianne Lauren, 'Anglo-Saxon Labours of the Months: Representing May – A Case Study', MPhil thesis, University of Birmingham, 2010.

Shippey, T. A., *Poems of Wisdom and Learning in Old English* (Totowa, 1976).

Sievers, Eduard, 'Collationen angelsächsischer Gedichte', *Zeitschrift für deutschen Altertum und deutsche Literatur* 15 (1872), 456–67.

Sievers, Eduard, 'Zur Rhythmik des germanischen Alliterationsverses', *Beiträge zur Geschichte der deutschen Sprache und Literatur* 10 (1885), 209–314 and 451–545.

Sievers, Eduard, 'Zum Codex Junius XI', *Beiträge zur Geschichte der deutschen Sprache und Literatur* 10 (1885), 195–9.

Sievers, Eduard, *Angelsächsische Grammatik* (Halle, 1898).

Siffrin, P., 'Das Walderdorffer Kalenderfragment Saec. VIII und die Berliner Blatter eines Sacramentars aus Regensburg', *Ephemerides Liturgicae* 47 (1933), 201–24.

Sisam, Kenneth, *Studies in the History of Old English Literature* (Oxford, 1953).

Skeat, Walter W., ed., *Ælfric's Lives of Saints Being a Set of Sermons on Saints' Days Formerly Observed by the English Church*, 4 vols., EETS os 76, 82, 94, 114 (London, 1881–1900).

Sokoll, Eduard, 'R. Imelmann, *Das altenglische Menologium* (Berlin, 1902)', *Anglia Beiblatt* 14 (1903), 307–15.

Stanley, Eric G., 'The Prose *Menologium* and the Verse *Menologium*', in *Text and Language in Medieval English Prose: A Festschrift for Tadao Kubouchi*, ed. A. Oizumi et al. (Frankfurt, 2005), 255–67.

Stokes, Whitley, 'Cuimmin's Poem on the Saints of Ireland', *Zeitschrift für celtische Philologie* 1 (1897), 59–73.

Bibliography

Stokes, Whitley, ed., *Félire Óengusso Céli Dé: The Martyrology of Oengus the Culdee*, HBS 29 (1905; repr. Dublin, 1984).
Swanton, Michael J., trans., *The Anglo-Saxon Chronicle* (London, 1996).
Sweet, Henry, ed., *The Student's Dictionary of Anglo-Saxon* (1896; repr. Oxford, 1976).
Ten Brink, Bernhard, *History of English Literature*, trans. H. M. Kennedy and W. C. Robinson, 2 vols (London, 1893).
Thornbury, E. V., *Becoming a Poet in Anglo-Saxon England*, CSML 88 (Cambridge, 2014).
Thurston, Herbert, 'Menologium', in C. G. Herbermann et al., *The Catholic Encyclopedia*, vol. 10 (New York, 1913), 191–2.
Toller, T. Northcote, and A. Campbell, eds., *An Anglo-Saxon Dictionary Based on the Manuscript Collections of the Late Joseph Bosworth, Supplement* (London, 1921).
Toswell, M. J. 'The Metrical Psalter and *The Menologium*: Some Observations', *Neuphilologische Mitteilungen* 94.3–4 (1993), 249–57.
Visser, F. Th., *An Historical Syntax of the English Language*, vol. 2 (Leiden, 1966).
Walkden, George. 'The Status of *hwæt* in Old English', *English Language and Linguistics* 17.3 (2013), 465–88.
Wallis, Faith, trans., *Bede: The Reckoning of Time*, Translated Texts for Historians 29 (Liverpool, 1988).
Walsh, Maura, and D. Ó Cróinín, eds., *Cummian's Letter De Controversia Paschali and the De Ratione Computandi* (Toronto, 1988).
Warren, F. F., ed., *The Leofric Missal as Used in the Cathedral of Exeter during the Episcopate of Its First Bishop A.D. 1050–1072 Together with Some Account of the Red Book of Derby, the Missal of Robert of Jumièges, and a Few Other Early Manuscript Service Books of the English Church* (Oxford, 1883).
Weinhold, Karl, *Die deutsche Monatnamen* (Halle, 1869).
Weston, Lisa Mary Colette, 'Cosmic Pattern and Poetic Order: Structure in Nine Old English Didactic Poems', diss., University of California, 1982.
Whitbread, L. 'Two Notes on Minor Old English Poems', *Studia Neophilologica* 20 (1947), 192–8.
Whitelock, Dorothy, 'On the Commencement of the Year in the Saxon Chronicles', in *Two of the Saxon Chronicles Parallel with Supplementary Extracts from the Others: A Revised Text*, ed. C. Plummer, reissued with a bibliographical note by Dorothy Whitelock, vol. 2 (Oxford, 1952), cxxxi–cxliid.
Whitelock, Dorothy, *English Historical Documents*, vol. 1: c.500–1042 (Oxford, 1955).
Whitelock, Dorothy, D. C. Douglas and S. I. Tucker, *The Anglo-Saxon Chronicle: A Revised Translation* (London, 1961).
Wilcox, Jonathan, ed., *Ælfric's Prefaces*, Durham Medieval Texts 9 (Durham, 1994).
Williams, B. C., ed., *Gnomic Poetry in Anglo-Saxon* (New York, 1914).
Wilmart, A., 'Un témoin anglo-saxon du calendrier métrique d'York', *Revue Bénédictine* 46 (1934), 41–69.
Wilson, David, *Anglo-Saxon Paganism* (London, 1992).
Wilson, H. A. ed., *The Missal of Robert of Jumièges*, HBS 11 (London, 1896).
Wilson, H. A., ed., *The Calendar of St. Willibrord from MS. Paris, Lat. 10837: A Facsimile with Transcription, Introduction, and Notes*, HBS 55 (London, 1918).
Wormald, Francis, ed., *English Kalendars before A.D. 1100*, vol. 1, HBS 72 (London, 1934).
Wormald, Francis, ed., *English Benedictine Kalendars after A.D. 1100*, 2 vols, HBS 77 and 81 (London, 1939 and 1946).

Bibliography

Wrenn, C. L., *A Study of Old English Literature* (London, 1967).
Wright, Charles D., *The Irish Tradition in Old English Literature*, CSASE 6 (Cambridge, 1993).
Wülker, Richard Paul, *Grundriss zur Geschichte der angelsächsischen Litteratur mit einer Übersicht der angelsächsischen Sprachwissenschaft* (Leipzig, 1885).
Wülker, Richard Paul, ed., *Bibliothek der angelsächsischen Poesie begründet von Christian W. M. Grein*, II.2 (Leipzig, 1894).
Zupitza, Julius, ed., *Aelfrics Grammatik und Glossar: Text und Varianten*, 4th ed. with an introduction by Helmut Gneuss (Hildesheim, 2003).

Index

Abingdon 7
Ælfric of Eynsham xi, 16, 27, 35–7, 42, 70–1, 96–7, 102–3, 116, 123–6, 187–8
   Catholic Homilies 16, 41–2, 45, 47–8, 61, 86–90, 92–7, 102–3, 107–8, 111, 113, 115–18, 120, 122–6, 128, 146–53, 183–4, 186–9, 193
   Lives of Saints 53, 61, 105, 107, 124, 183
   Grammar 27, 117, 184, 193
   De temporibus anni 35–7, 94, 110, 182–3
Æthelwold of Winchester 71, 94
Alcuin 123, 148, 160
All Saints' Day 29, 54, 85, 122, 135, 152, 177, 180
Andreas 60–1, 66, 87, 97–8, 103, 106, 109, 114, 116, 118, 121, 126, 128, 201
Andrew, St 28–9, 41, 85, 126, 135, 152, 178, 180, 201
Anglo-Saxon Chronicle xi, xii, 5–15, 33–4, 45, 53–5, 61, 69, 71, 86, 105, 111, 137, 183, 187
   C-text of xi, xii, 6–7, 10, 12–13, 33, 53–5
Annunciation 17, 28, 92, 94–5, 107, 117, 133, 136, 148, 160, 168, 190
Apollonius of Tyre 103
Assumption 29, 37, 113, 133, 150, 174, 180
Augustine of Canterbury, St 17, 41, 47, 79, 92, 103, 105, 133, 151, 170, 174, 201

Bartholomew, St 29, 37, 41, 81, 115, 133, 143, 150, 174, 180, 202
Battle of Brunanburh 13–14, 69–71, 89, 111, 120
Battle of Maldon 64, 118
Bede 35–6, 86, 89–90, 92, 100–1, 105, 111, 116, 118–19, 121, 124, 126, 147, 170, 182, 192, 198
   De temporum ratione 17, 27, 35–7, 45, 86, 89–90, 92, 94, 100–1, 105, 107, 111, 116, 118–19, 121, 127, 182, 184, 192, 198

   Historia ecclesiastica 10, 17, 93, 104–5, 148, 152
   Martyrologium 17, 124
   Old English Bede 104, 129, 183
beginning of the year 13, 45, 75, 86–8, 190, 197
Benedict, St 28, 41, 60, 71, 75, 93–4, 107, 110, 127, 133, 136, 141, 148, 168, 172, 178, 202
Beowulf 65–6, 70, 93, 95, 98, 104, 106, 109, 113, 115, 118, 123–4
Bible
   Acts 90, 111, 147
   Deuteronomy 129
   Genesis 50, 87, 94
   Luke 17, 50, 87, 90, 94–5, 107, 147
   Mark 17, 116
   Matthew 17, 116, 153
   I Timothy 150
bissextile day *see* intercalary day
Bosa of York 20, 143, 147, 151, 176
Byrhtferth ix, xi, 4, 35–6, 38–9, 50, 71, 91–2, 96–7, 100, 106–7, 112–13, 118, 122, 198
   Enchiridion 4, 16–17, 20, 35–6, 38, 49, 89, 90–4, 96–8, 101, 103, 106, 112, 118, 122, 183–4, 192, 198–9
calendars *see* liturgical calendar

Canterbury 7–8, 29, 31, 41, 103–5, 148, 161–3
Capture of the Five Boroughs 69, 71, 111
Christ A 95, 117, 121, 123, 128–9
Christ B 61, 66, 97, 115, 120
Christ C 102, 106, 118, 122–3, 130
Christ and Satan 66, 103–4, 112, 114, 129
Christmas xi, 28, 32, 34, 37, 44–5, 47–9, 86–7, 94, 107, 116, 128, 133, 135, 146, 179, 180
Circumcision 32, 43, 48–50, 86–7, 146, 166
Clement, St 17, 41, 60–1, 85, 123–6, 135, 145, 152, 178, 203
Coronation of Edgar xi, 64, 69, 71

225

Index

computus 27, 35, 37, 110, 187, 192, 194, 198–9
creation, the 17, 94
   of the sun and the moon 16–17, 92, 94
Cynewulf 102, 115, 147, 183
Cuimmin's poem on the saints of Ireland 23
Cuthbert, St 20, 43, 47, 51, 127, 133, 147, 168, 174

Daniel 66, 122–3
Death of Edgar 14, 20, 63–4, 67, 69, 71–2, 89, 94, 102, 104, 183, 187–8, 194
Death of Edward 13, 64, 120
De ratione computandi 37, 45
division of the year 25, 27, 33, 36, 38, 45–6, 49, 108
Dream of the Rood 95, 103
Dunstan, St 31–2, 43, 47, 94, 170
Durham 63, 100, 129

ecclesiastical calendar *see* liturgical calendar
Ecgberht of Ripon 20, 141, 169
Edward the Martyr 31–2, 43, 46–7, 71, 129, 168
Elene 53, 63, 89, 95, 102–3, 122, 128, 183
Enlaith betha 21, 23–4, 45, 156
Epiphany 13, 32, 43, 48–50, 88, 146, 160, 166, 180
equinox 17, 25, 27–32, 34–40, 45, 62, 77, 83, 92, 94–5, 107, 109, 116, 118–19, 127, 133, 135–6, 160, 181, 187, 190–1, 199, 203
Exodus 89, 103, 109, 122, 126

Fates of the Apostles xi, 65, 90, 102, 104, 108–10, 113, 126, 128
Félire Adamnáin 21–2, 24–5, 154, 156
Félire Óengusso 21–4, 45

Genesis A 58, 61, 90, 95, 98, 102, 109, 120, 123, 128, 130
Genesis B 104
Gregorian Sacramentary 45, 86, 118
Gregory I, St 17, 24–5, 38, 41, 46, 75, 79, 92, 133, 141, 147, 152, 155, 168, 205
Guthlac of Crowland, St 32, 48, 115, 121, 168, 174
Guthlac A 13, 89, 93, 103–4, 123, 128, 160
Guthlac B 13, 89, 103–4, 106, 120–1, 126, 128

Hewalds, Two 20, 151, 176
Holy Innocents 32, 43, 47–8, 54, 153, 179

intercalary day 50–1, 62, 75, 90–1, 202
Invention of the Cross 38, 47, 50, 102–3, 133, 170
Isidore of Sevilla 90

James the Apostle, St 29–30, 41, 47, 81, 110–11, 113, 133, 143, 150, 153, 173, 180, 206
Jerome 143, 146, 150–1, 176
John the Apostle and Evangelist, St 32, 43, 47–8, 107, 110, 133, 143, 145, 150–3, 179
John the Baptist, St 17, 36–7, 41, 79, 94, 106–7, 115–17, 133, 136, 141, 143, 149–50, 160, 206
Julian calendar, the
   original 29, 86, 94, 106–7, 136, 160
   revised 29, 31–2, 36, 94, 106, 136
Juliana 93, 115, 120, 128, 147

Lammas 32, 42, 47–8, 54, 81, 111–12, 133, 173, 205
Latin metrical calendar
   of York 17–20, 28, 47, 87, 89–90, 93, 95, 102, 107–8, 110–11, 113, 115–20, 122–4, 126, 128, 138, 149, 151, 164–79
   of Hampson 17–21, 42, 87, 89–90, 93, 95, 102, 104, 107–8, 111, 113, 115–20, 122–4, 126, 128, 146–53
   of Ramsey 19, 20–1, 47, 87, 89–90, 93, 95, 102, 104, 107–8, 111, 113, 115–19, 122–4, 126, 128, 146–53
   of Winchcomb 19
   of Wandelbert of Prüm 19,
   by Eugenius Vulgarius 19, 25, 45, 86
Laurence, St 29, 41, 81, 113, 133, 143, 150, 174, 180, 206
laws
   Geþyncðo 66, 91
   of Æthelred the Unready 31, 43, 46, 71, 129
   of Alfred the Great 46, 66, 91
   of Cnut 31, 43, 46
   of Wihtræd 184
leap year 50, 90–1
liturgical calendar xiii, 4, 7, 15–21, 25–6, 28–9, 30–33, 36, 38–45, 47–51, 53, 86–7, 89–91, 93, 95, 98, 102–4, 106–8, 111, 113, 115–20, 122–4, 126, 128–9, 146–53, 161–82, 184, 190–3, 198–9
liturgical year xi, xiii, 23–5, 27, 32–4, 36–7, 87–8

Index

Major Rogation 32, 38, 41–2, 44, 47–8, 50, 97–8, 100, 133, 169
manuscripts
  BL Additional 37517: 29, 31
  BL Arundel 60: 163
  BL Arundel 155: 162
  BL Cotton Caligula A.xv: 189
  BL Cotton Galba A.xviii: 19
  BL Cotton Julius A.ii: 193
  BL Cotton Julius A.vi: 19
  BL Cotton Julius D.vii: 19, 20
  BL Cotton Nero A. ii: 162
  BL Cotton Nero C.iii: 7
  BL Cotton Otho B.xi: 10
  BL Cotton Tiberius B.i: xi, 5, 10,
  BL Cotton Tiberius B.v: 19
  BL Cotton Tiberius E.iv: 19
  BL Cotton Titus D. xxvii: 162
  BL Cotton Vespasian B.vi: 18, 138
  BL Cotton Vitellius A. xii: 163
  BL Cotton Vitellius A.xviii: 163
  BL Cotton Vitellius E. xviii: 163, 189, 191
  BL Egerton 3314: 163
  BL Harley 3271: 26–7, 29, 189
  CCCC 9: 162
  CCCC 391: 162
  CCCC 422: 27, 42, 162, 182, 184
  Cambridge, Trinity College O.2.24: 18, 138
  Cambridge, Trinity College, R.15.32: 162
  Cambridge, University Library, Kk.v.32: 162
  Hauzenstein near Regensburg, Gräflich Walderdorffsche Bibliothek, s.n.: 161
  Munich, Hauptstaatsarchiv, Raritäten-Selekt 108: 161
  Oxford, Bodleian Library, Bodley 579: 7, 21, 29, 31–2, 48, 51, 161
  Oxford, Bodleian Library, Digby 63: 161
  Oxford, Bodleian Library, Douce 296: 162
  Oxford, Bodleian Library, Hatton 113: 163
  Oxford, Bodleian Library, Junius 27: 19, 20, 161
  Oxford, St John's College, MS 17: 15, 17, 19, 20, 47
  Paris, Bibliothèque Nationale, latin 7299: 162
  Paris, Bibliothèque Nationale, latin 10062: 162
  Paris, Bibliothèque Nationale, latin 10837: 161
  Rome, Vatican Library, Reg. Lat. 12: 162
  Rouen, Bibliothèque Manicipale, Y.6: 162
  Salisbury, Cathedral Library, 150: 163
Martin, St 41, 54, 60, 85, 123, 134–5, 143, 152, 170, 172, 177, 206
Martyrologium Hieronymianum 45, 86
Martyrologium Wandalberti, *see* Latin Metrical Calendar of Wandelbert of Prüm
Martyrology of Tallaght 21, 23, 156
Mary the Blessed Virgin, St 24, 37–8, 41, 46, 75, 77, 86, 90, 94–5, 107, 113–14, 117, 133, 135–6, 143, 150, 155, 175, 177–8, 180, 185, 206
Mathias, St 41, 47, 50–1, 60, 75, 90–1, 133, 136, 141, 147, 149, 168, 180, 206
Matthew, St 29, 41, 83, 90, 117, 135, 143, 151–2, 175, 180, 206
Maxims I 11, 122
Maxims II xi, 6, 8, 10–12, 14–15, 55, 66, 91
Menologium template 2, 15–16, 32, 39, 46, 49–52
Metres of Boethius 14, 61, 63, 89, 106, 128
Metrical Preface to the Pastoral Care 61, 93, 104
Metrical Psalms xi, 3, 16, 61 65, 70, 96, 111, 126, 129
Michael, St (Archangel) 24, 41, 83, 94, 118–19, 135, 143, 151, 155, 176, 206
Minor Rogations *see* Rogationtide
month system, Roman 20, 28, 53, 89

Old English Martyrology 1, 2, 20, 38, 42, 45, 61, 63, 86–90, 93–5, 98, 100–5, 107–8, 111, 113, 115–24, 126–8, 146–53, 183–5, 188, 192, 198–9
Old English *Orosius* 5–7, 10, 12–13, 15
Old Saxon 104

Paulinus of York 20, 143, 152, 176
Peter and Paul, SS 30–2, 41, 43, 51, 81, 90, 108, 110, 141, 150–2, 172
Philip and James, SS 41, 50, 79, 169
Phoenix 106, 115, 122–3, 128
Purification 28, 38, 41, 90, 133, 167, 180

Resignation 110
Riddles 61, 65–6, 69, 111, 118, 122–3, 126
Rogationtide 42, 100

Index

Roman year, the 37, 39, 45, 49, 52–53, 87, 146

seasons xi, xii, 11–12, 17, 21–2, 24–7, 35–40, 42, 45, 49, 52–4, 90–1, 101, 103, 112–13, 118–19, 121–3, 155
  autumn 24, 37, 81, 83, 85, 98, 112–13, 122–3, 133, 155, 205
  spring 24, 28, 37, 75, 90–2, 133, 155, 206
  summer 4, 24, 37, 53, 79, 81, 89, 101, 103, 106, 111–13, 122, 133, 155, 160, 208
  winter 4, 24, 37–8, 75, 85–6, 90, 119, 121–2, 135, 155, 210
Seasons for Fasting 14, 63, 88–9, 123, 183, 187–8
Seafarer 122, 160
Simon and Jude, SS 17, 29, 41, 83, 120, 135–6, 143, 152, 177
solar turning points: *see* solar year

solar year ix, xii, 17, 35–9, 45–6, 49, 52–3, 108, 118–19, 181
Solomon and Saturn 63, 113
solstice 25, 27, 32, 34–40, 45, 53, 79, 86, 94–5, 106–7, 118, 133, 135, 181, 190–1
Stephen, St 32, 43, 47–8, 145, 153, 173, 179

Tatberht of Ripon 20, 141, 147, 149, 170
Thomas, St 28–9, 41, 47, 60, 65, 85, 127–8, 135, 145, 152, 179, 180, 208
Twelfth Day 13, 75, 88

Vercelli Homilies 103, 110, 114

Wanderer 70, 95, 122
West Saxon Gospels 87, 116
Wilfrid I of York 20, 141, 147–9, 169
Wilfrid II of York 20, 141, 147–8, 169
Winchester 55, 71–2, 94, 98, 161–3
Wulfstan (Archbishop of York) 71, 91, 102

ANGLO-SAXON TEXTS

Volumes already published

1. *Wulfstan's Canon Law Collection*
edited by J. E. Cross (†) and Andrew Hamer

2. *The Old English Poem* Judgement Day II: *A Critical Edition with Editions of* De die iudicii *and the Hatton 113 Homily* Be domes dæge
edited by Graham D. Caie

3. Historia de Sancto Cuthberto: *A History of Saint Cuthbert and a Record of his Patrimony*
edited by Ted Johnson South

4. Excerptiones de Prisciano: *The Source for Ælfric's Latin-Old English* Grammar
edited by David W. Porter

5. *Ælfric's* Life of Saint Basil the Great: *Background and Context*
edited by Gabriella Corona

6. *Ælfric's* De Temporibus Anni
edited with a translation by Martin Blake

7. *The Old English Dialogues of Solomon and Saturn*
edited with a translation by Daniel Anlezark

8. *Sunday Observance and The Sunday Letter in Anglo-Saxon England*
edited with a translation by Dorothy Haines

9. *Anglo-Saxon Prognostics: An Edition and Translation of Texts from London, British Library, MS Cotton Tiberius A.iii*
edited with a translation by R. M. Liuzza

10. *The Old English Martyrology: Edition, Translation and Commentary*
edited with a translation by Christine Rauer

11. *Two Ælfric Texts: 'The Twelve Abuses' and 'The Vices and Virtues': An Edition and Translation of Ælfric's Old English Versions of* De duodecim abusivis *and* De octo vitiis et de duodecim abusivis
edited with a translation by Mary Clayton

www.ingramcontent.com/pod-product-compliance
Lightning Source LLC
Chambersburg PA
CBHW070801230426
43665CB00017B/2440